David Hicks scrapbooks

David Hicks scrapbooks

edited by Ashley Hicks

For my sisters, Edwina and India, this edition of our father's scrapbooks.

David Hicks: Scrapbook Artist

A few years before his death my father told me that he was unable to sleep from worry. He'd just realised that his library was a fire risk, with its open log fire, and that his precious scrapbooks could go up in flames at any moment. After all, they were the most important things in the house. They were his legacy and his monument. Paintings, furniture and people could burn, but not his scrapbooks! He quickly had shelves built for them in his flower room, which he considered fire-safe, with its door to the outside, and was able to sleep peacefully again.

His great work had reached 25 volumes by his death in 1998. They are standard black press-cutting albums but each one has scarlet leather labels, added to the spine by a bookbinder, stamped with 'David Hicks' and the date in gilt lettering. In my father's library at Britwell, they sat on a shelf above a black armchair on which he placed the scarlet leather cushion from Sir Ernest Cassel's motor-car, itself stamped with Sir Ernest's coat of arms in gold like the scrapbook labels. There was a comfortable sofa, and visitors (house guests, journalists or his children, home for the weekend from boarding school) could peruse the scrapbooks at leisure.

If he was at home and not jetting around the world, he would sit me down with the current volume so that I could 'catch up'. If he was away, I'd often sit there alone going through the older books, sharing his manifest delight in his own image and the perfection of his work. Putting the scrapbooks together was one of the great pleasures of his life. He was very particular about it. Everything was cut out freehand with scissors, carefully arranged and then glued in place with 'Scotch' glue which came from France (no ordinary English glue would do) and which had to be bought in bulk every summer in Nice while we were at our holiday house nearby.

He needed at least three copies of any magazine featuring his work: two to be ripped apart and his pages, front and back, stuck in, and a third to be kept intact. Even ripping the magazine up was a ritual: carefully peeling away first the covers, then sections of pages, and finally the precious ones starring Hicks himself. Rush the process, and they might tear. The first volume has a few magazine pages of other people's houses, like Groussay and La Fiorentina. Later on, these stop, because there was simply no room for anyone else, except perhaps his father-in-law. Asked if he had a press agent, he replied with typical modesty, 'I don't need one. Everything I do is news.'

The books are works of art, as was everything that my father did. Every detail of his life was considered and consciously designed, none more so than these books, which he consciously built into his monument. His scrapbooking style changes through the years, as does any artist's. Sometimes he would crowd pages with cuttings, pictures, ticket stubs and menu-cards, creating a layered, vibrant collage with every spread. At other times, he would simply crop a single photograph, magazine or newspaper cutting and position it carefully, in solitary splendour on the page, a minimalist gesture.

My father trained as an artist, at the Central School in London, and his first ambition was to be one. After a summer in Italy spent painting bold, graphic gouaches of Florence and Venice led to an exhibition in which he sold nothing, he decided to turn to decorating. Unlike most of his peers, he had little interest in his clients' comfort or convenience. What they wanted from him was style; what he wanted from them were images. He put together rooms as a contemporary painter might assemble a composition, blocks of intense colour resonating together.

Told by a timid client, 'I'm not sure my wife will like your clashing colours', my father responded: 'My colours do not clash, they vibrate; and your wife will find it – exciting!' When designing a scheme, he was always determined that it should be different from any he'd done before; within every job, indeed, each room had to be in sharp contrast to the others. This gave a richer and more varied look to the place, but importantly also gave its creator a whole batch of new, fresh images for publication and eventual collage into his scrapbooks. On their pages he worked as an artist, trying novel compositions, juxtaposing colour, texture and type.

The 25 books form a continuous, epic cycle: a life reflected, portrayed, sampled – the ultimate self-portrait. Like many an epic, what he left was a rambling, vast work that was challenging to enjoy: 25 unwieldy, delicate books that are still kept where he left them and must be handled with extreme care. I resolved to make it accessible, and spent weeks photographing all of his 3,068 pages on my kitchen floor, eventually paring those down to a selection of just over 300 that could fit in this single volume. It was a labour of love, but then so is everything to do with my father, somehow. He inspired it, as his style inspires so many, still today.

ASHLEY HICKS, FEBRUARY 2017

Part 1

1950–62

1950–62

Here we begin with childhood in suburban, stockbroker Essex, and end in an Indian palace with Jackie Kennedy. The first scrapbook opens with pages put together in 1954 when David has a bookcase to call his own, in the house on South Eaton Place that he decorates for himself and his mother. This begins with 3 colours of writing-paper and moves on to brightly painted rooms that launch his career when published in *House & Garden*. Here's his woven label 'David Hicks – London' sewn onto cushions and curtains; holidays at Rory Cameron's famed Villa La Florentina; the band tent for a ball at Claridge's designed by DH, and Charles de Besteigui's fantastic theatre at Groussay that clearly inspired it.

David in California, posing as a statue; David and Algy the pug, in Suffolk, just posing; his Christmas card design for Elaine and Vidal Sassoon. 'When a Hicks marries a Mountbatten' – 1959 – David marries up, up and away; and the property advertisement seen while flying up to Glasgow, for Britwell, the Georgian mansion that would crystallise the new country-house style. Here's David pushing the ceiling with an ageing Helena Rubinstein while builders drink their tea; here's her finished apartment and a swatch of the purple tweed from its walls; and 'Lucky wife June' standing at her garden fence when David limousines up and offers to redecorate her house for free.

At the end, David's first trip to India, March 1962, with Pammy, who had lived there as the last Viceroy's daughter. They coincide with Jackie Kennedy and Lee Radziwill, which means they have to leave Prime Minister Nehru's house (there they are, watching Russian dancers with him) and move to the President's – what had been the Viceroy's House, Pammy's former home. In Udaipur, a boat trip on Lake Pichola, where David takes a terrible picture of Jackie Kennedy; and a better one of Pammy, also in pink, standing on Shah Jahan's balcony in Agra, India.

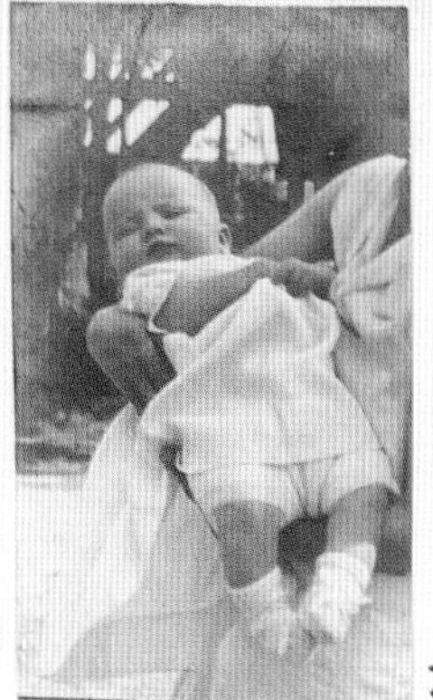

DH held by Faith

1948
R.A.E.C.

Peggy Lloyd.

14 Dec '48

DH as page

STATION: KELVEDON.
'PHONE: COGGESHALL 20.

THE HAMLET,
LITTLE COGGESHALL,
ESSEX.

1942

Herbert Hicks.

HICKS.—HERBERT HICKS, of Branwoods, Great Baddow, Essex, was born at Streatham, on February 17th, 1863. He is the eldest son of Thomas Hicks, a Past Master of the Salters' Company. He was educated at Winchester and Cheltenham, and married Miss Platten, of Essex. Mr. Hicks entered the Stock Exchange, and eventually founded the present firm of Messrs. H. Hicks and Faith, of which he is Senior Partner. He joined the Salters' Company about twenty-six years ago. He is a member of the Constitutional Club, the Gun Club, and the Chelmsford Golf Club.

"From the Guilds of the City of London and their Liverymen" in the Brickwell Library. DH.

DH

DH at 20

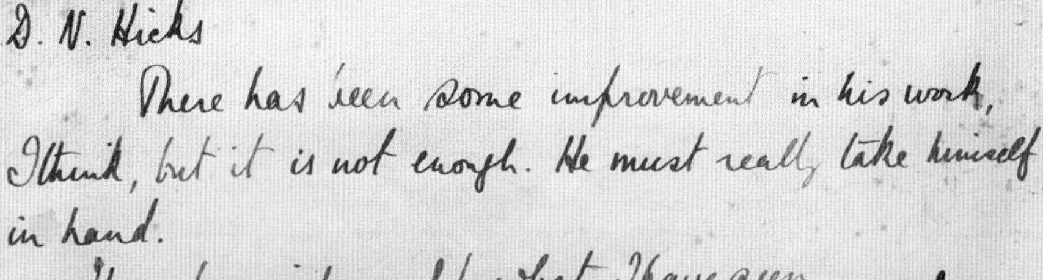

CHARTERHOUSE REPORT.

D. N. Hicks

There has been some improvement in his work, I think, but it is not enough. He must really take himself in hand.

I have been impressed by what I have seen of his work in Studio.

R Birley

Headmaster

DH

THIS PICTURE shows David Hicks, a twelve-years-old schoolboy at Barfield School, Farnham, and a member of the cricket first eleven. The year was 1941.

The same David Hicks — now a fashionable London interior designer — was married at Romsey Abbey to Lady Pamela Mountbatten last week. "He was not a wonderful athlete," recalls the headmaster, Mr. T. L. Griffith, "though he showed an early aptitude for art." At the age of eleven he executed a lino-cut for the cover of a school magazine produced that year. He was at Barfield from 1939 to 1942.

DAVID HICKS · SNELLS · GT. HENNY
SUDBURY · SUFFOLK

Grannie 1941

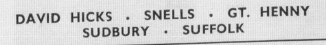

HICKS.—In ever loving memory of our beloved JOHN, who was killed in action in Italy, Oct. 14, 1944. He was the very dear elder son of the late HERBERT HICKS, and of Iris Hicks, and very near brother of David. He rests in Assisi.

John H

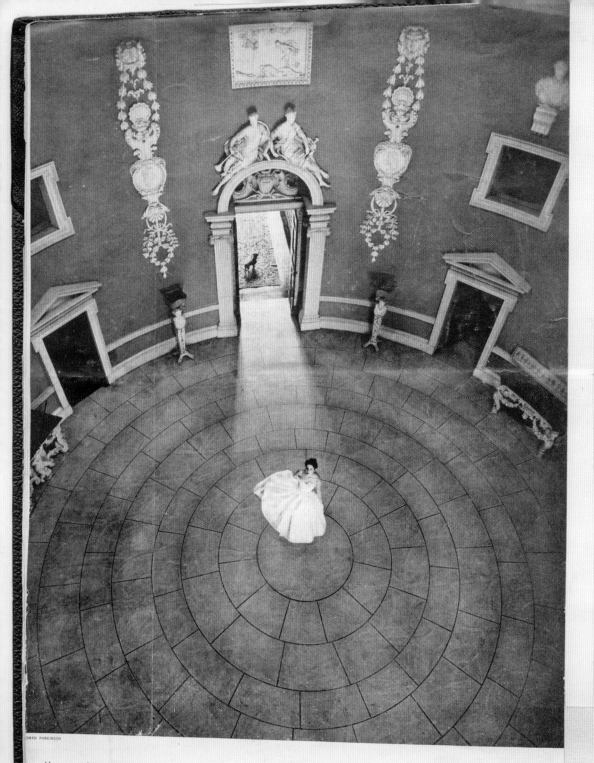

Above, we photographed her in the domed Round Hall, focal point of the house, seen also in the background, opposite, as she stands at the entrance of the orangery. Mereworth is being lent by Mr. Michael and Lady Anne Tree for the ball on June 6

THE WORSHIPFUL COM

OF

SALTERS

CORONATION YEAR DI

Tuesday, 7th July, 1953

AT

DRAPERS' HALL

(by courtesy of the Worshipful Company of D

Master:

JOHN DANBY CHRISTOPHER, Esq.

Wardens:

PROFESSOR WILFRID EDWARD LE GROS
M.A., D.SC., M.D., F.R.C.S., F.R.S.

LEONARD THOMAS SPENCER HAWKIN

Renter:

MALCOLM JOHN MORRIS, Esq.

Clerk:

WILLIAM REGINALD NICHOLS, Esq., T.D., M.A.

Mr. David Hicks and Miss Tanja Starr Busman had a glass of champagne together at 23, Knightsbridge.

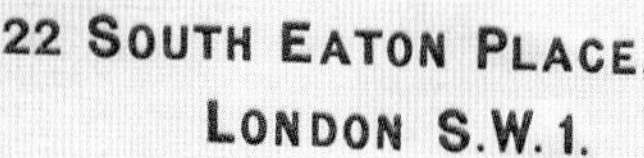

22 SOUTH EATON PLACE,
LONDON S.W.1.

22 SOUTH EATON PLACE.
LONDON S.W.1.

22 SOUTH EATON PLACE,
LONDON S.W.1.

1951
Peggy
Everard's
wedding

COURT CIRCULAR

1952.

BUCKINGHAM PALACE, Dec. 2

The Queen, Queen Elizabeth The Queen Mother, The Princess Margaret, and The Duchess of Gloucester were present at London Airport this afternoon upon the arrival of The Duke of Edinburgh and The Duchess of Kent.

Lady Palmer, Lieutenant-Colonel the Hon. Martin Charteris and Captain the Lord Plunket were in attendance.

The Hon. N. C. Havenga (Minister of Finance for the Union of South Africa) had the honour of being received by The Queen.

The Right Hon. Winston S. Churchill, M.P. (Prime Minister and First Lord of the Treasury) had an audience of Her Majesty this evening.

Dec. 2

The Lady Hyde has succeeded The Lady Jean Rankin as Lady-in-Waiting to Queen Elizabeth The Queen Mother.

Queen Elizabeth the Queen Mother will open the reconstructed picture gallery of Dulwich College on April 23.

Lady Isobel Gathorne-Hardy has moved to The Old House, Bradfield, Berkshire, which is now her permanent address.

Sir Richard and Lady Graham have left 24, Edwardes Square, W.8, for Norton Conyers, Ripon, Yorkshire, which is now their permanent address.

Lady (Wyndham) Childs has left Sidmouth and will be for a few months at 21, Carlyle Mansions, Cheyne Walk, Chelsea, S.W.3 (telephone: Flaxman 8796).

Mr. David Hicks has moved to 22, South Eaton Place, London, S.W.1 (telephone: Sloane 2818).

1952

Hicks

Leo d'Erlanger
at Home
s Tess d'Erlanger
Castle, Maidstone, Kent.
lay, June 6th 1952.

Dancing 10.30 p.m.

cretary.
nor Street.
W.1.

Please bring this invitation with you.

J. Walter Thomson
magazine

Miss Tess d'Erlanger at Mereworth Castle

Miss Tess d'Erlanger, seventeen-year-old daughter of Mr. and Mrs. Leo d'Erlanger, will have a ball in the Palladian magnificence of Mereworth. Her ankle-length white organza dress was a coming-out present from Mainbocher, for whom she worked in New York until recently

PERIOD PELMETS

By David Hicks

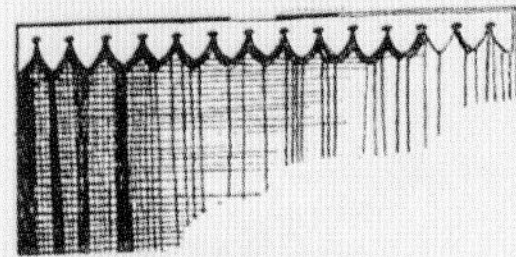

For a wide and shallow window, this design is effectively executed in ply or fabric. Happy hunting grounds for finding variations on this type of motif are Regency verandahs, Victorian conservatories, and platform roofs of the older railway stations and signal-boxes

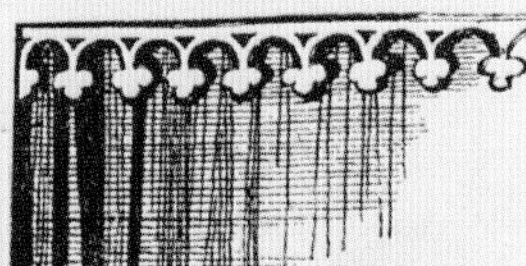

Cut a pelmet out of ply: use the design along the top of a wide and low window, making sure that there is an exact half-motif at either end. Curtains will hang better inside a window recess, their bottom just reaching the sill. Mount the pelmet itself approximately an inch in from the front of the window recess.

Use this in a room where the window comes very close to the ceiling. The idea can be carried out "in the flat" with the pelmet cut out by fretsaw. But it would repay more elaborate treatment: the upper part formed of a simple moulding and the pennant of fabric. If there is a cornice existing, repeat it above the pennant, instead of the moulding illustrated here.

Easily and cheaply this can be made by cutting out the entire shape in plywood and painting it a colour contrasting with

continued overleaf

The new bar at Monseigneur Restaurant, London.

Lounge and Bar Redesigned at the Monseigneur

An unusual and striking colour scheme has been used to great advantage in the recently transformed American bar and lounge at the Monseigneur Restaurant, Jermyn Street, W.1.

The ceiling of the bar is black and is dominated by a large circular black and white photostat reproduction of a painted ceiling. Two of the walls are blue and two are white. A beige and brown carpet provides a pleasing background for the vivid blues, reds and greens of the chair coverings. The tables are topped with bright woven fabric covered with glass.

and contrasts elegantly with crushed raspberry pink walls and ceiling arch. The carpet has a ground of the same pink, covered with a vari-coloured pattern and the windows have white venetian blinds. There is a gas-fired grill installed in the grillroom.

Mr. Andrea Gualdi is general manager of the Monseigneur. The decor was designed by David Hicks, and the work carried out by Hutchings & Keasley Ltd.

DAVID HICKS

ACCOUNT

22 South Eaton Place, London SW1 Sloane 2818

← Homes and Gardens magazine

JOHN FERER LTD, *Travel Agent* 1952

60 Ebury Street, London, S.W.1. Telephone: Sloane 1453

David HICKS, Esq.

London/Amsterdam, Friday 20th January BE 426

Report Waterloo Air Terminal 3:35 p.m.
Coach departs 3:50 p.m.
or
Report London Airport Central 4:50 p.m.
Take-off 5:20 p.m.
Arrive Amsterdam, Schiphol Airport 7:35 p.m.
Arrive Amsterdam, Museumplein 8:00 p.m.

Dinner is served on this flight.

P.T.O.

In the drawing-room of a Victorian house decorated by David Hicks for his mother, a multi-coloured collection of prints is arranged behind a lacquer-red sofa, with a green fringe and yellow cushions

DAVID HICKS, 22 South Eaton Place, London, S.W.1. Telephone: Sloane 2818.

House and Garden

DAVID HICKS

LONDON

House and Garden

A SPARKLING GATHERING. If it's glass you're after, the General Trading Co.'s glass department, at 5 Grantham Place, W.1, decorated by David Hicks, shows you the best at its best. Fine table glass in sets and individually, jugs, bowls, decanters, antique and modern, native and foreign, are gathered in an *embarras de richesse*.

Ann Coke Jane Willoughby Jane Stewart

Hicks

rs A. Courtauld

at Home

Saturday, May 26th

Dancing
9.0 o'clock.

Spencers,
Gt. Yeldham, Essex.

R.S.V.P.

acc.

The Countess of Ancaster

requests the pleasure of

Mr. David Hicks Company

on Monday, 5th December

at the Savoy Hotel (River Room)

R.S.V.P.
5, Westminster Gardens, S.W.1.

Dancing
10 o'clock.

1 2

4 5

Peter Coats at S.E.P.

SEP library

my bedroom

3

1. The library's Cherry Red blind, Cerulean Blue curtains, and violet-upholstered Regency Gothick chair, are all dominated by deep Flame walls.
2. In the drawing-room, a lacquer red sofa, fringed with green, has yellow cushions, and, with the multi-coloured arrangement of prints behind it, makes a concentration of colour against "dried-mud"-coloured walls and "mouse"-coloured carpet.
3. Another corner of the library has a bookcase designed by David Hicks; on the table is an interesting collection of chinoiserie.
4. A fine Tilliard Louis XV chair, in this part of the drawing-room, is covered in rose Tyrian velvet, blending with the "blotting-paper" pink, 18th-century tablecloth; white glazed percale curtains, a white lampshade, and white woodwork, lighten the room's neutral background.
5. Siamese Pink—for the partition and chair upholstery—contrasting strongly with the Leaf Green walls, makes an apt contemporary background for the Victorian rosewood desk and table

designed by John

Colour conversion

HOW A YOUNG DESIGNER USED MANY HOUSE & GARDEN COLOURS TO TRANSFORM AN EARLY VICTORIAN HOUSE

Colour is the key used by the young designer and decorator, David Hicks, to turn the interior of his mother's early Victorian house near Eaton Square into a setting of brilliant contemporary colours. A flair for using bold contrasts has enabled him to create an imaginative and successful background for antique furniture and works of art. In the writing-room, a Siamese Pink chair and one Leaf Green wall are heightened with Lemon Peel vases; Flame walls in the library surround engravings, prints, and brightly-bound books, and a brilliant Cherry Red blind accentuates curtains of white, glazed percale. Circular table-cloths are used in many colours, including a white one edged with black bobble fringe, and an emerald green flower trough is filled luxuriantly with flowers in many reds. To the decorator's sense of colour is added the designer's sense of form and awareness of texture—David Hicks successfully mixing mahogany with white-painted pieces, using felts, silks, and needlework to complete the final effect of richness.

ANTHONY DENNEY

House and Garden

Christmas Greetings from David Hicks

Staircase as I found it

UNE MAISON SUR LA

Danielle Waterpark

Clarissa Chaplin
Leslie & Mark Bonham Carter

The Pool

E K

Matchbox top

portico of Fiorentina

Mark Rudkin

Danielle

Lady Kenmare

Demand for £47,000

LADY KENMARE
News from the Chancery Court.

THE Countess of Kenmare —widow of my old colleague Lord Castlerosse—has received important news from the Chancery Court. Mr. Justice Danckwerts decided she is liable to pay £47,190 surtax for the years 1947-48. The principle of the decision will have wide implications.

Sonia Quennell

1956

...mo's villa

Le château de Groussay date des toutes premières années du XIXe siècle. Au bâtiment initial, M. Charles de Beistegui vient d'ajouter deux ailes auxquelles on accède par deux galeries en quarts de cercle. C'est dans celle de gauche (vue du parc) que se trouve la grande salle Louis XIII. Les agrandissements ont respecté l'ordonnance générale de l'architecture, notamment dans l'ouverture des fenêtres et des mezzanines de l'attique.

Au château de Groussay, Charles de Beistegui abandonne les grands courants à la mode pour redonner vie à un style tombé dans l'oubli

LE LOUIS XIII

Dans un article de mai 1952, *Connaissance des Arts* a montré l'influence profonde que M. Charles de Beistegui exerce depuis vingt ans sur les idées en décoration : il est à la source de la plupart des modes nouvelles dans ce domaine. Son prestige oriente les esprits vers les nouveautés. Ensuite il les impose dans l'histoire du mobilier avec la force d'une évidence.

Dans son livre « Cinquante ans d'élégance et d'art de vivre », M. Cecil Beaton consacre l'éminente place qu'on doit attribuer à M. Charles de Beistegui. On comprend donc pourquoi chacune de ses nouvelles entreprises a un retentissement si intense.

Juste avant la dernière guerre, M. Charles de Beistegui va chercher en Angleterre des meubles d'acajou de la fin du XVIIIe et du début du XIXe siècle. Il en décore tout son château de Groussay. L'acajou anglais était-il dans l'air ? Dans la haute couture parfois, une nouvelle ligne sort en même temps de tous les coins du monde. Assista-t-on à un phénomène de cet ordre ? En tout cas, après l'expérience de Groussay l'acajou anglais pullule chez les antiquaires de la rive gauche et certains décorateurs professionnels l'adoptent.

Le château de Groussay a été construit en 1802 pour Mlle de Touzel, gouvernante des Enfants de France, qui deviendra plus tard duchesse de Charost. M. de Beistegui a voulu l'agrandir. Il a confié ce soin à un architecte, M. Terry, qui a commencé les travaux en 1952. On a ajouté deux pavillons reliés par deux ailes au château primitif. La suture a été faite avec tant de grâce qu'un observateur non averti croirait que le château fut bâti ainsi au début du siècle dernier.

Nous ne nous occuperons ici que de l'aile droite. M. de Beistegui a fini de la décorer et de la meubler il y a environ un an.

Il a cherché son inspiration dans une époque dont il ne s'était pas occupé encore et qui pouvait servir son appétit de renouvellement. Il rompit avec les styles dont il avait joué ces dernières années et qui, pour le moment, avaient épuisé pour lui leur efficacité : le XVIIIe et le XIXe siècle. Il remonta plus haut dans le passé, jusqu'au début du XVIIe siècle, jusqu'au style Louis XIII. Il s'inspira de l'austérité, de la netteté des appartements qu'a représentés Abraham Bosse, et surtout des intérieurs hollandais de la même époque.

Une mode est lancée. On va sûrement l'imiter. Mais atteindra-t-on à sa grandeur ?

Une galerie longue de seize mètres, large de quatre, relie la salle à manger du château au pavillon de droite. Le style Louis XIII y obtient un effet de majesté.

M. de Beistegui a entièrement tendu un côté du mur de tapisseries de verdure. Il les utilise comme on faisait alors, en couvrant toute la surface d'un mur. Sur ces tapisseries mêmes, qui leur servent de fonds, il a accroché deux grands tableaux de chevaux qui donnent du mouvement et de la fierté.

Des tapisseries de verdure forment également les rideaux des cinq fenêtres. Le reste de la pièce est orné de boiseries grises auxquelles de très grosses moulures confèrent la force et la saveur.

Deux grandes portes en boiserie, peintes en gris, sont surmontées de potiches de Chine bleu et blanc, ainsi que la cheminée.

La décoration Louis XIII créée à Groussay rappelle le style de certains tableaux hollandais. Le sol en carrelage de marbre et de terre cuite est inspiré d'intérieurs d'églises peints par Peter Neeffs ; à leurs motifs correspondent les caissons du plafond, en bois peint gris. Les murs sont tendus de drap vert olive. Des carreaux de Delft bleu garnissent les ébrasures des hautes fenêtres et des mezzanines qui les surmontent. Cette association de bleu et de vert — chère à M. de Beistegui — est complétée par les grandes potiches en Chine et la garniture des sièges. A gauche, une table, couverte d'un tapis à dessin oriental, sert à la présentation d'objets d'art, selon la coutume des grandes demeures de la Renaissance. Au-dessus sont accrochés deux tableaux : l'Atelier d'Apelle par Willem van Haecht et un grand portrait d'Henri VIII de l'atelier d'Holbein. Pour reprendre un ancien usage Hollandais, un grand rideau rouge est fixé en haut du cadre ; ce système devait protéger les peintures contre les méfaits de la lumière.

requests the pleasure of the company of

Mr David Hicks

at Dinner

on Tuesday 18th June *at* 8.15 *o'clock.*

Reminder
~~*R.S.V.P.*~~

Spanish Embassy,
24, Belgrave Square, S.W.1.

Private Secretary.

IN LONDON LAST NIGHT

Twelve 'Slaves' fan dancers

Evening Standard Night Reporting Corps

MISS JACQUELINE ANSLEY had music wherever she went in Claridge's last night at a coming-out dance of Arabian Nights splendour given for her by her father, Mr. GEORGE ANSLEY.

There were four bands. Three played in the ballroom, decorated as a Turkish palace.

The bands took turns at playing in a scarlet and midnight-blue towered pavilion in the middle of the dance-floor.

A calypso trio beat out the rhythm in the supper-room.

A dozen pantaloon - clad "slaves" were posted round the floor waving huge fans.

Said Lord CECIL DOUGLAS: "I asked one of the slaves where he came from. The answer came back: 'Shoreditch, sir.'"

Lord Cecil Douglas's daughter, Miss SUSAN DOUGLAS, quipped: "They have probably been hired out from a debutante's delight's private harem."

Cha-cha

One of the bands, specially brought over from Paris for the occasion, introduced the Cha-cha.

After a few puzzled moments, the dancers were swaying to the music. Leading them was jive specialist, Miss FRANCESCA ROBERTI.

"This completes it as the best party of the season," she told Miss Ansley.

Watching the dancers beneath the candelabra were the Duke of MARLBOROUGH, the Marquess and Marchioness of BLANDFORD, the Countess of COVENTRY and Miss FRANCES SWEENY.

At one o'clock many of the debutantes looked towards the far end of the ballroom, half expecting the night club to open. But they were disappointed.

"I did not want one as it splits up the party and then the main floor looks empty and people start going home," explained Miss Ansley, who had been working since early morning on the decor.

"I want people to stay until six or seven o'clock," she said.

A fashion note for the men was set by Mr. IBRAHIM CHORBACHI who wore a red bow tie with his dinner jacket.

Mr. Peter Jankovic and Miss Sally Eaton dance at the Claridge's coming-out party last night.—See first story.

Salters Company Hall.

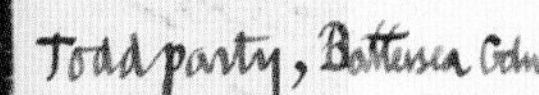

Todd party, Battersea Gdns

PLEASE NOTE THAT THERE WILL
BE NO ADMISSION TO THE PARTY
WITHOUT THIS CARD.

YOUNG FASHION GIRL. Lady Philippa Wallop, youngest member of HARPER'S BAZAAR's fashion staff, chose the clothes and supervised the sittings for the following five pages. She adores fashion, but not blindly, liking to sift and twist prevailing trends her way—less patient than their sheepish, war-conditioned elders, she and her friends sensibly protest when they don't get what they want.

MISS PENELOPE ANS[...] elder daughter of national banker George A[...] wishes to become an citizen.

"Just for income-tax poses, that is the main [...] I shan't spend a great de[...] time there," she says.

Her father, who posses[...] very large fortune, has be[...] Irish citizen for many [...] He has owned a house in D[...] since 1945, but he lives [...] in Paris.

In 1955 he spent se[...] thousand pounds on a co[...] out dance for his elder dau[...] And he spent as much [...] this year for his sec[...] daughter, Jacqueline.

Top: Miss Jacqueline Ansley and Mr. David Hicks

H&R decorations for Ansley Ball – Claridges.

Mrs. George Ansley
at Home
Monday, July 8th
Claridge's.

R.S.V.P.
1, Herbert Crescent,
London, S.W.1.

Dancing
10 o'clock.

Jaqueline

3'6"

2'

1'

Drapery.

Pelmet

DNH June 1957.

DANCE AT CLARIDGE'S

AGAINST the exotic background of a simulated Turkish night-club, guests enjoyed one of the most delightful dances of the Season. It was given by Mr. George Ansley for his daughter, Miss Jacqueline Ansley, at Claridge's Hotel, and among the guests were the Duke and Duchess of Marlborough, Earl and Countess Ferrers, the Earl and Countess of Coventry and Lord and Lady Edward Fitzroy

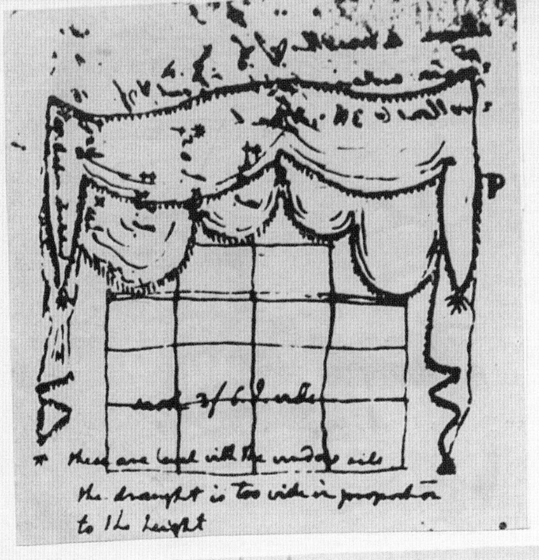

Jefferson's sketch for Curtains at Monticello

Reminder

Mr. and Mrs. Gilbert Miller

New Year's Eve

Tuesday, December 31st

Dinner

8.15

550 Park Avenue

N.Y.

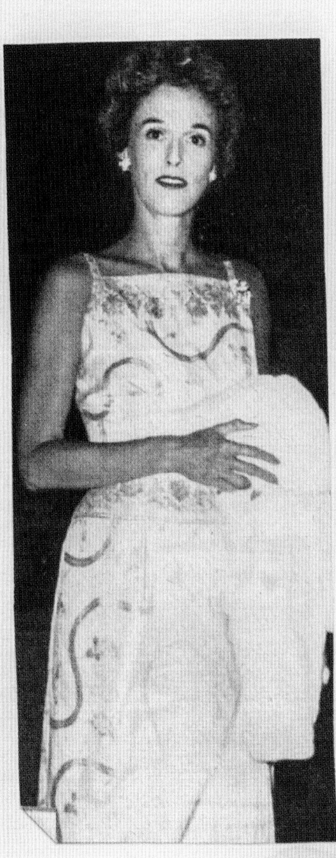

Mrs Paley

Mrs Fosburg

This is to make known that

DAVID N. HICKS

has traversed the skies over the Great Circle Route
in the regions of the Aurora Borealis on a **TWA JETSTREAM**

POLAR FLIGHT

FROM LONDON TO SAN FRANCISCO

ON NOV 19, 1957

In Witness Whereof, I have hereunto set my hand

TRANS WORLD AIRLINES, INC.

Lunching with Margaret Mallory in Santa Barbara California.

← DH in Wright Luddington's drawing room in Santa Barbara

Telegraph Hill, San Francisco

S.F.

WHEN he first started interior decorating, in 1952, David Hicks juggled with splashes of vivid colour, traditional antiques and ideas influenced by traditional methods of design. In six years, by a simple process of evolution, he has developed a style as individual as a signature. His mind is made up about colour—or rather non-colour, for he decorates in a whole range of neutrals; and about space, which he used lavishly and effectively, as if it were a tangible element. Many ideas were the outcome of a trip to America last winter, where he was impressed with the clarity of the light, the extravagant sense of space and the simple, almost stark treatment of the rooms.

His own drawing-room (this page) is an amalgam of all his ideas. He hates the "boring good taste" of rooms decorated in faithful reproduction of Georgian or Regency, preferring instead the challenge of mixing contemporary and antique, as he has done here. Colour has been reduced to its most negative value, whites, beige, sand and pale browns; even the books are arranged in blocks of one shade. This makes an excellent background for his fine collection of modern paintings and drawings, each of which is lighted individually. One of his innovations is in the mounting of pictures in glass, on slender steel frames, so that they stand away from the wall and can be lighted from behind, and can be easily moved without making indelible marks. He stands each object out in space, giving it new form and importance. This bare, spacious look demands careful lighting, which he considers half the battle in decorating any room; he often emphasises curtains, or bookcases, or a piece of furniture with tiny spotlights, or with lights in canisters shining upwards. On table lamps he uses solid shades, which shed pools of light rather than a harsh shine.

The Curzon Street flat (opposite page) is minute and here, too, colours are neutral. For the small drawing-room he chose only five pieces of furniture: the pair of Louis XV chairs covered in highly polished leather, an enormous marble-topped table which was specially made, a long cocoa-brown sofa against the opposite wall, a beautiful brass Queen Anne telescope. The windows are covered with white louvered screens that diffuse the light; at night lighting is done entirely by canisters on the floor. The curtains in both alcoves are oatmeal-coloured, in rough material, and the books are bound in white. With all this he has achieved a feeling of great elegance in a little space.

David Hicks is a young designer with very definite ideas—mainly about colour, and the use of space. He has a background of Central Art School, made his reputation by decorating his own house, and from there went on to redesigning houses of friends. In 1956 he joined Tom Parr in forming Hicks & Parr, now in Lowndes Street

Spacemanship

John Hedgecoe

1

2

3

1 Example of easy partnership of contemporary and antique: a landscape with figure by Dennis Wirth-Miller, in tawny yellows and browns; a white Berlin Pottery vase, and a pair of obelisks in white glass l.c.p.

Proof.

1959 Sunday Graphic

David Hicks, who is redecorating the rooms in the 17th century Portuguese castle where the Queen will stay in Ghana, is enthusiastic about red.

"I've just done a room in all red—red cotton walls, red velvet chairs, red taffeta radiator curtains (so much more effective and cheaper than metal cases) and red patterned chintz curtains."

There will be a great interest in paintings, he feels.

If you can't afford an expensive original (and there are few of us who can) try a drawing by a promising young painter. Who knows you may find a Picasso of the future?

'Lacks warmth'

Evening Standard.

Top interior decorator David Hicks thinks people have now had enough. "I notice a definite reaction against Contemporary with a capital C," he told me. "Possibly because it is too Scandinavian and not English enough. Possibly because it lacks warmth.

"I feel now that even if I were doing up the most modern flat imaginable—wildly plain, with concealed lighting, sheets of glass, masses of space—still somewhere I should want to have an enormous deep sofa covered in silk taffeta, with a buttoned back, elaborate fringes, piles of cushions and two deep armchairs standing alongside—to give the room warmth, character and receptiveness."

THEY FOLLOW

Daily Express.

Says young decorator-designer **David Hicks**: "Decorating fads follow fashion fads." And I see this mixing and matching of rooms as a direct steal.

Mr. Hicks's prize dual-purpose room is a dining-living room in the flat of Mr. and Mrs. Vidal Sassoon. Key to its conversion is a Napoleon marble coffee-cum-dining table just 18in. high.

Mr. and Mrs. Sassoon's dinner guests sit on cushions on the floor to eat.

The room is done in neutrals—white, cream, sandalwood and brown—with one bright touch: an orange silk cushion.

"Monotone decorating is another fashion follow-up," said Mr. Hicks. "Remember when women were wearing one-colour ensembles?"

assoon send you greetings
best wishes for 1959

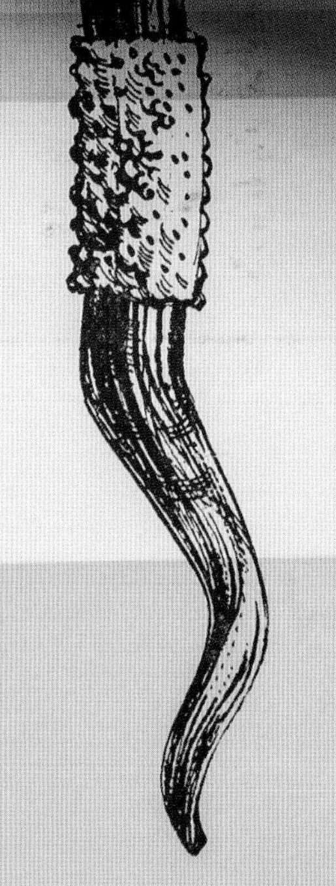

Drawn and designed by DH.

H&P chairs: Arthur Jeffress flat.

Elaine Sassoon

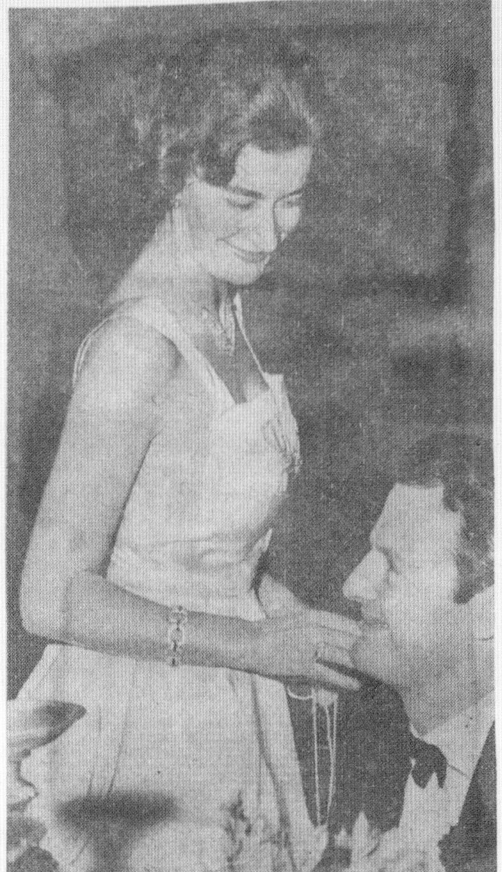

A CURTAIN-RAISER TO THE YEAR'S MOST TALKED-ABOUT SOCIETY WEDDING

When a Hicks marries a Mountbatten

by DONALD EDGAR

ROMSEY, Tuesday

TOMORROW David Hicks will marry Lady Pamela Mountbatten in the magnificent old Abbey of Romsey.

And already this charming little town has got out its decorations — Union Jacks, bunting, heraldic pennants. It all looks very gay, festive and a little feudal, in a rather quaint way.

But then Romsey has always been a little feudal towards the owners of Broadlands, the splendid Palladian mansion which looks down with 18th-century elegance and pride on the Test, one of the finest fishing rivers in the country.

The link

ONCE the master was Lord Palmerston — that stout defender of British rights during the 19th century. And his brother-in-law, Lord Melbourne, spent many a week-end here when he had given up his premiership and with it his affectionate relationship with the young Queen Victoria.

Queen Victoria — it is strange that there should be this link, for the present master is Lord Mountbatten, whose grandmother was a daughter of Queen Victoria.

Everything is being done on a splendid scale—it will be the biggest Royal wedding in this country since that of the Queen in 1947. Nearly all our Royal family will be here.

Unfortunately, the Queen will not be able to come because she is expecting her third child soon. But Prince Philip, with Prince Charles and Princess Anne, are travelling overnight from Sandringham in the Royal train.

This will be a very special occasion for Princess Anne. She will be performing her first public function.

She will be a bridesmaid along with Princess Clarissa, who is 15, and Princess Frederica, who is five, both daughters of Princess Sophia of Hanover, the Duke of Edinburgh's sister.

Everybody is looking forward to seeing Princess Anne.

It is rather hard luck, in a way, that the Queen will not be here to see her daughter's performance—and also not to visit again Broadlands, where she spent part of her honeymoon.

The honeymoon was an idea of Lord Mountbatten, who is Prince Philip's uncle.

Two trains

THE Queen of Sweden, Lord Mountbatten's sister, is expected. So are many of the German connections of the Mountbattens—who before the 1914-18 war were the Battenbergs.

Two special trains are bringing down many of the thousand guests from London and there will be two receptions—one at the house and another outside the grounds for the villagers and the tenants of the 6000-acre estate.

But it is expected that the bride and bridegroom, together with the Royalties, will visit this second party.

Lady Pamela—"Pammy" as they call her—is having her dress from Worth. It was her mother's choice of couturier, for she has always dealt there and has an implicit faith in its taste.

Lady Pamela Mountbatten and Mr. David Hicks an engagement picture.

Born in Spain

LADY PAMELA has played her part in life—especially in India when her father was the last Viceroy.

But she is a quiet person.

Her full names are—Pamela Carmen Louise.

The Spanish-sounding Carmen is a souvenir of her birth in Barcelona.

Lady Mountbatten was accompanying her husband whilst he was serving in the Mediterranean.

They were in a storm off the Spanish coast in a small chartered craft. It was a nerve-racking experience. A little later they arrived at Barcelona.

The child was not expected for another two months

seem that David Hicks, who has an interior decorator's shop off Lowndes Square, Knightsbridge, might be overwhelmed.

His father was a stockbroker. His mother is a retired actress. They have been comfortably off—but no more.

He was at Charterhouse and then went on to art school.

But, in spite of a background of middle-class comfort, it could be overwhelming to find yourself about to be related by marriage to the Queen, Prince Philip and all the surviving royalties and princedoms of Europe.

But the cards are not all against him

who was at one time Chancellor of Germany, one episode in his mem

He shows that on the side the Mountbatten trace their descent to called Haucke, who was service of a Count Bruel 18th century.

This Haucke, a Saxon, the daughter of a Germ and confectioner in W

Their descendants fin a daughter who became of honour of the wife Tsarevitch in St. Peter

She fell in love Prince Alexander von They were exiled fo

Stansted Park

The Moroccan Ambassador
& Princess Fatima Zahara
request the pleasure of the company of
Mr. David Hicks
on Wednesday 25 March 1959 at 8.15 p.m
at 23, Wilton Crescent S.W. 1

Buffet Supper
(Informal)

R.S.V.P.
~~23 Wilton Crescent S.W. 1~~
To remind

Colchester: summer 1959.

Wirth-Miller. "But they hung it upside-down."

Standard

EARL MOUNTBATTEN'S naval brevity seems to have affected Mr. David Hicks, who marries Lady Pamela Mountbatten on Wednesday. He has sent telegrams to his ushers which read: "Report Romsey Abbey at 1.30 Wednesday. David."

BROADLANDS

Painting by Felix Kelly showing (to the left) the North Front restored to its 1760 architecture.

Admiral of the Fleet
Earl & Countess Mountbatten of Burma
request the pleasure of your company
at the Wedding of their daughter
Pamela
with
Mr. David Hicks
at Romsey Abbey at 3.0 p.m.
and afterwards at Broadlands
on Wednesday, 13th January 1960

R.S.V.P. Private Secretary,
Broadlands, Romsey, Hants.

Watch My Line

By NICOLAS BENTLEY

"Doesn't she look sweet?"

Paul TANFIELD . . . investigates the fascinating world of the man who is to marry Lady Pamela Mountbatten

The exclusive life of the exclusive Mr Hicks

Lady Lewisham was jolly excited about the announcement yesterday of the engagement of **Lady Pamela Mountbatten** and **Mr. David Hicks.**

"Actually," said Lady Lewisham, "Mr. Hicks is doing my hall."

Mr. Hicks has been described up to now as "an interior decorator." Mr. Hicks is in fact just about the most exclusive interior decorator in the whole exclusive business.

FRAMING LADY L

"He's awfully nice," said Lady Lewisham. "For instance, whenever a cartoon of me appears in a paper I get hold of the original and send it along to Mr. Hicks. He has designed a special frame in black and white with an egg-blue mounting."

This is by no means the full extent of Mr. Hicks's creative ability.

"He did my curtains and pelmets," Lady Lewisham said. "They're marvellous. They never move out of place or hang wrongly or do any of the horrible things that curtains usually do."

PAPERING LADY L

On the day his engagement became official Mr. Hicks spent several hours designing even more curtains, carpets, and wallpaper for Lady Lewisham's hall.

The people who call in the brilliant 30-year-old Mr. Hicks and his firm make an impressive list.

Lord and Lady Bessborough asked him to decorate their new attic flat near Marble Arch. He turned the place into a blaze of colour—yellow, blue, coral, and green.

Mrs. Douglas Fairbanks sought his advice when she moved into her Kensington home. So did **Lord Beatty** when he wanted to change the decor of his country house in Buckinghamshire.

MARRYING LADY P.

But perhaps his most notable achievement was when he flew to Ghana on a near-secret mission to prepare the Governor's former palace for the visit—later postponed—of **the Queen.**

What of his marriage to Lady Pamela?

Certainly it will raise no difficulties in his relationships with his clients. For he has discreetly acquired a considerable social standing of his own.

His financial position? Mr. Hicks's services are expensive. Very expensive.

LADY PAMELA MOUNTBATTEN . . . and MR. DAVID HICKS

After her honeymoon, Lady Pamela Mountbatten is going to live "over the shop."

The flat which she and her fiancé, Mr. David Hicks, are preparing for themselves is above the premises he uses for his interior decorator's business in South Eaton Place, Belgravia.

THE FLAT IS UPSTAIRS
The Hicks home in Belgravia.

Lady Pamela Mountbatten, daughter of Earl and Countess Mountbatten, IS going to marry David Hicks, the Mayfair interior decorator.

Today's official announcement puts an end to speculation started two months ago.

Lady Pamela (pictured above as Commandant of the Girls' Nautical Training Corps), is 30. She and Mr. Hicks, three years younger, were often seen together.

She was a bridesmaid at the Queen's wedding.

A hard-working girl too. She was a lady-in-waiting to the Queen on her Commonwealth trip to Australia six years ago.

And she is rich. She has access to a large fortune

When will Lady Pamela name the day?

PERHAPS IT WILL BE SOMETIME IN NOVEMBER

WHAT WILLIAM HICKEY SAID LAST WEEK

founded by her great-grandfather, Sir Ernest Cassel.

Mr. Hicks, the son of a stockbroker, has built up a thriving business from his shop in Belgravia.

Lady Pamela, fair-haired and slender like her mother, has three times denied engagement rumours.

First, in 1951, it was said she would marry Lord Ogilvy, heir to the Earl of Airlie. Then it was Prince Bertil of Sweden.

Finally, before Mr. Hicks came along, there was Mr. George Arida, son of a Lebanese textile manufacturer.

There were no denials to the latest rumours. Neither was there confirmation—until today.

Town's gift

The people of Romsey, Hampshire, have been asked by their mayor, Councillor H. G. Mackrell, to subscribe to a wedding present for Lady Pamela Mountbatten, who marries interior decorator Mr. David Hicks in Romsey Abbey next month.

Local banks and shops are accepting subscriptions. And anyone contributing more than a shilling is invited to put their signature on a list.

✦ ✦

These lists will be bound into one volume and presented to Lady Pamela with the town's gift—a painting of Romsey by Royal Academician Mr. Richard Eurich.

Says Mr. Mackrell: "The painting is in hand, and will be completed in time for the wedding. When the fund is closed, in a week or two, I think it will be found that a very good proportion of Romsey's 6,500 inhabitants have contributed."

PRINCESS ANNE TO BE A BRIDESMAID

Buckingham Palace confirmed last night that Princess Anne will be a bridesmaid at the marriage of Lady Pamela Mountbatten and Mr. David Hicks at Romsey Abbey in January. Lady Pamela Mountbatten was one of the Queen's eight bridesmaids.

Princess Anne, 9, Will Be Bridesmaid Next Month

Associated Press.

LONDON, Dec. 7.—Princess Anne, pretty, honey - blonde daughter of Britain's Queen Elizabeth II, is going to be a bridesmaid for the first time.

The wedding at Romsey Abbey next January will unite Lady Pamela Mountbatten, 30, daughter of Earl Mountbatten, and David Hicks, 27, one of Britain's top interior decorators.

"The wedding is all she talks about these days," said a friend of the 9-year-old princess.

Although it is expected that there will be at least two pages, Anne's brother, Prince Charles, will not be one. The entire royal family has been invited to the wedding; one of the biggest society events of the year.

Lady Pamela, slender, fair-haired heiress to her mother's fortune, was one of the Queen's eight bridesmaids and also her lady-in-waitng on her visit to Australia six years ago.

THE MOUNTBATTEN WEDDING—More pictures page 3

Wilcock Woodward

1. THE WEDDING OF LADY PAMELA MOUNTBATTEN AND MR. DAVID HICKS

The couple left Romsey Abbey in a snowstorm

Two weddings, one in Paris, the other in Hampshire, have each excited a nation with their demonstration of

Marrying in the grand manner

UARY 13, 1960, will be a day to remember in the Mountbatten family—and no mistake. It was the day Lady Pamela got married, ing together a fabulous collection of people in the 12th Century at Romsey.

was also the day when so many things nearly went wrong. After al dry, crisp days it snowed—and hard. It was the day the ing veil nearly didn't arrive in time. It was the day the power at the Broadlands reception and toasts were proposed by candle-

nd it was the day when the bridegroom and best man nearly got t Winchester and Pc Keith Fuller turned chauffeur and came to rescue.

he ceremony was timed for 3 pm and the minutes were ticking when, over the police radio network, came the news that the ey road out of Winchester was blocked. Snow and slithering vehicles had made that route to Romsey temporarily impassible. The alternative way was through Otterbourne and along Poles-lane.

Pc 442 Fuller was patrolling that section of road and he was detailed to escort the bridegroom's car to Romsey. Two royal cars were expected to pick up the bridegroom, best man and some other guests who had spent the night at the Southgate Hotel, Winchester. But only one car put in an appearance. It was now 2.10 pm.

So into the police patrol car with its familiar "Police" notice piled Mr. Hicks and Lord Brabourne (best man), smiling and thoroughly enjoying the unexpected lift behind "chauffeur" Keith Fuller. Like the veil incident, this unrehearsed, unexpected episode lent a touch of excitement and informality to the occasion.

Hampshire Police seem to have a knack of helping out in times of difficulty with royal cars. It was about two years ago that the Queen Mother was given a lift to Romsey when her car broke down before reaching Stockbridge. She rode in the police escort car for the remainder of her journey.

Curtis & Henson Banbury 3295

By direction of the Executors of the late Major C. G. Whitaker

OXFORDSHIRE CHILTERNS—LONDON 50 MILES

THE BRITWELL HOUSE ESTATE

WATLINGTON

FOR SALE FREEHOLD
BY
PRIVATE TREATY
WITH

ABOUT 578 ACRES

(OR POSSIBLY WITH A SMALLER AREA BY ARRANGEMENT)

THE EARLY 18th CENTURY HOUSE OF EXCEPTIONAL QUALITY AND DISTINCTION

WITH ORIGINAL PINE AND OTHER PANELLINGS AND A NOTABLE STAIRCASE AND CEILING

is secluded in a small timbered park and enjoys open views over unspoilt country.

HALL, 4 RECEPTION ROOMS, 10 BEDROOMS ALL TOLD ON TWO FLOORS AND 3 BATHROOMS
STAFF WING WITH 2 BATHROOMS
AND A SELF-CONTAINED FLAT
COMPRISING THE NORTH WING.

OIL-FIRED HEATING

Private electricity and water supplies but mains available.

3 SERVICE COTTAGES

BRITWELL HOUSE WITH ABOUT 100 ACRES IS IN HAND AND AVAILABLE WITH VACANT POSSESSION

THE REMAINDER OF THE ESTATE IS LET

Full particulars available from:
Messrs. J. CARTER JONAS & SONS
11, King Edward Street, Oxford (Tel. 48205),
and JOHN D. WOOD & CO. (REF. R.R.)

Solicitors: Messrs. EVAN BARRACLOUGH & Co. 9, Orme Court, London, W.2

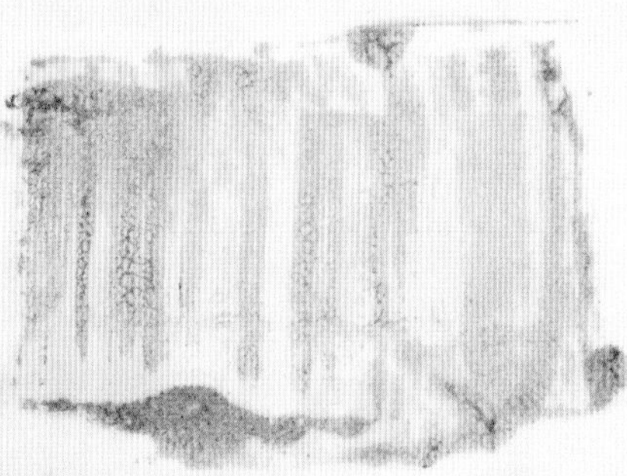

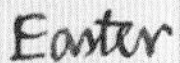

Easter

HOME FOR THE HICKSES

—or the house that Lady Pamela bought

THIS IS Britwell House, which wealthy Lady Pamela has bought for herself and her new husband, interior decorator Mr. David Hicks.

It is a fine eighteenth century mansion in Oxfordshire, and it cost her £80,000. Though Lady Pamela and her husband cannot get vacant possession until the autumn, I hear they plan to move a good deal sooner than that.

But they will live only in the north wing, which is self-contained.

And from this vantage point, Mr. Hicks will no doubt plan what improvements he can make when at last he gets to grips with the interior.

Interior decorators, like surgeons and detectives, tend to lead fairly anonymous lives. Their clients, so to speak, are the people who usually get into the headlines: their own job, even when spectacularly successful, is likely to be smothered by their clients' egos and/or news-worthiness.

Recently, however, interior decorators have been getting into the news on their own account. Mr David Hicks got married among the crowned heads and the headlines. Mr Oliver Messel got almost as much publicity as his patron for the elegant neo-Regency shoe shop he redesigned in Bond Street. Mr Tom Parr announced to the Press that he was severing his partnership with Mr Hicks and joining forces with Mr John Fowler, perhaps the most fashionable of them all.

Mr Hicks and all that

Certain popular papers, in their determination to revamp the Cinderella story, pretty well implied that Mr Hicks was decorating bed-sitters before he met Lady Pamela Mountbatten, but the truth is that, at thirty, he was (and still is) one of the top men in his lucrative, hard-working profession. His recent fame is, of course, proving no handicap in his career.

David Hicks—tall, dandyish, uncommonly assured—was as determined to be a decorator as Menuhin was to play the fiddle. After Charterhouse and the Central School of Arts he had a brief stint in the studios of J. Walter Thompson, the London-American advertising agency, but moved on to (or rather into) interiors. He is now one of the major arbiters of taste in the fashionable world. Amongst his recent commissions have been designing a flat (eighteenth century) for Lord and Lady Bessborough and another (twentieth century) for Mrs David Mischon. (Photographs of these flats will be published later in *House & Garden*.) Mr Hicks is intensely ambitious, takes his work and himself with deep seriousness and already talks, almost not jokingly, of 'Hicks Traditional' and 'Hicks Modern'. He believes that the stylish London interior is about to enter a grey-and-white phase, using nothing but washable, cleanable fabrics.

House & Garden.

● I PRESENT the most talked of horse in town. Life-sized, life-like, it has been staring glassily at Belgravia out of David Hicks's glossy window. Alluringly reminiscent of a Marini sculpture, it has a price considerably lower on its head—a mere £100. Keenest bidder: The Tower of London. Victorious bidder: Shirley Conran, better half of the Terence Conran husband-and-wife design team. She plans it for a spacious new office—"just me, the horse and a couple of acolytes."

Hicks and Parr and Guirey

With Tom Parr, David Hicks designed this drawing-room for Princess Guirey. The high points include panels striped in white and scarlet, a sofa in red towelling, Louis XIV chairs, red and black lacquer tables

about four guineas.

DAVID HICKS: "I would say the new feeling is for chalk-white walls with brilliant colours against them. And more material is being used on walls. This is expensive and impractical unless it is a dark.

The Times Feb 26th: (Seen in aeroplane to Glasgow)

By direction of the Executors of the late Major G. C. Whitaker

OXFORDSHIRE CHILTERNS—LONDON 50 MILES

THE BRITWELL HOUSE ESTATE, WATLINGTON

For Sale Freehold by Private Treaty with about 578 Acres

(or possibly with a smaller area by arrangement).

THE EARLY 18th-CENTURY HOUSE OF EXCEPTIONAL QUALITY AND DISTINCTION with original pine and other panellings and a notable staircase and ceiling is secluded in a small timbered park, and enjoys open views over unspoilt country; hall, 4 reception rooms, 10 bed rooms all told, on two floors, and 3 bath rooms; staff wing with 2 bath rooms, and a self-contained flat, comprising the North wing; oil-fired heating; private electricity and water supplies, but mains available; 3 service cottages.

BRITWELL HOUSE, with about 100 ACRES, is in hand and available with vacant possession.

The remainder of the Estate is let.

Full particulars from J. CARTER JONAS & SONS, 11, King Edward St., Oxford (Tel. 48205); and JOHN D. WOOD & CO.

the secret of serenity

by ANNA NEAGLE

Repose is hard won and comes usually at the end of a lifetime

One charming young exception is Lady Pamela Mountbatten, the daughter of Earl Mountbatten, now married to Mr. David Hicks.

I have met her about half a dozen times, the last occasion at a luncheon given in aid of the Forces Help Society. I was again struck by her calm, serene expression, just as I was when we met for the first time, about ten years ago, when she was very young.

Lady Pamela is new Burma Star President

Lady Pamela Hicks, daughter of Earl Mountbatten has agreed to become President of the Southend-on-Sea and District branch of the Burma Star Association. This was announced at the monthly meeting of the branch at the Burma Bar, Grand Pier Hotel, Southend, last Thursday.

Lecturer

INTERIOR decorator **Mr. David Hicks** looks like becoming a professional lecturer.

I can tell you that he is off to Australia in October for a three weeks' lecture tour, sponsored by a big Sydney store.

His wife, **Lady Pamela,** will go with him.

Mr. Hicks has been lecturing in this country a good deal recently, and in Australia he will give advice to housewives on how to make their homes more attractive.

Who told you that?

GIVE a husband enough rope and he'll be tied up at the office.

Mr. Hicks tackles a room at the top

While the men carrying out the work break for tea, the two other figures in the picture give the task some thought. Interior decorator Mr. David Hicks makes some measurements while his client, millionairess Helena Rubinstein, sits on a carpenter's bench and asks herself that age-old question—what will it look like when it's finished? (see first story).

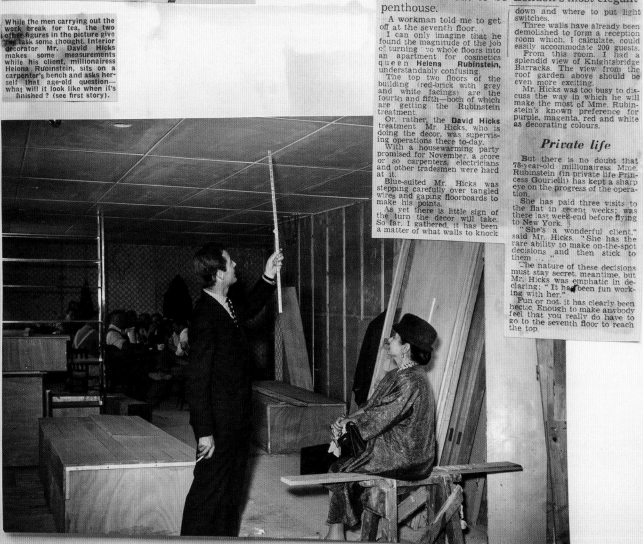

I TOOK the lift to the top floor of a Knightsbridge mansion to-day for a peep at what should turn out to be London's most elegant penthouse.

A workman told me to get off at the seventh floor.

I can only imagine that he found the magnitude of the job of turning two whole floors into an apartment for cosmetics queen **Helena Rubinstein,** understandably confusing.

The top two floors of the building (red-brick with grey and white facings) are the fourth and fifth—both of which are getting the Rubinstein treatment.

Or, rather, the **David Hicks** treatment. Mr. Hicks, who is doing the decor, was supervising operations there to-day.

With a housewarming party promised for November, a score or so carpenters, electricians and other tradesmen were hard at it.

Blue-suited Mr. Hicks was stepping carefully over tangled wires and gaping floorboards to make his points.

As yet there is little sign of the turn the decor will take. So far, I gathered, it has been a matter of what walls to knock down and where to put light switches.

Three walls have already been demolished to form a reception room which, I calculate, could easily accommodate 200 guests.

From this room, I had a splendid view of Knightsbridge Barracks. The view from the roof garden above should be even more exciting.

Mr. Hicks was too busy to discuss the way in which he will make the most of Mme. Rubinstein's known preference for purple, magenta, red and white as decorating colours.

Private life

But there is no doubt that 78-year-old millionairess Mme. Rubinstein (in private life Princess Gourielli) has kept a sharp eye on the progress of the operation.

She has paid three visits to the flat in recent weeks; was there last week-end before flying to New York.

"She's a wonderful client," said Mr. Hicks. "She has the rare ability to make on-the-spot decisions and then stick to them . . ."

The nature of these decisions must stay secret, meantime, but Mr. Hicks was emphatic in declaring: "It has been fun working with her."

Fun or not, it has clearly been hectic. Enough to make anybody feel that you really do have to go to the seventh floor to reach the top.

Madame Rubeinstein

WEDDING BREAKFAST

following the Marriage of

THE PRINCESS MARGARET

with

MR. ANTONY ARMSTRONG-JONES

BUCKINGHAM PALACE

FRIDAY, 6th MAY, 1960

M A.A-J

DH MOJB PH
Broadlands. Nehru

The Lord Chamberlain to
Queen Elizabeth The Queen Mother
is commanded by
Her Majesty

to invite Mr David and Lady Pamela Hicks

to the Ceremony of the Marriage of
Her Royal Highness The Princess Margaret
with
Mr. Antony Armstrong-Jones
in Westminster Abbey
on Friday 6th May, 1960 at 11.30 o'clock a.m.

An answer is requested addressed to the Lord Chamberlain to Queen Elizabeth The Queen Mother, Clarence House, St. James's, S.W.1.

Dress:- Morning Dress
Serving Officers - Ceremonial Day Dress
Ladies:- Morning Dress with Hat.

Brian Blaire DH

: Summer 1961

DECORATION

David Hicks tackles suburbia

Client and consultant: Mrs. G. V. Galwey eloquently explains the problems of semi-detached living to decorator David Hicks

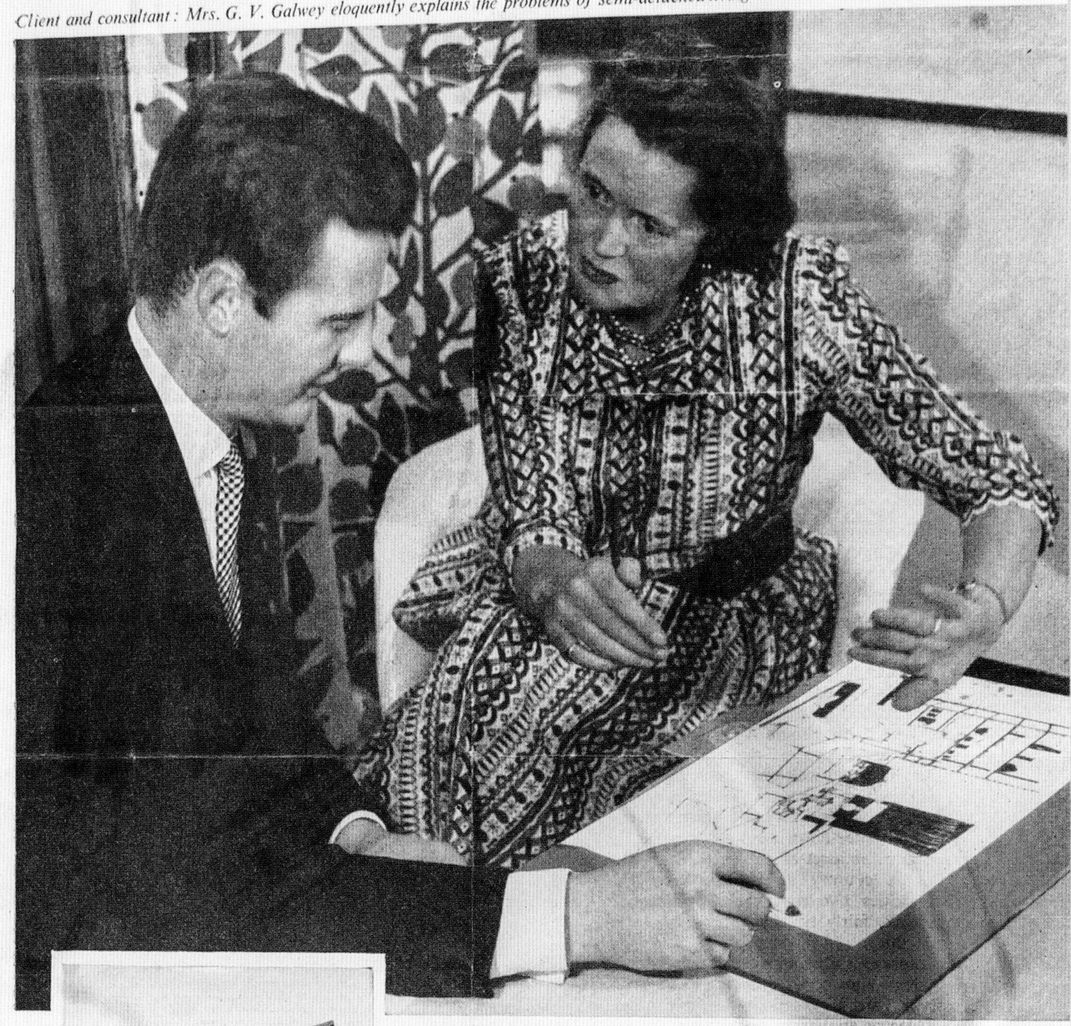

How "common" is the common touch? Can a decorator who graduated in fashionable flats and private yachts make the leap from Mayfair to Mayflower Way? Says David Hicks: "A room is a room — anywhere." Witness what happens when he re-schemes this semi-detached in an Essex suburb

Continued overleaf

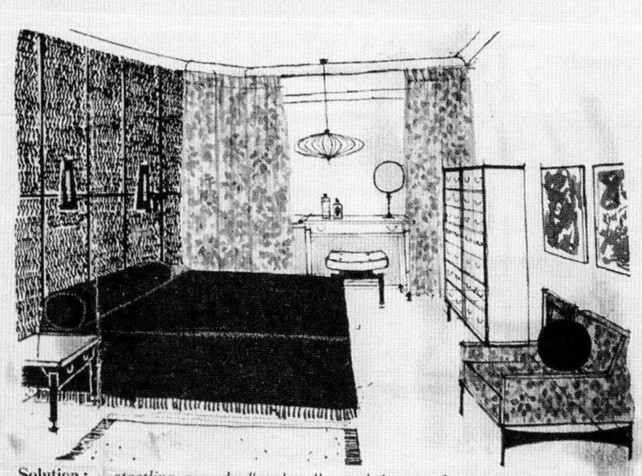

Solution: *a startling cane bedhead wall, a subtle use of pattern and a double bed completely transform the bedroom. You'll find more details in the text block below*

Solution: *seen from the now eliminated doorway, the dining-room re-emerges in black and white. Further details of the change are given at the foot of the page*

Blueprint in words of Hicks's solution

THE " AFTER " SKETCHES below and on the next page show David Hicks Associates' scheme for the three main rooms in the Galweys' house. They incorporate many of the ideas that Hicks has developed into his personal decorating signature during the last eight years.

White backgrounds for small rooms, with colours used dramatically and definitely on slip covers, curtains and accessories. He sticks to tones of one colour or at most two. Limiting these strong colours to furnishings (practical cottons, repps and felts), rather than furniture, his approach is ideal for the budget-minded.

Furniture is picked for a purpose, not to clutter up corners. Money is concentrated for comfort on chairs and sofas. He feels strongly about pattern, or rather its absence, and keeps it to one surface.

The living-room below has the only structural alteration—removal of the wall and glass doors separating it from the dining-room. This heightens the illusion of space and light.

He extended the arched alcove to the ceiling and inset a long mirror to add width to the room. Double-backed curtains can divide the two areas.

The Moorish-type fireplace has been kept but painted white so it isn't so strident.

Hicks's favourite white is used for walls, paintwork and ceilings to give a cool, enlarged look. With his unified colour scheme ideas, he here used tones of brown with black and white spiced with yellow and orange. Close-fitting chocolate-brown carpet sweeps across the living-room floor, matching a brown linoleum in the dining end.

A white rug in front of the fire isn't as impractical as it sounds—it's made of cotton (another Hicks favourite) and washes in a minute.

As always, Hicks trimmed furniture to essentials: a sofa, covered in black tweed, cinnamon-coloured armchairs, low metal-and-glass coffee table, a teak storage unit for sewing, games and clutter. To hold the Galweys' 1,001 books he prescribed industrial shelving, painted brown, black and white. Mr. Galwey's do-it-himself window seat (for rarely needed odds and ends) is dressed up with cinnamon cushions.

To give a unified look from outside, the designer used Pinoleum blinds both here and in the bedroom above.

...and after

Footnote . . . the black-and-white headquarters of David Hicks Associates at Harrison Gibsons. Again the cool, clean look that is typical of Hicks's ideas

Before . . .

三間堂

Japan

I watched a new series yesterday—"Rooms in View," about planning rooms in the house, and even Polly Elwes, one of the nicest of the BBC's young women, failed to emerge as more than a cipher. She and the rest of the team seemed to feel it would be indelicate to express a strong opinion.

Too courteous

Franklin Engelmann, Joan Gilbert, David Hicks and Mai Zetterling did have some criticisms of each others' ideas, but they delivered them with such courteous understatement as to be dull, when quite obviously some of the ideas needed to be firmly smothered.

My only favourable reaction to the programme, apart from that created by Mai Zetterling, who is always good to watch, was that Joan Gilbert was even more likeable than in the old days when she was the extremely able mainstay of the BBC's women's programmes, before being suddenly and inexplicably dropped.

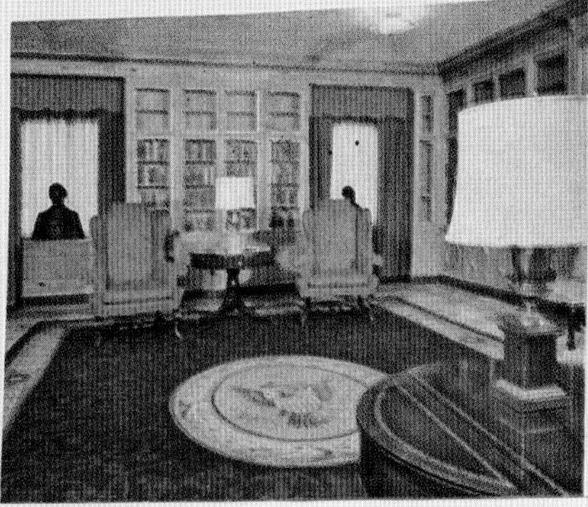

WHAT WOULD YOU DO WITH THE WHITE HOUSE?

If you were the wife of the new American President, what would you do with the White House? Mrs. Kennedy, the youngest First Lady for many years to keep house in the White House, is unlikely to revolutionise the public rooms although she may hang some modern American paintings in them. But Mr. Bob Roberts, whose firm is in the running for the interior decorating, says that she has important plans for the private apartments. All we know about these is that she loves pale blues and greens. If Mr. Roberts had his way, he would change the official apartments as well—at least to the extent of getting in some fine eighteenth-century American Heritage pieces. But what would an English interior decorator do? The views of three of them are on the following pages.

David Hicks comments:

If Mrs. Kennedy intends that the White House should retain the flavour of a royal palace anywhere in Europe, then basically the Blue and Green Rooms are quite handsome, but certain details, I feel, should be changed.

BLUE BALL ROOM Starting from scratch, I should want to eliminate all the small objects which are cluttering up the room, and not in any way helping the scale. The scale of the damask in the Blue Room—and the design—is of a rather uninspiring type, and I feel that it would be far more stylish to have a very broad striped silk Regency design. The curtains should not only touch the floor but should have more fullness. The draperies are not deep enough for the height of the window, and I think that the height of the room should be accentuated by raising the eagles on the pelmet poles so that they would appear in silhouette over the cornice. The chandelier chain should be wrapped in silk of the same colour as the wall damask, and the furniture grouped with more style, not just placed round the edge of the room. There should be a large oval table in the centre with a cloth of the same material as the walls, falling to the ground. The flower arrangements seem to be very vague and should be much more elegant. On the chimneypiece there should be neat tight arrangements as one sees in engravings of the period: and rather than have one puny palm tree in the window, I would like groups of them beside the fire place.

GREEN ROOM Ideally the material on the walls should be of a bigger and bolder design, and nearer the date of both the White House itself and the Aubusson type carpet. The chief eyesores in the Green Room are, to my mind, the curtains—they do not come to the ground and are too mean at the base. There should be more fullness. A thicker interlining would give more substance. The sofa and chair are of poor quality and the covering of these should be of the same material as that used for the walls. The log basket seems to me to be out of scale and could well be improved. The room generally lacks sufficient furniture, and I think could be made extremely attractive and comfortable by the addition of an occasional table and of *bibelots* and *objets*. The table supporting the pier-glass between the windows is insufficiently solid and could well be replaced by a massive Buhl piece.

LIBRARY This seems to need the most attention. The pine panelling is boring and looks as though most of it is modern and made up. It might be an attractive idea to copy some of the early American painted panelled rooms, making the doors covering the books solid, and using stencilled decoration. Ceiling lights, of course, would have to go, and the wing chairs could be exciting if recovered. However, the room as it stands seems hardly worth retaining, and I would think it would be interesting to gut it completely and create a modern interior, using some of the exciting modern American action painters, hung if possible on walls of coarse off-white linen. I would retain the diamond-patterned grey and white marble floor. The pictures could be lit by recessed spot-lights in the ceiling and the furniture could all be of advanced modern American design. Instead of curtains at the windows, it would be exciting to see two huge pieces of relief sculpture mounted on steel or iron legs stretching from floor to ceiling. These could be mounted a couple of feet out from the windows so that light would filter round them, and at night they would sufficiently screen the dark windows.

UP IN ARMS are the interior decorators of the United States (where they are called "interior designers"), stung by recent comments on the White House by some of their English opposite numbers who, presented with coloured photographs of the public rooms, wanted to do away with the woven-in presidential seal on the fitted carpets, along with much else, and to substitute concealed lighting for the ornate ceiling clusters. Interviewed by the New York *Herald Tribune*, they have been taking it out of Buckingham Palace in return.

"Throw out half the furniture!" was one American comment, from an interior decorator with the not, we thought, particularly American name of T. H. Robsjohn-Gibbings, who also wanted to "do away with the insipid pastels and use only the brightest sunshine colours to counteract the fog." He omitted to say whether he meant inside or outside. "More of a casual, comfortable look," was what another American designer demanded: "they ought to mix a few upholstered pieces with all those stiff chairs,"—imagining, no doubt, that droppers-in chatted with the Queen while slouching on the base of the spine, with their legs crossed.

On the whole, though, the Americans were less ruthless with Buckingham Palace than David Hicks and Michael Inchbald were, for instance, with the White House, one of them wanting to do away with the splendid pine panelling in the library, and the other recommending a white marble floor with brass inlays. But then it is in the Anglo-American tradition that they should be kinder than we are: no American has yet done to Buckingham Palace what we did to the White House in 1812—burn it to the ground.

THE ROSETTA STONE

Egypt

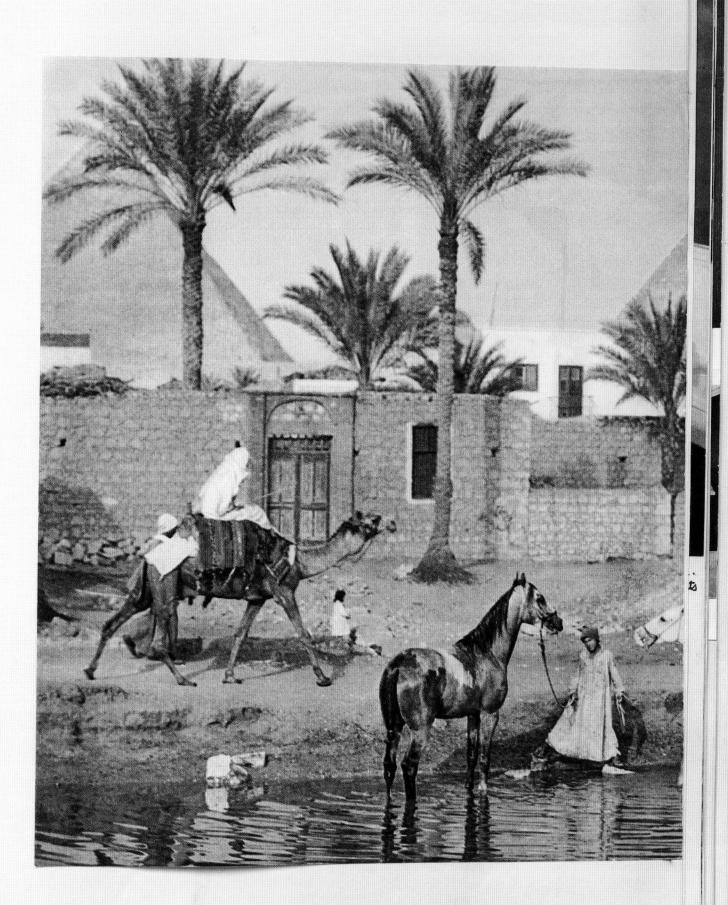

J. Juel : Glyptotek : COPENHAGEN

Rubenstein flat preview sketch in 'Queen'

FABULOUS!

WOMAN'S OWN takes you inside the luxurious London home of Helena Rubinstein designed by David Hicks

ONE of the most fabulous homes in London, that's the new Knightsbridge flat of Helena Rubinstein. Perfectionist in all things, Madame Rubinstein insisted on the world's finest craftsmanship, and the most beautiful materials, then with the help of the day's most famous young interior designer, David Hicks—who has also designed for WOMAN'S OWN—she created for herself a penthouse palace.

And here she shares her pleasure in it with WOMAN'S OWN readers.

Rich red, gold and black greeted us in the hall with concealed lighting behind the exquisite Chinese ebony frames which were bought in Hong Kong.

And this luxurious use of colour, we found, is the keynote to the whole flat. Boldly, purple, cerise and lots of brown are mixed in a living-room where tweed is used for walls and blinds as well as banquettes. (The material matches a favourite Balenciaga suit, she told us.)

Glowing pimento warmly welcomes guests to the spare bedroom, where a richly carved bedhead is the centrepiece, with closely grouped pictures above it.

Her own bedroom—with bright yellow walls and violet silk furnishings—is every woman's dream of an elegant boudoir. The bed itself comes from Portugal and is delicately carved, its beauty emphasized by white bedside tables and white shantung curtains.

As the head of a world-famous cosmetic empire, Madame Rubinstein never completely escapes the cares of business, and it is here that she likes to work.

Hall

Mrs Coopers bedroom : sitting room

main 'reception' room:

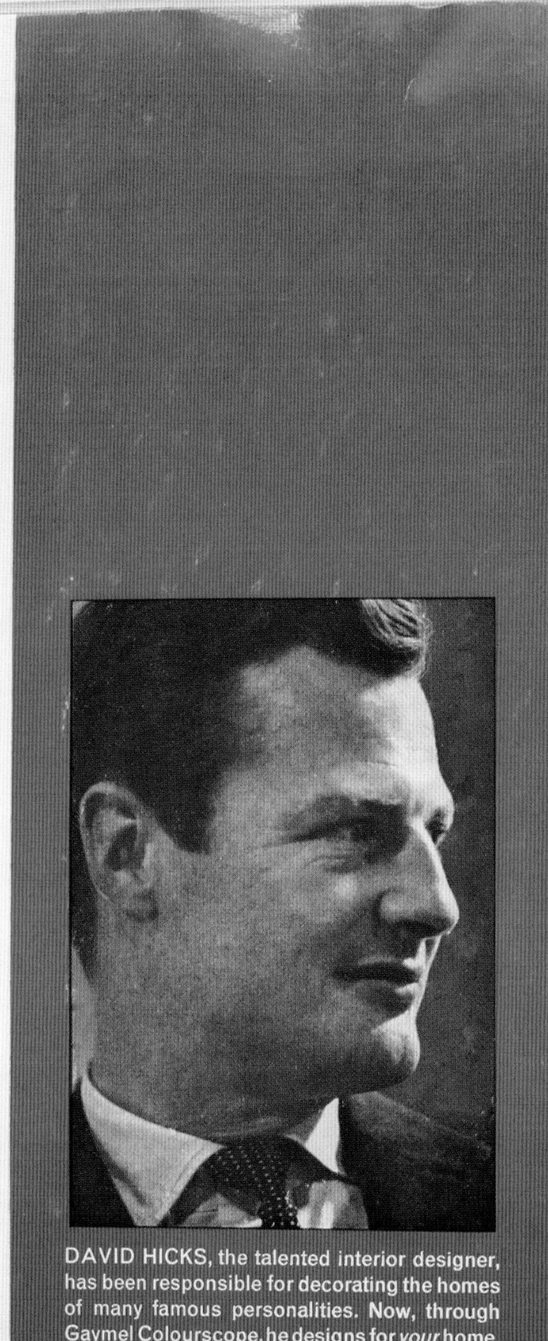

DAVID HICKS, the talented interior designer, has been responsible for decorating the homes of many famous personalities. Now, through Gaymel Colourscope, he designs for *your* home.

The rooms which I have chosen for this Gaymel book are real rooms, in average houses and flats.

I began, as I always do, by trying to rearrange the furniture, only re-covering if it seemed unavoidable, and I also tried hard, as each "scheme" evolved, to get new value out of existing curtains and carpets. In one or two cases I have chosen new curtains, or replaced a carpet, but generally I have proved, by giving special thought to paint colours, how successfully this can be avoided.

The Gaymel colour range will give you unlimited scope in this way, help you to inject change, freshness, and an altogether new atmosphere into your rooms.

David Hicks

rith
ex North

LUCKY WIFE JUNE GETS A RIGHT ROYAL GIFT . .

TERIOR decorator David Hicks, husband of the Queen's ousin, Lady Pamela Mountbatten, walked into a Surrey burban garden and gave a young couple the Christmas esent of their lives. And what a Christmas present!

appened like this: A young and pretty housewife, June Mears—she is twenty - eight—was leaning over the wooden garden gate of her semi - detached house at Kingston-on-Thames, Surrey, chatting to a neighbour. Wives have been known to do this.

June's children, fourteen-month-old Suzanne and three - year - old Christopher, were playing in the garden.

A chauffeur-driven limousine passed them slowly. Then it idled past again—even more slowly.

"I wonder what they want," said June Mears to her neighbour.

The car came round a third time—and stopped by the two women.

Reply

A pleasant-looking young man, immaculately dressed, got out of the car and said to June: "Do you want your house decorated inside and out? It will cost you nothing."

To be on the safe side, June made a typically feminine reply of an offer of something for nothing. "I wouldn't mind," she said. "Incidentally, who are you?"

The husband of the Queen's cousin then introduced himself.

"I have a client who is particularly interested in my idea of re-decorating 'lived-in' houses in various social categories." said David Hicks.

Difficult

You don't know how difficult it has been to get people to allow me to use their houses," he went on. "I have been driving around for two days trying to get hold of the right type of suburban house.

People have been so suspicious. It has been like trying to sell £5 notes for a penny."

David Hicks went over the house.

"I will make suggestions," he said. "If you don't like my colour ideas—then we will have a conference about it."

New

Said June: "The inside and outside walls will be painted and I am being given new curtains and a new bedspread. My white carpet will be washed as well."

How did her car salesman husband, Brian, react? He is waiting to see the result—and looking forward to a happy and newly-decorated Christmas.

IE MEARS . . decorations 'on the house.'

Jean Barrett *transfers a traditional strap design for the David Hicks Organisation onto squared paper. She is a versatile designer.*

Gaymel Colourscope

Nehru's guests

LADY PAMELA MOUNTBATTEN left London Airport for India today. She will be the guest of Mr. Nehru at his home and will then journey to many places which her mother Lady Mountbatten visited as Vicereine—Udaipur, Benares, Agra and Jaipur.

Lady Pamel's husband, Mr. David Hicks, is going with her. He said: "We don't want to lay much emphasis on the invitation to stay with Mr. Nehru. We will be with him for 48 hours on a private visit.

"The main purpose of my journey is to help the Indian Government on merchandising of goods for overseas markets—things like cloth and goods produced from what you might call cottage industries."

Off to help

LADY PAMELA HICKS flew from London to-day on a journey that will evoke both sad and happy memories.

She will be the guest of **Mr. Nehru** at his home, and will then journey through many places where her mother, Countess Mountbatten, was so popular with the Indian people—Udaipur, Benares, Agra and Jaipur among them.

With her has gone her husband, **Mr. David Hicks,** who said: "We will be with Mr. Nehru for 48 hours on a private visit. The main purpose of my journey is to help the Indian Government on merchandising goods for overseas markets.

"The Minister in charge has asked me to see if I can help."

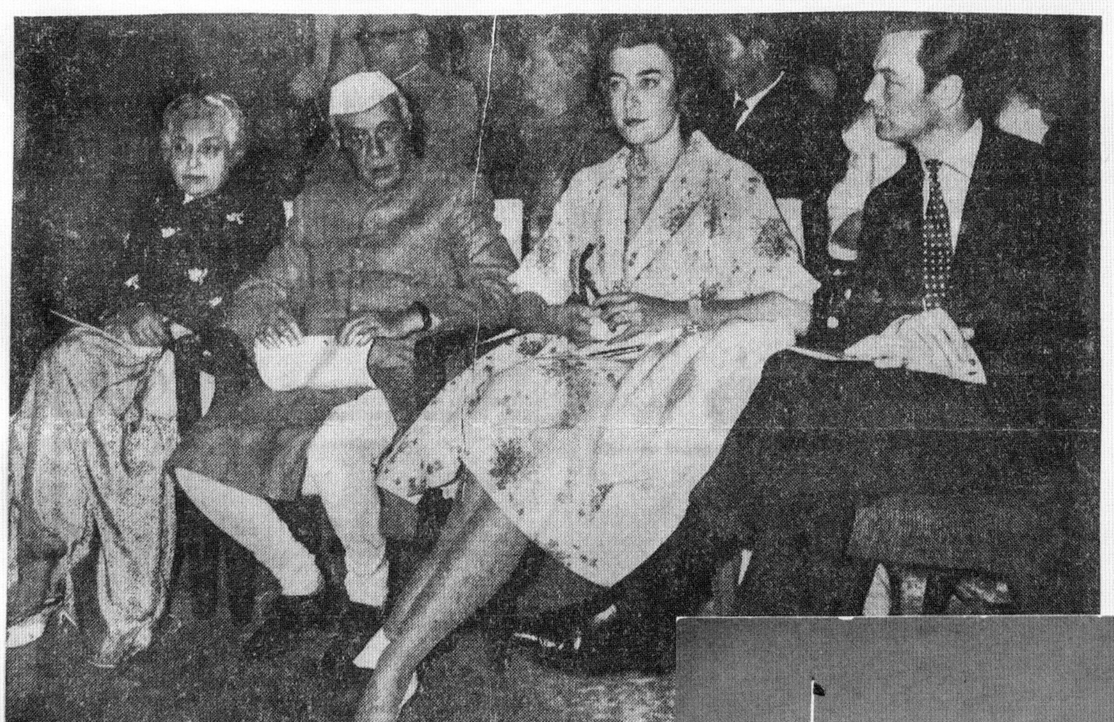

Rashtrapati Bhavan

MONDAY: In the morning the President drove in State and addressed the Joint Session of Parliament. In the afternoon the President received Mrs. John F. Kennedy. Lady Pamela Hicks and Mr. David Hicks have arrived.

SUNDAY: In the morning the President received the Prime Minister. In the afternoon the President received:—Chief Minister of Bihar, Shri B. B. Varma.

SATURDAY: In the afternoon the President received Shri B. K. Nehru. The Governor of Gujarat and party arrived in the morning and left in the evening.

The Lt.-Governor of Himachal Pradesh and party have left.

IN MOTHER'S FOOTSTEPS —LADY PAMELA

IN New Delhi's National Stadium Lady Pamela Hicks, daughter of the late Countess Mountbatten, watches a touring team of Russian dancers.

With her are her husband, Mr. David Hicks, India's Premier Nehru, and his diplomat sister, Mrs. Pandit.

From New Delhi Lady Pamela set out to visit places where her mother stayed as Vicereine of India in 1947.

In honour of
Mrs. John F. Kennedy

The Prime Minister

requests the pleasure of the company of

Mr. David Hicks & The Hon'ble Lady Pamela Hicks

at Dinner

8-30 p.m. on Tuesday, the 13th March, 1962.

R.S.V.P.—
Reception Officer,
Prime Minister's House.

[P.T.O.

DINNER PLAN

Tuesday, the 13th March, 1962.

—:o:—

Major Mohd. Mirza.	Shrimati Laj Yunus.
Shrimati Pamela Kochar.	Shri G. S. Pathak.
Mr. David Hicks.	Shrimati Helen Chaman Lall.
Shrimati Krishna Hutheesing.	Dr. Homi Bhabha.
Shri Surjit Singh Majithia.	Shrimati Vijayalakshmi Pandit.
Princess Radziwill.	H.E. John Kenneth Galbraith.
The Prime Minister.	**Shrimati Indira Gandhi.**
Mrs. John F. Kennedy.	H.H. the Maharaja of Patiala.
Shri B. K. Nehru.	Mrs. Galbraith.
H.H. the Maharani of Patiala.	Diwan Chaman Lall.
Lieut.-General R. K. Kochar.	The Hon'ble Lady Pamela Hicks.
Shrimati Tara Sahgal.	Shri Gautam Sahgal.
Shri Mohd. Yunus.	Shrimati Syeda Mirza.

ENTRANCE

Time

She sat at Nehru's right and her sister at his left in a simple, teakwood-paneled dining room. The 23 other guests at the long, narrow table included Lady Pamela Hicks, daughter of India's last British viceroy, Lord Mountbatten; her husband, David Hicks; and the Maharajah of Patiala.

The menu consisted of consomme; stuffed pomfret, an Indian river fish; roast chicken; sweet potatoes; French beans; chocolate cake, and fruit salad. There was no wine, in keeping with Nehru's generally austere style of living.

UDAIPUR, Saturday.

MRS. JACQUELINE KENNEDY ended her week of dutiful public appearances and stereo-typed sightseeing from he Taj Mahal to Benares burning ghats last night in the airy-tale splendour of feudal India.

She is guest of the Maharana of Udaipur, premier prince of he Rajputs, whose seat is a fantastic 17th century marble pile of lomes, balconies and crenellated walls set beside pale blue lakes and agged greeny-brown hills and ame forests.

She is among India's version of er own kind of people, the cream f Hindustan's ancient nobility, ultured, travelled, fond of the hase and, above all, rich.

Her fellow guests are her sister rincess Lee Radziwill, wife of a ondon business man, Lady Pamela licks, Earl Mountbatten's aughter, and her husband Mr. avid Hicks, the interior decorator.

Among excursions planned for Irs. Kennedy was a visit to an land palace which the Maharana tends to develop as a luxury otel.

Maharana of Udaipur   Maharanee

Queen Louise Patricia Rory Cameron P

PH JK

Part 2

1962–66

1962–66

David in action, on the phone in his studio, while Pammy reads the papers in her new drawing room at Britwell. David, 'Decorator of Today', leaning on a Kjaerholm chair in his modern room; the hall with dogs; the splendid dining room; Pammy in a ballgown and tiara – all at Britwell. A weekend at his father-in-law Dickie's with Grace Kelly, now Princess Grace, and other royals gives David a chance to photograph the famed beauty, who tells her host that he had been her college pin-up and gives him her picture, which he keeps by his bed ever afterwards. Then, to the South of France and David's new Riva named 'Les X' – The Hickses in French.

Visiting Ethiopia, where David photographs the Jubilee Palace from the Imperial Chevrolet, and a leopard chained to the steps outside. Pammy's place-card from lunch, seated on Emperor Haile Selassie's right. David on TV with a client and his fabric printer; his house for the Londonderrys in Hampstead; with Pammy at Yves Vidal's York Castle, Tangier and Drumlanrig Castle, Scotland. Christmas guest rooms at Broadlands and assembled staff at Britwell, with a smoking Noel Coward.

The timeless cover of *L'Oeil* with Christina Cholmondeley's London hall and braided shower-room; David's Jaipur-inspired dining room in Chelsea, and Jenny Samuel's house next door with its famed green silk velvet walls. Dickie gives a garden party with Rex Harrison and Shirley Maclaine. David buys an Ellsworth Kelly for his Coca-Cola lacquered walls in London. Britwell in Vogue, David Bailey pictures, Horst-style; and David included in the cool young London set in Bailey's *Box of Pin-Ups* before being looking slightly less modern in Francis Marshall's sketches ...

David Hicks provided one of the highlights of the Cotton Board Exhibition with this spanking modern living-room (right) and adjoining dining-terrace

DAVID HICKS, whose crisp modern approach to interior design has brought him ready acclaim, has given simplicity and the clean clash of clear colours to his 'Modern Living Room and Dining Terrace'. He thinks British designs could be simpler and has used only one printed pattern, a glazed floral chintz in clear blue and green on a white ground. His other patterns reflect his preference for a clean unfussy statement of tone and line.

in cotton

ur Design and Style Centre

David Hicks

DECORATOR OF

TODAY

In the last few years David Hicks has become Britain's most celebrated decorator. Here, we show the first pictures of his new house in Oxfordshire, and overleaf Janice Elliott examines his talents and achievements

Photographs by Terence Donovan

Left: design and garden room at Britwell Salome, the Hickses' Oxfordshire home. Here curtains are eliminated—unpainted pine screens conceal ungainly windows and radiators; plaster walls are left bare. Chairs are by Poul Kjaerholm, the Buddha is Chinese.
Above: a bathroom serves also as a study. On the table are a Swedish porphyry vase, modern Swedish pottery containers, a 1730 bronze plaque of horses being shod. The base of the lamp is a Bristol blue chemist's bottle.
Right: wallpaper specially made for the staircase area at Britwell. The design was taken from a fragment of late 17th-century fabric, probably Portuguese, found at a rag-merchant's.
Below: the long, low, panelled breakfast room, decorated in tones of honey and straw. The carpet on the polished chestnut floor is 18th-century Spanish, the curtains are by Donald Bros., and the early Victorian serving table belonged to David Hicks's grandfather. The dining table is decorated, when not in use, with 18th-century dairy dishes, and Whieldon plates. Cane-seated dining chairs are painted green.

Sunday Times
Colour Supplement

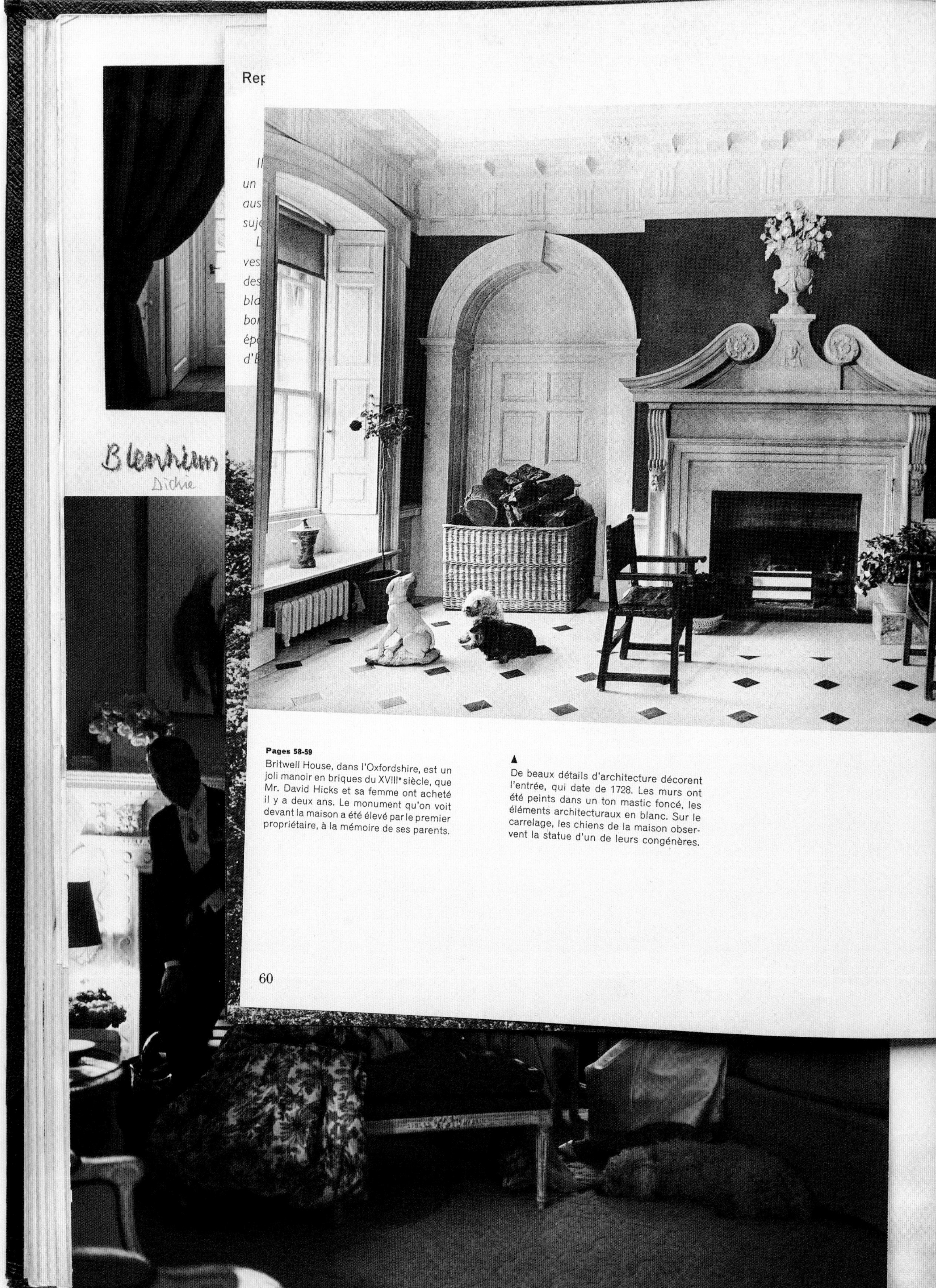

Pages 58-59
Britwell House, dans l'Oxfordshire, est un joli manoir en briques du XVIIIe siècle, que Mr. David Hicks et sa femme ont acheté il y a deux ans. Le monument qu'on voit devant la maison a été élevé par le premier propriétaire, à la mémoire de ses parents.

▲
De beaux détails d'architecture décorent l'entrée, qui date de 1728. Les murs ont été peints dans un ton mastic foncé, les éléments architecturaux en blanc. Sur le carrelage, les chiens de la maison observent la statue d'un de leurs congénères.

Nottingham

The Peacock Bar
Nottingham.

HOME DECOR Employing an interior decorator at all is incredibly ROGUE. But if you must, among the least ROGUE are John Siddeley, David Hicks and John Fowler. Antique is GO if borrowed. Aubusson carpets are ABORT. Owning original paintings is ROGUE, unless they were inherited when they become ABORT. The most GO painting to have at the moment is Goya's Duke of Wellington.

The Marquess of Queensbury invites you to see

Rosenthal exhibition

His day

PROPPED in front of the cornflakes bowl on **DAVID HICKS'S** breakfast table was a typed postcard from his secretary with a list of the day's nine appointments — which ranged from visiting the young Duchess of Rutland to checking his new silver designs.

"Get more razor blades. Cancel *The Times*," was scribbled on the pigskin-covered notepad which lay by his two boiled eggs supported in stiff-collared new eggcups.

Pale, shiny bentwood chairs with woven cane seats stood round the circular table covered by dark grey and deep blue wide-striped cotton.

Round a central glass cylinder of cornflowers stood sturdy white breakfast china with a bright blue smudge pattern, wooden bread platter, pepper and salt grinders.

IT'S OBVIOUS: Hicks is practical, well organised, sophisticated. The impact of the inexpensive objects used showed wit and imagination.

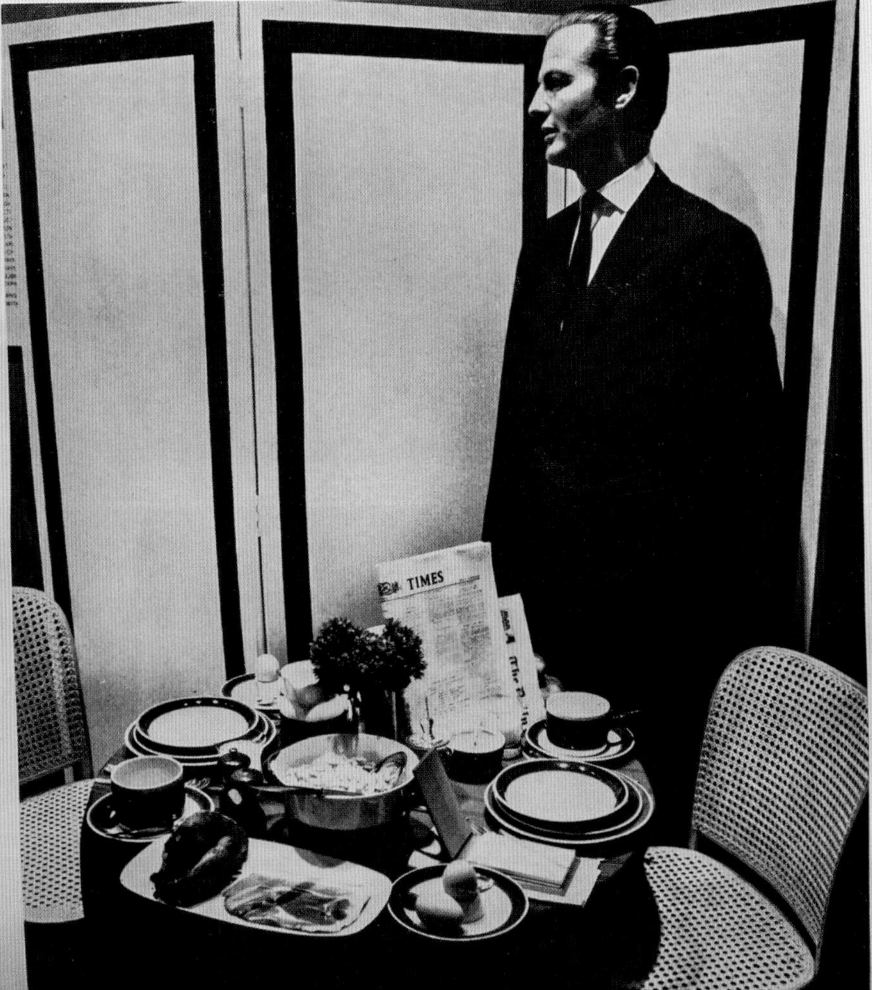

David Hicks's table set for breakfast (*see above*).
What he put on it: Rorstrand's lively blue & white set called Koka—the big breakfast cups are really soup cups that look like rather smart coffee mugs. What pulled it off: the bang of blue against blue—blue china, blue cornflowers, blue striped cloth.
What he likes for breakfast: fruit juice, cornflakes, boiled eggs, cold game or ham, coffee, toast & marmalade.

The Princess of Hesse and the Rhine (for whom Doreen Lady Brabourne stood proxy) is godmother to the infant son of Lord and Lady Brabourne who was christened Philip Wyndham Ashley by Canon Douglas A. Duncan at St. John the Baptist, Mersham, yesterday. The other godparents are the Hon. James Dugdale (for whom Mr. David Hicks stood proxy), Mr. C. H. W. Troughton, and Mrs. Peter Leng (for whom Lady Pamela Hicks stood proxy).

P

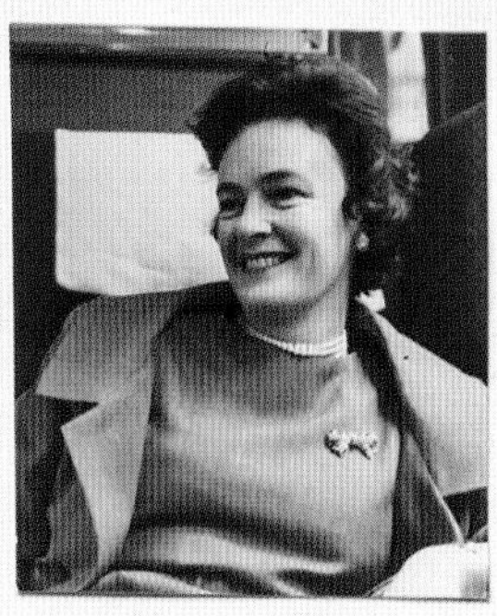

Sosh Troughton

On the way down in the train.

Blenheim dress

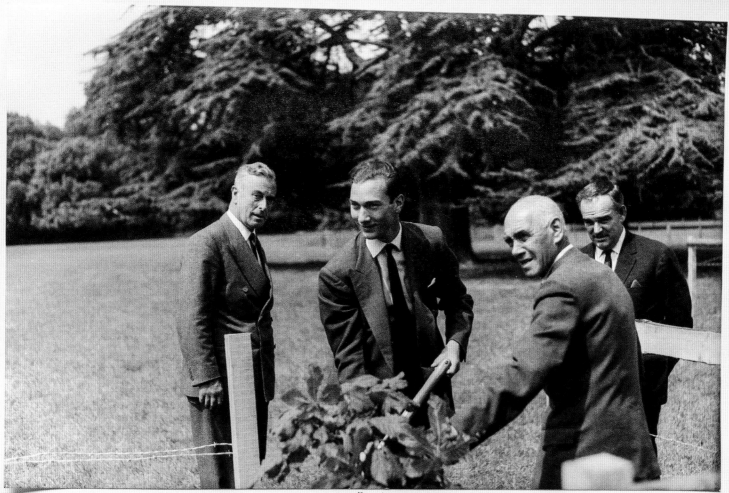

P. William Harold P. Rainier

Broadlands weekend

Johnny Dalkeith

P. Maria Beatrice of Italy

P. Rainier of Monaco

P. Grace of Monaco

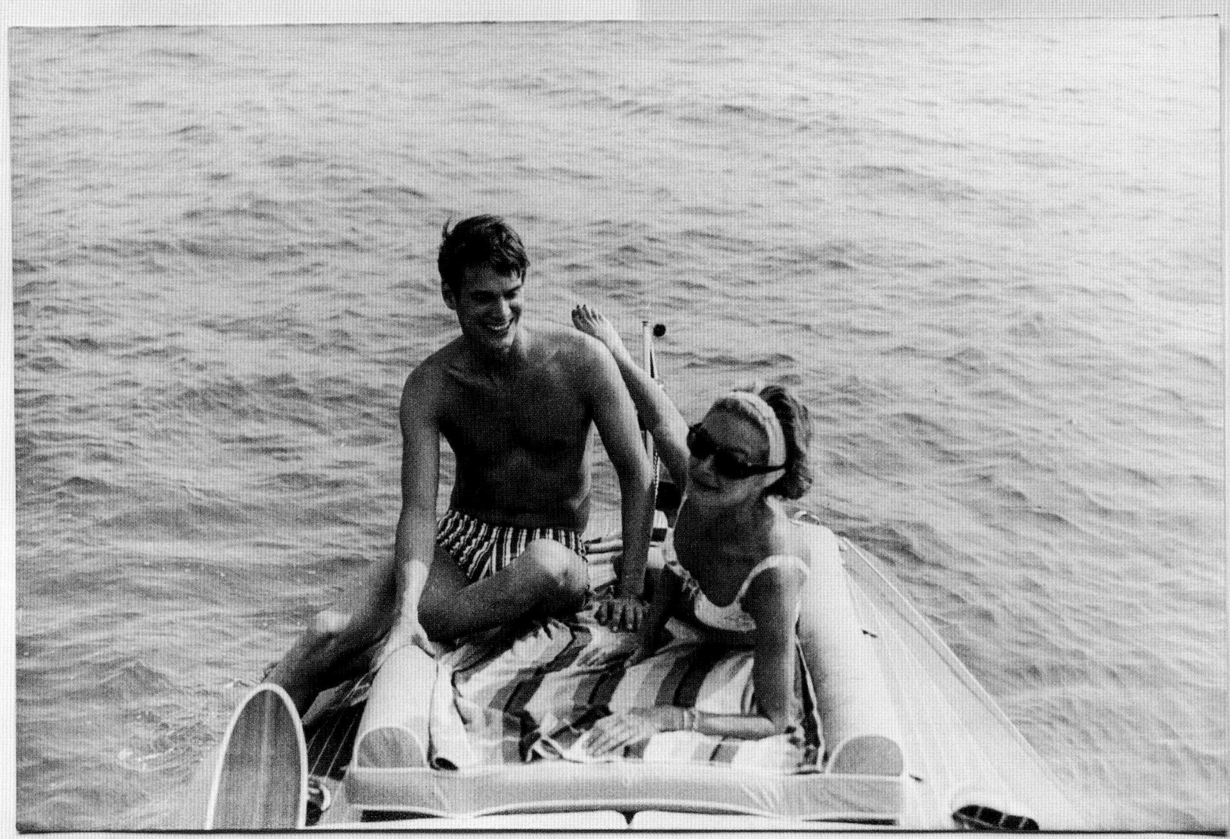

Billy McCarthy   Battista Stewart   on Les XS

in Le Roc – the Cholmondeley villa

DESIGN FOR LIVING
BY **PRISCILLA CHAPMAN**

Sunday Times supplement

Peter Keen

Jenni Sammel's dining room

Left: pattern on pattern carries the fight against shape starvation about as far as it can go. In this London dining room David Hicks uses precise, geometric patterns with matt surfaces: heavy brown cotton curtains with a border in thick red, blue and green wool; red carpet, designed for the house by Mr Hicks; Welsh woollen rug permanently covering a table which is only a wooden frame; on the walls a stencil border adapted from American colonial decoration

the vase in new york vogue

staying on Corisande with Phyl Drummond

St Tropez awning

Versailles

December

laff

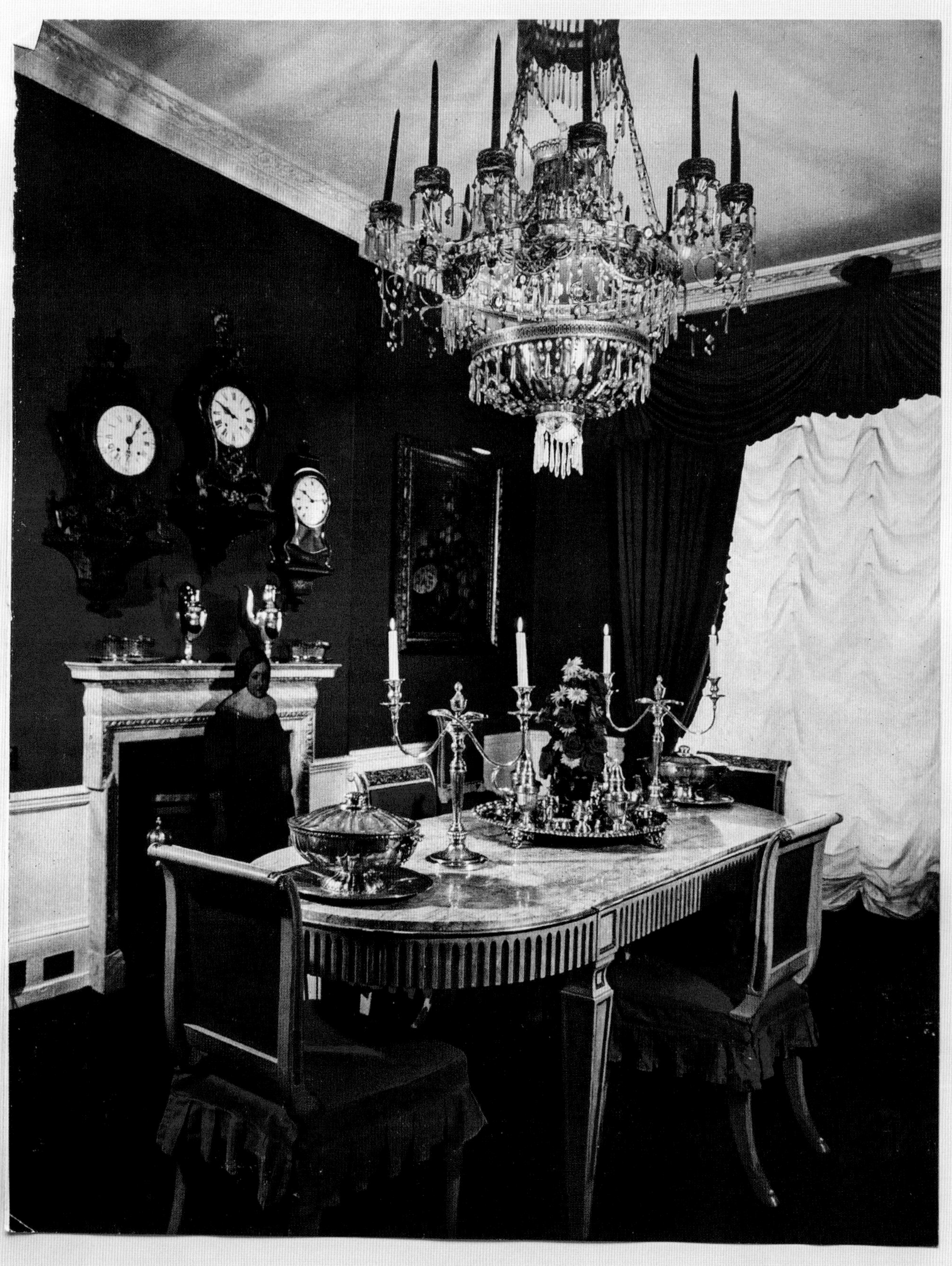

Carla Venosta's dining room : Chester Sq DH.

Thanksgiving : New York

Jubilee Palace
Addis Ababa

12th February, 1964

Dear Lord Mountbatten:

It was a pleasure to receive your letter of 22nd January and to know that all is well with you.

We would have liked to have the opportunity of welcoming you again to Ethiopia accompanied by your daughter but, as this is not possible, We will be pleased to receive your daughter and her husband next month in Addis Ababa and We trust that the date of the proposed visit will be communicated to Us.

HAILE SELLASSIE I
EMPEROR

Earl Mountbatten of Burma, K.G.,P.C.,G.C.S.I.,
Chief of the Defence Staff,
Ministry of Defence,
Storey's Gate,
London, S.W.1.

Grand Palace

HIM Grants Audience

His Imperial Majesty Haile Selassie I graciously granted audience yesterday at the Grand Palace to Lady Pamela and her husband Mr. D. Hicks.

Lady Pamela and Mr. D. Hicks are here as Guests of His Imperial Majesty Haile Selassie I.

Ethiopia

arriving at Jubilee Palace

LADY PAMELA HICKS

ENTRANCE

lunch plan

guarding the door ......

gin and tonic

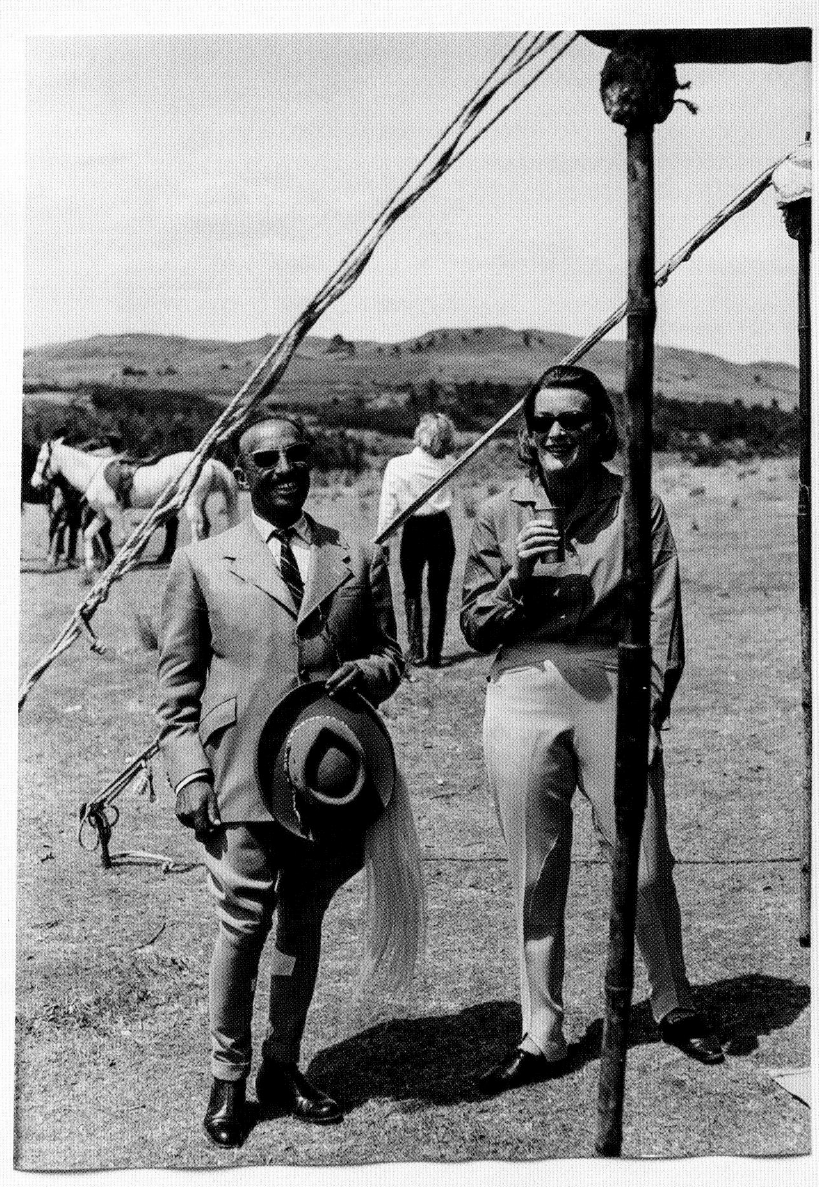

the master of the Imperial Horse

sday, July 23, 1964

David Hicks plays it so crisp and cool

THE top people, it seems, like their furnishings crisp and cool. This was the theme running through a full-length BBC television feature starring **David Hicks.** What a bonanza for this elegant young consultant the programme turned out to be . . .

Mr. Hicks smiled at suggestions that furnishing the Hicks way was expensive. Why, he had even prepared a scheme for a small room for as little as 25 guineas! What had the client got for that? A coloured sketch of Mr. Hicks' ideas!

Mr. Hicks told us he wants to wholesale some of his fabric and carpet designs; he is writing a book to help ordinary people furnish with good taste.

When a fabric salesman called on him it was as though the rep was consulting an oracle, rather than selling.

"Messy," said Mr. Hicks—and the offending design was whisked away. Ah! that's better. In fact Mr. Hicks liked it. It was crisp, and cool.

One of his clients was starred too. She spent several thousands on decorating and furnishing a room for relaxing in. She was a very charming girl—cool and crisp.

35 minute T.V. programme.

PADDY

BBC CAMERA SCRIPT

OUTSIDE BROADCASTS

SITE: DAVID HICKS LTD.,
25 Lowndes Street,
London, S.W.1.

- David Hicks has glanced at this – he's not got a copy in his possession. I got the impression that he may wander in his replies. But I think he'll be good, & generally fairly easy to talk to. See you Tuesday morning.
Cheers.
[illegible]

"ALL SORTS TO MAKE A WORLD"

"THE INTERIOR DECORATOR"

RECORDING: Tuesday 29th June, 1964
Wednesday 1st July, 1964.

PROJECT NO......72/1/4/4182
VIDEOTAPE NO....VT/4T/GW1551

ES EDITOR..........Max Morgan-Witts
UCER...............Max Morgan-Witts
. ASSISTANT........Alec Nisbett
. SECRETARY........Sonja Thomas

E MANAGERS.........Ronnie Pantlin
David Collison
Murray Marshall
Bob Joner

S.TEL.E...............Clive Potter

Crew No...............London Unit 3

Scanner 'Phone No......BEL: 6887

TRANSMISSION: Wednesday 15th July, 1964
7.00 - 7.35 p.m.

REHEARSAL AND RECORDING SCHEDULE - see over page

PARTICIPANTS..........David Hicks
Hon. Mrs. Anthony Samuel
Mr. Thorpe of Warner & Son Ltd.
Mr. Conroy of Conroy & Slipper Ltd.
Peter Evans

PAISLEY DAILY EXPRESS, SATURDAY, JULY 1

TELEVIEWS

WELL-DONE DOCUMENTARY

UNDYING gratitude to the BBC for this week's episode of "All Kinds To Make A World," featuring interior designer David Hicks. It is nice to think that someone, somewhere, last winter had foresight and pity enough to prepare such a series to enliven the otherwise prevailing summer diet of re-heats and left-overs. Maybe it is the novelty, in these days of finding a programme with any sense of direction that has not been screened before, but Paddy Feeney's prying little session into the lives of Mr Hicks and his clients did seem extraordinarily well done. Meeting rich and sophisticated people on TV is always fascinating—particularly in situations where the exotic side of their personalities has scope to expand. Certainly there was scope here—a large empty room, and unlimited resources to spend on furnishings. The programme seemed to be crammed with fascinating facts and pieces of film — in fact, it was slightly disappointing the number of promising situations that had to be skipped through or curtailed so that the whole story could be contained. Production was really crisp, with "still" flashes cleverly used to convey a sense of urgency, as well as to compress the unwieldy mass of material. Hats off to Paddy Feeney—he is almost as relaxed and respectful with the fearfully-upper-class as Alan Whicker—and we can think of no higher praise.

Dinner party for Luton Hoo Ball at Britwell

Charles Rutland Johnny Dalkeith

Campanula Pyramidalis! Tomislav of Yugoslavia Jane Dalkeith Margarita Frances Rutland

Billy McCarthy Sarah Wilson P.H.

THE LONDONDERRYS continued

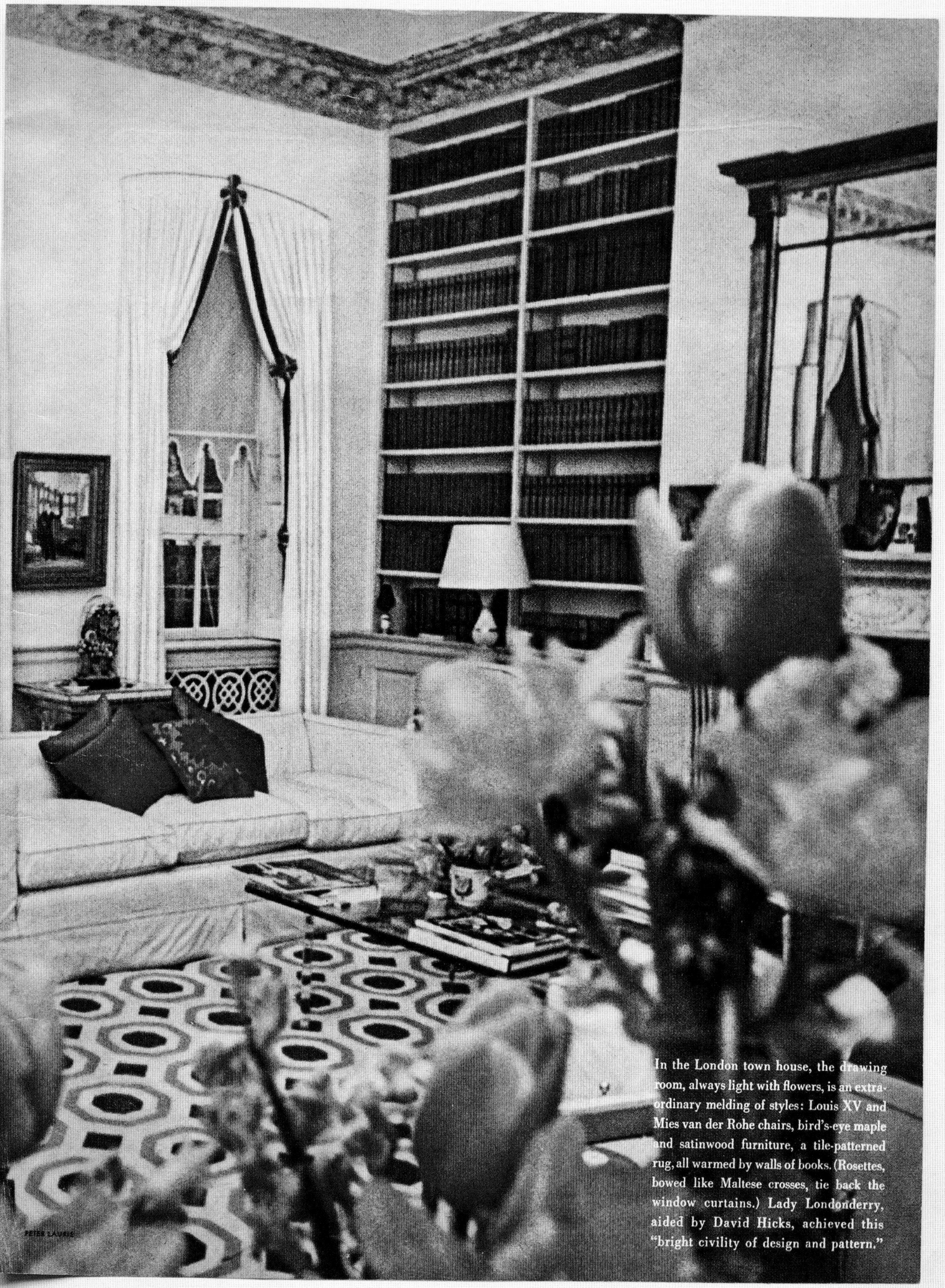

PETER LAURIE

In the London town house, the drawing room, always light with flowers, is an extraordinary melding of styles: Louis XV and Mies van der Rohe chairs, bird's-eye maple and satinwood furniture, a tile-patterned rug, all warmed by walls of books. (Rosettes, bowed like Maltese crosses, tie back the window curtains.) Lady Londonderry, aided by David Hicks, achieved this "bright civility of design and pattern."

this shot also in English 'Vogue'

Once in London, up through the twisted back streets of Camden Town to the open hill of Hampstead. Here, the Londonderrys' Georgian town house that stares with the blank self-confidence of perfect proportions onto a tree-lined lane, is the hub of a vivid and various life. It resounds with Lady Londonderry's passion—pop music. A surprised Hampstead record shop, that usually does brisk business in Shostakovich, has a standing order to deliver to her the newcomers to the British and American Top Twenties every week: she thinks of backing a pop group from across the river, and auditions them in the drawing room. Or, leonine and energetic, she teaches her daughters—the Ladies Sophia, five, and Cosima, two, the niceties of Association Football and the offside rule on the walled lawn. Tiring of this, she leaps into her Alfa Romeo—also fitted with a gramophone and awash with pops—and plunges down the hill to London to the strains of Elvis or the Beatles. With her husband, she is to be found in many milieux: at the newest nightclub, at film premières, or, for instance, when Robert Kennedy paid a visit, at the Ambassador's table to meet him.

One joint passion of the Londonderrys' is horror films—to hear them savouring and comparing *The Curse of Frankenstein* against *The Brides from the Mummy's Tomb* is like hearing two ancient gourmets ruminate over vintages. The other is travel. They went to the Egyptian Temples last spring and to Thailand in May. But always back again to Hampstead, where Lady Londonderry and David Hicks produced a bright civility of design and pattern that makes the intricate old house a machine for modern living. One of the striking things about the house is the way it keeps the integrity of texture and function that got lost in the pomp of Victorian England. For example, the sixteenth and seventeenth centuries thought of a house as something to be lived *on* as well as *in*—one reads of Pepys, or earlier, Lord Chancellor Francis Bacon, walking and meditating on the leads of their houses. So, here, leaving the twentieth century, and the thump of blue beat behind, one emerges at the top of the house onto a white-railed quarterdeck, to stare across the windy miles to the Thames, where St. Paul's and Westminster still cruise low and dark like ships on the horizon.

american vogue.

Jane Dalkeith

Britwell pool

THE LONDONDERRYS

The country gentleman's park and seat is one of the finer achievements of the English mind. This rehandling of nature—the flowing turf, trees grouped to please the eye, tufts of pine or oak counterpointed by a scarp of temple or an obelisk, warm live cows grazing neither too bunched nor too spread, a lake glinting between branches, and the big house neatly at the focus of all—seems like a painting, setting out man's estates in a due order and harmony. So one muses as the blue bullet rolls softly through a landscape that is in its way a small masterpiece.

Withdraw the mind's eye: up, away from the car, over the cows that look now like black pen scratches on the turf, over the woods like soft green lace, high above the lake that ruffles brown and vertiginous. Duck and coot swim small below; in the autumn swans come creaking down and slice across it in creamy swathes like children cutting into coffee cake. The lake was dredged last year, but already the reeds, tender green brush strokes from Dürer's hand, are rearranging themselves along the margin. The woods hang darker green over the water; the lake, like a huge Y, holds the house in its arms. The blue Buick passes over a stone lion-guarded bridge, the blank sweep of windows gazes out over the waters to the rounded slopes on the other side—this arm of the lake trails off up a valley, between pine and laurel, and under a crumbling grassy bridge grown over with ivy. High above that bank are the graves of the Londonderry pets: Hambletonian, the sire of trotters, lies under a Romanesque casket; mossy dog funerary statues peer gloomily out of their shiny-leaved (Continued on page 121)

THE LONDON HOUSE OF THE LONDONDERRYS. 1. Lady Londonderry, in the dining room, sitting on an inlaid Maltese marble table in front of a portrait by Sir Thomas Lawrence of Lord Stewart, the husband of Frances Anne. 2. Lady Londonderry in the music room, which holds Lord Londonderry's definitive collection of musical literature. On the floor, one of many tile-patterned rugs loomed for the house by England's clever, successful young designer, David Hicks, who by keeping "the integrity of texture and function turned this old house into a machine for modern living." 3. The dining room, with white plasterwork on lemon-yellow walls, a Waterford crystal chandelier, rush matting on the floor; over the mantel, a portrait of Lord Seaham by Sir Thomas Lawrence. 4. The Georgian house with its private lawn the size of a cricket pitch. 5. In a guest room, an *oeil de boeuf* window; wallpaper and curtains of the same Paisley print in deep Victorian shades. 6. An abstract painting, "Another World," by Kenneth Noland over a Louis XV chest signed by Macret; on the Louis XV chair, stencilled white sacking. 7. Lady Londonderry with her two young daughters, the Lady Cosima Maria-Gabriella Vane Tempest Stewart, aged two, and the Lady Sophia Frances Anne Tempest Vane Stewart, aged five.

PETER LAURIE

our bedroom

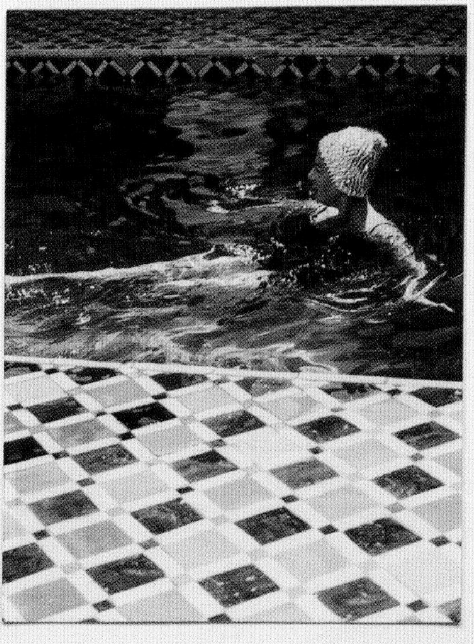

Pammy in the pool at York Castle

Staying with Molly Buccleuch : Drumlanrig

her sittingroom

the Gloucesters

Charles de Bestegui
the Duke of Buccleuch

Count ? C de B Tina & Sonny Blandford

Staying at Marchmont

after lunch at Alnwick

Staying with the Telfer-Smollets

Christmas '64

LIST OF VISITORS ROOMS FOR CHRISTMAS

The Lord Brabourne	PORTICO ROOM
The Lady Brabourne	LADY LOUIS' ROOM
Doreen, The Lady Brabourne	GREEN ROOM
Mr. David Hicks	GARDEN ROOM
The Lady Pamela Hicks	PALMERSTON ROOM
Mrs. Hicks	CANOPY ROOM
Sister Helen Rowe (with twins)	FUCHSIA ROOM
The Hon. Norton Knatchbull	INDIA ROOM
The Hon. Michael John Knatchbull	BERMUDA ROOM
The Hon. Joanna Knatchbull	ADEN ROOM
The Hon. Amanda Knatchbull	CYPRUS ROOM
Nannie Bowden & Philip	WEST ROOM
Miss. Edwina Hicks	BLUE ROOM
Nannie McKibben & Ashley	FOUNTAIN ROOM

from an eighteenth-century carved stone urn, which stands in front of the house, to a towering cedar

Britwell: Christmas 1964

David Hicks doing up 'nurseries' at Windsor

William Hickey

MR. DAVID HICKS, the interior decorator, has received a royal commission for his work. He has been redecorating the rooms of **Princess Anne** and **Prince Charles** at Windsor Castle. Princess Anne was a bridesmaid at his wedding four years ago when he married **Lady Pamela,** daughter of **Earl Mountbatten. The Queen, Prince Philip,** and **the Queen Mother** were among the guests.

Quietly Mr. Hicks moved into Windsor Castle with his own team of plasterers, painters, and furnishers to alter the decor in the rooms which Anne and Charles have on the second and third floor of the Queen's Tower.

The rooms are above those used by the Queen and Prince Philip.

The work is all but complete and the Queen, who moved into the castle yesterday for the rest of April, was able to inspect his handiwork.

Mr. Hicks goes about his work with a definite flourish. For the late Helena Rubinstein, the cosmetics queen, he provided a coarse tweed of deep purple for the walls of her Knightbridge apartment.

The children's suites in the royal apartments at Windsor —known to the family as the "nurseries"— are much less sophisticated.

Easter at Easton Neston '65 with Kisty →

New York
Herald Tribune

The Complete Country House

Photographed for the Herald Tribune in England by JILL KREMENTZ

L'ŒIL

NUMÉRO SPÉCIAL: LE DÉCOR DE LA VIE

Christina Cholmondeley's hall

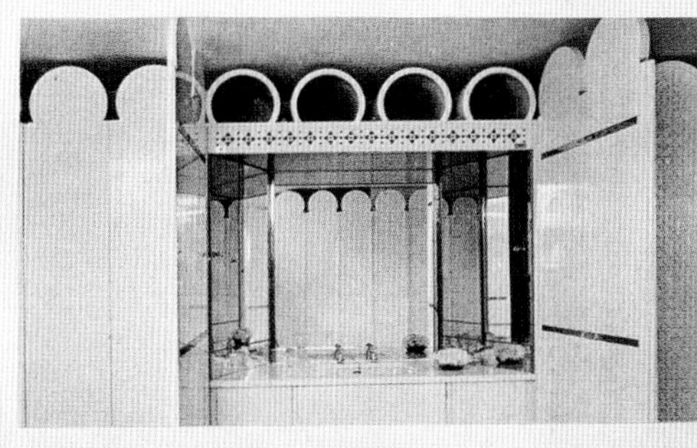

1. Cette salle de bains des Mille et Une Nuits a été inspirée par les voyages au Maroc de Lady Londonderry et de David Hicks. Ayant visité le pays à quinze jours d'intervalle, tous deux eurent un coup de foudre pour les moucharabiehs marocains. C'est après de longues recherches pour trouver des artisans capables d'un tel travail que David Hicks (en collaboration avec William Mc Carty) put créer cette pièce en bois laqué blanc et glaces. Lady Londonderry ayant isolé sa chambre au maximum — on doit traverser la salle de bains pour y accéder — il fallait donc donner à celle-ci un caractère de pièce de réception. Les 28 moucharabiehs qui l'entourent dissimulent les placards de rangement et les appareils sanitaires. Le trou au sommet de chaque moucharabieh est destiné à un chapeau.

2. La baignoire laquée blanc est placée au centre de la pièce selon une disposition chère à David Hicks. Le mur du fond est fait de six panneaux de glace maintenus par des tiges de bronze doré; les deux panneaux du milieu ouvrent sur la chambre de Lady Londonderry. Le siège est une banquette de nursery 1860 capitonnée de 122 boutons et recouverte d'un imprimé de feuilles de trèfles bleues et verte.

3. Quatre des moucharabiehs dissimulent un lavabo. Derrière les deux faces latérales du grand miroir, un placard.

4. Un monte-plat est dissimulé derrière deux autres moucharabiehs. Les grilles au-dessous de chaque panneau autour de la pièce sont des bouches de chaleur.

5. Un coin de la salle de bains de Lord Londonderry. Le store fait dans un imprimé hollandais brun et blanc est assorti aux rideaux du dressing-room (voir page 6). Le lavabo de marbre brun a été encastré dans le renforcement de la fenêtre donnant sur le jardin. Un large galon rouge borde les murs mastic. Un spot vertical éclaire le lavabo.

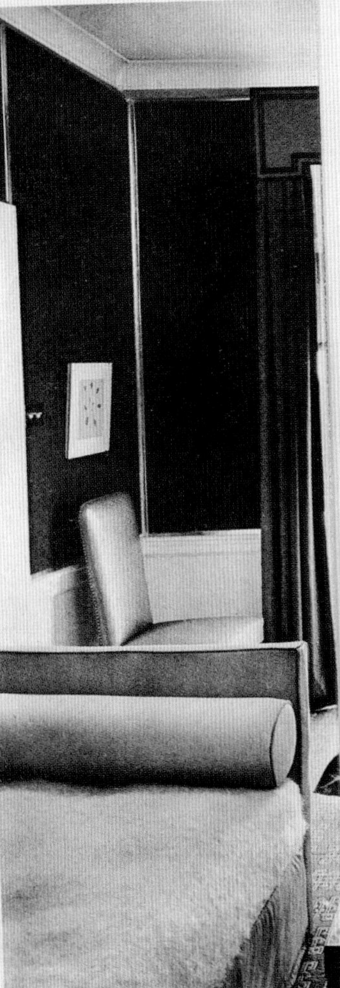

1 2

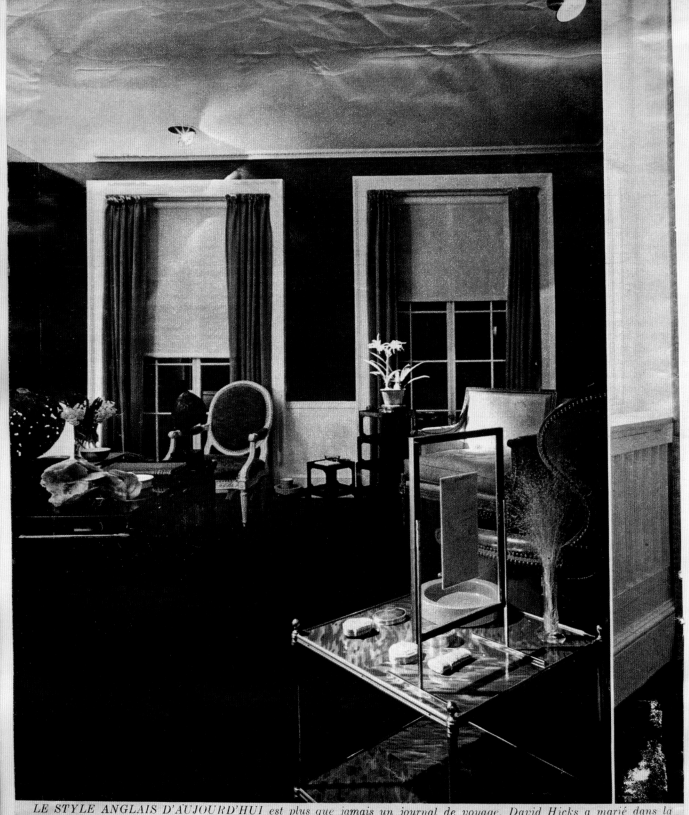

LE STYLE ANGLAIS D'AUJOURD'HUI est plus que jamais un journal de voyage. David Hicks a marié dans la

LE CONFORT ANGLAIS

(suite)

ROGER GAIN

lumière de Londres ses trouvailles du monde entier, ses audaces et la technique de l'an 2000 (détails page précédente).

CONFORT BRITANNIQUE STYLE JEUNE ANGLETERRE, nous l'avons photographié (page 126) chez Mr David Hicks, décorateur • Dans le living aux couleurs de Londres (bronze, gris sombre, ocre) voisinent des fauteuils français et danois, des tapis espagnols et des bibelots d'Orient. Les fenêtres changent de rideaux à chaque saison : bruns à l'automne, rouges pour Noël, jaunes au printemps et blancs l'été. Murs et sol en peinture vert bronze vernie, éclairage par spots encastrés. • Pour la salle à manger (page 127), couleurs soleil, ocre, crème, corail, orange, mauve, une table en contre-plaqué toujours drapée, des cotonnades très bon marché, toujours fraîchement repassées, des copies de chaises « Queen Anne » peintes en rouge mat. La lumière entre (sur mesure), filtrée par le store blanc intérieur (Holland). Rien au mur que des panneaux peints en trompe-l'œil et une lanterne XVIIIe indo-portugaise.

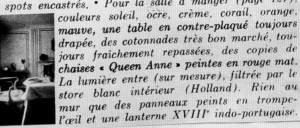

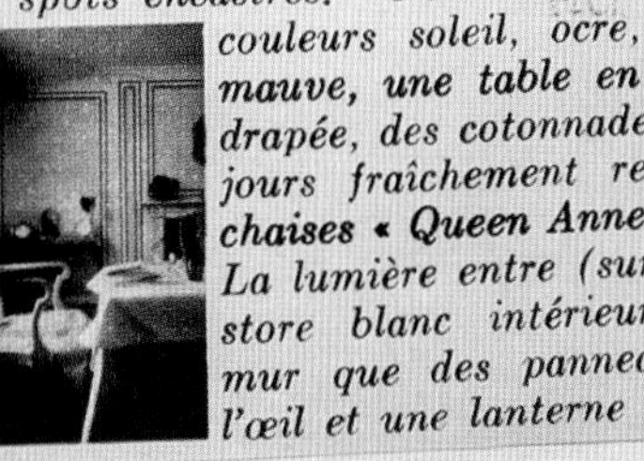

St Leonard's Terrace

"Elle" magazine

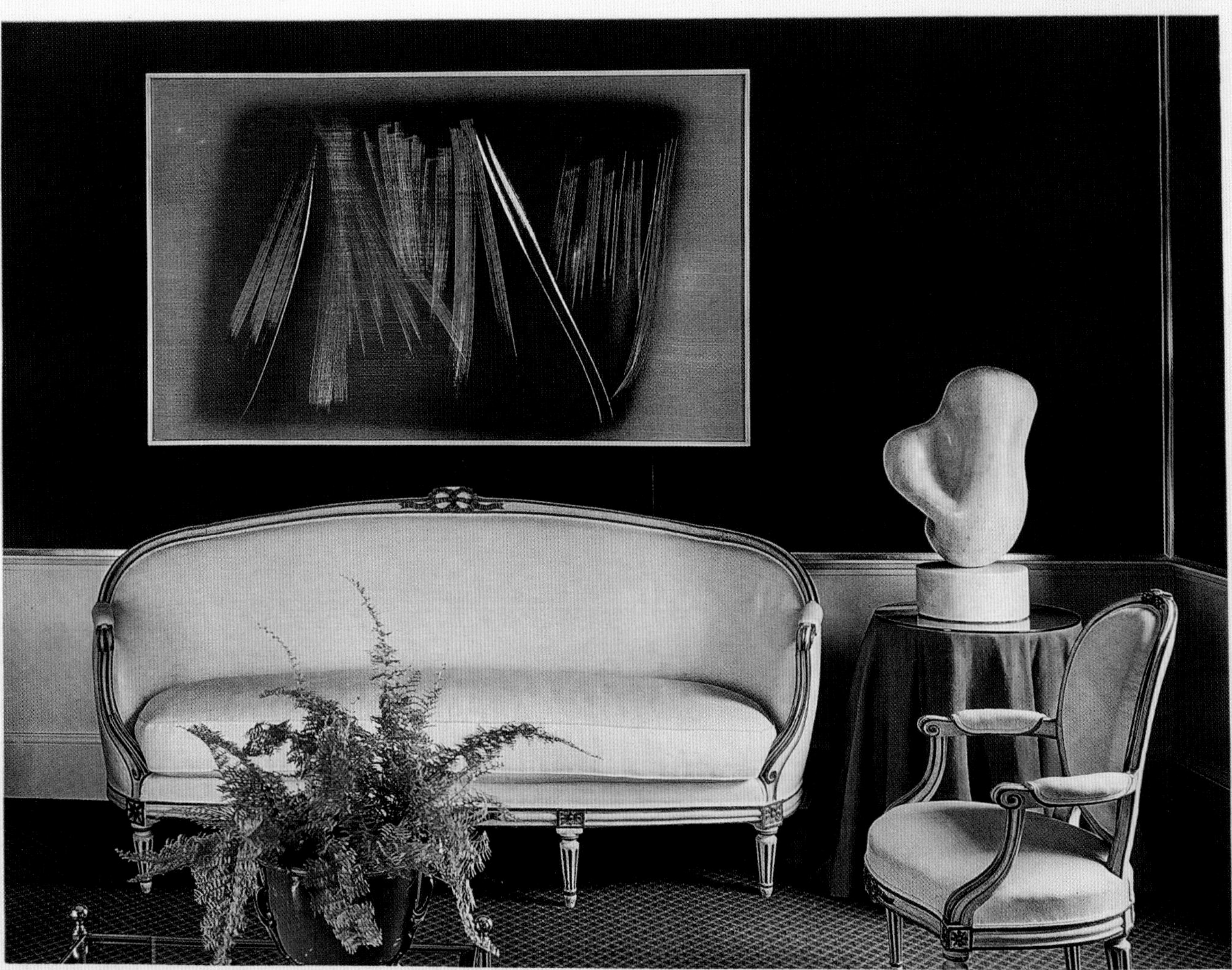

Un autre détail du salon « du soir ».
Le canapé et les fauteuils anglais XVIIIe,
peints en vert et blanc, sont recouverts
de toile blanche. Au-dessus du canapé,
une huile de Hartung (1962) dans des tons
turquoise, brun et noir. Sculpture de Arp.
La moquette, verte et turquoise, a été
spécialement dessinée pour cette pièce
par David Hicks. Il a également créé
la table de verre et de laiton (au premier plan),
sur laquelle est posé un cache-pot chinois
avec une monture Louis XV de bronze doré.

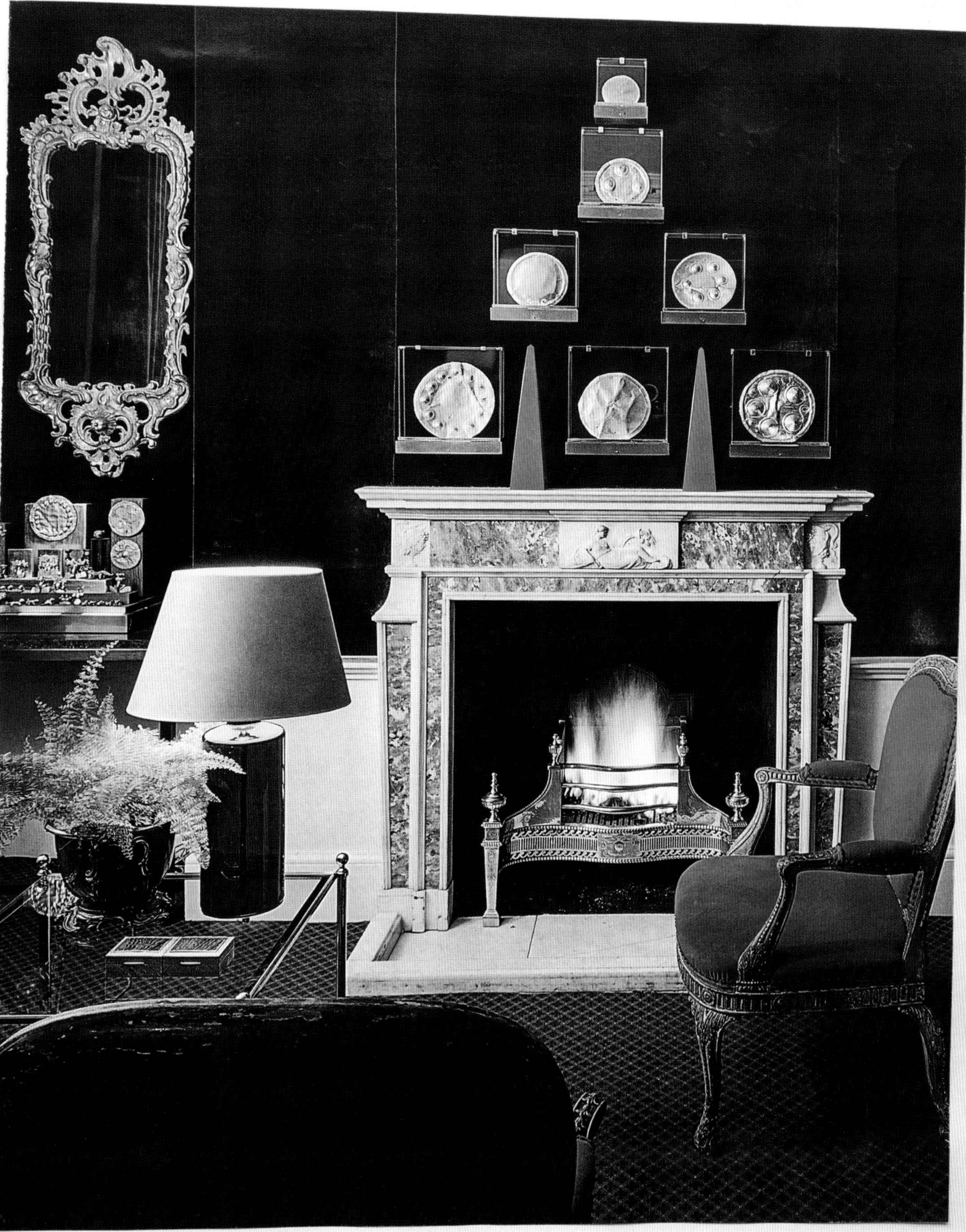

midsummer '65 —
David Hicks.

24 LOWNDES STREET,
LONDON S.W.1.
BELGRAVIA 5954.

BRITWELL SALOME
OXON
WATLINGTON 314

23 ST LEONARD'S TERRACE LONDON SW3 SLOANE 4652

23 ST LEONARD'S TERRACE LONDON SW3 SLOANE 4652

DAVID
HICKS
LIMITED

23 ST LEONARD'S TERRACE LONDON SW3 SLOANE 6288

DAVID HICKS ASSOCIATES 23 ST LEONARDS TERRACE LONDON SW3 SLO 6288

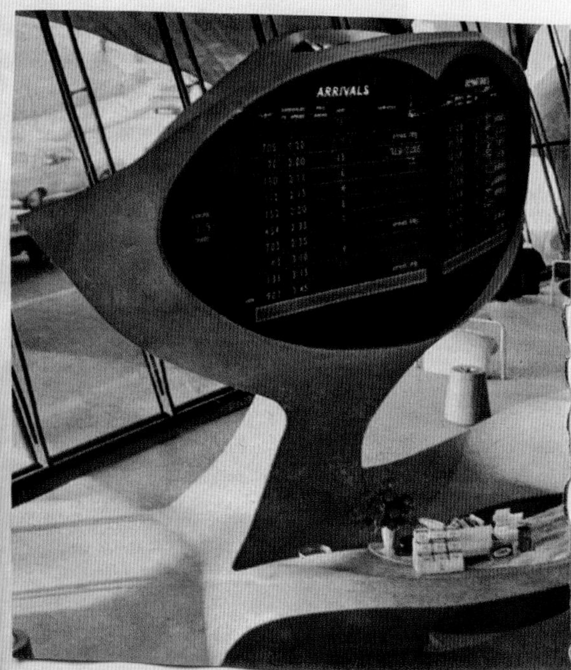

TWA Kennedy going to Virgin Islands.

FIVE

SOCIETY: THE INDEX

WHO? WHY? WHERE? WHEN?

*For the majority of his life, every Englishman carries round with him, like some haemophilic strain, a delicate sense of what is acceptable and what is not. What is done and not done. From birth, his parents, his school and university, his social milieu provide him with a subtle gauge which enables him to place his fellows in a proper (however prejudiced) perspective. Once learned, it helps the Englishman to sort his attitudes into compartments. Once learned, it never stops whirring. One hears it everywhere. It always adopts an easy and superior tone. When actually expressed, it usually takes the form of a subdued epithet. 'Basically, he's quite sound,' for example, or 'By God, the man's all right. He played cricket for * * * * didn't he?' During the last few years, these attitudes have been based almost exclusively on money. And as the common wealth has been more evenly distributed, the main theme has tended to become muffled due to an excess of variation. Now, although the old attitude prevails, it disguises itself under the mercurial cloaks of old money versus new money; fashion versus vulgarity; the old aristocracy versus the new; the with-it opposed to the unwith-it. The new social attitudes rely on shifting perspective. As fast as the unwith-it discover the with-it, the with-it scurry frantically on to the super-with-it. One never quite becomes the other. And since the old hard and fast rule no longer applies generally, certain modern desperations are set up. What to do, where to do it, how to do it, and who to be once the rest have been accomplished. Therefore, in order to ease the minds of Englishmen in anguish, we have compiled the Index which follows. At best, it represents the social milieu of the moment. At worst, a complete guide for the aspiring snob. It is said that beauty is fashion running away from vulgarity and afraid of being caught. Please adjust your rate of progress accordingly. The expiration date, of course, is September 1st.*

Art Galleries to buy from

YES	NO
Kasmin	Agnew
Hanover	
New Art Centre, Sloane Street	

Art Galleries to be seen in

YES	NO
Marlborough	O'Hana
Robert Fraser	Trafford
McRoberts and Tunnard	

Jewellers

YES	NO
Arthur King	Asprey
Cartier	Ciro
Collingwood	
Hooper Bolton	
Gosschalk	
Garrard	
Wartski	

Where to buy Furniture

YES	NO
Partridges	Harrods
Mallet	Mrs Shields
Aram	
Habitat	
Heal	
Ciancimino	

Artists to have at your party

YES	NO
Nolan	Merton
Sutherland	Anderson
Bishop	Bratby
Daintrey	Annigoni
McEwen	
Freud	
Whidborne	
Hockney	

Artists to have on your wall

YES	NO
Bacon	Elwes
Piper	Scott
Sutherland	de Lazolo
Hockney	Coldstream
Passmore	Russell Flint
Richards	
Nicholson	P. Blake
Hutchins	
Auerbach	

Auctions to be seen at

YES	NO
Christies	Harrods
Sotheby	Druce & Co
Bonhams	Sotheby (at evening sales with Early Bird coverage)
Tattersalls at Newmarket	

Gambling Houses

YES	NO
Clermont	Le Cercle
	The Sporting Club
	Curzon House
	Crockford's
	Casanova
	Quent

Wine Merchants

YES	NO
Berry Bros and Rudd	Smeeds
Justerini and Brooks	Victoria Wine Co
H. Allen-Smith	
Mayor, Sworder and Co	
Christopher's	

Barber Shops

YES	NO
Alan Cooke	Thomas
Morris Stanton	Trumper
Robert James	Truefit and Hill
Vidal Sassoon	
The London Barbers' School?	

Hostesses

YES	NO
Lady Pamela Berry	George Weidenfeld
Miss Fleur Cowles	
Lady Antonia Fraser	
Mrs David Bruce	
Mrs Jack Heinz	
Mrs Gilbert Miller	

Embassies to be posted to for pleasure

YES	NO
Athens	Bonn
Rio de Janeiro	Saigon
Beirut	
Bangkok	

Embassies to be posted to for prestige

YES	NO
Washington	Reykjavik
Bonn	
Paris	
Moscow	

Ministries to go into

YES	NO
Treasury	Ministry of Science and Technology
Dept of Economic Affairs	Post Office
Ministry of Public Building and Works	Foreign Office

Banks for Private Accounts

YES	NO
Rothschild	
Bank of England	The Big Five
Hambros	
Coutts	
Hoares	
Mayfair London Bank	

Queen magazine

YES	NO
Lambton	Hamilton
Jenkins	Sandys

Architects

YES	NO
Lasdun	Phillimore
Cadbury Brown	Spence
Drew	Price
Becket	
The Smithsons	
Shankland	

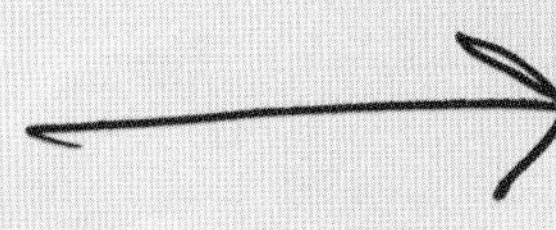

Interior Decorators

YES	NO
Hicks	Semple
McCosh	Siddeley
Underdown	
Bannenburg	
Fowler	

Comedians

Country Life

2.—CAFE-CURTAINS COMBINED WITH BLINDS. A bathroom in Mr. David Hicks's London house

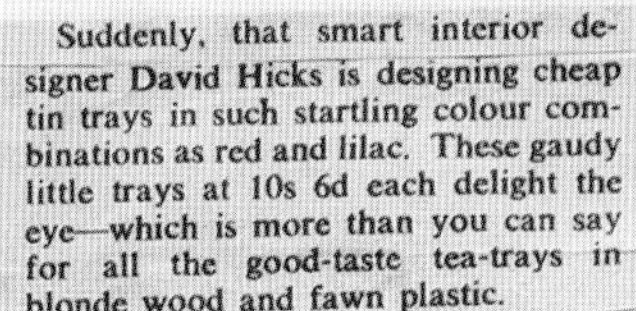

Suddenly, that smart interior designer David Hicks is designing cheap tin trays in such startling colour combinations as red and lilac. These gaudy little trays at 10s 6d each delight the eye—which is more than you can say for all the good-taste tea-trays in blonde wood and fawn plastic.

Broadlands

the Marines beat the retreat

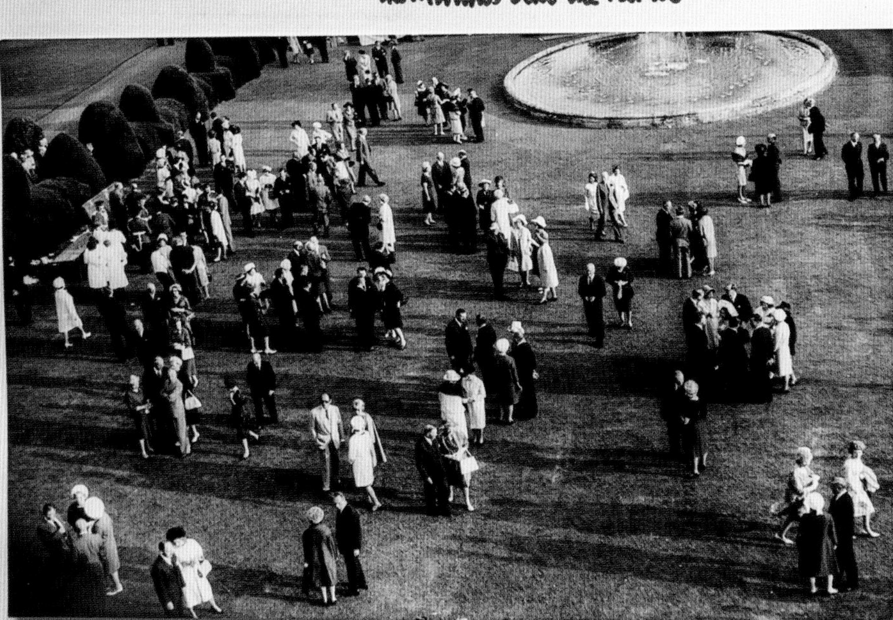

the end of the party

Dickie's standard

the Fairbanks arrive

Pammy receiving

Rex Harrison Shirley Grandpapa Rachel Roberts

Shirley M

Auch London liebt Farben

Vorurteile über Engländer – vor allem darüber, wie sie wohnen – gibt es bei uns viele. Wie sehr man sich täuschen kann, zeigen die Wohnungen, die der Londoner Innenarchitekt David Hicks gestaltet hat. Nichts von grauen Regenfarben, auch nicht nur konservative englische Stilmöbel (deren Imitationen bei uns fast beliebter sind als in England selbst). Leuchtende Farben, die der Dekorateur für Stoffe und Tapeten, Teppiche und selbst für die Bilder an den Wänden aussuchte, bringen südländische Helle und Freundlichkeit ins Haus, die im nebligen London allmählich Schule machen. Jedoch in so bedächtiger Weise, daß aus dieser, vorerst nur in wenigen Fällen erkennbaren Farbenfreudigkeit kein neues Vorurteil abgeleitet werden darf. Die Häuser, aus denen wir auf den folgenden Seiten einige Fotos zeigen, sind typische englische Reihenhäuser, wie man sie straßenweise in London oder in einer anderen Stadt findet.

1
Schwarzbraune Wände, mit glänzender Ölfarbe gestrichen, schwarzer Fußboden und dunkelbraune Decke, dazu ein verblüffender Kontrast: das weißgelbe Gemälde von Kelly. Der Raum wird durch geschickt angebrachte Punktstrahler hier und da effektvoll aufgehellt.

2, 3, 4
Drei Hauseingänge – alle drei typisch englisch. Überraschend farbenfroh aber und unenglisch für unsere Vorstellung ist das Innere dieser Londoner Wohnungen.

5
Durch ein sehr einfaches und keinesfalls teures Verfahren erhält das Eßzimmer Stil und Wärme. Die aprikosenfarbenen Wände werden von weißen, schwarz umrandeten Leinenbändern in Felder aufgeteilt. Tischtuch und Vorhänge (in dunklem Orange) sind auf die Wandfarbe abgestimmt.

6
In diesem Wohnraum harmonisieren verschiedene Grüntöne miteinander, die man gewöhnlich als »beißend« empfinden würde. Die Wände wurden mit tiefgrünem Velours bespannt, der gemusterte Spannteppich ist fast grasgrün, und das Gemälde über dem weiß bezogenen Louis XVI-Sofa weist hauptsächlich blaugrüne Töne auf. Die weiße Plastik von Jean Arp auf dem Tisch mit einer türkisblauen Decke kommt vor dem dunklen Hintergrund sehr gut zur Geltung.

HICKS HOUSES

by Emma Booker

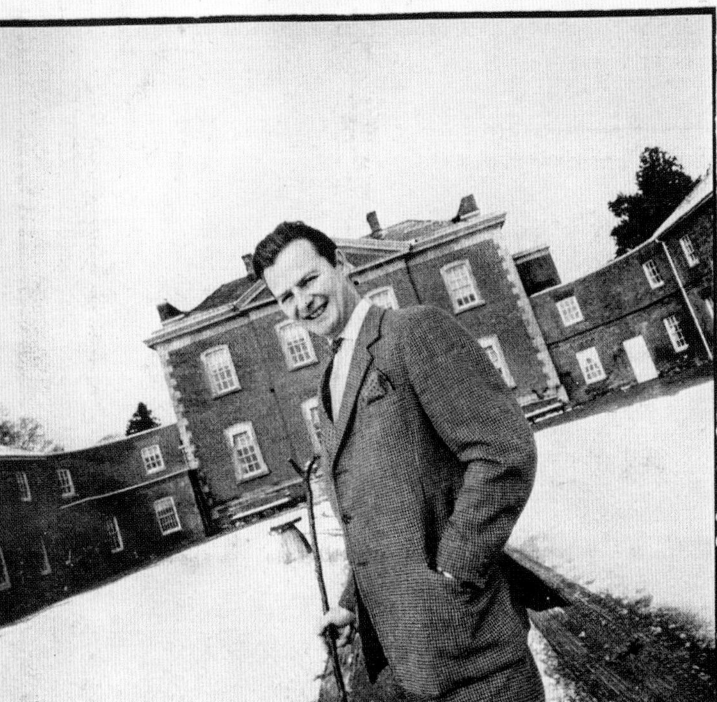

London A house in a row, but a house that looks out on green trees, and straight ahead the Soane entrance lodge to the Royal Hospital; David Hicks is a great admirer of this early 19th-century architect's work. From the outside the house, though pretty, is ordinary enough. Only the "Entryphone" by the front door, which is designed in an intricate pattern of "H's" like the Napoleonic N, gives a clue to the character of the man who lives inside. One feels that there may be a surprise or two in store.

"I dictate and telephone in the garden, and there is a greenhouse for growing incense plants and bananas. Do you like the staircase?"

The front door has opened with an angry buzz and David Hicks, who is a handsome man in his early thirties, seems for a moment to be floating above the dazzling geometric pattern of his carpet. The walls of the hall and staircase are whitewashed and the dizzy black and scarlet stairs stretch ahead: already all conventional ideas of a terrace house have disappeared. The rooms, of course, are in their usual places—a small dining-room on the ground floor, L-shaped drawing-room on the floor above, and over that the bedroom and bathrooms. But the sensation in the house is more of having been caught inside an abstract painting than a collection of rooms.

"What do you notice most in the drawing-room?" After looking into the tiny dining-room downstairs and seeing that the table was lit by only one spotlight, which is focussed on the gilt candlestick in the middle, it seemed probable that the answer had something to do with the lighting. The walls of the drawing-room are dark and shiny, a sort of Coca Cola colour, and the woodwork is a matt white: why, in spite of this, does the room seem relatively un-dark—there is none of the oppressive feeling of a deep green or red room. "The windows; they're made of dark glass. Look." Hicks opened a window and a shaft of green light fell into the room, making it for some reason dark and depressing. "I will not suffer the tyranny of this English light," he said with triumph. Now one of his obsessions became clear and it was possible to see why his house resembled a big modern picture or sculpture: apart from the geometry of his design and the grouped objects and paintings, nearly all of them by contemporary artists, which in the drawing-room in particular are so well placed, the house itself is lit and presented as if it were an exhibit at a show of modern work in the Tate. Dark glass, spotlights, sun-blinds, control the light throughout the day and the year; the passing of the seasons can be noticed by the changing curtains which at Christmas are scarlet, in the autumn brown, and in spring and summer are white and yellow respectively. Onto them filters the odd subdued light from the outside world.

Strangely enough, the effect is not stuffy. A great Ellsworth Kelly, all yellow and white, seems to give out a light of its own against the near blackness of the walls; a vase of green weeds, picked in the garden and spotlit on a modern table, looks like a small jungle. The fabrics, and these, reasonably enough as he designs them, are another of his obsessions, melt into the room and do not interfere with the paintings and sculpture: chairs are upholstered in very soft leather or in plain brown.

Upstairs the main bedroom is covered with material—everywhere, on the walls and on the bed, soon, one feels, printed on the eyeball, is the somersaulting design of abstract flowers on a background of dazzling white. "To give the effect of someone running quickly through a garden with a bunch of wild flowers that they have just picked." It is very pretty; designed by Hicks himself; a spotlit vase of scarlet wheat increases the illusion of having strayed into a field at the end of the rainbow. Now for his dressing-room, a strange contrast to the unreal summer of the room where he sleeps: to go in there in the early morning must be like leaping, half-awake, into a pool of deep black treacle. Walls are black and framed with gold, they part to show a row of sober suits and soft shirts, they close again and open somewhere else to disclose a lavatory, an intercom machine, a tiny lift. "Ah, my iced water comes up in there while I change." The window over the oval basin is made of two-way mirror glass and tinted dark; to shave he has only to open it a crack and there is his reflection and the light to shave by—a most economical idea!

The house is alive with telephones and tape recorders, and messages hum there all day long, for it is his office too. At the weekends he goes to Britwell Salome, his country house near Oxford, to relax: what could this be like?

English Vogue ↑

English Vogue

Country

Britwell Salome is sixty minutes distance from London and stands in surprisingly unspoilt country above a little village of the same name. The house has what David Hicks refers to as an early, "gutsy" façade and was built in 1728 in a soft pink brick; once inside the hall the softness ends and the "gutsiness" becomes intensified. Unlike his London house, the atmosphere here is one of light and airiness, but, as always, the colours are strong. The hall staircase is papered in a vivid blue and white design copied from a fragment of Portuguese woven linen of the year 1700, the drawing-room walls are covered with a pale English linen, but against them are sharp modern pictures and tables laden with blue lapis lazuli and hefty porphyry slabs. Colours are grouped together, so that on one table are a lump of cornelian, a piece of modern African sculpture, and Mogul dagger-heads; colour: browns and greys; on a Leleu commode are a 17th-century Chinese head, a Turkish helmet of the same date, and a spattering of Aztec bracelets—colour: gold and deep grey. The blue objects, either lapis lazuli or 18th century Bristol glass, and

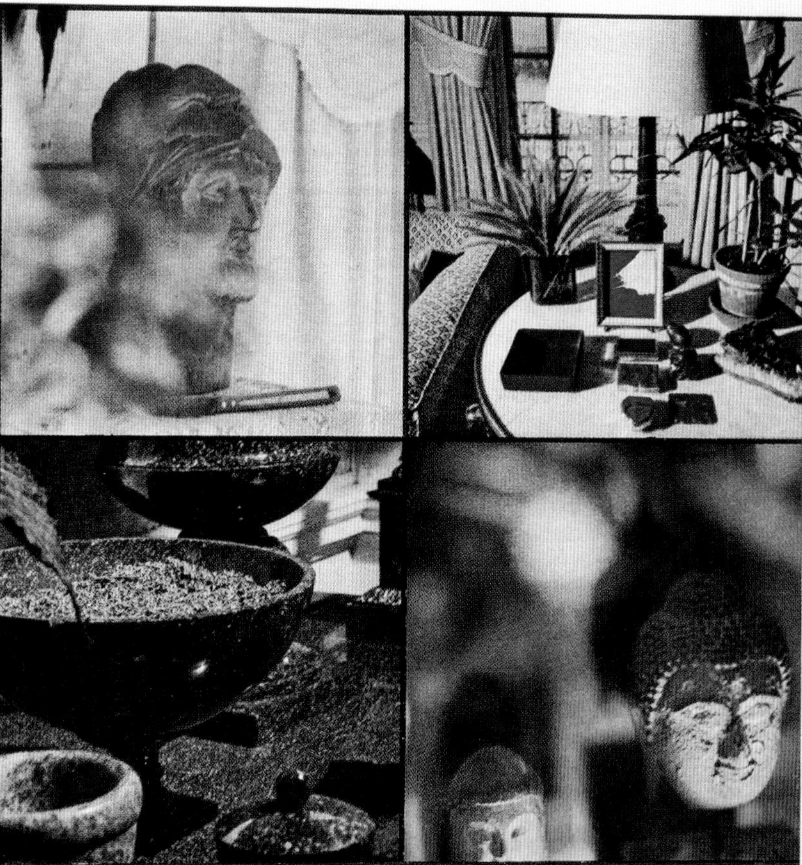

Left: The drawing-room at Britwell Salome. Above the sofa, a Dante Leonelli painting. Bergère chairs in cream silk velvet. Walls and curtains in cream and white English linen. Sofas covered in printed cotton designed by David Hicks. Carpet from Cogolin. The plant is a Spasmania Africans. Top left: Giltwood heroic head from the prow of an 18th-century ship. Bronze gladiator's scraper. Table covered in cobra skin. Top right: On a gilded metal table with marble top: dried purple wheat and Daphne, a Peter Upward miniature, mahogany lamp, blue Bavarian glass box, Bristol glass, 18th-century Persian inkwell in lapis lazuli, faux lapis egg, a lump of topaz. Above left: A collection of porphyry on a Kent table with Scagliola porphyry top. Above right: Siamese heads in a brass and glass vitrine

DAVID BAILEY

A LONDRA E IN CAMPAGNA LE CASE DI DAVID HICKS

Italian Vogue

From Smooth Society ... Raw

THE EXPRESS this week is presenting, in widely ranging variety, the work of the man who is currently the most quoted photographer in Britain: David Bailey.

The pictures come from his shortly-to-be-published book "David Bailey's Box of Pin-ups."

Today PHOTONEWS highlights vividly — contrasting personalities as seen through the Bailey lens—personalities representing the polar extremes from the smoothest of smooth high society to the star exponents of the Beat World.

ON THE LEFT: Interior-decorator-to-the-artistocracy, David Hicks.

RIGHT and BELOW: Gordon Waller of Peter and Gordon with companion, model Celia Hammond.

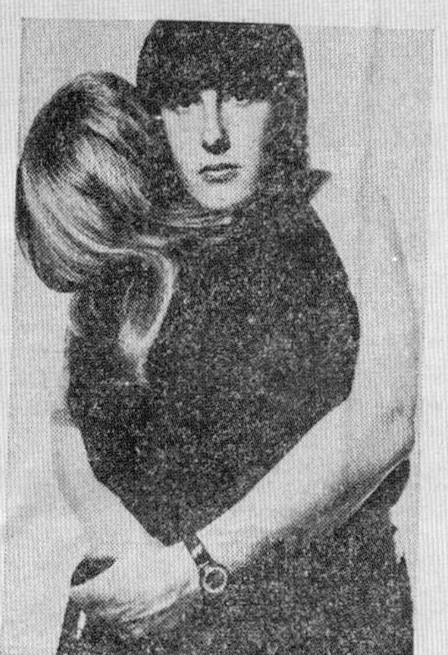

HE HAS ESSENTIALLY TO BE A DEALER IN ILLUSION

DAVID HICKS, interior decorator, has a polished look, like a well cared for piece of furniture—smooth, shiny, cold to the touch, and inlaid with gold.

Every interior decorator is to some extent a dealer in *trompe-l'œil* [illusion].

A Hicks garden will contain an avenue of trees distorted to resemble wooden toys.

★ ★ ★

Out-of-doors becomes indoors, while indoors (though upholstered in large, bright floral patterns and embellished by exotic plants) remains resolutely indoors as well.

Bathrooms are for party-giving, with the bath placed sociably in the middle of the room.

It may be that David Hicks himself is another piece of *trompe-l'œil*—that his glacial, cautious exterior conceals passion and daring, that his elegant personality is poised in perpetual tension between fantasy and reserve.

Daily Telegraph

ALICE HOPE reading a book for the design-minded

Yes—but let's see some humbler homes!

TASTE in the council home seems to have made more progress in the last few years than in the old middle-class homes in the better streets. This is the view of Viscount Eccles, in a foreword to a lush book on interior decorating which comes out this week.

The book is a directory of interior design, edited by Jacqueline Inchbald, and I for one would have liked to have seen some modest homes in it. After all, David Hicks did a big job on working-class interiors a few years ago.

Instead, we get a portfolio of grand rooms furnished with complete disregard for cost—a dream world for most of us.

Not that we don't all like to browse vicariously among such splendours as a country house bedroom in France, or an English ensemble circa 1750.

And I for one was fascinated by a view of Cecil Beaton's drawing room that shows his curtains to be several inches longer than they should be.

I observed, too, the name of the designer who did the interior of Peter Sellers' country home and I note that we are told where to buy *toile de jouey* paper or to seek out the name of a firm which does marbling and graining.

So this is a useful book, especially in that it brings together for the first time the names of the leading interior designers with examples of their work.

Some of the lesser-known names are here too: Derek Parker, who has decorated some of the great houses of Scotland, Mary Fox Linton, an American married to Peter Bernard, an antique dealer, and Lex Aitken, an Australian who trained as a sculptor in Melbourne.

* "*Interior Design and Decoration*" (*Michael Joseph, 5gns*).

DAVID BAILEY'S 3 BOX OF PIN-UPS

at

Daily Express

Design & Decoration '66 Book

+ actually opened as 'Raffles'.

David Hicks

David Hicks was born in 1929. He describes himself as being "half educated at Charterhouse and the L.C.C. Central School of Arts and Crafts, and half by travelling widely and looking at every conceivable piece of furniture, museum, house, building and painting". He started by decorating his own house, and his achievement quickly led to his first commission—a flat for Lady Benson. This was followed by numerous other commissions, the best known being Helena Rubinstein's London penthouse; the Marquis and Marchioness of Londonderry's Hampstead house; and Lord and Lady John Cholmondeley's London penthouse. He also designed the decorations for Mr. Felix Fenston and Lady Dashwood's dance.

David Hicks has also worked widely in the commercial field, where his commissions include ten Peter Evans' Eating Houses, the first of which was the *Gay Gordon* in Glasgow, and the latest a nightclub called *Peter*.+ For another restaurant group he designed the *Carosse* in Chelsea, and a second called *The Garden*.

Apart from his work as an interior designer and decorator, David Hicks has worked widely in a number of related fields. For a year, he ran an advisory service at Harrison Gibson in two provincial cities. He has lectured in Australia and compiled a report on design for the Indian Government. He has designed a range of carpets for Crossley; a number of fabrics of his design are now being released in England in simple washable cotton; and he has decorated the interiors of three yachts.

David Hicks is consultant to the architectural practice of Garnet, Cloughley and Blakemore, and with them is at present designing two large country houses and a London mews house. His other commissions in hand include the remodelling and decoration of a house in Scotland for the Hon. Anthony Samuel, and Kelvedon Hall in Essex for Mr. and Mrs. Paul Channon. He is also a painter and has recently finished a number of paintings for an exhibition of landscapes. David Hicks is now writing a down-to-earth book on decoration for the ordinary householder.

Illustrated is a sitting-room recently completed for the Duke and Duchess of Rutland in London. The walls were painted white and the white marble chimney-piece (circa 1800) was installed. The carpet is *tête de nègre*. The chair is covered in Chinese yellow tweed and the sofa in turquoise blue suede cloth. The brass column lamp has a plain white opaque card shade. The two urns are from Bangkok and the cushion is in a fabric designed by David Hicks.

Below: Sitting-room in the Duke and Duchess of Rutland's flat in London. (*Photograph Guillemot—Conaissance des Arts*).

Ideal Home '65

Britwell Salome, near Watlington, Oxfordshire. The centre block was built in 1728 and the column in the foreground erected in 1764. In Regency times, the house was a nunnery

WHEN A DESIGNER DESIGNS FOR HIMSELF

What happens when a man, normally limited by the wishes of others, is himself calling the tune? Artist Francis Marshall provides an answer with a vivid picture of well-known interior decorator David Hicks and his family in their beautiful Oxfordshire house

In the drawing-room, Edwina Hicks adjusts a cowslip in her father's buttonhole. The sofa material is one of a range designed by David Hicks at Goods and Chattels

NATURAL good taste needs no laborious research into which goes with what. It is simply a matter of having a good eye, plenty of courage and a lot of common sense. What is your attitude to life? What is the room to be used for? If the answers are honest, the room will express your personality.

David Hicks has a good eye and all the other qualities. In a very short space of time, he has become one of the most successful interior decorators in Europe. He travels constantly on business and always returns with objects that others might well have overlooked and which he uses imaginatively in his schemes of decoration.

The result of all this is splendidly

Part 3

1966–69

1966–69

David's decoration in his architect partner Patrick Garnett's London house, and lovely Nico Londonderry in hers, with a telegram from Pammy's Uncle Gustaf, King of Sweden. 'The missing ingredient in a modern room is strong colour', says David, although there is little in Keith Lichtenstein's Chelsea flat, full of Bacons and antiquities. David relaxes in Mallorca, while Pammy is photographed by the fire with their children. Twinkle, twinkle, little stars. A first book, a library in Hawksmoor's Easton Neston and blinds for Mary Quant.

On set in California, David gives notes on the improperly executed pelmet for Julie Christie's bed that he designed for 'Petulia'. In London, David shows his 'Portrait Drawings and Sculptural Objects' before jetting off to New York to show his first carpet designs with an invitation typed on his brown wrapping-paper writing-paper. David buys a house in the South of France; Pammy's all-white bathroom there makes another L'Oeil cover. On the last page of a scrapbook, David pointing: 'If you're a real glutton for punishment – see next volume.'

'David Hicks opens shop: lights flash: chairs take new shape', *Vogue* reports. David with carpet samples; with Yves Saint-Laurent; with Pammy at his Red Party. Everything goes in the scrapbook – everything interesting – like the label from two brace of pheasants sent from the Queen, and the wine list from her dinner table. David turns 40, goes around the world and back; designs the nightclub on the QE2; thinks Fortnum & Mason is frightfully common. His beach house in the Bahamas complete, he is photographed outside it in a leather jacket, but Tiffany spell the island's name wrong on the writing-paper.

29 Royal Avenue SW3

Lady Londonderry (*right*) *lives in a house in Hampstead. It was built in 1780 and was bought three years ago by the Londonderrys. David Hicks decorated the sitting-room in cool pale colours with flashes of bright. The carpet, designed by him, is a small geometric design in white and pale coffee; the settees are covered in off-white cotton.*

1966 92

PASSERKORT

TILL

KUNGL. SLOTTET

ULRIKSDAL

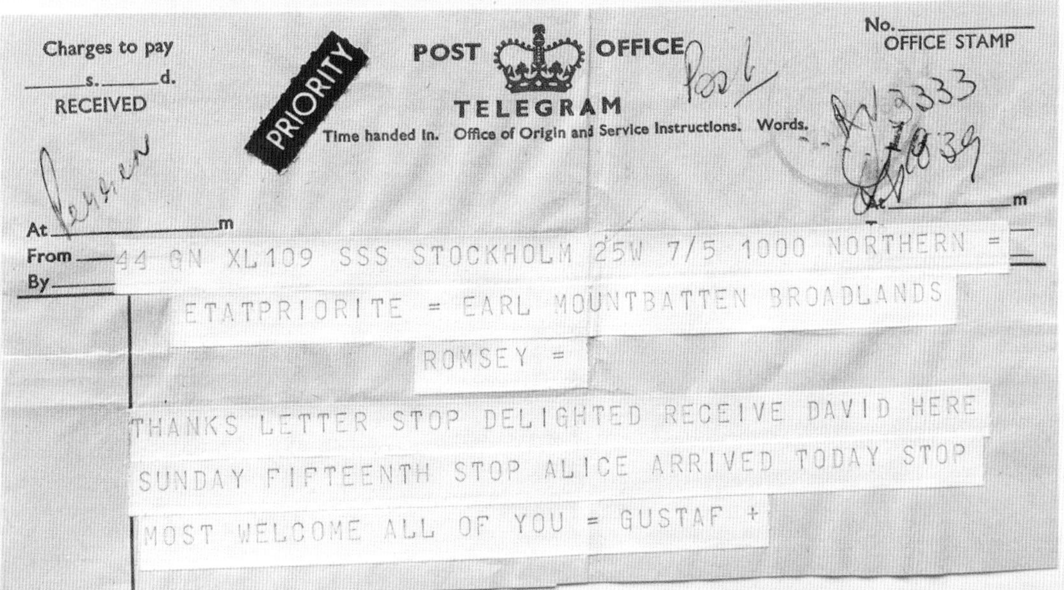

Charges to pay ____s.____d.
RECEIVED

PRIORITY

POST OFFICE TELEGRAM

Time handed in. Office of Origin and Service Instructions. Words.

No.______
OFFICE STAMP

At______m

At______m

From 44 GN XL109 SSS STOCKHOLM 25W 7/5 1000 NORTHERN =
By______

ETATPRIORITE = EARL MOUNTBATTEN BROADLANDS
ROMSEY =

THANKS LETTER STOP DELIGHTED RECEIVE DAVID HERE
SUNDAY FIFTEENTH STOP ALICE ARRIVED TODAY STOP
MOST WELCOME ALL OF YOU = GUSTAF +

King Gustaf

"The Times"

PHOTOGRAPHS BY RAY WILLIAMS

Guide to decorating

Interior decorating is fast becoming one of Britain's major industries: consider the countless hours of time and thought that go into converting houses and planning colour schemes, and the energy that is expended in painting walls, choosing furnishing fabrics, and laying down floor tiles. As a result, we are assailed on all sides with conflicting advice from advertisers, manufacturers, and magazines on every aspect of decoration from restoring country cottages to refurbishing dark interiors.

David Hicks, one of our leading interior designers, has now compiled a comprehensive guide to this ubiquitous subject, which is published this week and will undoubtedly appeal to distraught decorators in need of sensible and practical information. The book—simply entitled *David Hicks on Decorating*—has all the undeniable qualities of a coffee table best seller, and the excellent advice is convincingly teamed with lavish colour pictures of the real thing. There are sections on colour planning, lighting, fabrics, and carpets, as well as a detailed guide to decorating kitchens, bathrooms, and tackling problem areas, such as halls, staircases, and rumpus rooms. The book is published by Leslie Frewin, price 4gns.

Far Right: The library in David Hicks's country house in Oxfordshire. The two doors are ingeniously screened in studded black felt.

Top: Detail of the library shelves—a simple combination of scrubbed wood and steel supports.

Bottom: Still-life study of a table arrangement in the drawingroom.

Magic Mr. Hicks

Daily Express

THAT versatile interior decorator David Hicks (he's tackled everything from private suites at Windsor Castle to the G.P.O. Tower) gives some valuable advice in his new illustrated book, "David Hicks on Decoration" (Leslie Frewin, 84s.).

Decorating the Hicks way need not be expensive. Everyone can afford a luxury home, he claims, because luxury does not mean high cost, it means quality plus taste.

Wise but daring use of colour is one way to achieve maximum effect with minimum cost. And how about a fitted carpet in the bathroom for an extra touch of luxury — quite practical even with children if you use a large bath mat?

He confesses that his most daring innovation — brilliant purple tweed for the walls of the late Helena Rubinstein's London drawing-room—was not really his idea at all.

One day when he was consulting Madame Rubinstein she sent for a pair of scissors, lifted her skirts and promptly snipped a purple strip of silk off the hem of her Balenciaga dress. "Weave tweed to this exact colour for the walls," she commanded. And so it was.

Peter Grosvenor

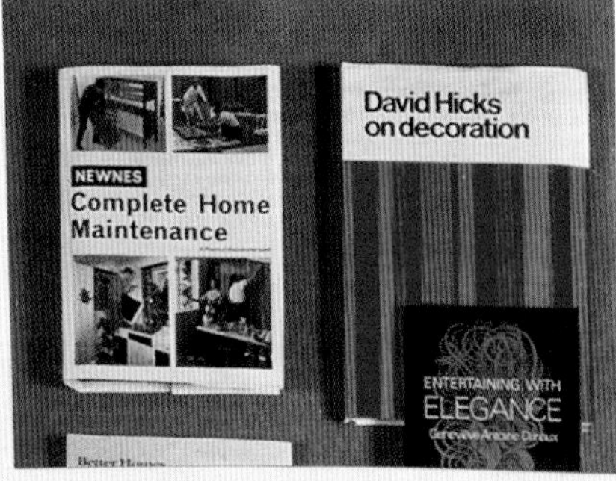

Home and garden

DAVID HICKS ON DECORATION
DAVID HICKS Covers every aspect of interior design and includes colour, lighting, furniture, fabrics and carpets. There are also fascinating chapters on some of the world's most exciting homes and gardens. 32 pages of full colour photographs and some 120 in black and white. *Frewin 50/- Oct*

"Luxury is a beautifully rounded wooden bowl which may cost sixpence in a Japanese bazaar but is luxurious because of its simplicity and polished finish."

—from David Hicks on Decoration, published today by Trewin, 4 gns.

The Sun

SUCH VULGAR SATIN CURTAINS..

TWO NEW how-to-do-it books will be in the shops tomorrow

Good Housekeeping Children's Cook Book (Ebury Press, 18s.) miraculously explains the mysteries of cooking in words and photographs. It is meant for children, but the simple recipes in this book make an ideal starting point for innocent grown-up cooks, too.

Sophisticated cookery writers tend to forget that beginners are baffled by commands to "fold in" the ingredients.

This book explains what it means and there are photographs of every move in every recipe.

David Hicks on Decoration costs four guineas (published by Leslie Frewin) and is worth every penny. If you buy it before you re-do the sitting room or move into a new house you'll likely save twelve times that amount.

Mr. Hicks is a top interior decorator (he did the private suites at Windsor for Prince Charles and Princess Anne) with the sort of ideas you could use in homes where the only kind of suite is a three-piece one.

He gives a foolproof colour guide: "All reds go together, all pinks go together, just as all blues, greens, yellows, browns and all greys do . . ."

Plywood

The book is full of colour pictures of rooms Mr. Hicks has decorated and it's nice to see that his own dining-room table has a plywood top which he covers with a cloth to the ground.

"I place on the top a separate cover of the same material which can be laundered frequently. Between the two cloths I have a piece of plastic to prevent stains."

Most people employ interior decorators because they are not sure of their own taste—or even what good taste is. Read this book and you don't need an interior decorator, for David Hicks devastatingly defines what good taste isn't.

"It is not gilt chandeliers and crimson velvet. It is not magenta orchids nor deep pile carpets and satin curtains, not gold-plated fittings on a car, not a heated lavatory seat nor an electric toothbrush, not a cocktail bar in a house nor an imitation log fire, not onyx ashtrays, nor refrigerators disguised as walnut cabinets, not gold candles, chiffon lampshades, table cigarette lighters, new wrought-iron gates or tapestry upholstery."

Sunday Mirror

Hicks' country home, above; right, modern paintings bove favourite objets d'art. Pictures by TERRY GIBSON

LICE HOPE'S
OME PAGE

VID HICKS is married to a kinswoman of the Queen wife is Lady Pamela, ter of Earl Mount-. He lives in the manner with an site country house and ne in London. But in of all this he has some good ideas when it s to home decorating. has just produced a called "David Hicks Decoration*." It is a y big, coffee-table in glorious colour and d it out on the bed- brigade, the office aries who after all are oung home-makers of ature. ey were completely siastic. They all said y had four guineas they l buy it. And it really does talk sense especially on such things as colour and making a lot out of a little.

Good taste, he says comfortingly, is in no way dependent on money. "I detest gladioli in expensive cut-glass vases. Instead I prefer a wide basket tightly packed with marguerites. Similarly, expensive antiqued velvet is hideous yet plain coarse linen is inexpensive and elegant."

Saying that colour means more to him than any other of his raw materials, Mr. Hicks gives a set of loose rules which cannot fail. They were evolved by the American decorators in the immediate post-war period and roughly they are that:

"All reds go together, all pinks go together, just as all blues, greens, yellows, browns and all greys do. All reds and pinks will mix and most blues and greens will. Yellows, oranges and browns all blend attractively. All mauves and blues look well and olive and emerald greens can be used with them.

"Shocking pink and magenta will work with orange, with greens, with browns and reds but not with blues. White and black are the great mediators.

"Scarlet will look wonderful with royal and midnight blue but this is strong stuff as are red and brilliant yellow or emerald green and vermilion red. Because of this they are not suitable for most private houses.

"Some colours vibrate when they are used together and I often use them to make a dull corner sizzle.

"For instance in a room mostly containing beiges, browns and yellows I would add clashing pink and orange silk cushions."

The really important thing about colour, the writer goes on, is not so much selection as a collection. Select a rough palette in the yellow brown range. First choose the basic colours which are the carpet, the wall colour and the curtain colour.

If the three are chestnut brown, golden yellow and a print in two yellows, begin collecting accessory colours and subsidiary furniture colours such as orange, vermilion, shocking pink and apple green.

"It seems to me," says David Hicks, "that some of the best modern interiors lack strong use of colour and I am sure that this is the missing ingredient that makes many people think of them as cold and inhuman."

When I saw Mr. Hicks at his home in Oxfordshire he showed me how he has carried out this precept by using in his own drawing room, which has a pale cream background and traditional antique furniture, bold modern paintings in vivid clear colours on each wall.

This is a traditional English country house and furnished as such. The one all-mod room is a garden extension. Here there is a leather sofa flanked by plain pine cube tables, with a long table which has a rosewood base and a plate glass top.

Objets d'art there are in plenty all around the house but there are also what Mr. Hicks calls his *objets trouvé*. These include a well-polished drain cover and a piece of broken wood from the top of a farm gate—they seem to be much loved.

In his London home David Hicks uses mostly modern furniture and his lighting is specially interesting. He declares that standard lamps are absolutely hideous and for reading lamps the best is an adjustable arm, "preferably just a brass strip."

For the rest his room is entirely illuminated by "down-lighters" placed at strategic points on the floor. These are simply tin cans with a series of concentric rings inside to split up the light which then shines on whatever spot you direct it.

He wants us to stop doing things like putting little wall lights up. "These are ideas taken from stately mansions and all these homes are so utterly out-of-date that even the people who own them can't live in them."

*ed by Frewin, 4gns.

The missing ingredient in a modern room, by DAVID HICKS

FROM A TOP DECORATOR, EASY RULES FOR HANDLING COLOUR LIKE A PROFESSIONAL

the Telegraph

OINT OF VIEW

LOT of people would as soon look for help to the devil elf as consult an interior rator. One sees quite clearly To call in Mr. Hicks or of his confrères is to con- one's own inadequacy in a liarly humiliating way.

suggests firstly that you n't any taste of your own secondly, that you haven't rited a lot of good stuff of own. It suggests thus in way or another that you are rvenu, without background reeding, a sort of M. Jour- starting from scratch and e to make an awful ass of self at every stage.

What answer has Mr. Hicks? aps this: that, if you actu- did have ancestors of taste means they would not have ashamed to call in the ners Adam, say, to design e rooms for them, with stick of furniture and h of fabric part of the me.

nd if the first gentleman in pe was not too proud to let do the whole Pavilion for inside as well as out, why ld you be too proud to ring Mr. Hicks?

Telegraph again

... badsarkofag omgiven av öppen spis, svart guldbeslagen läderstol, alabasterlampor, tavlor ... badalkov uppfiffad med röd heltäckande matta, runt, duk-täckt bord, avkopplingsstol i ocean av rosa/gröna blommor ... Vilket föredrar Ni?

... och hur matchar purpurröda väggar? Duka i orange, gult, rosa? Arrangera sänghimmeln? Utnyttja kobraskinnet från senaste safarin? ... DAVID HICKS härliga bok ruskar verkligen om vårt inredningstänkande ... inspirerar, kanske CHOCKERAR ... Och vad den är vacker och inspirerande! —

Fråga på Presentsalongen och på bokavd. Hamngatan och Farsta. Titta samtidigt på Presentsalongens runda, dukade salongsbord med thaisidendukar ned till golvet ... Ni förstår varifrån vi fått idén ..

Swedish review

2

Papier d'emballage et flanelle grise

Photos Marc Lavrillier

A Londres
un jeune
collectionneur
présente
ses tableaux
sur des fonds
inattendus

Keith Lichtenstein, un jeune Néo-Zélandais qui habite Londres, dirige un petit restaurant très couru dans King's Road. Il désirait habiter au-dessus, parmi ses tableaux de Francis Bacon et sa collection de sculptures classiques. Mais les locaux disponibles, dans cette maison toute en hauteur, étaient des pièces minuscules resserrées comme les alvéoles d'une ruche, avec une cuisine au-dessus. Appliquant ses propres idées sur l'aménagement de l'espace, et avec le concours de David Hicks comme décorateur, le maître de maison a enlevé les murs et les cloisons, supprimé ou déplacé les portes. Le résultat est un petit appartement dont le volume principal est occupé par une belle salle de séjour-salle à manger et par une cuisine, dissimulée derrière des panneaux de persienne. Une différence de niveau apporte un élément de variété dans la distribution de la pièce et détermine le coin repas. David Hicks, qui aime généralement utiliser des couleurs vives et contrastées s'est limité ici à une gamme de tons neutres, bruns, noirs et blancs, pour laisser toute leur importance aux œuvres d'art. Les sculptures sont mises en valeur par des spots incorporés au plafond ou posés sur le sol.

L'oeil

3. Vue générale de la partie salon.
La nuit, les persiennes intérieures fermées forment une paroi continue de lames de pin non vernies. Tables dessinées par David Hicks. Le sofa de cuir noir vient d'Italie. Lampes de cuivre de San Francisco.

4-5. Le coin repas et le passage menant à la chambre à coucher et à la salle de bains. La cuisine est masquée par les panneaux de persienne répondant à ceux qui garnissent le mur opposé de la pièce. Cette partie est située sur un niveau plus bas, séparé par une balustrade de bois. Deux peintures célèbres de Francis Bacon sont accrochées côte à côte. Chaises anglaises en hêtre de style « gothique » milieu du XVIIIe. (L'une est d'époque, les autres sont des copies). Lustre anglais XVIIIe en étain.

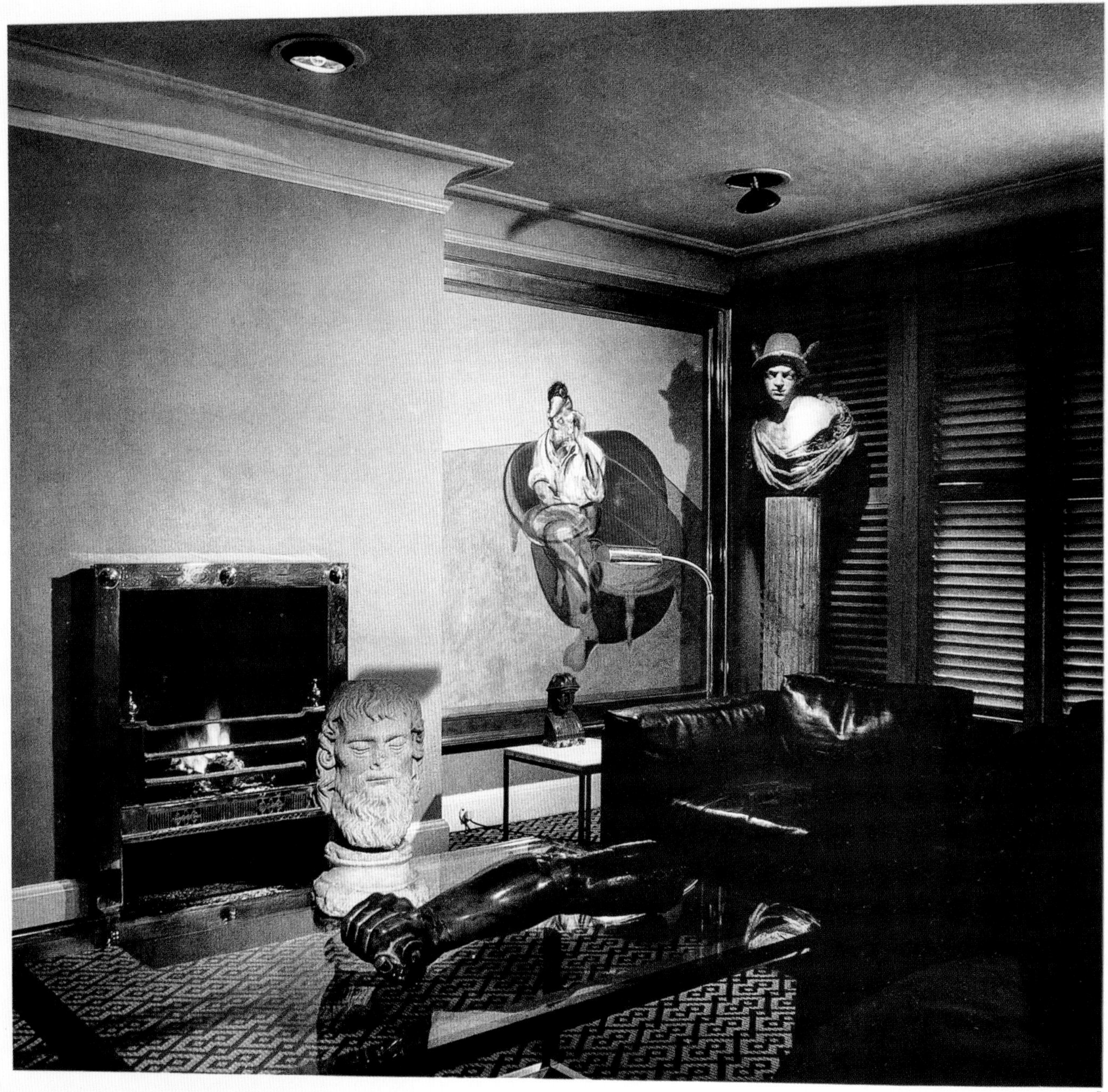

1

1. Un coin de la pièce principale, donnant sur la rue. Les murs sont recouverts d'un simple papier d'emballage dont les chaudes tonalités font parfaitement ressortir les tableaux. Une peinture de Francis Bacon occupe entièrement l'une des parois. Sur la table basse, un bras romain en bronze. Sculptures de marbre antique.
2. Un autre angle de la même pièce. Le tapis à motifs géométriques, en deux tons de brun, a été dessiné par David Hicks. Le portrait romantique à droite et les bustes antiques sont éclairés par des projecteurs placés sur le sol et au plafond.

6

6. Dans le salon, sur la belle console en bois doré de William Kentz, des bustes romains forment un contraste étonnant avec les trois peintures de Francis Bacon accrochées au-dessus.

7. L'aménagement du toit-terrasse est un exemple typique du goût de David Hicks pour les effets décoratifs obtenus par les moyens les plus simples: des lattes de bois peintes en blanc masquent une vue sans intérêt. Des coffres de bois carrés avec des coussins de toile et de caoutchouc mousse constituent des meubles de plein air à l'épreuve des intempéries.

7

Above: *the room has ample cupboard space.* **Below**: *the sleeping-area and the large light-giving window*

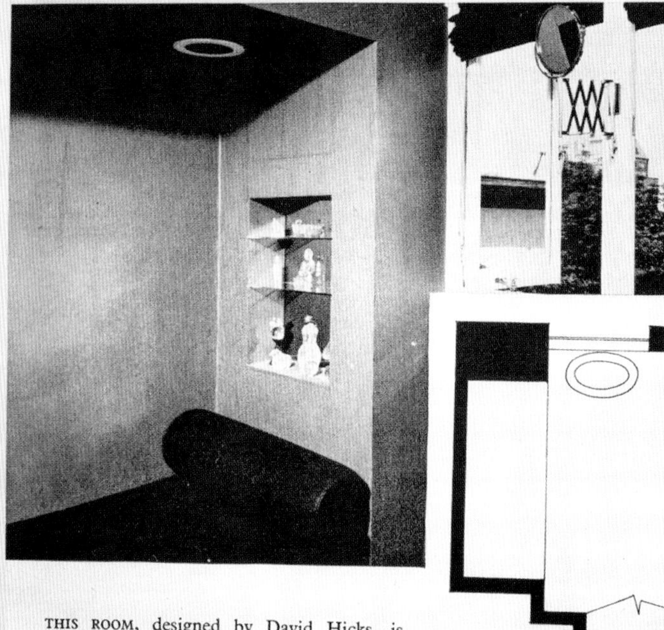

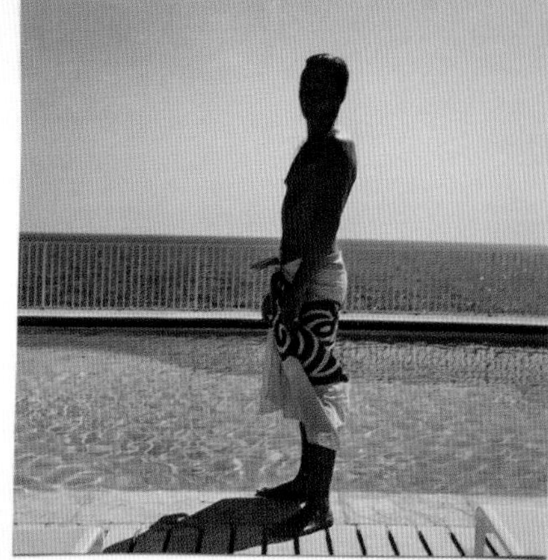

DH in Majorca

House and Gardens view of my dressing room at St Leonard's Terrace!

As small as they come (for one man)

THIS ROOM, designed by David Hicks, is currently used as a man's dressing-room (and occasional bedroom) on the top floor of an eighteenth-century Chelsea house and it is undoubtedly one of the most skilfully planned and well equipped rooms of this order in London.

Yet its basic equipment and layout could well serve as a prototype for a series of self-contained bed-sitters in any University hostel, or as a concentrated but mildly luxurious cabin in any ocean-going yacht. Although all this equipment has been inserted into a smaller-than-small room (almost on a space-capsule basis), it is as comprehensive a one-room home as anyone could demand. Every single piece of equipment has been designed to do its job within the minimum space. A bed, full storage and wardrobe space, wash-basin and adjacent shower are all here. The careful planning and detailing of each piece of equipment bodes well for the design work which Mr Hicks is doing for the projected new Cunarder Q 4.

Cynthia Sainsbury at Gardeo

DH working on plans of Roquebrune staying with Gilbert Millers on Majorca.

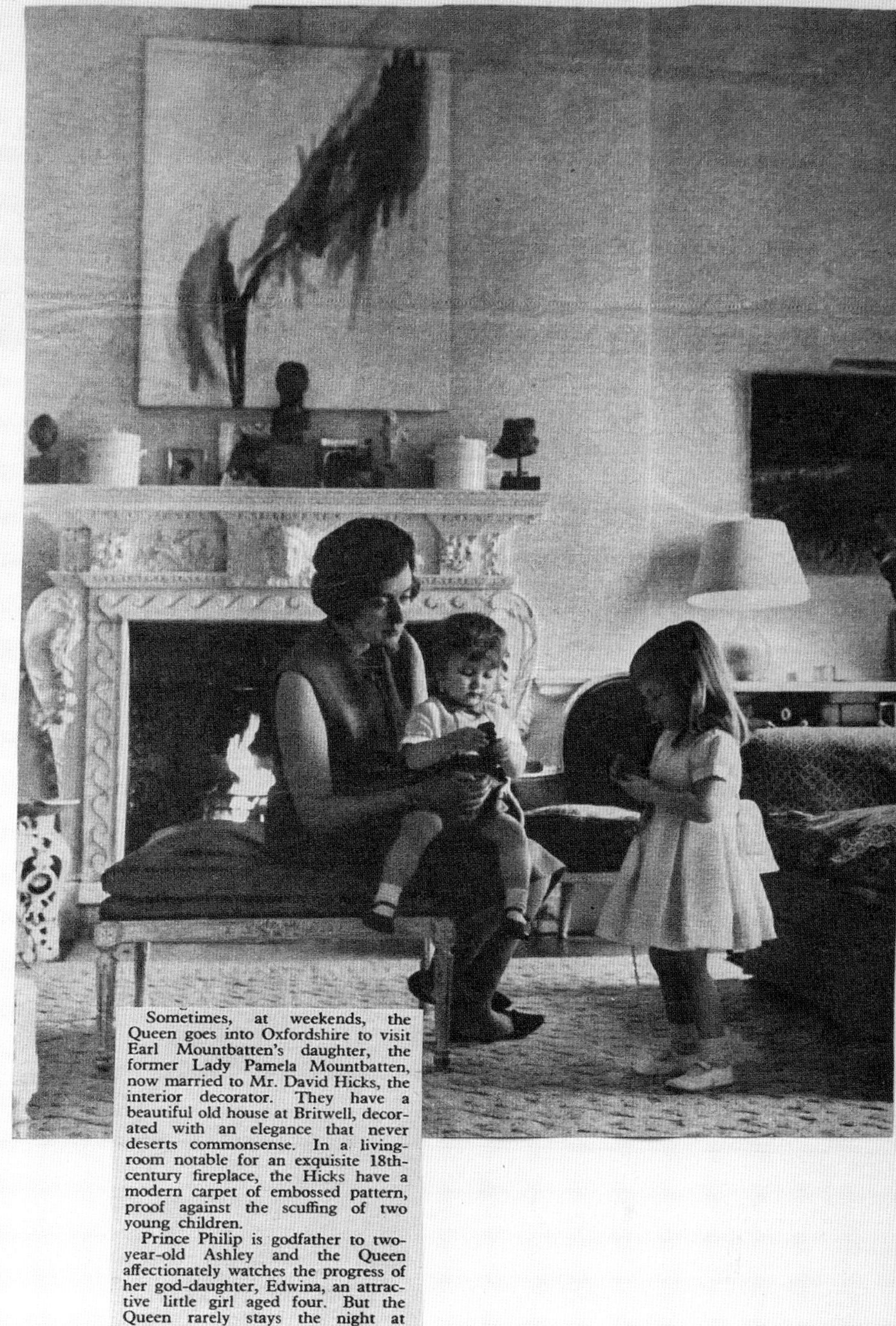

Sometimes, at weekends, the Queen goes into Oxfordshire to visit Earl Mountbatten's daughter, the former Lady Pamela Mountbatten, now married to Mr. David Hicks, the interior decorator. They have a beautiful old house at Britwell, decorated with an elegance that never deserts commonsense. In a living-room notable for an exquisite 18th-century fireplace, the Hicks have a modern carpet of embossed pattern, proof against the scuffing of two young children.

Prince Philip is godfather to two-year-old Ashley and the Queen affectionately watches the progress of her god-daughter, Edwina, an attractive little girl aged four. But the Queen rarely stays the night at Britwell, for she well understands the difficulties of an overnight guest for a busy couple.

On choisit donc deux événements amicaux, l'anniversaire de Maurice Jacquin et l'au revoir à Paris de Maria Frias qui partait rejoindre l'ambassade du Brésil à Damas. Cravates noires, robes longues et signées, silhouettes aussi internationales que parisiennes, le jerk au dernier étage, les causeries et les flâneries au rez-de-chaussée. Le Tout-Paris se retrouvait et s'agglomérait dans l'île déserte. Ci-contre, quelques insulaires : de gauche à droite et à partir du haut, Maurice Jacquin, Estelle von Schinkel et Henri d'Origny, puis Natti Abascal, Paolo Bassevi, Hervé Dugardin et Marie-Christine Boulart, puis Pascal Busson, le prince de Baroda, Eric Patenôtre et Béatrice de Mareuil, puis David Hicks, Lady Pamela Hicks, Mme Conrad Henkel et Yves Vidal. En bas, à gauche, Mme Louis Malle, à droite, Charete del Castillo et Guy Letellier.

French Vogue

Ball at Moulin des Courbeaux.

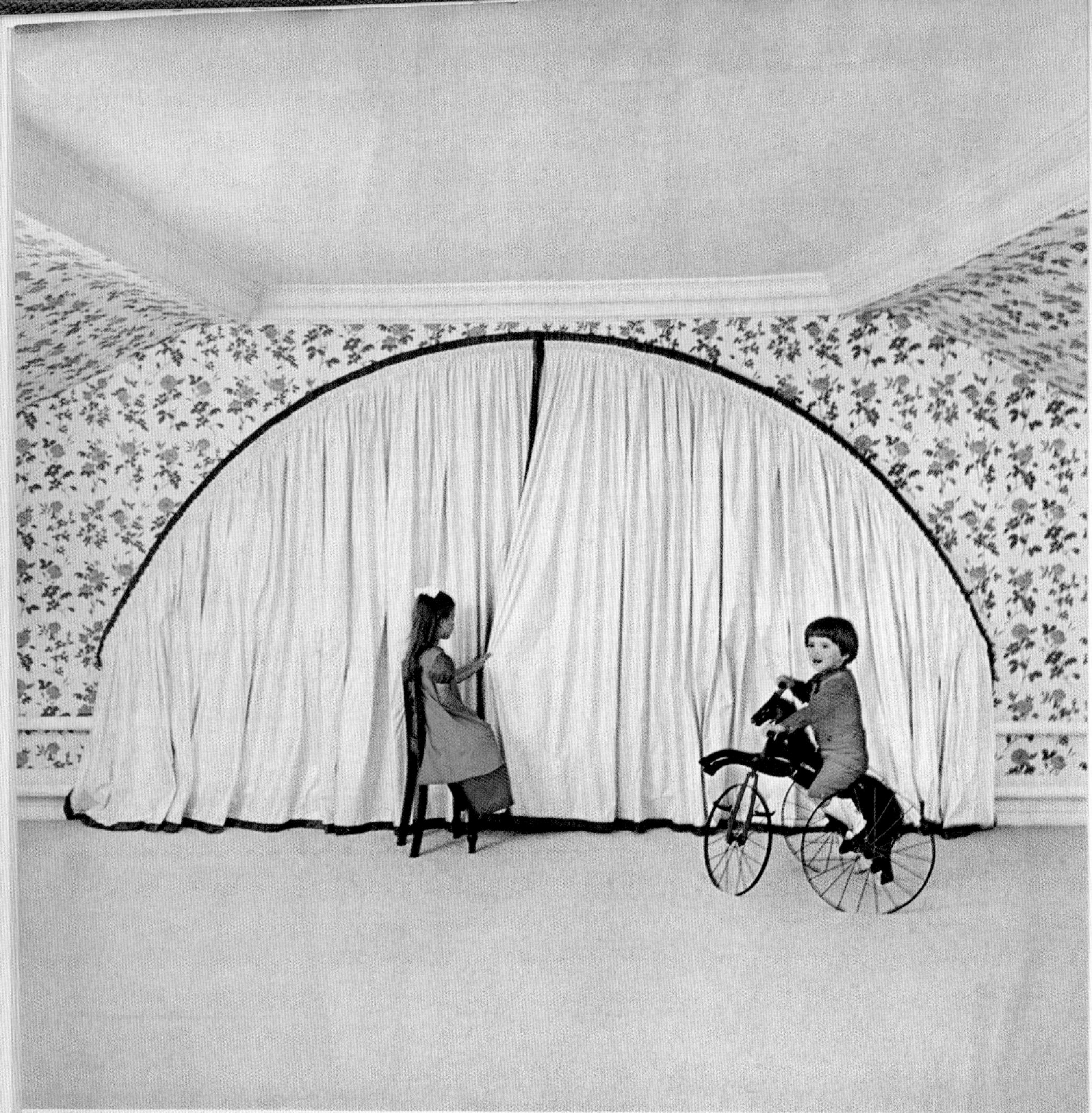

TWINKLE, TWINKLE, LITTLE STAR
HOW I WONDER WHAT YOU ARE!

Peeping out between the curtains of the night nursery, Edwina Hicks questions the Little Star while Master Ashley rides carelessly by on an antique toy-horse tricycle. Edwina wears a turquoise poplin pinafore tucked over a bright green poplin dress. Master Ashley companions her in poplin shirt, a jerkin, knee breeches of corduroy. The children are the son and daughter of Mr. David Hicks and Lady Pamela Hicks. Mr. Hicks is the prominent interior decorator; Lady Pamela, the daughter of Lord Louis Mountbatten and a cousin of the queen. Their home, decorated by Mr. Hicks, is the brick, early Georgian, Britwell Salome, in Oxford.

RHYMES IN AN
ENGLISH

NURSERY

American 'Harpers'

David Hicks On Decoration

At 37, David Hicks is Britain's top interior decorator. His work covers a wide range from the private suites at Windsor of the Prince of Wales and Princess Anne to rooms in modern semis. He has just published a book, "David Hicks on Decoration" in which the Daily Post has acquired serial rights. Every day this week, the Daily Post will publish an illustration from the book and tips from David Hicks to guide the ordinary householder in his own decorative schemes.

TO-DAY—CHOOSING YOUR COLOURS

IS bathroom and HERS

HERS is fabulous but you should see HIS. Royal weaver Peter Saunders and his 29-year-old wife, Didi, decided to do something special with their bathrooms.

They called in David Hicks.

Saunders, who makes tweeds for his old school friend, Prince Philip, said: "The bathrooms were a problem—all so dreary with lino on the floor." The house is a stone mansion in Easton Grey, Wiltshire. In the 1920's it belonged to the Prince of Wales, now the Duke of Windsor.

Didi's bathroom is all pink and orange and Portuguese tiles.

And HIS, in aubergine, is a second home. It has a sofa, black leather armchairs, a desk, drinks cupboard and radiogram. "I often use it as my private office," says Saunders.

There's a bath somewhere around, too. David Hicks thinks of everything.

BEVERLEY GOODWAY took the picture

Daily Mail

Britwell Salome garden "before"!

New wing of hotel opens

Over 130 guests were entertained to a buffet luncheon at the Izaak Walton Hotel, Dovedale, yesterday, to mark the opening of a new £30,000-£40,000 wing to the hotel.

The extension, with a decor by David Hicks, is built in Derbyshire stone which blends well with the existing building.

The hotel is owned by Rutland Development and the guests were welcomed by the Duke of Rutland.

"Izaak Walton"

Interior Decoration

DAVID HICKS ON DECORATION. *Leslie Frewin*, 84s. 1966. 31·5 cm. 152 pages. Illustrations.

One of the most accomplished and successful interior decorators of the last decade has here compiled a book which distils his experience, methods and preferences. The general tone is one of luxury and opulence but a strong undercurrent of practical common sense gives balance and reason to what otherwise might appear, at first glance, to be a series of glossy photographs. Closer inspection reveals that the rooms here illustrated have been designed with scrupulous care and intelligent appraisal of their potentialities or of the needs of their owners. Colour, texture, furnishings and even flowers are used to maximum effect. Though Mr. Hicks is a little severe on 'clutter' and the proliferation of inferior, if personally valued accessories, his own style, with its several typical features such as louvred screens and spotlights, is so attractive and fresh that nobody looking through this book could fail to regard his own surroundings with new and much more critical eyes. (747)

British Book News

David Hicks has set the scene: Black walls covered with spot-lit prints of bygone beauties, candle-lit tables to seat about 70, a comfortable armchair in front of a log fire, a small dance floor and a table spread with magazines.

The overall atmosphere is one of chi-chi homeliness, even to cases of "books" . . . about 1,500 book spines glued to the wall.

And they say they have the only doorman in Chelsea.

"Raffles"

CHELSEA'S first luxury nightclub, named after Raffles, the amateur cracksman, has a drawing room atmosphere designed by **David Hicks.**

Express

Advertisement in the 'Queen'

Liz Whitney (Mrs. Cloyce) Tippett, and also the Michael Phipps were there. The Phipps are just finished a stunning French house in Palm Beach and Molly has decorator David Hicks coming over from London. He is the son-in-law of Earl Mountbatten of Burma.

San Francisco Chronicle Feb 11th

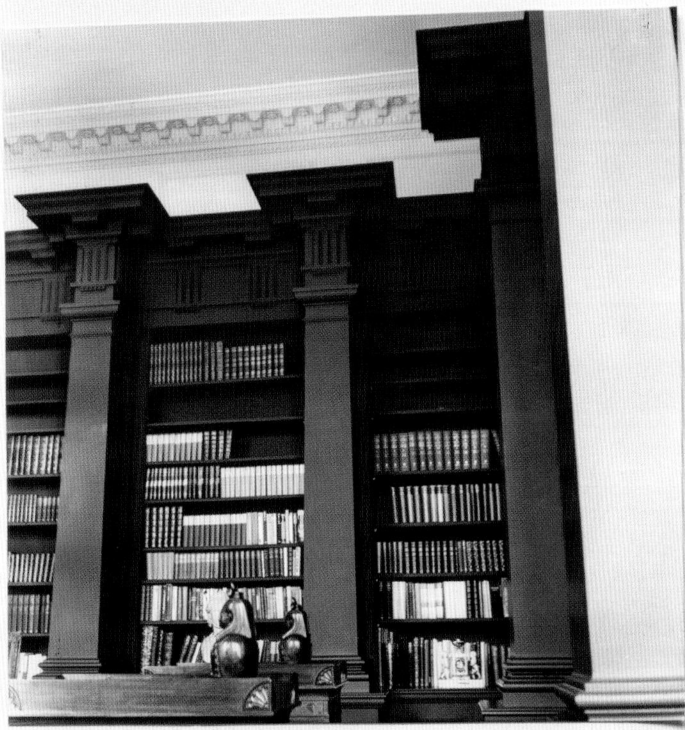

My library for Kisty at Easton Neston

The problems the BBC have in mind are those that have been tackled often enough in *House & Garden:* what to do with the attic; how to decorate a business girl's bed-sitter; how to brighten and streamline a small, out-of-date kitchen. And so on. The designers they have asked to solve these problems include Natasha Kroll, Alan Irwin, John Heritage, Sylvia Reid, John Brookes, David Hicks, Liz Goldfinger.

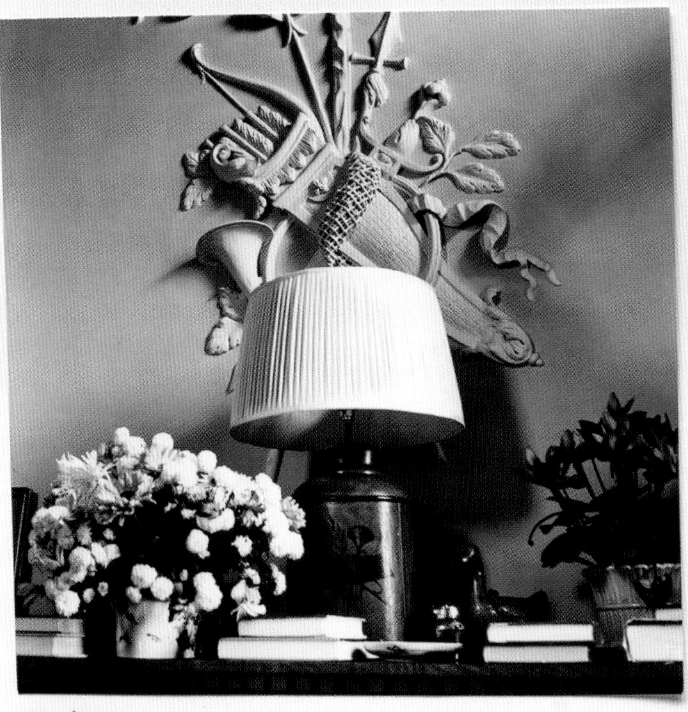

Easton

Q4's casino has had its chips

SIR BASIL SMALLPEICE, chairman of Cunard, has cancelled the plans for a casino aboard the Q4—the liner now nicknamed Princess Anne by those who think they know what she is to be called.

This follows an experiment in the liner Franconia which was "not a success" and withdrawn after three months.

It means that the much-publicised David Hicks's work for the Q4 has been considerably reduced. He was to have designed the casino and the night-club.

"Now he is just doing the night-club," says the design co-ordinator, Dennis Lennon, who between dealing with the Q4 is turning his hand to such landlubber's pleasures as the London Steak Houses.

for Mary Quant's flat

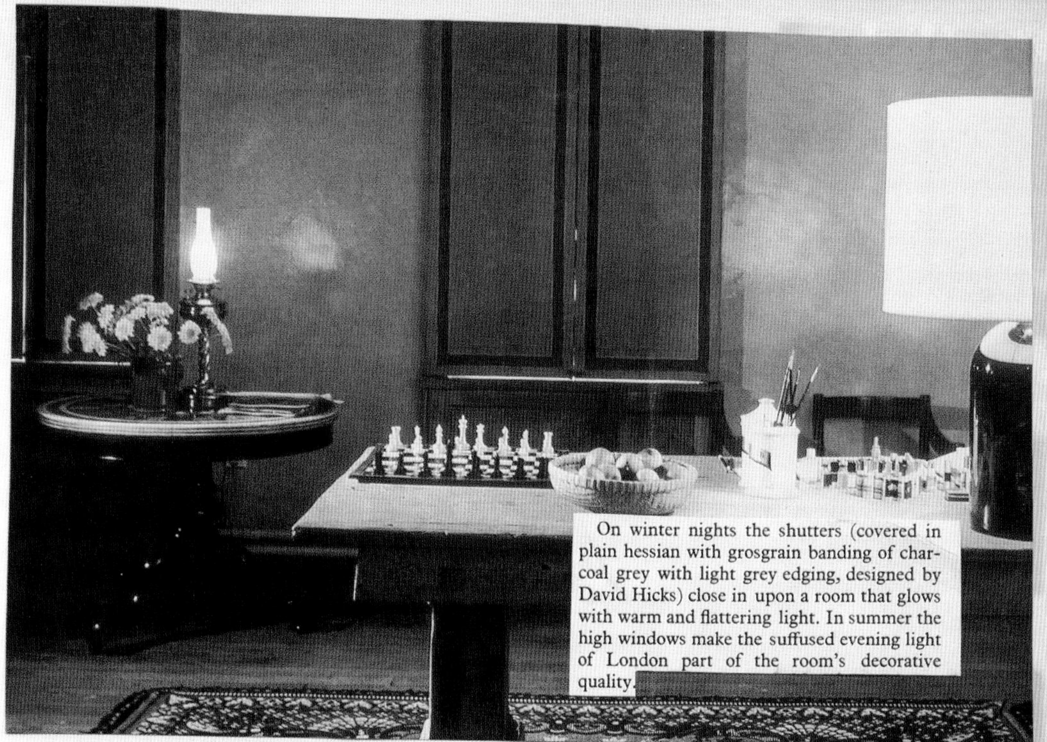

On winter nights the shutters (covered in plain hessian with grosgrain banding of charcoal grey with light grey edging, designed by David Hicks) close in upon a room that glows with warm and flattering light. In summer the high windows make the suffused evening light of London part of the room's decorative quality.

for Carla Venosta in Milan

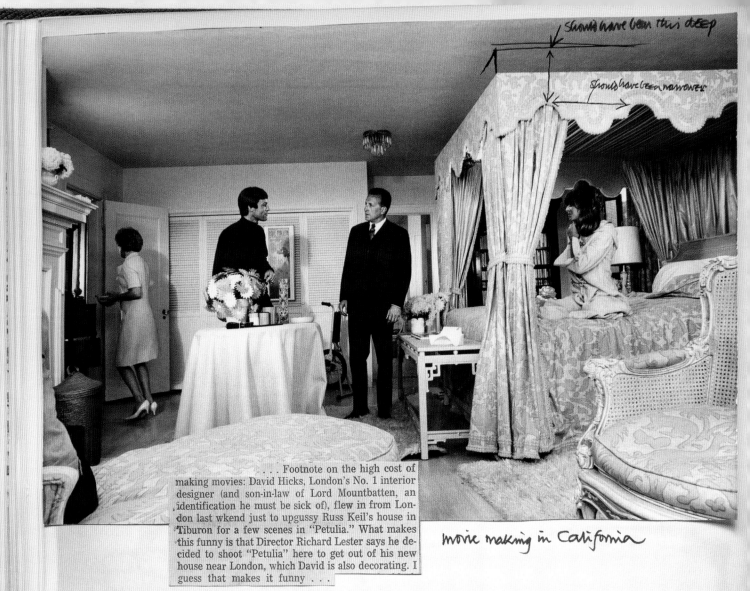

Should have been this deep

Should have been narrower

. . . Footnote on the high cost of making movies: David Hicks, London's No. 1 interior designer (and son-in-law of Lord Mountbatten, an identification he must be sick of), flew in from London last wkend just to upgussy Russ Keil's house in Tiburon for a few scenes in "Petulia." What makes this funny is that Director Richard Lester says he decided to shoot "Petulia" here to get out of his new house near London, which David is also decorating. I guess that makes it funny . . .

movie making in California

Der Markgraf und die Markgräfin von Baden
und
Markgräfin Theodora von Baden
bitten

David Hicks Esq.

zum Empfang anläßlich der Hochzeit
Seiner Großherzoglichen Hoheit des Prinzen Ludwig von Baden
mit
Ihrer Durchlaucht Prinzessin Marianne von Auersperg-Breunner
am 16. Oktober 1967 um 21 Uhr in Schloß Salem/Bodensee.

U. A. w. g.
bis zum 1. Oktober 1967
Bitte die Einladung mitbringen

Frack (Orden), Smoking
Abendkleid (Diadem)
Wagen 03 Uhr

Twiggy Enterprises Limited

21st July, 1967

David Hicks, Esq.,
23 St. Leonards Terrace
Chelsea, S.W.3.

Dear David,

Both Twiggy and I would like you to know how much we enjoyed meeting you and would like to thank you for the book, which was a super gift.

Yours,

T & J

Twiggy and Justin

22 Little Portland Street
London W1
Telephones:
London: (01) 580-9651
Paris: 073-56-29
New York: Plaza 34610

Daily News Record USA.

Verve and Versatility Blended in David Hicks

David Hicks

SAN FRANCISCO. — "I'd like to see very long overcoats — about 4 inches from the ground.

"I go pheasant-hunting in winter and I have a tweed outfit with a coat that sweeps the ground. It's marvelously warm. I'm having a town version made with a deep velvet collar —like Beau Brummel's."

This from opinionated English decorator David Hicks — the man who put scarlet tweed on the Queen of England's gallery walls and who brought color to drab-weather England.

Film director Richard Lester brought Hicks to San Francisco "to do a few rooms" for "Petulia," which has been filming in San Francisco and which stars Julie Christie and George C. Scott. Hicks recently completed decorating Lester's "modern glass box" of a house in London.

Still talking about clothes, Hicks says: "I'm keen on capes and cloaks, too.

"I like coats with concealed buttons and no pocket flaps. I like high-styled collars. I believe trousers should have slits up the side to accommodate boots. I think all men should wear boots—they make any outfit sit better."

Then he says: "I really must apologize, but with this weather and mucking about looking at houses for the film, I couldn't bring myself to go beyond something casually simple. Hicks was wearing a lightweight black jacket with the look of a silk blend, linen-looking trousers, beige cashmere V-neck pullover, light blue shirt open at the neck. His footwear was antique brown moccasins.

Hicks' projections of masculine elegance appear even stronger against the background of his decorating preferences. (His new book, "David Hicks on Decoration," will appear in the United States soon, as well as a series of brilliantly colored, geometric-design carpets, somewhat resembling tapestry weaves.)

"There's no more flowery chintz," explains Hicks. "There's no reason for it. The whole world is available. You can match wallpaper to straw and straw to wallpaper. The home is going to be more architectural and edited. And I'm glad."

He cites a house he's decorating on Windemere Island in the Bahamas—a modern stone tower with poured concrete walls a la Corbussier. Black glass vertical windows, plus extensive use of aluminum and plastics in the interior heighten its industrial mood.

Hicks recently signed on as consultant with the New York decorating firm of Mark Hampton, Inc. His first job will be the Mark Hamptons' apartment.

"One room will be all black," announces Hicks.

He's doing a house for himself and his family in the south of France that sounds even wilder.

"It's a Louis XVI farmhouse . . . I'm going to whitewash all the walls and use no chairs at all. Just great shapes of foam rubber covered with brilliantly colored fabrics. That's the message I bring to England."

Of apparel designers, Hicks favors Pierre Cardin "but only for the very young man or woman." (Hicks turned 38 while he was in San Francisco.)

He goes on to say: "I hate the mini on any woman who doesn't have matchstick-thin legs and isn't under 20. I think Balenciago is marvelous, but my wife [he's married to Lady Pamela, daughter of Earl Mountbatten of Burma] never goes to the collections in Paris.

"Couture goes out of date so fast no one can afford it any more. Besides, there are so many exciting things in ready-to-wear these days," adds the man who somehow found time to return to an early love—portrait painting. He'll have a show in New York in the fall.

Story and photo by ALBERT MORCH

DAVID HICKS

PORTRAIT DRAWINGS AND SCULPTURAL OBJECTS 1967

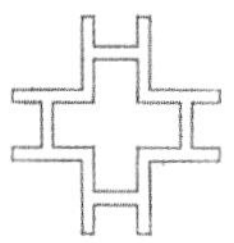

VASA 31 LOWNDES STREET LONDON SW1

PORTRAIT OF FATHER-IN-LAW. Mr. David Hicks with his portrait drawing of Earl Mountbatten, his father-in-law, at the opening of an exhibition of his work in London yesterday. Mr. Hicks, who is married to the former Lady Pamela Mountbatten, is best known as an interior decorator.

Mountbatten unlimited

Many prominent persons have been quick to form unlimited liability firms under the new Companies Act. Recently particulars appeared at Companies House of three anonymous-sounding companies re-registering as unlimited. They were M. Securities, B. Securities, and H. Securities. Closer investigation revealed that M., familiar James Bond initial, stood for Lord Mountbatten, the Queen's cousin. B. and H. are the former defence chief's sons-in-law, Lord Brabourne, film producer, and David Hicks, designer. A few weeks ago *Business Diary* was able to reveal that Lord Snowdon had also formed an unlimited company.

The main advantage of the unlimited company is that it drops a curtain of secrecy over the affairs of the firm. The drawback of being unlimited is that shareholders are liable to the last penny in insolvency, which means that in that unlikely event Lord Mountbatten would lose his estate at Romsey with its salmon river and pheasant shoot.

M. Securities has a nominal capital of £100, of which 98 per cent is owned by Lord Mountbatten. Its object is "to hold shares, stocks and other securities." The family trusts are major shareholders in Lowland Investment Trust, which has a market capitalization approaching £1,400,000.

Lord Brabourne's film producing interests are in a company with Olivier and Fonteyn, which has not become unlimited. His earlier films had a strong nautical flavour, stemming perhaps in part from his father-in-law, but his latest production is Romeo and Juliet, whose first night the Queen is attending next week.

BACKWORD

The name David Hicks has been synonomous with post-war decoration for so long, that most people overlook, or are unaware of, the creative virtuosity which first set him on his present course. Having studied painting for four years under Keith Vaughan at the Central School of Art and Design, he came to the conclusion that he would be much more usefully employed in decoration. And indeed, although an excellent and original draftsman as can be seen from his series of portrait drawings, he has proved himself right. He has a rare eye for the decorative, a depth of knowledge, and a fertility of ideas that has raised his work to an art form in itself.

This present exhibition—like many of his ideas for furniture, textiles and lighting—was originally conceived as a practical and unpretentious way of filling a need. The drawings were done because currently, there did not seem anyone to record the young and attractive in an acceptable mode. The perspex-mounted objects are glorifying the ready-made, creating a new thought for the subject, in much the same manner as Marcel Duchamps, though with considerably less irony of expression. Always a superb arranger of objects into still-lifes, he has found here a substitute for sculpture that is light, amusing and engaging. David Hicks is a master of controlled ingenuity. A decorator in the best and fullest sense of the word.

MARY GILLIATT

anti-Hicks!

VISCOUNT LEWISHAM has been kept pretty busy in his first few days at Oxford.

Most of his time has been spent scotching rumours put about by malicious scandalmongers, who deserve only my contempt, that he is going to have his oak-panelled Peckwater quad room decorated by society designer David Hicks.

Casually clad in corduroy jacket and running a hand through a mane of blond hair, the youthful lord told me: "To have this room decorated by David Hicks would, with all respect to him, be like putting a skyscraper in the middle of the college lawn."

It seems Christ Church's latest aristocratic freshman is more enamoured of his traditional college room than contemporaries.

"I love my oak panels. So does my mother," he said. For those not up in these things, "Mother" is Lady Dartmouth of "Ulysses" fame.

He added: "Even if every other room was decorated by David Hicks I'd keep mine the same.

"I'm not going to change it at all. I'll probably get a new lampshade and hang up my Durer print."

Do come and drink champagne at the private view of my exhibition of Portrait Drawings and Sculptural Objects between noon and midnight on October 18th at Vasa, 31 Lowndes Street, S.W.1.

It would be so nice if you could manage it.

David Hicks

RSVP (David Hicks) 23 St. Leonard's Terrace S.W.3.

PS. The exhibition will remain open on October 19th, 20th, 23rd, 24th and 25th between 9 am and 6 pm.

DAILY EXPRESS WEDNESDAY OCTOBER 18 1967

David Hicks, selling his father-in-law (left) at £200

rd Mountbatten . . . Hicks' style

ONE of the more acceptable aspects about being an artist is that there are always little money-making sidelines to be explored. For instance, **David Hicks,** the interior igner who is married to **Earl Mountbatten's** daughter **Lady nela,** is about to launch out into the picture-selling business.

The same Hicks hands that have sketched out beautiful and intricate carpet, ain, and wall designs recently gone to on 45 pointillist wings of famous le.

ey are on show today at rst-ever exhibition being d at Vasa, the Lowndes t store. Price: £200 With a range from gy to Mr. Hicks's father-w Lord Mountbatten elf.

he object," said 38-year-old Hicks simply, "is to sell The only two of the 45 aits not for sale are those rince **Philip** and the ess **of Kent.**

it I have done some of the aits in poster form which ell at 20s.—which is, of e, rather a new-image range for me."

QUICK

Hicks spent five years at entral Art School and is btedly an accomplished tsman. The technique he sed here has been one of ing sittings.

he subjects have posed for or five minutes' worth of fire photography. And he rawn the portraits from hotographs.

is just a new way of cing original drawings," he "Most people don't have or three-hour sittings two ee times a week. Using echnique I can get similar in a few minutes."

"I know you like it, dear, and I'm quite fond of it myself . . . but I'm positive David Hicks would loathe it."

NOT FOR SALE: THE 'ANTIQUE' JACKET

BARGAIN HUNTERS at an antique shop in the Somerset village of Beckington have been puzzled by a naval jacket which has been on display inside.

The jacket, complete with an impressive array of decorations, belongs to Earl Mountbatten.

But it was *not* for sale.

Says the embarrassed antique dealer Mr. Tom Stewart: "I took the jacket inadvertently when I collected a bundle of antiques and soft furnishings from Lord Mountbatten's son-in-law, Mr. David Hicks — for whom I work as an accountant two days a week.

★

"I only realised my mistake when I arrived home and discovered the jacket in the bundle.

"I hung it on the clothes stand, to keep it safe.

"There is no danger of it being sold. I am returning it to Lord Mountbatten very shortly."

THE SUNDAY TIMES, 19 NOVEMBER 1967

TURTLENECKING By HAROLD CARLTON

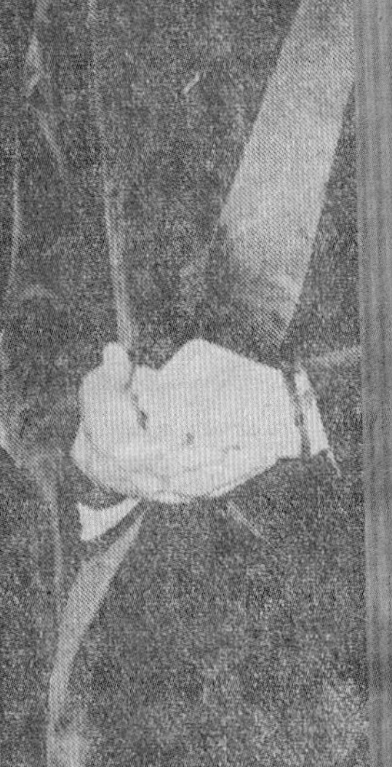

IN LONDON, Lord Snowdon ... with a dinner jacket for a Cov...

IT IS said that the voice of the turtle was first heard a year ago when David Hicks dined at a country house wearing a deep red turtleneck sweater with his dinner jacket. Some people call them "polo-necks," a nice rich chukka-sounding name, but the new turtleneck craze is dressy rather than sporty. Because the new turtlenecks are made in crêpes and silks, they now fall halfway between a shirt and a sweater. Turtlenecks for evening were given the royal okay last March when Lord Snowdon wore a black silk one with a dinner jacket for a party following a Covent Garden first night. It proved that it's not what you wear but *who* you are and *where* you wear it.

Lord Snowdon's turtleneck made headlines. Time magazine raised its eyebrows but was forced to lower them when the two Senators Kennedy (Bobby and Ted) began wearing white

---

23 ST LEONARD'S TERRACE LONDON SW3 SLOANE 4652

I am going to be in New York on the 25th October and am giving a Cocktail Party in the Decoration and Design Building at 979 Third Avenue in the Rug Gallery of the Harmony Carpet Corporation at 5 pm. It would be very nice if you were able to come as I should like to meet you and show you my new carpet designs and my books - 'David Hicks on Decoration' and 'The Highland Clans', my portrait drawings, prints and sculpture.

Perhaps you would drop my secretary a line to say whether you are able to come at the Harmony Carpet Corporation 979 Third Avenue N.Y.

I shall very much hope to see you.

David Hicks

DAVID HICKS

Men's clothes are no joke

DAVID HICKS leant back on the complicated patterned pink sofa and talked about male fashions. "It must be a wide tie and a thick knot," he said. "Matching handkerchief, of course."

Mr. Hicks, curiously enough, happened to be wearing a wide tie, thick knot and matching handkerchief.

Tapered trousers, too. No turn-ups. Double-breasted suit. Six buttons. White shirt.

"I think flowered shirts are, on the whole, on their way out. I wore one in Paris two years ago, and I am expected to wear one at a flowered shirt party again in Paris this Friday. But I think I will go in a turtle-neck sweater."

I looked a little surprised.

Square

"The trouble with you is you're square," he said, friendly enough. "I don't want to make you feel square, but you obviously still think of men's fashions as a joke market."

He thinks overcoats are right out.

"It is such a bore having to fish inside your overcoat and not finding a handkerchief, and you can't possibly have two because it makes too much of a bulge. So I have ordered a cloak. Two inches above the ground. Box cloth. Velvet collar."

He takes his clothes very, very seriously indeed. His cuff-links he designed himself: rubies set in a clear gold disc. Cigarette holder gold too. This time with an emerald set in the case. On his wrist a gold chain.

Marriage

"You can't take it off," he said. "It symbolises five years of marriage (he is married to Lady Pamela Mountbatten). I had it put on by the goldsmith at Cartier's in Paris."

In fact, he would rather like to become a couturier.

"I am negotiating with two top fashion houses at the moment. I would really love to design clothes. I hope they are going to use my geometric patterns for shirts. Evening shirts need to be changed, too. They are going to be black and white poplin with stiff white collar."

It seems we men are all just a little bit out of date.

David Hicks in Newcastle yesterday.

NORTH-EAST IDEAL FOR PROJECT, HE SAYS

Designer David wants to 'do' council house

By JEANETTE ROBINSON

DAVID HICKS, acclaimed as Britain's leading interior decorator, would like to decorate a council house somewhere in the North-East.

Today he made an open invitation to all Tyneside authorities—an invitation which could give council house tenants a chance to jump into the world of sumptuous luxury.

Mr. Hicks, who married Lady Pamela Mountbatten in 1960, has designed some of the most beautiful and revolutionary apartments and houses in the world.

During the past few weeks, he has been designing the interior of Montagu Court, a block of luxury flats in Gosforth. Today, one of the finished products—a £13,500 double flat—was on show.

The theme of the flat is unashamed luxury with a brash boldness typical of the 20th Century "jet set."

Tribute

Although Mr. Hicks spends most of his working life enveloped in an atmosphere of unlimited wealth, today he paid tribute to the industrial city of Newcastle and supported a plan to push the North-East to the top of the interior decorating poll.

He described Newcastle as one of the most beautiful, exciting and dramatic cities in the country.

"From the regular Victorian terraced rows to the dramatic blackness of the City buildings—it is all so wonderful," he said.

"Ever since I came first to the North-East 18 years ago I have loved it.

"I have never designed the interior of a block of flats like this before, but when I heard it was in the North-East I jumped at the chance.

"I admit I have been bold, brash and daring in the colour scheme. This counteracts the dullness of the North-East climate."

avid Hicks, designer, in the show flat with the builder, Philip Cussins.

MR. DAVID HICKS, the interior design consultant, with Mr. Philip Cussins, the builder, at a Press showing of the new exhibition flats at Montagu Court on the edge of the Town Moor, Newcastle.

EXECUTIVES' LUXURY HOMES GO ON SHOW

North Eastern papers

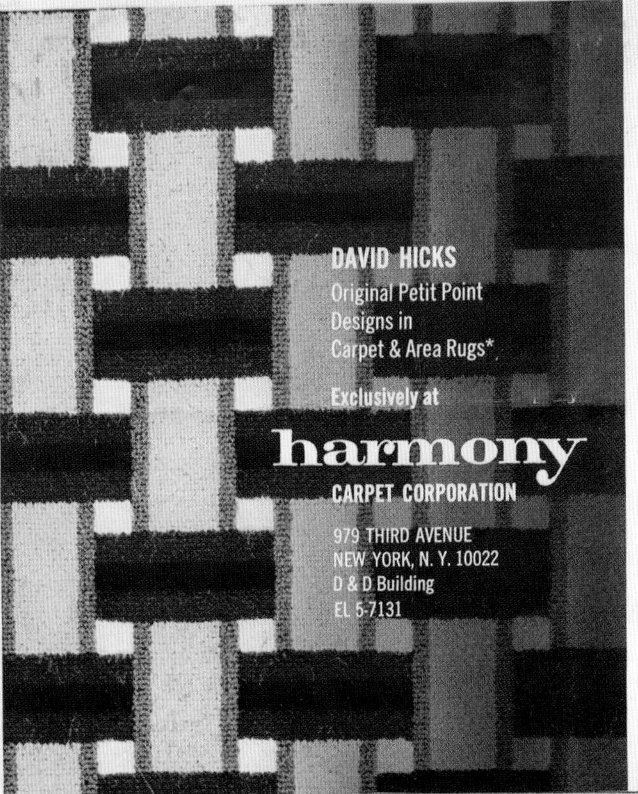

A Princely Carpet Can Make a Home a Castle

By RITA REIF

Shop Talk

A STRIKING medallion-patterned carpeting, which David Hicks, the British interior designer, created for Prince Charles's apartment at Windsor Castle, has just arrived in adapted form at the showrooms of the Harmony Carpet Corporation, 979 Third Avenue (at 59th Street). The blue and off-white octagonal design comes without the British crests that center the medallions in the Prince's version. Another outstanding carpet in the collection is a motif of circles and squares that Mr. Hicks designed for a restaurant but would be at home anywhere.

Other carpets with clover, basketry, stripes and geometric motifs in vivid colors and flat weaves are also being introduced. All the carpeting is $30 a running yard measuring 27 inches wide. The showroom may be visited by decorators or architects and their clients.

Medallion-patterned carpeting (above) is adapted from design by David Hicks for Prince Charles of Britain. $30 a yard at Harmony Carpet showroom.

New York Times

For Your Information

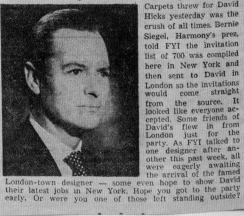

DID YOU SEE DAVID? It was the industry bash of the year. If you think the preview parties at Bloomingdale's for the model rooms get a bit crowded, the party Harmony Carpets threw for David Hicks yesterday was the crush of all times. Bernie Siegel, Harmony's prez, told FYI the invitation list of 700 was compiled here in New York and then sent to David in London so the invitations would come straight from the source. It looked like everyone accepted. Some friends of David's flew in from London just for the party. As FYI talked to one designer after another this past week, all were eagerly awaiting the arrival of the famed London-town designer — some even hope to show David their latest jobs in New York. Hope you got to the party early. Or were you one of those left standing outside?

H.F.D

VOGUE'S DECORATING FINDS AND IDEAS FOR

FASHIONS IN LIVING

Here: Scoop decorating news with top Christmas gift snap.

Right: The young Mark Hampton's new apartment introduces, to New York, décor by London designer David Hicks; and former museum man Mark Hampton as his New York associate. Expanding the small living room, shown here, open-ended white Plexiglas cube tables, the perspective of the geometric rug showing through. Banker's grey suiting-flannel walls recede softly, while shiny silver leaf screens heighten the window wall of washable white vinyl Roman shade. Louis XVI open armchairs, painted flat white, surprisingly upholstered in bold black-and-white Welsh bedspread cotton, flank luxurious black hopsacking sofas with squashy white cotton cushions. To order through decorators: David Hicks's rug, Harmony Carpets, 979 Third Ave., N. Y. 10022; David Hicks's 20" cubes, approx. $200 ea., Mark Hampton, 166 E. 63rd St., *Left:* Lumia, an electronic instrument, 24" x 32", by nuclear physicist Earl Reiback, "paints" hypnotic images in swirling colour and light. Just plug it in. $1,500. Plexiglas cube table, 24" x 32", $195. Both, at Laverne Assoc., 979 Third Ave., N. Y. 10022. Velvety wool "Wickerwork" rug through decorators, Patterson, Flynn & Johnson, 50 E. 57th St., N. Y. 10022.

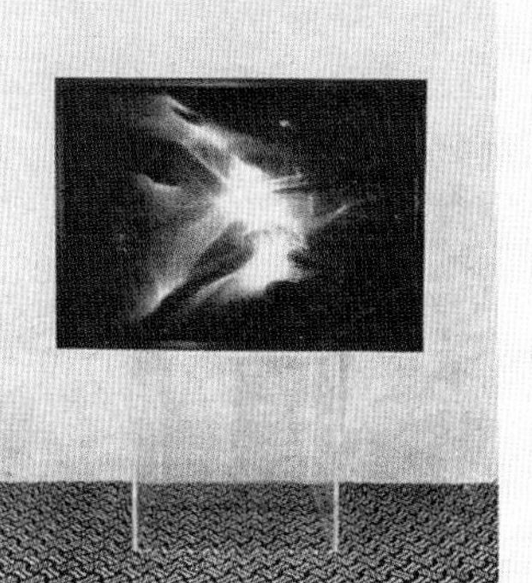

The geometric rug... see-through tables... the chair with a difference

Below: Spacemaking for a small dining room, an "invisible" dining table. Of 1/2" Plexiglas with 3/4" plate glass top, 36" x 72", it seats 8-10. This remarkable design by Roe Kasian seems not to be there at all. $875. His all-Plexiglas moulded chair is springy and sturdy, might pull up anywhere. $295. Both to order from Bloomingdale's, 59th St. at Lexington Ave., N. Y. 10022.

Above: Two Games For One: Make 163,840,000,000,000,000,000 designs with shiny black and white paper-covered 3 1/8" cubes. See two at left. Box of 16 Doty blocks, $10.50, Scarabaeus, 223 E. 60th St., N. Y. 10022. Plexiglas chairside-cum-Solitaire table holds the giant marbles on its rim. Reversible top. $175, Belgravia House, 225 E. 57th St., N. Y. 10022. Wool rug by David Hicks, Harmony Carpets, 979 Third Ave., N. Y. 10022.

Below: Superb chrome steel and glass library-backgammon table. The glass lifts off the red-white-black leather playing bed. $1,650. Folding steel benches, $390 ea. John Vesey, 969 Third Ave., N. Y. 10021. Smashing wool rug by Tom Isbell, to order, Stark Carpets, 979 Third Ave., N. Y. 10022.

Bottom, below: British officer's chair is news with zebra slings. $175. Chrome tubing table plus clips to hold a top, $21. Bronze Ibex, from a James L. Clark sculpture, $1,150 . . . Catalogue, $2. All, Hunting World, 247 E. 50th St., N. Y. 10022.

Above: David Hicks's wool rug. Fur pillows: left, natural deerskin, $50; calf in brown or black and white, $60. Right, black opossum, $68, black Borrego, $60. All, through decorators, Harmony Carpets, 979 Third Ave., N. Y. 10022. Luxurious leather Italian trunk-table by designer Moreddi, $242. Scandinavian Sun, 1714 Walnut St., Philadelphia, Pa.

DAVID MASSEY

American Vogue Nov 67.

pattern explosion

Hampton apartment on

At the Grand Rapids Showroom

Exhibitor's Building

The red and white carpet is a David Hicks design.

RECOGNIZE THEM?

By now everyone who is following design trends in the floor coverings industry should know that these small all-over patterns are the handiwork of David Hicks.

A few sources who were known to say "they're only ugly old linoleum patterns" several weeks ago—are now busy getting their competitive designs off the drawing boards. (One firm will reportedly come out approximately 20 designs by December).

Three new designs shown here are from the Hicks collection at Harmony Carpets.

"The trend to pattern has been coming for two years," Helen Marcus points out. Patterned goods are sold almost equally well for both residential and contract work, but with the big emphasis on residential "unless it is a no budget contract job," as Bernie Siegel points out. His carpets, designed by David Hicks and others, run about $30 retail per linear yard in the 27-inch width.

And what are these big selling patterns?

The vast majority are the mini geometrics, small stylized flowers, contemporary plaids (away from the Tartans), interlocking squares, spaced out flowers joined by inch-wide bands and variations on the snowflake and fleur de lis perennial motifs.

Of course, a major portion of the pattern game is the matching or contrasting border. Patterson, Flynn & Johnson likes the plain border, while Harmony goes in for the matching variety.

THE WAR OF GEOMETRICS IS ON: One decorator supply house after another is trying to cash in on the geometric explosion in floor coverings. Cries of "copy!" and "knockoff!" are heard from floor to floor in 979 Third Avenue and its environs.

Who had what first is hard to establish. After all, small all-over geometric patterns have been around since the middle ages and anyone can go to the public library and find a great pattern.

One of the leading decorator supply houses in New York (the one that doesn't like to show its designs to the press "because they will be copied") has been the most flagrant copies of them all.

Just about every has heard the name David Hicks and when his book on interior design appears in the States Oct. 23 (it's already out in England), the geometric explosion is sure to reach from coast to coast.

The elite Londontown designer has not only designed 30 or more geometric patterns, but he has the name and substance to put them across. And with the help of Harmony Carpet, who has a fantastic tiger by the tail, the small all-over pattern has become THE fashion item among interior designers today.

But now that the trend has started, is there any need for one firm to copy patterns line for line, color for color, and try to say it was the first and claim to prove it only to back down when pressed? (See designs shown here.)

The world of design—any type of design—needs creativity and ingenuity. Adapting someone else's idea is fine to a point—even David Hicks adheres to this philosophy wholeheartedly. But downright flagrant copying helps no one—least of all, the ones who do it.

DH on Bay Orchid.

GUE'S TEBOOK

and Mr Fish arranged
g party and fashion show for charity

of the Playboy Club were taken over by Annacat and fashion show organised by the Keystone Committee National Association of Boys Clubs. Bunny girls sold to guests most of them wearing romantic dresses e occasion. 1. Miss Janet Lyle of Annacat with tman and Mr David Hicks. 2. Lady Anne Tennant. Michael Vaughan and Miss Arabella Churchill. nt of Glin and the Hon. Mrs Michael Brand. 5. illes wearing an Annacat dress in the show. 6. Mr ns with The Hon. James and Mrs Ogilvy. 7. Lord aulieu with Mr Patrick Macnee. 8. Mrs Paul Channon.

2

3

5

8

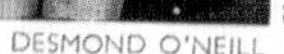

DESMOND O'NEILL

5 Hickses by Patrick Lichfield.

L'OEIL

numéro spécial
le décor
de la vie

L'oeil oct 67 :

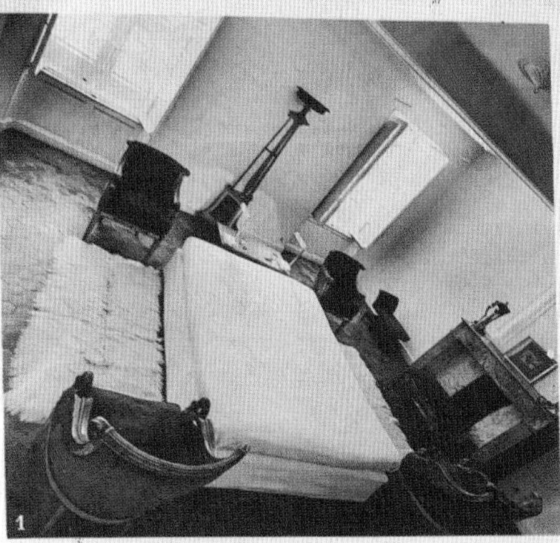

book
icks

ars ago, David
Mountbatten's
n-in-law—was
hat he wasn't
ch as people
ink and that
nmissions.

that his first
Hicks on
as helped to
t.

me that he
t ten major
s a result of
says his pub-
Frewin, who
ing to bring
David Hicks
h Taste.

e 5 gns. and
than last
de photo-
g the taste
n homes of
e Duchess
ord John
nd mail-
Saunders.

1 *Dans la chambre à coucher principale, autour du lit recouvert de blanc, quatre fauteuils Directoire aux accoudoirs en col de cygne. Tapis blanc et carrelage ancien sur le sol. Sur la cheminée Directoire, un brûle-parfum de même époque, en bronze doré. Entre les fenêtres, une torchère anglaise portant une coupe de marbre qui provient de Londonderry House.*
2 *Vue latérale du salon. Au premier plan, sur un tapis brun et blanc d'Addis-Abéba, une colonne et une coupe blanche.*
3 *Vue de la bibliothèque vers le salon. Sur la table à écrire, des céramiques blanches de David Hicks. Près d'un bouquet de tubéreuses, six vases de jade dans une monture de Perspex. A gauche, une pendule de voyage 1900. Au fond, un dessin de Jack Smith.*

4 *Parmi les objets disposés sur la cheminée en marbre gris moucheté de la bibliothèque, une poterie italienne aux tons bruns et crème, des vases d'ambre chinois, une miniature moghul et des boîtes de bois. Au-dessus, une toile de Peter Sedgeby aux tons rouges. Les coussins capitonnés sont recouverts d'un tissu orange assorti à la couleur du tapis. A gauche, sur une table anglaise XVIIe, une collection d'étains du XVIIe siècle. Chandelier de porcelaine blanche.*

5 *Un autre aspect du salon. Sur la cheminée du XIXe siècle, en marbre safran, une collection d'objets blancs: des émaux de Norvège, un relief abstrait de Michaël Fussell, des objets d'ivoire. A droite, des roseaux vaporisés de blanc dans une simple soupière d'acier inoxydable. Le panier, près de la cheminée, contient des sarments de vigne. A droite et à gauche, deux lampadaires de cuivre. Les céramiques blanches ont été dessinées par David Hicks, l'été dernier, à Roquebrune.*
6 *Un Bouddha chinois en bois du XVe siècle, trouvé à Kyoto, est posé sur une table de verre et de bois laqué blanc. A droite et à gauche, deux chaises de Kjaerholm à piètement chromé, tendues de toile blanche. Des colliers tahitiens en coquillages offerts à Lord Mountbatten sont accrochés au mur à côté d'une peinture de Peter Sedgeby et composent avec une collection de poteries blanches d'époque Ming et des herbes séchées de Provence une harmonie de tonalités crème et blanc.*

If you're a real glutton
for punishment -
see next volume

Alberto Arbasino / David Hicks / Piero Ottone / Carla Venosta alla Milano Libri martedì quattro giugno alle ore diciotto e trenta per presentare **David Hicks on decoration**

Milano Libri / via Giuseppe Verdi 2 Milano / telefono 875871

Milano Libri / via Giuseppe Verdi 2 Milano / telefono 875871

White will be worn . . . even by the men

DAVID HICKS could hardly be expected to ease himself quietly into the world of commerce. Such a momentous step demands to be marked by something unusual, not to say bizarre.

Thus for the opening of his London shop tomorrow night he has arranged a somewhat unusual party. All the guests have been asked to wear white. Not just women guests: men guests, too.

Of course, one understands the reason. The motif of the shop—which Hicks is opening with Neil Zarach—is white and you can't have a motley lot of guests spoiling the effect by wearing any old colours.

Still, problems have arisen. Simon Dee, the teleperson, has announced that he's not going to wear white unless he feels like it and Hicks has said in that case he jolly well can't come, so there.

'One has to be ruthless about these things,' says Hicks, more in sorrow than in anger.

Other guests have been more accommodating. Patrick, Earl of Lichfield, the photographer, will be wearing white. So will film director Dick Lester.

Daily Mail

In our Infancy

DURING a party given the other day by David Hicks, at which both men and women guests were asked to wear white, an irreverent passer-by stopped to look at the spectacle.

"Wot's this," he inquired, "'Eaven?"

Kenneth Rose

Robert Stokes *ARIBA*
Dip Arch (Birm) England
in association with
David Hicks *Interior Decorator*
London, New York and Nice

Robert Stokes Associates
PO Box 4812
Nassau, Bahamas
telephone 21542

All in White, Even Margaret

David Hicks, such a nice, regular-featured chap, is married to the former Lady Pamela Mountbatten, and hence his papa-in-law is the renowned seadog, Earl Mountbatten of Burma. But being [illegible]ted to a pack of titles by marriage was never enough for David. A talented, hustling interior decorator, he has done some of the best houses and nobbiest restaurants in London and the countryside.

And now with the London season in full swing, David has just launched his new all-white decorating shop in Chelsea with an all-white party. No one could get in the door unless attired in something pure as the driven.

Even Margaret, Duchess of Argyll, who is forever swooping into cocktail paties in little black Paris numbers, followed instructions. She was tripping around, cool as a cuke, and getting herself photographed with Indian Prince Ali of Murshidabad in a pristine new Balenciaga. "I'm only wearing white because David and Pammy insisted," she said gaily. It seemed like a fairly good reason. Prince Ali wore a white rajah coat. I suppose he's entitled.

Among the Most Popular of Diplomatic Couples

The duchess, along with the Queen of England and Prince Philip and a few others of lesser degree, has sat for David Hicks' latest brain wave, the photo-portrait. This consists of taking hundreds of photographs of the subject's face and assembling them all to paint a composite portrait. Do you see how that works? Oh, well. Oh, well.

Anyhow, Margaret Argyll was escorted to the all-white affair by the Spanish ambassador, the Marques de Santa Cruz, called Pepe by everyone who loves him. He and his super-spirited consort, Casilda, are among the most popular of London's diplomatic couples. They give big smashing crowded parties in the far-flung Spanish Embassy where it's worth your life to get a chair, but where you see everybody in London who counts.

Also poking through the new Chelsea shop were romantically beautiful Evangeline Bruce, wife of the American ambassador, in a white flowered hat, and Britt Gertsen, secretary to Hicks' associate, Neil Zarach, with a lot of bare Scandinavian middle showing between her white crocheted pants and her skimpy crocheted top.

Suzy "Daily News"

Mr David Hicks.

SHOOTING PROGRAMME
BROADLANDS 1968/69

Sat. 19 Oct.	1st Park	* Sir Brian Mountain * Mr Charles Williams	
Sat. 26 Oct.	1st Luzborough	* Mr Potter * Mr Morris	
Sat. 2 Nov.	1st Busheyleaze	Duke of Kent Prince Moritz of Hesse	Duchess of Kent Princess Moritz of Hesse Princess of Hesse
Sat. 9 Nov.	2nd Park	Sir Harold Wernher Mr Ambler	Lady Zia Wernher Princess Margaretha King Gustaf Lady Delamere
		NSB	
		NSB	
		Prince Philip Lord Brabourne Mr D vid Hicks	The Queen Lady Brabourne Lady Pamela
		NSB	
		* Lord Montagu * Lady Brecknock	
		Lt. Cdr. de Pass Nr Noel C-Reid	Mrs de Pass Mrs C-Reid
		NSB	
		King of Greece Prince of Wales	Queen of Greece Princess Anne
			Xmas House Party
			Xmas House Party

VOGUE'S DECORATING FINDS AND IDEAS FOR

FASHIONS IN LIVING

DAVID HICKS OPENS SHOP; LIGHTS FLASH; CHAIRS TAKE NEW SHAPE

At last David Hicks, *above*, **has opened his own shop, seen distinctively black and white.** In the Fulham Road, called Hicks + Zarach (he is in partnership with Neil and Andrew Zarach of the Sander Mirror Co), it is small but uncluttered, spotlessly white for the moment only as colours will change with the seasons, and carpeted in sharply patterned black on white. This is one of about thirty designs, just part of the stock of beautiful furnishings all carefully selected or designed by David Hicks himself, all simple, practical, imaginative. Like the stacking Perspex tables, *above*, £61 10s for a set of five; or the white ceramic ashtrays in the foreground, triangular, 12s. 6d, circular, 25s. Elements for an arrangement, *right*, Perspex column, £29 13s; topped by a blob of glass, 40s; knot of glass, 19s 6d; standing frame of glass and aluminium £7 13s. 9d. *Below:* octagonal Perspex stool or table, £25 8s. 9d.

PETER RAND

◀**More impeccable design from Hicks + Zarach.** *Left:* white and rounded pressed paper table and chairs by Hull Traders, £11 17s and £9 1s each; rectangular Perspex vase on the table, £5 3s. *Right:* lacquered black library steps or ladder inspired by an eighteenth-century French design seen by David Hicks in the Musée des Arts Decoratifs in Paris. Fine and light but strong, they snap to decisively for easy storage, £42. All from Hicks + Zarach, 110-112 Fulham Road, S.W.3.

There was, in the close-knit but highly competitive New York decorating field, a sense of some dramatic change — the beginnings of a sensational trend, which had its origins a few years ago when Mr. Tommy Marchetti, then Design Director with Crossley Carpets, suggested to David Hicks that he might like to produce some carpet designs.

Something in the nature of a revolution seemed to be called for — and that's exactly what was started last autumn, when the famous London design trio — David Hicks, John Fowler and Cecil Beaton — were asked to develop a small collection of striking new carpet designs for the U.S. market. From David Hicks came the geometrics; John Fowler supplied elegant 18th century designs in muted pastels; Cecil Beaton adapted free-wheeling abstracts from his original ideas in oils and

When the news of what was afoot first leaked out, London's *Daily Mail* described the Hicks designs as "meticulous geometrics in bold colours."

David Hicks himself called them "those tight geometric patterns."

Lord Garnock, Crossley's marketing director who had commissioned them, forecast: "They'll be something of a shot in the arm for the American decorators."

Left: The flat of Mark Hampton David Hicks' New York associate.

Right: One of David Hicks' geometric designs used in the lounge of a house in Italy.

from a house magazine article of Crossleys'.

CORNER TABLES

HER name is Britt and she works at the shop in London's Fulham Road owned by David Hicks and Neil Zarach. Britt is leaning against a very modern nest of tables—they are made of red plastic and can be used either as pure decoration—say, stacked like this in the corner of a room—or for utility purposes.

In fact, nearly everything in this picture is red. Britt is toying with a red plastic "love-knot" — a fun-design for Christmas. The red plastic boxes (scattered around the floor with other love-knots) have clear acrylic lids. The clock (perched on the table in foreground) though not red, is very way out. It is electric and numbered. It might take you some time to learn how to tell the time from it—but at least your guests would notice it.

Daily Telegraph

'A'

Asked about the children, he named three . . . "Edwina, 6½, Ashley 5, and India, our youngest who received the name because it's lovely, don't you agree, and of course it relates to her grandfather—Lord Mountbatten, who, you know, was the last Viceroy and first Governor General to India with residence in New Delhi."

LADY PAMELA, his wife, "likes Courreges for clothes . . . probably my influence of the geometric clean-cut look . . . she has no part in my work, rather she spends her time in charity things, child welfare, and is especially interested in "Save The Children" organization."

Lady Pamela's interest in worthy causes AND CLOTHES comes naturally—from her mother, Lady Edwina Mountbatten, who in younger days could afford to indulge every whim fashionwise. She was rated as the wealthiest woman of the world. At one period was known to travel with 40 or 50 trunks and extra cases when on tour in Europe.

Lord Louis Mountbatten, Pamela's father did not travel in his wife's shadow by any means. Prior to England's entry in World War II, he was described variously as, among the "best dressed, a social lion, and leader in merriment in swanky circles around fashionable London."

But by fall of 1941, there was little trace of the 'merriment' in either one. Lord Mountbatten became Chief of Com-

now go to 'B' on facing page

EMPIRE BUILDERS of a unique order in 'royal toast' at Wright-Hepburn-Webster Gallery in New York. Left: Yves Saint-Laurent, world-famed French couturier whose theatre sketches for recent one man show at gallery may be seen in-part in the background. Right: David Hicks, dynamic British interior decorator whose drawings contingent to his field are currently on display. It's a first time for such an opening.

DAVID HICKS' design of the great tester bed for the Duchess of Rutland at Belvoir Castle, England.

PENTHOUSE LIVING ROOM for Lord and Lady Cholmondley, pictured, is a graphic example of David Hicks' talent as an artist and interior decorator. Sketch shows glimpses of his geometric type carpeting, some of the squashy-cushioned couches with straight sides and backs, glass and metal furniture he designs.

...nts.

Edwina & Ashley go to Ireland

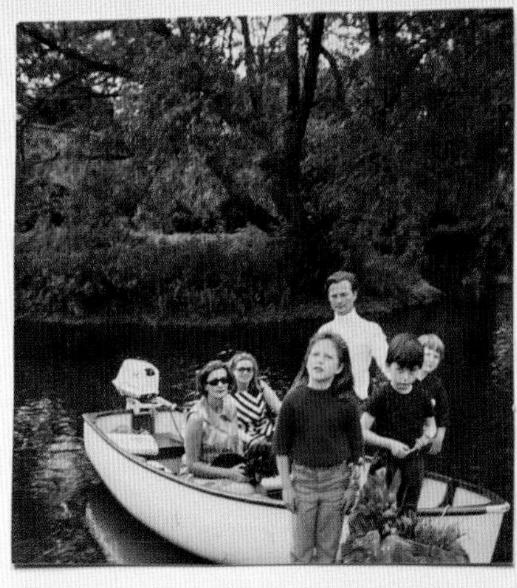
Spend a weekend on the Thames + D... Ha...

...go to France and play

in their garden.....

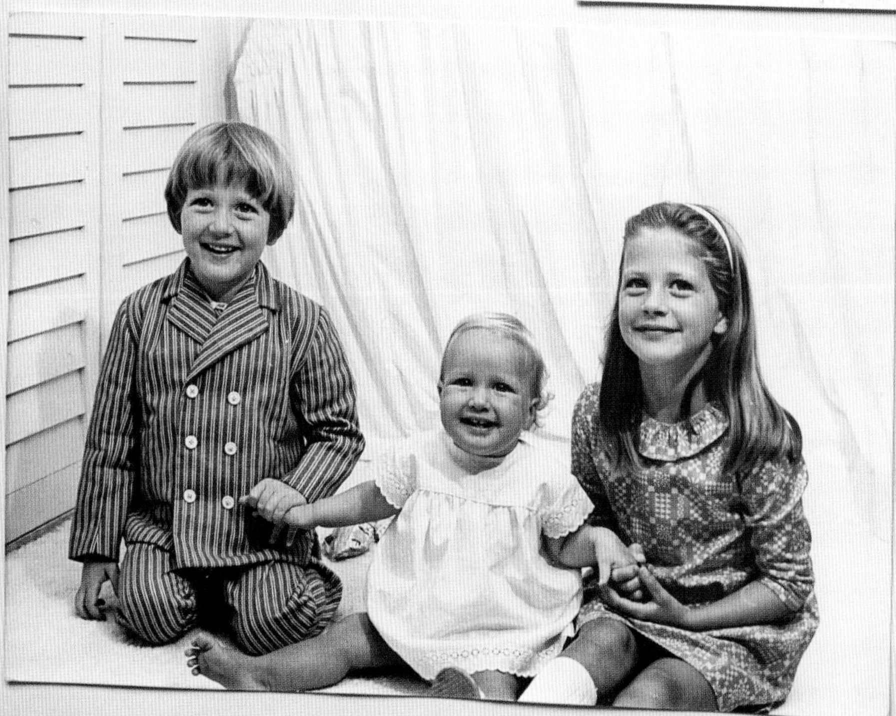
and return to Bretwell to see India!

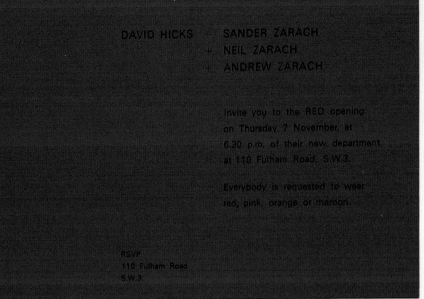

DAVID HICKS + SANDER ZARACH
+ NEIL ZARACH
+ ANDREW ZARACH

Invite you to the RED opening on Thursday, 7 November, at 6.30 p.m. of their new department at 110 Fulham Road, S.W.3.

Everybody is requested to wear red, pink, orange or maroon.

RSVP
110 Fulham Road
S.W.3

6

Q4 ROOM — Night club

❝**The Q4 room:** this room looks aft, and has a viewing on to one of the outdoor swimming pools. We asked David Hicks for a design that would provide an informal lounge during the day, convertible at night into a night club. His solution includes dark grey flannel panels on the walls, edged with metal on a gold-leaf background; a dance floor and space-dividing screens designed by Rory McEwen and made of perspex rods sandwiched between polarized glass—really very pretty. Banquettes line the walls, and the atmosphere can be immediately changed at night by drawing brilliant red shutters across the windows.❞

David Hicks on Taste

The title itself of David Hicks' new book, **Living – with Taste** (Leslie Frewin, 5 gns) is ambiguous. Is it a book of tasteful interior decoration, or a manifesto for the personal taste and dogmas of David Hicks? If it is the former, it is rather too limited in its scope to serve any great purpose; but as the latter, it is a magnificent publicity hand-out, though overpriced.

It is certainly true that many of Mr Hicks' interior designs are extremely tasteful (noticeably, those for his own houses) and it could also be said that there are quite a few decorating tricks to be picked up from the book. But one's enjoyment does depend on whether or not one goes *all* the way with Hicks.

The credits are very discreet; few other people are mentioned, those who are being mostly assistants and clients. On the pages devoted to those examples of modern furniture blessed by inclusion, there are chairs by Breuer, Scarpa and Colombo, without a word about the designers, but then one senses that Mr Hicks is not exactly at home with modern design, preferring pastiche to the real thing.

John Vaughan

WHEN interior decorator David Hicks opened his Fulham Road shop in June he threw a party with the proviso that all guests must wear white. This rather angelic opening will be followed with another party next week to celebrate the opening of an extension. This time guests must be in red. Not, I am assured by Hicks's business colleague Neil Zarach, that the shop's accounts are.

Express

GWEN ROBYNS has made a successful first effort as a biographer with her life of actress Vivien Leigh, "Light of a Star." It is now in its second printing after only a few days of publication. This New Zealand-born former journalist has a busy time ahead until May. She must then deliver biographies on actress Dame Margaret Rutherford and designer David Hicks plus a book on the women of the Royal Family.

PERSPEX MOVES up into the luxury class with some exciting new designs launched by David Hicks last week. The perspex he uses is thick, solid, and elegant with smooth edges, and when it's combined with glass or chrome gives a lovely lightness and floating delicacy to modern furniture. Everything is so simple one wonders why no one has thought of it before.

There is a lamp base made of a single cylinder of clear perspex with a chrome base and top; a bookcase in scarlet opaque perspex on a chrome base; and a table with two sheets of clear perspex crossed to form a base, with a sheet of plate glass making the table top.

ELEGANT

There is a really elegant modern clock the size of a small carriage clock. A hexagonal box of clear, brown perspex with one clear, colourless side, the clock itself is two revolving cylinders, one marked with the hours, the other with the minutes. You read the time by means of a static needle on the clear perspex side.

There is a book rest for those who like to read in the bath. Made in a single curve of thick, white perspex, your book rests on the curl at the bottom, and the black perspex base stretches across the bath.

Tall square vases in perspex in almost any colour you can think of are made from eight inches high and four inches square, right up to any height you like. Photograph frames are made of two sheets of glass which slot into two square stubby perspex feet. There's a jig-saw puzzle to puzzle the experts, since the whole thing is made in clear perspex so you can't tell which is the back.

All these are still at rich man's prices. For example the lamp base is £45. A coffee table 24in. by 24in. costs £27 7s. 6d. The clock is £15 15s. The book rest £18 15s. The vases from £4 3s. The photograph frames £1 17s. 6d., and the puzzle £3.

But the ideas are such a stunning mixture of good design and common sense that they should be copied at prices all of us can afford.

★

Sunday Express

← Oxford pa

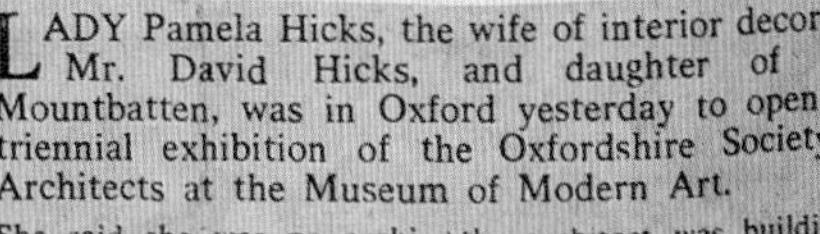

LADY Pamela Hicks, the wife of interior decorat Mr. David Hicks, and daughter of Ea Mountbatten, was in Oxford yesterday to open t triennial exhibition of the Oxfordshire Society Architects at the Museum of Modern Art.

She said she was no architect, but her architectural background went back to her childhood, when she lived at Broadlands, Hampshire, which was designed by Capability Brown.

Later her parents built what she thinks must have been the first penthouse in London, looking over Hyde Park.

"It had five reception rooms which could be joined together to make a ballroom or cinema," she said, "and a lift, which went berserk when Queen Mary visited us, and took her up and down and up."

Lady Pamela said she had learnt that architecture was essentially about people, whether the architect was building a university or a three-roomed house.

It was not true, she ad that modern architecture looked alike or that houses spoilt old villages. was only true if the design at fault. "If there is real e ity, old and new can live gether," Lady Pamela said

Christmas at Broadlands:

Heads of departments and household staff.

Broadlands.

Happy Xmas and New Year
to you and yours
from
uncle [signature]

King of Sweden

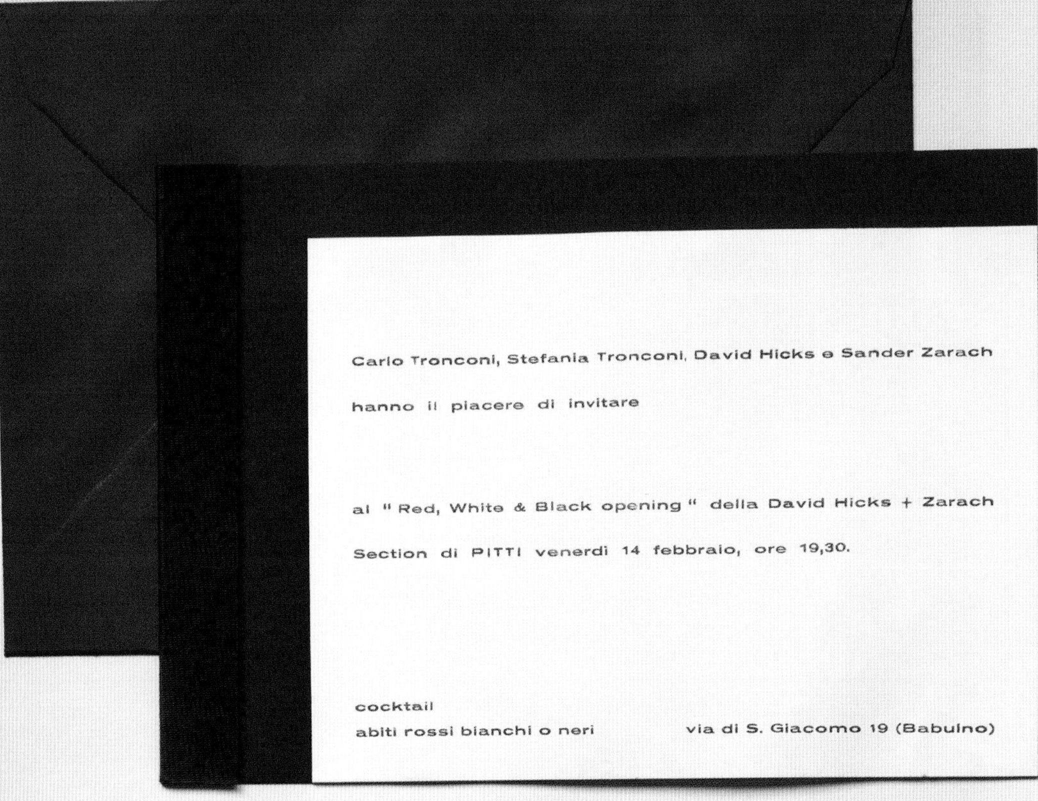

Carlo Tronconi, Stefania Tronconi, David Hicks e Sander Zarach

hanno il piacere di invitare

al " Red, White & Black opening " della David Hicks + Zarach

Section di PITTI venerdì 14 febbraio, ore 19,30.

cocktail

abiti rossi bianchi o neri

via di S. Giacomo 19 (Babuino)

PEOPLE

THE Duke of Westminster, who is campaigning in Ireland for Captain Terence O'Neill, is 'not taking seriously' a threat telling him to 'Watch the bullet . . . the gunman will be in Fermanagh after Monday.' . . . Naturalist **Peter Scott** is to compete in the National Gliding Championships in his £3,000 glass fibre sailplane. . . . **David Hicks** and his wife, **Lady Pamela,** fly off to Rome today for the opening party of his new furnishing boutique there, where all the guests are invited to turn up in red, white and black.

EARL MOUNTBATTEN'S son-in-law, David Hicks, 39, was host in Rome last night at a party for the opening of his latest enterprise, a shop devoted to interior design on the lines of the one he has in London's Fulham Road. It was a red, white, and black affair; Mr. Hicks likes pure colours for his parties. He was wearing a black velvet suit and red polo-necked sweater when he and his wife Lady Pamela welcomed guests. Those invited included King Constantine of Greece. But one important figure was absent—our Rome Ambassador Sir Evelyn Shuckburgh, 59. He has just had his appendix out.

We invite you

to meet

DAVID HICKS

Among the glamorous bolt-holes offered for your inspection is ex-model Bettina's wild white beach house in Sardinia, where the library is tiled and timbered in aromatic cedar and juniper wood; David Hicks's lushly idyllic village house in the South of France, which had been uninhabited (except for the village *curé*) for more than 30 years when he found it.

Daily Mail review of H&G Holiday houses book

The decor, where it is completed, as in the bright silver beige and white Queen's room, is breathtaking.

There is the wicked luxury of the room designed by David Hicks in red, black and grey of the Midships Bar, stunningly relieved by the bright green of the carpet and sofas.

Le « designer » anglais le plus à la mode, David Hicks, ouvre un magasin à Paris, Rive gauche bien sûr. Tous les objets, tables, tissus, tapis, cendriers, lampes, etc., ont été dessinés par David Hicks lui-même.

DH new years eve 1968

★★ **La Carrosse,** 19 Elystan Street, sw3, 584-5248. David Hicks' decor, and one of the most comfortable restaurants in London. Downstairs, with its enormous library table partitioned by books, is less sumptuous. But the food's the same, and very good too.

David Hicks, top interior decorator, is a man with strong and sometimes provocative opinions on colour and taste. But his comments make sense when one looks at the wealth of photographs of rooms he has designed in his stimulating new book **David Hicks on living—with taste** (Frewin, 5 gns.).

FOR CHRISTMAS READING AT CAERNARVON PUBLIC LIBRARY

"Valentino", by Irving Schulman. Illustrated biography of the screen idol of the 'twenties.

"David Hicks on living—with taste", by David Hicks. Deals with flower arrangements, tablescapes, style lighting and general decor.

Homes

And how will our homes be? I had a chat with interior-designer David Hicks, who forecast a return of more "elegant simplicity" with people going right off gimmicky things like blow-up furniture.

David predicts that there'll be a return of black, white and dark brown in decorations, but the wallpaper people at Sandersons see a big move towards cool blues and greens in living rooms with fantastic tiger skin papers in bathrooms!

AND MORE WE COULDN'T BEAR TO LEAVE OUT:
La Carosse—elegant David Hicks decor, three star food, in Chelsea.

Womens Wear Daily: NY.

YOUR COLOUR COUNTS WITH MR HICKS

385 words

From ANNE-MARIE RENDELL in London

WHEN David Hicks, the interior decorator, gives a christening party for a new shop, he states the colours he wants the guests to wear. When he opened a new floor in the London shop, Hicks + Zarach, everyone had to wear red, pink, orange or maroon.

David Hicks only just made the party; he flew in from New York in the afternoon. He wore a fine black gaberdine suit with a high Mao stand-up collar. His red polo neck wool evening sweater added the required colour. Lord Montague of Beaulieu, who owns that famous museum of veteran and vintage cars and motor cycles, added the required colour by his pink shirt worn with a business suit.

Lady Pamela Hicks' contribution to the colour scene was her bright petunia pink latticeweave wool dress. Mrs Evangeline Bruce, the beautiful wife of the US Ambassador to London, Mr David Bruce, swept into the party wearing a full length fuschia pink and black printed chiffon gown trimmed with black ostrich feathers.

Even Margaret, Duchess of Argyll, who is said to favour more sombre colours for the evening, complied with the instructions on her invitation. She wore brightest red chiffon and added some of her famous jewellery. In fact she wore a three-strand necklace of pearls, pearl and diamond earrings, a large emerald heart brooch surrounded by diamonds; a large emerald ring encircled by diamonds and an imposing diamond and emerald bracelet.

Mrs Dominic Ewes disappointed everyone at the party by turning up in a tweedy trouser suit which did not seem to include any of the stipulated colours. She is also an interior decorator, under her maiden name of Tessa Kennedy.

Lord Litchfield, the society photographer, who includes the Royal family among those he has photographed, was also at the party. Others all wearing one or more of the stipulated colours were the Marchioness of Dufferin and Ava and Lord Cholmondeley.

Australian paper

with the same.

Despatched	From
19/1/1969	HER MAJESTY THE QUEEN, SANDRINGHAM.
Pheasants Partridges Hares Wild Duck	Mr David Hicks

H & S B

SANDRINGHAM NORFOLK

CHAMPAGNE.	KRUG.	1952.
HOCK.	DORSHEIMER BURGBERG.	1964.
BURGUNDY.	CHARMES CHAMBERTIN.	1961.
PORT.	DOW.	1945.

on the table

AMONG the Queen's guests at Sandringham this weekend were Earl Mountbatten, his daughter Lady Pamela and his son-in-law interior designer David Hicks (right). But Mr. Hicks appears to have arrived a little late to extend his professional services.

The modernisation of the 99-year-old house has just been completed, after five years of re-wiring, installing central heating and removing the fireplaces. As the house has 365 rooms, one for every day of the year, no doubt Mr. Hicks found a few small alterations he could advise on.

Daily Sketch.

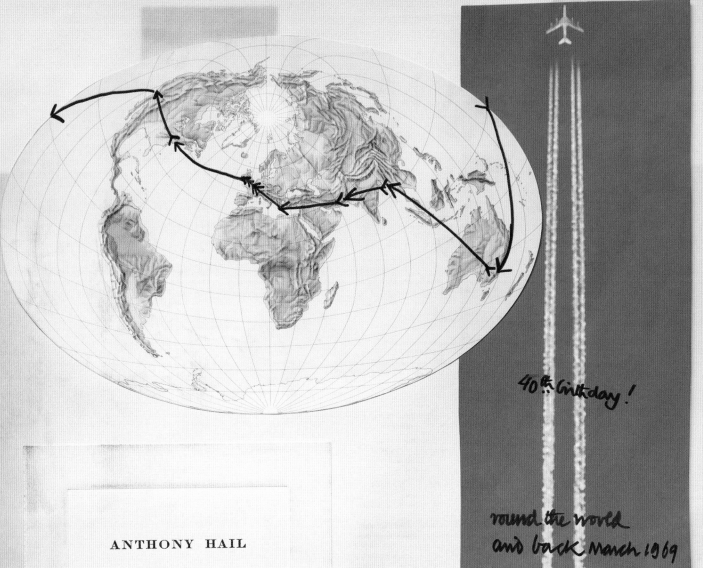

40th birthday!

round the world and back March 1969

ANTHONY HAIL

CORDIALLY INVITES YOU TO ATTEND AN

OPEN HOUSE

FOR

DAVID HICKS

ON SATURDAY, THE FIFTEENTH OF MARCH

NINETEEN HUNDRED AND SIXTY-NINE

AT SEVEN O'CLOCK IN THE EVENING

PIER 35 - SAN FRANCISCO

↑ 'so why the other?'

THE OTHER guest of honor was decorator David Hicks of London, who is being wined and dined during his stay here . . . Mr. Hicks spoke Sunday in the Brundage Auditorium of the M. H. de Young Memorial Museum . . . his talk was sponsored by the Northern California chapter of the American Institute of Interior Designers . . . at Tony Hail's party he wore a brown leather jacket, coral turtleneck, matching slacks and love beads.

LONDON decorator David Hicks, who shared honors at party given by Tony Hail, chatted with Mrs. John A. Vietor and Matthew Kelly

San Francisco Chronicle

April 75¢ '69

House Beautiful

EMOTIONAL DECORATING

5 houses that speak of love, happiness, nostalgia, and high drama

How to create mood with lights, music color, décor

David Hicks' tablescape, Oxfordshire

TRUMAN CAPOTE *describes his fascinating and curious possessions in a six-page color portfolio*

The cover
Treasured *objets*, arranged by Decorator David Hicks for his wife, Lady Pamela Mountbatten. Many were gifts from her grandmother, not to be opened until her wedding day. Story, page 90. Photograph, Michael Boys.

Half an hour later Mr. Hicks, in the borrowed dinner jacket, is holding court in a Darling Point bachelor flat. "This is the best I've seen yet," he is saying, "basic, understated, and simple," and begins a story about the Rolling Stones then stops halfway; it would be unfair if it ever got back to them. Besides, he is doing their house. He has a word to say to everyone and leaves in a flurry of midnight-blue trousers, wide cut, which luckily match the jacket with its electric-pink handkerchief in the pocket. He is late for his next dinner party. In fact, he says, Hannah Lloyd Jones will already have arrived . . .

There is whisky and soda at the Press party next day, and a hard core of Society of Interior Designers drinking it. "I knew if I looked hard enough I'd find something better than champagne," says one, watching Mr. Hicks relaxing into a smilescape before the lens. "The thing about that man is he's a decorator's decorator. Don't you think?"

THE BULLETIN, April 5, 1969

Q4 ROOM
Designer: David Hicks in association with Garnett, Cloughley, Blakemore Associates

The two rooms which follow, like a number of others, are totally different in character and by different designers. They illustrate the diversity of styles on the ship and Dennis Lennon's undoctrinaire approach to design coordination ('. . . we tried to create a climate in which designers could work'). The Q4 room, situated aft on the quarter deck, serves the dual role of bar to the first class outdoor pool by day and night club at night. The walls are covered in small projecting panels of dark grey worsted framed in aluminium trim, with the spaces between panels in gold leaf. Against this restless background a carpet of a bold black, grey, white and red check design (also by Hicks) stretches from wall to wall. Coulsdon chairs and built-in seating round the walls are upholstered in black, but this gloom is relieved by shocking pink and grey tablecloths during the day, and by window shutters in broad stripes of black, white and pillar box red by night (when tablecloths will be black and grey). Rory McEwen's ingenious screens of perspex rods sandwiched between sheets of polarised glass (made by ICI) are unfortunately too small to play a positive part in the design as a whole.

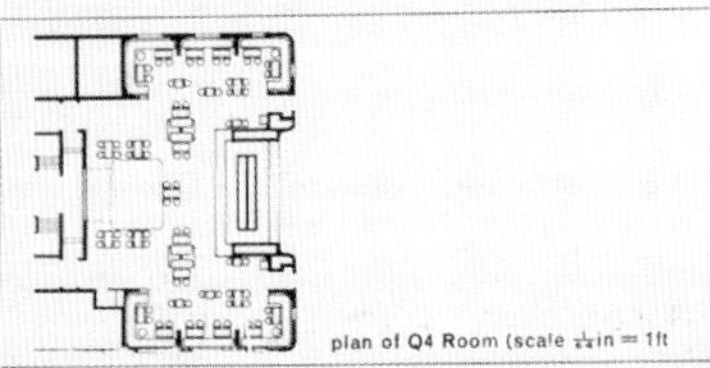
plan of Q4 Room (scale 1/32in = 1ft

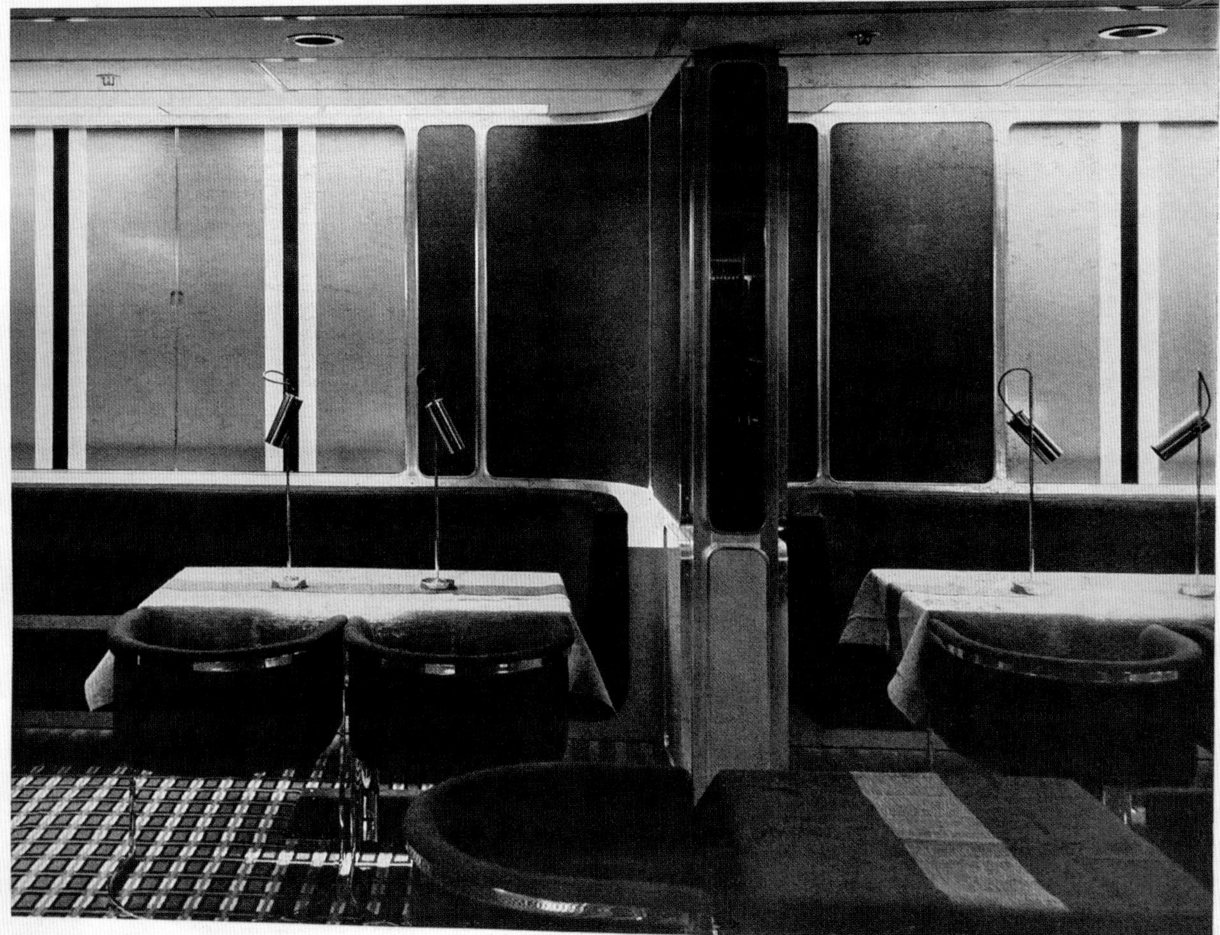

Architectural Review:

Rēalitēs
Juin Numéro 281
'69

décoration

les 7 idées qui font le succès de David Hicks

propos recueillis par Hélène Demoriane

Le décorateur dont Londres raffole commente lui-même pour nos lecteurs ce qu'il considère comme son apport le plus original à l'art de vivre de ses contemporains.

Dans le petit monde clos de la haute décoration l'Anglais David Hicks se plaît, depuis dix ans, à ouvrir des fenêtres et à provoquer des courants d'air. On a crié au « scandale » parce qu'il plantait des baignoires au milieu des salles de bains, parce qu'il recouvrait de jute les bergères Louis XVI, parce qu'il arrachait l'Angleterre à ses salons bleu pastel et vert d'eau pour la faire vivre dans les couleurs des collages de Matisse. Rajeunir les décors traditionnels par l'emploi insolite de tons fauves, de matériaux naturels et d'objets contemporains, ainsi se résumait sa méthode.

Très vite, le succès est venu. Aujourd'hui, à quarante ans tout juste, cet impertinent est sans doute le décorateur le plus « en vue » (et le plus envié) non seulement du Royaume-Uni mais d'Europe et peut-être d'Amérique. A Londres, c'est un personnage célèbre. L'aristocratie le revendique, les Rolling Stones le réclament, la reine Elisabeth elle-même lui a confié l'installation de la « suite » du prince héritier à Windsor Castle. Sa maisonnette de Chelsea est devenue le centre d'un réseau d'activités de plus en plus variées, de plus en plus cosmopolites. Associé à Milan avec Carla Venosta, à New York avec Mark Hampton, David Hicks n'hésite pas à ouvrir des chantiers à Athènes ou à Genève, à Chicago et aux Bahamas. Mais surtout il organise la diffusion à travers le monde par ses boutiques de Londres, Rolle (près de Genève), Rome, Sidney, des objets qu'il crée : petits meubles ou bibelots en perspex, cotonnades imprimées, tapis à motifs géométriques. « Les décors passent, dit-il, mais les objets restent. »

Charmant, grand, svelte, David Hicks a l'apparence et les cravates d'un dandy mais l'activité et l'ambition d'un homme d'affaires. Quoi qu'en disent ses ennemis, ce dynamisme le sert beaucoup plus que son mariage avec la seconde fille du dernier vice-roi des Indes, Lady Pamela Mountbatten, cousine de la reine d'Angleterre. Sa force? Avoir su, avec des moyens très simples, se créer un style personnel qui, sans renier le passé - « J'ai des goûts très orthodoxes » - corresponde à l'époque et fasse la part belle au géométrisme, à la peinture contemporaine, à la gaieté, à la jeunesse.

« J'ai passé mon enfance en province, dans une maison victorienne, où tout était sombre, triste, poussiéreux, dit-il, je sais exactement ce qu'il ne faut pas faire. » Il prétend aussi savoir ce qu'il convient de faire. Le 7 mars dernier, à San Francisco, il exposait ses idées devant cinq cents confrères américains. Quelques jours plus tôt, par un calme dimanche, il avait montré aux spectateurs de la télévision britannique, comment on peut, avec un budget de cinquante livres sterling, transformer un deux pièces-cuisine de H.L.M. en un appartement « cosy » et « up to date ». En effet, contrairement à la plupart des décorateurs, David Hicks divulgue ses secrets.

Il analyse pour « Réalités » quelques réalisations mettant en lumière sept idées qui définissent le « style David Hicks » et ont fait son succès.

Grandpapa

CLARENCE HOUSE
S.W. 1

7th May, 1969.

Dear Lady Pamela,

I am commanded by Queen Elizabeth The Queen Mother to write and ask if you would both like to come to the Horse Guards to watch The Queen's Birthday Parade on Saturday, 14th June, this year.

As in previous years, the best route i[s]
The Mall and Admiralty Arch to Whitehall.
be open to Mmebers of the Royal Famil[y]

The Police have asked i[f]
a Crown, and set down pass
Entrance to the Horse G

The fol[l]
receive H

Queen of Italy

pour mémoire

Week-end du 20, 21 et 22 Juin 1969

Des places ont été réservées dans l'avion quittant LONDRES (HEATHROW) le 20 Juin à 10 heures 20 L'embarquement est prévu à 9 heures 30. Une hôtesse vous accueillera à l'aéroport.

...tre arrivée à Nice, nous vous guiderons vers une voiture avec chauffeur.

...ous venez par vos propres moyens et par ailleurs avec votre chauffeur et votre voiture personnelle, nous vous serions reconnaissants de bien vouloir nous le faire savoir.

Une chambre d'hôtel vous aura été réservée.
Un coiffeur est prévu à chaque hôtel.

...vendredi 20 Juin à 21 heures dîner à Eze (robe longue - smoking)

Le samedi 21 Juin à 11 heures rendez-vous à Eze (robe habillée et chapeau-jaquette), à midi messe, suivie d'un déjeuner.

...s vous prions de nous confirmer également les places que nous avons ...s à votre intention dans l'avion quittant Nice le 22 Juin à 15 heures 35
L'embarquement est prévu à 13 heures 35.

...es détails de votre séjour vous seront adressés par un prochain mot.

R. S.V.P. Tél. 222.62.85 et 222.62-86

Maria Gabriella

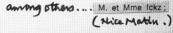

among others.... M. et Mme Ickz; (Nice Matin.)

Our client is internationally famous as a freelance designer. In order to allow him and his staff to concentrate their skills on design, and to expand the company, a business manager is to be appointed. His responsibilities will be very wide, including the negotiation of contracts and licensing agreements—often overseas—marketing and public relations, and the day to day running of the business. Candidates should be around 30, with exceptional business acumen and flair, who do not want the routines of a large corporation. They need not be specialists, but a legal or accountancy background, combined with a commercial career, is probably ideal. The starting salary will be negotiable up to £4,000, and success will bring considerable financial advancement within a matter of months. (Ref. GM32/3639/ST)

Sunday Times.

Roquebrune ←

Londoners talk about their village

store. Vidal Sassoon treats it with respect. David Hicks thinks it's frightfully common. Mick Jagger calls it up when he's present-giving. And to let you decide for yourself, Laurence Marks takes you on tour behind the richly laden counters of Fortnum and Mason. Step out of Fortnum's back door and you are in the heart of St James's.

David Hicks

I only go to Fortnum's now to get my chamois leather moccasins. But my first visit probably made me become an interior designer. I remember Adam green décor based vaguely on a lost 18th-century grandeur – everything I now loathe. I think Fortnum's is frightfully common. I'd love to make it great again – for instance they have a letter there from Florence Nightingale complaining about the quality of boots they supplied to the Crimea. I'd play that up like mad

Savannah is finished July 1969

SAVANAH
WINDEMERE ISLAND
ELEUTHERA
B W I

wrongly spelt paper by Tiffany

House Beautiful

Suede-on-the-walls, opposite, as mounted by Decorator David Hicks in Mr. and Mrs. Chester H. Roth's drawing room. Soft peach of the suede squares is spiked by a cyclamen-pink chair. Rug and table designed by Mr. Hicks. Painting by Braque. New York associate, Mark Hampton.

O. PHILIP ROEDEL

↑ Roth dining room at the Pierre Hotel by DH. (House Beautiful)

Shock of pleasing contrast—brilliant red draperies against lacquer-bright, shiny egg-plant walls—is offered in room designed by David Hicks and Associate Mark Hampton, left. Furniture, crystal chandelier express traditional 18th-Century English elegance.

Except for David Hicks or historical names such as Chippendale, Saunier, or Jacob, contemporary designers have rarely been properly merchandised.

Town & Country: see twice overpage 'designer names'

U.S. House & Garden

Part 4

1969–72

1969–72

Let's start with David's all-mirrored bathroom for Betsy Theodoracopoulos, which 'helps a dazzler get ready to dazzle in twenty minutes flat'. A visit to Eleuthera, Bahamas, and his cement-walled beach house dotted with Perspex cube tables, before rushing back to London to photograph the Peeresses' Lavatory in the House of Lords for 'David Hicks on Bathrooms'. A kaleidoscope of carpet designs; decorating rooms for the young Prince of Wales at Buckingham Palace; using his 'Midas Touch' on polyester.

'$1,000 an hour... British Interior Designer Fast and Expensive' Dickie swimming in his 70th birthday present, watched by most of European royalty. 'I don't really like people,' says David. 'I like objects.' Dinner at the White House ('I was especially struck by the clumsiness of the servants, and Mr Nixon's pancake makeup'); 'Lucky America! David's got designs on you...' As part of a promotional campaign by his American licensees, all the Hicks beds are hung with curtains using his new printed bedlinen collection. The President is photographed rolling a strike in his bowling alley under the Old Executive Office Building, hung with Hicks wallpaper.

A Swiss bathroom with panels of chrome-framed mirror on scarlet lacquered walls; an all-white bedroom in Long Island; David's own London dressing room with tweed floor and walls, lined with chrome and scarlet panels (that inspired this book's cover). David puts his geometric monograms on everything, from ties ('A moment of glory for the American male') to writing-paper. Family holidays in the Bahamas and Stockholm; the Queen, opening New South Wales House in London, asks David: '... and you designed the interior?' A glamorously modern apartment in Athens opens with a stainless-steel alcove for an ancient marble statue.

Mirrors, mirrors on the walls, also on the ceiling, from which lights cascade to the white Formica floor. Betsy Theodoracopulos and decorator David Hicks designed this beauty workshop together. Its wild mosaic of mirrors keeps its user well-informed on every angle of her, helps a dazzler get ready to dazzle in twenty minutes flat.... A window curtained in silver beads overlooks Central Park. A glass shelf holds rock crystal prisms and obelisks. A mirrored vanity, brushed steel and granite stone, conceals in its drawers her makeup and gadgets, all neatly arranged in wicker baskets. A hair dryer lowers from the ceiling.

BETSY THEODORACOPULOS:
NO SECRETS IN HER BATHROOM, A REFLECTION POOL OF MIRRORS

U.S. Vogue

The techniques and discipline that keep her looking as though she'd just been plucked from a spring-fed pond may be American, but the man who helped her design her spectacular beauty workshop-bathroom is an Englishman, David Hicks. More on this, next page.

993 FIFTH AVENUE NEW YORK CITY 249-8984

January 7th, 1970

David,

shall be in London for a few days on busine

Betsy's writing paper by Tiffany that I designed.
DH.

TEMPLE TO THE SUN IN THE BAHAMAS:

A designer team creates a holiday sanctuary on a dune in Eleuthera

Reaching back toward the dawn of architecture for their inspiration, co-designers David Hicks and Robert Stokes have brought an essence of the Nile Valley to this winter residence on the Bahaman Island of Eleuthera, British West Indies. Their design alludes to the clean cubism of the Temple of King Zoser, built at Saqqâra nearly 5,000 years ago by the great Egyptian architect, Imhotep. Tall, cool, and contemporary, it suggests, rather than imitates, its ancestor. Its glass-pierced outer simplicity is the direct expression of its inner reason for being—to provide a restful, mini-maintenance holiday sanctuary for escaping metropolitans.

"Savannah," as it is called by its owners, commands the sea and beach from atop its own private Sahara—an acre of sand dune cleared of native growth. Its storm-safe concrete-block walls are coated with plaster mixed with honey-colored limestone dust from a local quarry and textured with seashells. The house is surrounded by a light raft-like walking deck anchored at its outer edges by occasional low-standing parapets of the same plastered masonry. A detached guest pavilion is at right, above. The grand entry, opposite, flanked by freestanding pylons, leads through a fountained forecourt to the screened porch beyond (inset).

HANS NAMUTH

High-ceilinged interiors, cool-hued, sheltered from the tropical sun

Understatement and easy care were basic requirements in the planning of the house, its surroundings, and its accoutrements. The interior space treatments are definitive examples of needs well fulfilled. Soft and cool, they are easy on the eye—and the housekeeper. The high-ceilinged living room, this page and opposite, is typical, and starts from the floor with plain, scratchy coconut matting in natural color. As outside, the plastered walls are shell-textured. Opaque white roller shades give instant, diffused light control at the crook of a finger. All night lighting is indirect. Overhead fans paddle the air to give comforting visual support to hidden air conditioning. The bold sculptural paintings by Bruce Tibbetts dominate walls and form striking focal points for seating groups. The low-slung English chairs are of chromed steel with mailbag canvas slings.

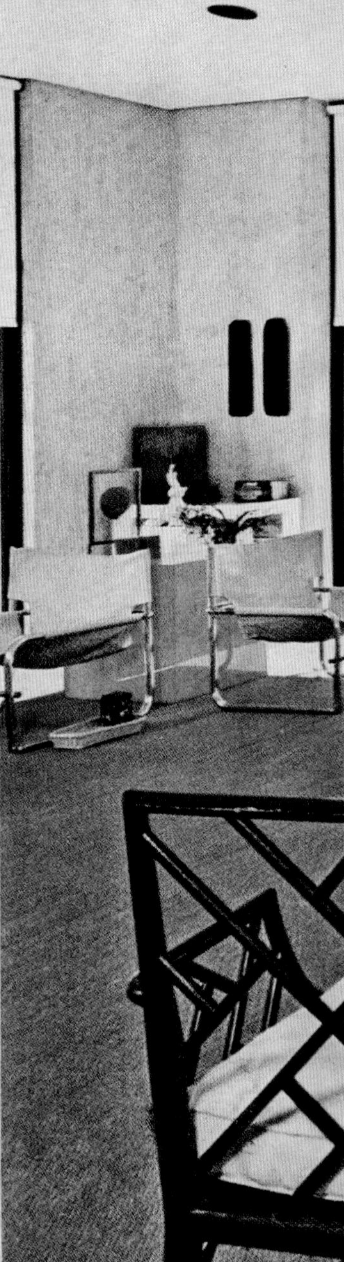

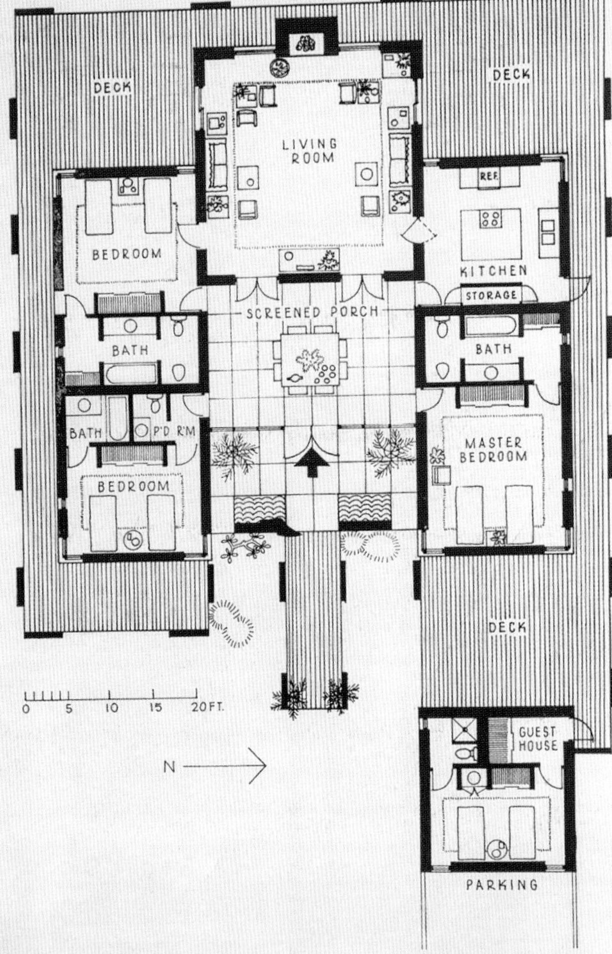

The living is easy, and guests come and go in privacy

The floor plan, left, is beautifully organized for casual living, yet allows guests and householders to come and go with great privacy. A careful study of the plan shows how the foot-thick masonry walls are turned within to give complete sound separation for the three self-contained bedroom suites. The master bedroom, below, left, is similar to the other bedrooms in the house. They are without lamps, curtains, or frills. Each is simply and soothingly fitted for all-out relaxation, differing from the others in mood by quiet variations on a pastel palette. The comparatively few windows (and their slenderness) help keep interior spaces cool and reduce tropical glare—but the sea is still there. Bedspread fabrics and marine collages designed by David Hicks.

M.7 9.

Available for date shown only

HOUSE OF LORDS

PERMIT TO TAKE STILL PHOTOGRAPHS

APPLICANT MR. DAVID HICKS

DATE & TIME OF PHOTOGRAPH 2.30 – 3.00, MONDAY, 17TH NOV. 1969

PLACE PEERESSES GALLERY (RETIRING ROOM)

DETAILS, ETC. TO PHOTOGRAPH LAVATARY

No sketching or photographing is allowed while either House is sitting. This includes the three-quarters-of-an-hour before the sitting.

K. L. Mackintosh.

SERJEANT-AT-ARMS

(83109) 6/65

HARMONY WITH HICKS

By MONICA MEENAN

NEW YORK. — Harmony Carpets is taking the retail route—establishing a retail program with major department stores across the country.

"We're busy setting up our patterned carpet for a retail program," said Bernard Siegel, Harmony owner. "We'll have only one large store in each city with the line exclusive to them, such as Rich's in Atlanta and Woodward & Lothrop in Washington, D. C. However, in New York, there are several stores who carry our patterned carpets . . . Bloomingdale's,

See HARMONY, Page 13

PATTERN DIRECTION: "Patterns are getting away from the very small geometrics. David Hicks' newest patterns are large in scale, more open, more dramatic, even bolder in color. (The photo on Page 1, of the newest Hicks pattern at Harmony, illustrates this point.) Consumers are seeing more of these patterns every day. In its better dress department, Bloomingdale's just installed one of Hicks' first patterns.

otos by Pierre Venant

1 Books on the subject sell well considering that they are usually gloss productions and fairly expensive. David Hicks' last book, for example, sold the entire print of 15,000 copies at 4 gns each within a year.

A subsidiary role of the interior decorator is often to shake people up and make them think things out afresh. David Hicks, for example, blends ultra modern with antique in a way that has made it his special handwriting. Periods which were formerly thought to be irreconcilable are shown to get along very well.

He is, however, turning increasingly to commercial work such as the Q4 room of the QE 2 liner (panels of grey flannel framed by polished aluminium, separated by strips of gold leaf),

David Hicks—shock blending of the old and new.

2 for which he won considerable acclaim. His company, which he founded nine years ago, has designed projects all over the world, and his latest venture is a restaurant and hotel complex in Malta.

"Time & Tide"

Previously just another decorator industry supplier, Bernie Siegel is the man who brought David Hicks and his patterned carpet designs to the United States over three years ago. Now Harmony not only sells these patterns to decorators and architects but to department stores.

"Each store is setting up a Designer Pavilion similar to the one at Sloane's here in New York." It's the boutique approach to selling and Siegel believes in it enthusiastically. An area is set aside within the rug department for displaying the samples and several rugs are made up with correlated borders.

"DEPARTMENT STORES ORDER through us and the carpet is supplied from our $200,000 stock in Long Island City. Custom colorings are also available."

On the lookout for years for that something "different" and with the professional opinion of designers Mrs. Henry Parish, Billy Baldwin and Everett Brown . . . the first people in New York to see any David Hicks designs . . . Siegel quickly closed the deal in London to be the exclusive agent in this country for the much acclaimed, much talked about Hicks carpet patterns.

Harmony has over 200 carpet designs in the narrow 27-inch width. Most of them are by Hicks, but Siegel has also added designers Seymour Avidgor, Everett Brown and Burt Wayne to the roster. Though the patterned carpets represent only 10 per cent of Siegel's volume, they have put Harmony on the map.

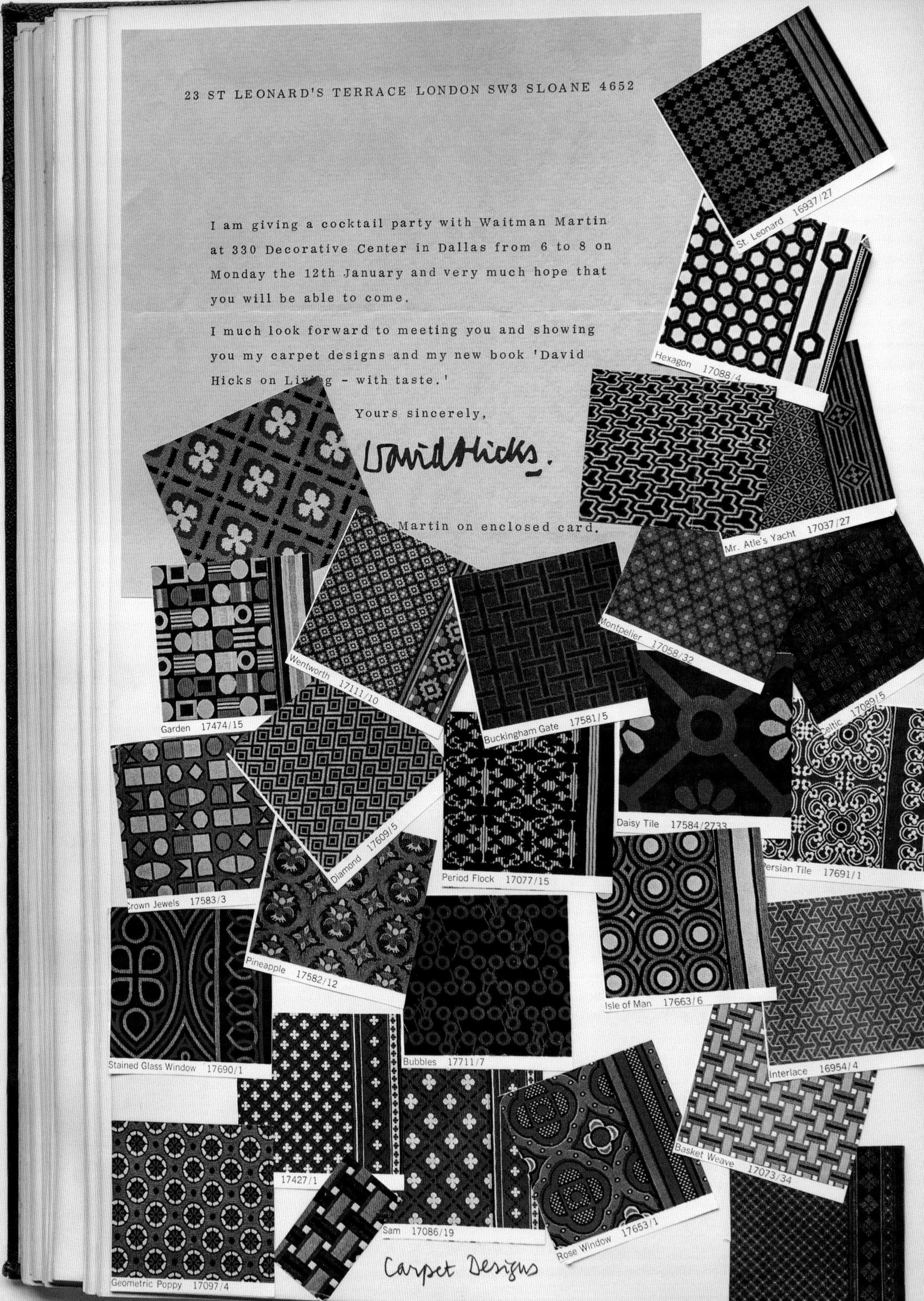

23 ST LEONARD'S TERRACE LONDON SW3 SLOANE 4652

I am giving a cocktail party with Waitman Martin at 330 Decorative Center in Dallas from 6 to 8 on Monday the 12th January and very much hope that you will be able to come.

I much look forward to meeting you and showing you my carpet designs and my new book 'David Hicks on Liv ng - with taste.'

Yours sincerely,

David Hicks.

Martin on enclosed card.

Crossbridge 17491/4
Rushes 17065/4
Waist-Coat 17210/3
Interlock 17162/5
Sammy 17427/24
Fourstar 17490/5
Lord Monty 17079/15
Londonderry 17156/4
Simeon 17298/4
Chantilly 17080/24
Teatime 17087/24
Distributors ↓
Moonstone 17129/2
Chess 17654/2
Maltese Cross 17026/3
Diamond 17150/4
Prince of Wales 17477/3
D.H. Carpet designs!
Bob Mitchell Designs,
125 N. Robertson Blvd.,
Los Angeles, Calif.
213 272-7395
McCune Showroom,
42 Hotaling Pl.,
Jackson Square,
San Francisco, Calif.
415 982-7221
Ellouise Abbott,
1911 West Alabama,
Houston, Texas
713 529-8465
George & Frances Davison,
420 Boylston,
Boston, Mass.
617 CO 6-0072
Bob Collins, Inc.,
120 N.E. 39th St.,
Miami, Fla.
305 754-5026
Decorators Walk,
6-136 Merchandise Mart,
Chicago, Ill.
312 329-1510
Forrest C. Gearhart,
2325 Chestnut St.,
Philadelphia, Pa. 19103
215 561-1491
Waitman Martin, Inc.
330 Decorative Center
Dallas, Texas 75207
214 747-4247
harmony
CARPET CORPORATION

IN NEW YORK HOMES, EVEN THE TOOTHPASTE MATCHES THE DECOR

By JUNE FIELD

IN New York the decorator is king. When the average couple decide to set up home or redecorate their existing one, they seek professional help.

"A decorator knows where to save money and when it is best to spend a little more. He can save you time, he knows where to find the things *you* want, and he has the background knowledge of finishes, fibres and construction so important in the wilderness of new products today," Paul Hould, president of a fabrics firm, told me. I visited him at the incredible Decorating and Design Building in New York's Third Avenue.

Incredible . . . because this vast many-floored emporium houses the showrooms of an enormous number of manufacturers in the home decor field, and you can get in only if you are accompanied by your decorator.

Decorators in the United States are often designers too, and Britain's David Hicks is one of the big names there as a designer of wall-coverings and fabrics.

His designs for these items, incidentally, do not necessarily match, but they co-ordinate or integrate: two totally different materials related in colour or pattern.

Mr Hick's big, bold geometrics sweep across a wall to give total coverage achieving a wild, wonderful exuberance of pattern. His colour combinations for the seventies are black, grey, and white, brown and white, and "occasional sorties into brilliant hues."

He feels that the whole concept of bold colour and pattern in the home has not yet really got under way in Britain.

"There is so much you can do to transform a room if only you are brave enough to use both," he insists. His latest projects include a château near Mont Blanc, a boutique in Brussels, two houses in Australia, and numerous eating places.

The smart new decoration colours for the Seventies as decreed by the American glossies are mouth-watering and delectable enough for us all to copy.

Beach Plum is a pungent reddish hue coming in on the new purple wave; African Violet is half-pink and half-purple; Pink Coral a soft, luscious rose; Lettuce a cool, sharp yellow bordering on green; Mercury a velvety new grey; Golden Rod a magnificent amber; and Space Blue will make your ceiling look as if it is part of the great outdoors.

The living-room of the Manhattan apartment I stayed in was decorated in soft shades: cream walls, butter - coloured carpet, magnolia curtains. This cream "shell" made an ideal frame for bright upholstery and colourful paintings. "Area rugs" defined seating areas, conversational grouping.

The "in" phase in American decor is the conversation piece. Conversation pieces include massive sofas covered in brilliant splashy prints; couches available in three zipped-together sections that can be folded up to make a single chair—and old travelling trunks rescued from the attic and covered in fabric or wallpaper with their wooden strips painted black, and their hardware gilt; their new-found glory making them into coveted coffee tables. All to sit or squat by—conversationally.

A giant settee flanked by bookcases, desk and drinks cabinet qualifies as a conversation lounge.

Accessories range from do-it-yourself Tiffany lamp kits, which you assemble piece by piece on a plastic base, to old wicker hampers painted white and used as umbrella stands. Other ideas to copy are brightly-patterned wall-paper - covered folding screens used as room-dividers.

Pattern is everywhere. Daisy-printed non-stick ironing-board covers, floral-patterned toilet rolls, tissues and even toothpaste tubes.

Shower towers are the last word in luxury for the bathroom, with enough controls to make a jet pilot happy. In the tower are two shower heads, one below the other—for bathers of different heights. There is an automatic timer, too, for turning off the water when the tub is full.

End-to-end bathtubs and twin lavatories complete what is called the bathroom / dressing-room/bedroom complex.

Wall to wall—and even up the wall. It's the kind of decor New Yorkers are queueing to consult their decorators about. Wallpaper design is by David Hicks (pictured).

BIRTHDAYS TODAY

Lieutenant-Colonel Sir Michael Bruxner, 88; Lord Hemingford, 66; Mr. David Hicks, 41; Major-General S. W. Joslin, 71; Sir Geoffrey Keynes, 83; Mr. David Lean, 62; Sir Charles McDonald, 78; Sir Bernard Miller, 66; Sir Frank Newson-Smith, 91; Sir Kenneth Peppiatt, 77; Sir George Pope, 68; Major-General Sir William Scott, 71; Mr. A. J. P. Taylor, 64; Sir Owen Wansbrough-Jones, 65.

An away winner

JANATHA STUBBS, the Littlewoods Pools heiress—her father is John Moores—and her husband, Paddy, are opening a £12,000 restaurant here designed by Lord Mountbatten's son-in-law, David Hicks.

Stubbs explains: 'Hicks was going to design a house for us in London, but then we moved out here. But we like his work and we thought he would be the right person for this scheme.'

Fortunately for their English friends, Dolph and Gaby Bentinck not only kept open house in Paris but frequently returned for a day or two to their Eaton Square flat decorated by David Hicks.

★ *LORD Mountbatten's two daughters, Lady Pamela Hicks and Lady Brabourne, are to be neighbours in the Bahamas. The Brabournes haven't started yet, but the Hicks house is already up. Betty Kenward, who writes Jennifer's Diary in Queen magazine, reports in the next edition that David Hicks designed his on 'ultra-modern lines which would not be my choice.'*

Pammy and Edwina

Queen and Edwina Hicks.

at Jellicoe wedding

Ashley by the new canal.

"Thank you, David Hicks."

Eight carpets from our famous Kensington Brussels range have won an award in the Council of Industrial Design Awards for 1970.

They were all designed by David Hicks, assisted by the Crossley team of Colin Royle and John Palmer. To them we say, "Thank you".

The winners from the range are: **Nico, Wentworth, Hexagon, Daisy Tile, Montpelier, Maltese Cross, Crossbridge, Large Quatrefoil.**

Thursday, 2nd July 1970 837

Palace of   *Westminster*

OPENING OF PARLIAMENT

Admit Master Ashley Hicks *(one person only)*

TO

ROYAL GALLERY (STANDING)

Ladies: Day Dress with Hat
Gentlemen: Morning or Service Dress or Lounge Suits

NORMAN PORCH ENTRANCE

Doors will be opened at 10.00 a.m. and closed at 10.45 a.m. precisely
Places are not reserved

Cholmondeley
Lord Great Chamberlain

ROYAL PARTY
TELEGRAM

From: Buckingham Palace — 251310Z Mar.

To: Royal Party On Tour — Date: 25.3.70.

Recd: 1314Z.

Bow No 38

For H.R.H. The Prince Of Wales

From: Mr. David Hicks

The work on your suite is up to schedule and providing we have no unforseen delivery problems all that you have approved should be in place by 5 pm London Time April 14th. Mr Tims in my absence in America will confirm on Monday 6th April

David

251310Z

Chief Clerk Private Secretary's Office,
Buckingham Palace (2)

Mr David Hicks
The Court Postmaster
Sir M.Charteris

PJH/180

ROYAL PARTY
TELEGRAM

"What will it cost?"

– who could blame JON BANNENBERG for coming on like the David Hicks of boat design at a recent Earls Court spectacular for those who, like Slickey, go down to the sea in ships when the urge is upon them?

Queen

News Round-up

Prince of Wales to have own suite in Palace

THE Prince of Wales is to have his own private suite, comprising a sitting room, bedroom and bathroom, at Buckingham Palace. Its decoration will be supervised by David Hicks, son-in-law of Earl Mountbatten.

The Prince has previously had accommodation on the second floor of the Palace.

He has said that he wants his suite to be in a "traditional and quiet decor."

A Palace spokesman said last night: "The Prince comes down from Cambridge in June, and will be spending more time at the Palace. It is thought that he needs his own suite."

Telegraph

Today's engagements

Prince of Wales arrives at Heathrow from Japan, 6.30 a.m.

Charges to pay
____s.____d.
RECEIVED

POST OFFICE
TELEGRAM

No.____
OFFICE STAMP

Prefix. Time handed in. Office of Origin and Service Instructions. Words.

25 MAR. 70

At____m
From
By

At____m

23 TSO/HB206 5.30 ROMSEY SO 20 RETRANS =

DAVID HICKS 23 STLEONARDS TCE LONDONSW1 =

BEST WISHES FOR A HAPPY BIRTHDAY JUST RETURNED FROM PARIS FRENCH SERIES EXCELLENT = DICKIE +

23 ~~FOR SW3 PSE +~~ ~~TS 651~~

51-1504 J.P.

... "TELEGRAMS ENQUIRY" or call, with this form at office of delivery. Other enquiries should be accompanied by this form, and, if possible, the envelope. B or C

→

SIR BASIL SPENCE, David Hicks, Sir Hugh Casson, Ove Arup, Lord Holford, David Mlinaric . . . ten of Britain's top architects and designers are being invited to stop work on plans for great mansions and prestige buildings to lower their sights for a day.

Nico, from the Brussels range of carpets designed by David Hicks with Colin Royle and John Palmer.

"The Grange" .... the Queen.

The David Hicks decor is elegant, too, and it was probably indigestion that made the mock Old Masters round the walls look like the TV Munster family painted by a failed pupil of Sir Joshua Reynolds.

A shaggy loo for David Hicks

Daily Mail July 9 70.

WHAT a leading interior decorator does in his own house has a habit of becoming the design fashion of the year. So let me tell you about David Hicks's bathroom.

He is having his walls, ceiling and floor covered in Harris tweed.

Earl Mountbatten's 41-year-old trend-setting son-in-law points out that he's always searching for new uses for old materials and new ideas for old problems.

'This way I'm combining both,' he says.

'Consider the elbow of a Harris tweed jacket. It takes years to wear out, so it must be an excellent material for a bathroom floor. I'll be wrapping it round blocks of wood about 18in. by 14in. It should prove quite pleasant on bare feet.'

He has ordered 90 yards of Harris tweed — a chocolate colour known as Stornoway Bourneville—at 32s. a yard to do the job. Mind you, the managing director of the Yorkshire firm supplying it was distinctly taken aback. 'It came as a surprise to hear it was going on a bathroom floor,' says Mike Burrows.

★

THE DUKE and Duchess of Kent are about to be converted. Not religiously, but they are going over to natural gas at Coppins, their Buckinghamshire home next week. 'It will take a day,' reports the Gas Board, which will deal with three cookers, one refrigerator, two water heaters and the central heating system.

Hicks to Use His 'Midas' Touch On Hystron's Polyester Designs

By KATHLEEN MOORE

NEW YORK.—David Hicks, originator of the gutsy geometric look and international interior designer, will be guiding the Trevira Era into the home environment.

"The ink is still wet on the contract," he said yesterday, as Hystron Fibers officially announced that Hicks has been signed on as consultant for the use of its polyester fiber in home furnishings.

Hystron hopes Hicks' touch will be visible in products introduced at the Chicago home furnishings market next January.

They may be upholstery, carpeting, wall coverings, decorative fabrics, bedding, curtains and draperies, area and bath rugs—or something else.

They will be aimed at the volume market but which fabric and furniture producers surface first with Hicks designs is still a moot question.

So, too, is the method by which they'll be merchandised. Hicks designs are currently presented boutique-style at W & J Sloane, New York. But whether more boutiques are in the cards for the Trevira designs is a question nimbly fielded by George O'Connor, marketing manager for home furnishings at Hystron.

Before the Hicks-Hystron venture turns into actual products, David Hicks will be making two other debuts in America—with the publication here in September of his third decorating book, on bathrooms, and with a new line of fabric designs for Connaissance Fabrics in the fall.

The suave London resident who describes himself as "the international living-in-a-jet ...cks" because of his constant traveling and international assortment of clients, is most excited by the book and the Hystron assignment.

They both represent firsts.

The book is his third, but the first (in what he envisions as a nearly endless series of decorating books) to concentrate on particulars instead of generalities. He chose the bath because "it's the most neglected room"—and also, for the first time, has included interiors by other designers and examples from the past that offer inspiration for the present.

"HYSTRON HAS bought more than just a name, a merchandising peg—not to mention any names," inserted Leslie Button, president of the firm that looks after Hicks' interests. "He's not like a couturier doing apparel, then moving into towel design."

While neither Hystron nor Hicks wants to be at all specific about plans, both hint at total environments will be important ... that Hicks' talent as an interior designer (as well as a product one) is going to be utilized to make the average lady's decorating chores easier and their result ...e smashing.

The idea of working with a man-made

DAVID HICKS

fiber has Hicks delighted. He says he's discovering that textures and colors can be achieved that would be impossible with natural fibers. And everything designed by Hicks in Trevira—regardless of the product manufacturer—will coordinate.

Gutsy geometrics, pattern-on-pattern and unexpected color combinations—all Hicks' hallmarks—can probably be expected to appear in Trevira.

"ANYTHING I'M involved in is part of everything else," he comments, adding that he thinks the potential of the geometric look has barely been scratched.

From the "haute couture point of view in decorating," Hicks adds: "Geometrics may be waning a bit, to be replaced, perhaps, by more curvaceous, romantic, less rigid forms and patterns."

As for color, Hicks is thinking pastel: "The almost cosmetic colors—faded banana yellow, pale, pale almond green—are gradually creeping into my work.

"There was a tremendous fashion for dark living rooms—my own was dark, lacquered colors. Billy Baldwin's was. Mine's now shiny white . . . Baldwin will probably change his, too."

The pales could well be important in Hicks' plans for the volume market—though he adds, hastily, that they won't predominate in carpet. "A carpet has got to hold the room down, to be dark."

At this point, Button inserts another hint of Hicks' plans for the Trevira Era: "What David's doing with the carpet fiber should be quite startling."

Trevira Over-Counter Drive Opening Jan. 1

By JOANNE GAMLIN

NEW YORK. Hystron Fibers, Inc., which has made its Trevira polyester a household word in ready to wear, will hoist that name high in the over-the-counter home furnishings fabrics field come Jan. 1.

And the companion name to Trevira will be that of David Hicks, originator of gusty geometrics, in the boutiques, said Adrian Butash, director of marketing.

"By Jan. 1, we expect to have our Hystron home furnishings fabrics boutiques in a number of fabric specialty chains," he said, noting that chains approached with the idea have indicated assent. He explained that the boutiques will be concentrated in specialty chains rather than department or mass merchandising outlets.

Next year, in fact, will mark the start of the Hystron drive to become broadly significant in the home environment field, Butash asserted.

During his association with Hystron, Hicks, who as reported in Home Furnishings Daily signed a three year contract last May, will be producing a spectrum of products said Butash. He named some: "Decorative fabrics, upholstery and bath rugs."

BUTASH ALSO indicated that Hicks will be working with furniture designers to produce the right melding of curvaceous contemporary furnishings and pattern lines.

In the home furnishings fabric boutiques, Hicks designs should contribute about 20 per cent of the total fabrics, estimated Butash. The rest will be Trevira fabrics, sidetracked from their usual destinations of jobbers or manufacturers.

Prices on the home furnishings fabrics will be competitive between approximately $3 and $8 a yard.

Butash went on to speculate that boutiques built of Hicks products such as carpeting and upholstered furniture may emerge.

To accessorize the over-the-counter fabric boutiques, major pattern manufacturers are being approached on the question of putting out patterns on home furnishings products.

"We see the bedroom as a hot area," said Butash, elaborating: "With home sewing recognized as a fashionable, do-your-own thing kind of pursuit, we envision women sewing pillows, bedspreads, sleeper covers, throws and even draperies."

INDEED, HOME sewing will burgeon even larger in the 70's, he contended. "Kids look at making their own clothes—and their own home furnishings products—as means of expressing their personalities and life styles."

He indicated Hystron expects to promote its home furnishings boutiques in the style it gave to ready to wear.

Butash reflected: "We envisage photos of David Hicks along with those of table clothes made in his new 1971 geometrics in consumer shelter books."

What's more, Hystron's giant apparel piece goods 1971 promotion whose theme is "The Girl Who Makes It, Makes It in Trevira," will embrace home furnishings fabrics.

As for Hicks geometrics, Hystron is betting that with 1971 modifications they are due for a lusty second breathe.

"In the 70's, consumers will be wearing more geometrics which will supplant the ubiquitous florals. And when consumers view these patterns on the clothes in their closets, they will accept them more easily on their beds or at the windows."

In Hystron's view, he said, nothing gives glamor and sales turns to home furnishings fabrics as swiftly as a name designer.

"The problem in the home furnishings industry has been that it takes $1 million to develop that name."

Hystron is well satisfied with David Hicks.

"The urbane Londoner typifies what we want to say to the home furnishings world," Butash asserted.

"He is the Man of the Trevira Era."

$1,000 an hour

Flamboyant Britisher is 'Midas' of interior design

NEW YORK — (NEA) — Money is tight? Not if you are a client who wants a few apartment rooms or a house in Manhattan, Athens, Paris, Nassau or the Bahamas spiffed up by David Hicks.

Hicks is a phenomenon in a sense. He is a magnificently flamboyant Britisher. Understatement is not his medium. And under the close scrutiny all the drive, flair and self-appreciation hang together for this international leader in interior design.

On his corporation conference room bulletin board was scribbeld: "Midas Hicks, Esquire."

IN THE shadow of the "Midas" sign, Hicks revealed he was in the city to promote his new assignment as design consultant for Hystron Fibers' home furnishings division.

"As you know, I work fast," he explained. "My fee is $1,000 an hour as an interior design consultant. A woman here wanted me to consult on four rooms for a Fifth Avenue apartment. After we talked for four hours I reminded her of the fee and she said, 'Keep talking. It's so fascinating. I'll pay extra.' "

To him this pinpointed a basic difference in approach to decorating the home of an American as opposed to that of a European.

"IN EUROPE, most people know what atmosphere they want," Hicks says. "Men and women in the U.S. tell me, 'My God. What am I paying you for? You're the professional. That's why I came to you for advice.' "

Hicks is making financial tracks with this American attitude. He will help direct design and color use of Trevira polyester in upholstery, carpeting, decorative fabrics, wall coverings, bedding, curtains and draperies, area and bath rugs. Some of his fine design thoughts should surface during the January home furnishings market in Chicago and be in the stores for Mrs. Average Consumer in Spring '71.

These will show a strong geometric design trend. He is fond of geometrics because they are classical and helped move them into mass prominence almost 10 years ago in British carpet and rug design.

HICKS LIKES pattern-on-pattern — a room in his Oxfordshire country home is brown, black and yellow Victorian with 18 different patterns. This, the 41-year-old businessman shares with his wife, Lady Pamela Mountbatten, and their two girls and a boy. She is the daughter of Lord Mountbatten of Burma and a cousin of the Queen. Hicks recently redecorated Prince Charles' four-room apartment in Buckingham Palace.

"I want to make geometrics palatable to the general public," he said. I would like to work with mobile homes. I'd put in geometrics but they would soft and wooing."

He defniitely is thinking in terms of pastels, such as faded banana yellow and pale almond green, and shifted the color of his dark, lacquered living room in one of his homes to white. His summer house in the south of France is "all whitewash, with rushes, modern paintings and antiquities, while the master bathroom in our Chelsea (London) townhouse has a clear Plexiglas tub, walls covered in bronze khaki Trevira and a wood-burning fireplace."

HIS PROBLEM in getting his color and design thoughts into more moderately priced homes is reaching the "mid-buyer or home furnishings coordinator.

"The man on the street generally has no taste, good or bad, and home furnishings suffers from 'the ditherers' who don't know which way to go," he explained.

"I did tea trays that retailed for $3 about three years ago. I saw them in the pantries of my moneyed and titled friends. Good design is recognized anywhere, no matter the price."

David Hicks puts design and color to work for the internationally famous. He's currently working as a home furnishings fabric design consultant. Insert illustrates his favorite motif — geometric designs.

< Some of the syndication headlines

British Interior Designor Fast And Expensive

British decorator with a Midas touch

Need To Consult An Interior Decorator— At $1,000 An H

Decorated Prince Charles' apartment

His 'grand' fee is for 'spiffing up'

Interior Decorator's Fee A Spur To Do-It-Yourself

Need an Interior Decorator at $1,000 an Hour?

British interior designer David Hicks is an original who puts design and color to work for the internationally famous. He's currently at work as a home furnishings design consultant for the makers of Trevira polyester on co-ordinated fabric designs for the American mass market. Insert illustrates his favorite motif—geometric designs.

M. of B.

P.o.W.

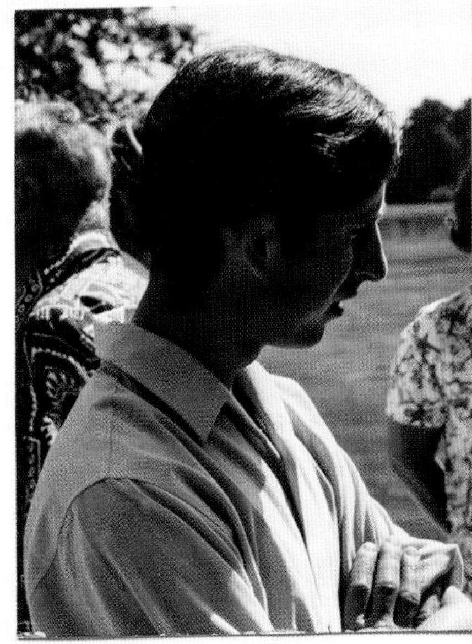

70th birthday party: Sunday

Clubmen to leave home

THE City of London Club, at £100 still the most expensive British gentlemen's club to join, is leaving its historic Broad Street home to make way for a bank development.

But its 880 members—"they are mostly hard-headed business men," says an official—are not too sad. The deal with the National Westminster will be worth around £1 million.

The bank will demolish the 140-year-old club building to make room for development around its 600ft. high headquarters. But before that it will put up a new home for the club just down the street—at a cost of about £500,000.

LEVELLED

That should leave the club another half-million, and I understand half of that may go towards having the place done up in style by designer **David Hicks**, whose wife **Lady Pamela** is a cousin of member **Prince Philip**.

The demolition of the City of London Club in some three years' time will upset many preservationists. It is the work of architect Philip Hardwick, whose famous Euston Arch was levelled by British Railways not many years ago.

Daily Express

Dickie's 70th birthday party weekend: Sat: lunch.

The Lady

Above: *After opening the 31st Chelsea Antiques Fair, Lady Pamela Hicks admired the Exhibit of Dolls loaned by Mrs. Jackie Jacobs.*

DAVID HICKS, internationally renowned designer, has been named Design Consultant for Hystron Fibers' Home Furnishings Division. He will work with Hystron to expand the use of Trevira as the premier fashion fiber both for residential and commercial applications.

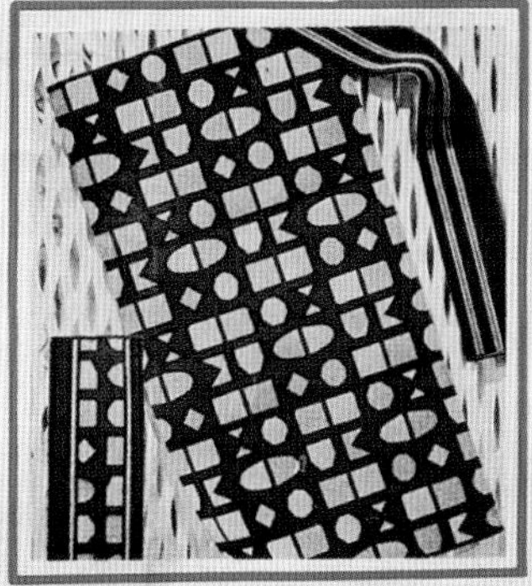

PICTURED ARE representative examples of geometric carpet patterns designed by David Hicks, Hystron's Home Furnishings Design Consultant. He will be interpreting "New Environments of the Trevira Era" in upholstery, carpeting, decorative fabrics, wall coverings, bedding, curtains and draperies, and area and bath rugs.

Sunday Times advertisement: Michael Joseph.

Fort Worth Morning Star-Telegram

"DAVID HICKS ON BATHROOMS" (World, $15) focuses on a specialty of the famed designer. Convinced that most bathrooms are too clinical, Hicks offers a survey of design ranging from the historic to the prophetic. The book is well illustrated.

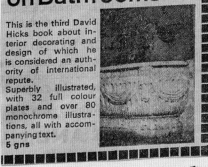

★ David Hicks, designer son-in-law of Earl Mountbatten, nearly had a road named after him. But not quite. Solicitors clerk Norman Burton suggested that a road at Coggeshall, Essex—where Hicks was born and brought up should be called Hicks Road or something similar. But council chairman Stanley Haines said that Hicks wasn't sufficiently connected with the place to warrant that. So it has become Windmill Close. And Hicks still waits for his highway posterity.

Daily Mail.

LEBENDIGE STILLEBEN

David Hicks zeigt, wie er liebenswerte Kleinigkeiten arrangiert

Die Kunst, Objekte so zu zeigen, daß sie Aufmerksamkeit erregen, ist nicht neu. Aber daß ein Innenarchitekt wie David Hicks zu seiner Freude so meisterhaft komponierte Arrangements gestaltet, ist wenigen bekannt. Uns allen wird selten Gelegenheit zu kreativer Betätigung gegeben. Versuchen Sie es doch einmal selbst mit Mut, Phantasie, Geduld und Humor! Es gibt keinen festen Plan, nehmen Sie das Vorhaben nicht zu ernst. Wichtig ist, daß Sie Kontraste bilden, Breites zu Schmalem, Hohes zu Niedrigem, Altes und Modernes in Spannung zueinander setzen. Die Kunst ist zu erlernen! Ein Tisch in einer abgelegenen Zimmerecke, ein nicht benutzter alter Schreibtisch, eine Kommode mit einem Bild, welches in die Komposition mit einbezogen wird, oder ein leeres Bord in einer Bücherwand können den geeigneten Untergrund für das Werk ergeben.

Die abgebildeten Arrangements von David Hicks sollen Ihnen Anregung geben. Im Foto unten sehen Sie: Kontrast zwischen Natur- und Kunstformen, zwischen starrem Material und bizarren Pflanzen. Akzent: das Bild mit Kampfszene

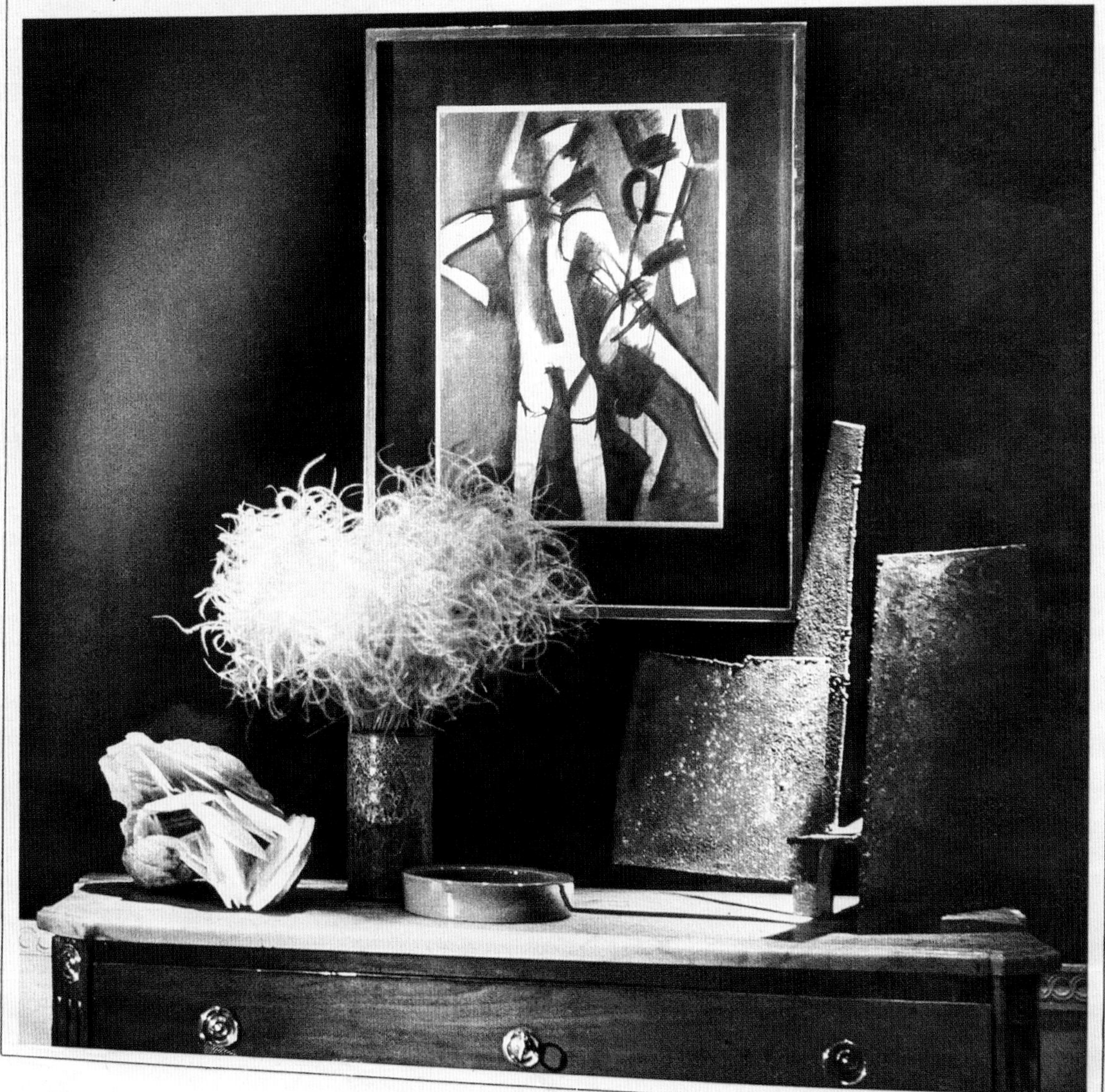

Architektur und Kultiviertes Wohnen : Winter 70/71.

STILLEBEN

Fin-de-siècle-Stimmung mit getrockneten Blumen und Gräsern, zerknitterter Schleife, Kostümfest-Helm, geschnitzter Architektenspielerei; Hähne, Dosen, Steine; das Blau der Vase, rosa Elefanten und der Messingglanz als Farbkontrast (links). Modernes japanisches Bild, Porzellanreiher, Buddhakopf; die Goldreifen sind Reproduktionen von Grabgaben (ganz oben). Statische Komposition von Rundformen der Steinschalen und Längsformat der Lederetuis über barock geschnitzten Tischfüßen (oben).

Antik wirkende Holzplastik einer alten Schiffsdekoration, moderne italienische Keramik in Gelb und Orange, getrocknete Ähren auf dem schlangenhautbespannten Tischchen. Darüber Abstraktion im Stil Hartungs (ganz oben). Schreibtischatmosphäre eines Edwardian Gentleman: grüner Lampenschirm, Bernsteinstempel, Uhr und Silberdose, Steinschalen. Verfremdung durch den zarten Hauch der Distel (oben).

Bar auf der Marmorplatte: nach Art und Größe gestaffelte Drinks unter tomatenrotem Plakatstil-Bild. Überraschungseffekt des Pop-Arrangements: Fragment eines Bischofskopfs (ganz oben). „Oval und eckig" überhöht von antikisierender Vase als Lampenfuß. Fröhliches Bric-à-brac von Emaildosen, Jugendstilschmuck, griechischem Miniaturkopf auf einem Glaswürfel und bunten Marmoreiern (Bild oben).

Fotos: Michael Boys (1), Jacques Schumacher (7)

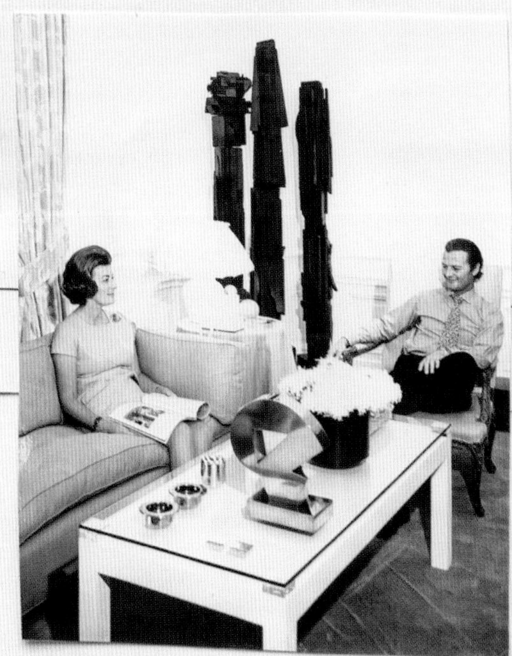

PH & DH in newyork DN sinte!

"I don't really like people —I like objects"

DAVID HICKS

In a world where self-effacement seems to have become one of the greatest virtues, David Hicks may be one of the last egotists.

Hicks is the London decorator who brought us geometrics, shiny walls and the pattern mix. One of his more recent commissions: the redecorating of Prince Charles's four-room apartment in Buckingham Palace.

He is a man of energy as well as ego. Example: He now travels to New York monthly in his role of general consultant to Hystron Fibers on matters concerning the company's Trevira fiber and its application–as wall and floor coverings, apparel, luggage and in airplane and automobile interiors.

By his definition, Hicks has stopped being a "decorator" and has become an "interior designer." He considers his work close to artistry and divorces business acumen from creativity.

"Artists have had to develop a business sense because life is jolly expensive. But it's not the artist–or me–who has the real business sense. It's our business managers. We're the dreamers. I think it's a disaster when a designer becomes too involved in the business side. He should be totally detached from it."

Forthrightly, without a trace of humility, Hicks describes his rise from England's "dull, sane, middle class" to–he can't quite detach himself from business–his position as an international designer-financial success.

He studied design at the Central School of Arts and Crafts, followed by two years in the army. He says of his stint in the service:

"It was good for me to be with all those awful lorry drivers, to know what really bad food is, to get away from one's mother, to be deprived of flowers and live in hideous rooms. All that is terribly good for one's character."

Following the army, Hicks spent two years wandering around the world, painting and studying architecture, "really passionately exploring the whole world. You know, the eager culture vulture."

The exploration ended in favor of a job. He returned to London and spent six months in the creative department of an advertising agency, "drawing blowups of tractor tires and corn flakes." Reaction: "Advertising people just drink gin and tonic and talk a lot of nonsense."

Then came the turning point. Hicks decided to buy a house in Eaton Square and proceeded to decorate it "absolutely as I wanted." It was at a time when imaginative wallpaper and carpeting were difficult to come by.

"I relied entirely on color–of course, I used it in a stunning way."

The results were immediate. The house was published in an English magazine and suddenly "people rang up to ask, 'Will you do my house?' So really that was my big breakthrough. I then specialized in doing private homes for the upper class . . . but now I do that only through my associates."

What are David Hicks's decorating guidelines?

"I do believe there are certain classic rules to which one must always [Continued on page 152]

← House Beautiful

P.152 H.B.

stick, whether traditional or modern. One must have all four walls the same. One cannot have a fabric on one wall. You can, however, use a wall of mirror in a justifiable case, such as in an entrance hall. All ceilings have to be painted white. I strongly disapprove of dark ceilings except in nightclubs. Dark ceilings are an eccentric gimmick left over from the 30s."

His associates currently carry out this credo. While Hicks may consent to the initial consultation with a client, the associates execute the work, with Hicks dropping by at the finish to say, "Marvelous–but why don't you hang the pictures there?"

He is married to the former Lady Pamela Mountbatten. At home, as in business, he applies total control ("not through discipline but through charm, intelligence and explanation") to the rearing of their three children. "I adore my children, but, of course, there I'm molding. I've created them, for one thing. One is dressing them, teaching them about life."

He admits to not having much use for people. "Occasionally I long to redo somebody's hair or their smile, but less than I long to redo things. I don't really like people very much. They bore me. I like objects."

He qualifies: "If people are intelligent, then I'm interested in them. But if they are intelligent, then I'm not sufficiently interesting to keep up with them. I have about three friends."

Hicks has the same number of houses as friends–two in England, one abroad. "In my houses in England, town and country, it's pattern on pattern because one needs the interest in a cold country. But in the south of France, where I spend the summer, everything is white–beds, floors, walls, awnings, louvered shutters. I get away from the pattern mix." The latter, he says, is preferred by the young. "Older people are more staid, inclined to go for the well-groomed, well-tailored, plain, safe look–only one pattern to a room."

He is pleased with his private life. "If you have a country life as I do, you know, it's very full." He deplores gladiolas, cut glass, Cadillacs, the breakdown of the servant class, the war in Vietnam and his "impossibly dreary" hotel room. But, dislikes notwithstanding, he admits that, for the most part, all's well with his world. "I do have a varied, marvelous life. I've got a divine wife and three marvelous children. I'm very blessed with having so many possessions.

"I adore possessions." ■

ADDRESS BOOK

By Epsie Kinard

Who'll paint a miniature of my tablescape?

This St. Louis reader, inspired by Decorator David Hicks's tablescapes in the April 1969 issue of House Beautiful, has created a stylized grouping of sculpture, carvings, snuffboxes, antique animals and other treasures.

BOOK MAKING

'David Hicks on Bathrooms'

LONDON-BASED DECORATOR DAVID Hicks has written two books on decorating — and taste. Now he thinks it's about time to specialize.

His third book, and the first of a projected series, takes up the subject of bathrooms. Subsequent volumes will deal with carpets, textiles and so on.

"David Hicks on Bathrooms" (World, $15) is handsome enough to qualify as one of those coffee table volumes. It's lavishly illustrated, as book blurbs love to say. In this case it's true of the black and white as well as the many color photographs. It's a well designed volume, too, with easy to read text.

Hicks, because he's worked for so many of the famous and rich (among them his father-in-law Earl Mountbatten of Burma), may have the reputation for dealing in only expensive projects. He puts this to rest immediately in this book.

It's a very personal kind of book with, naturally enough, Hicks' own likes and dislikes. Among the things he does not like — black basins, over-mannered taps, plastic lace headrests. There's an imposing list of clients and lots of title dropping. And some charming little reminiscences in which Hicks recalls bathrooms he's known and loved from childhood.

It's also a practical, "how to" book with simple, easy to follow advice on how to go about planning a bathroom, deciding where to put the fixtures, how to plan the lighting. Hicks points the way and then lets the photographs show the possibilities.

He breaks his bathrooms down into three categories — historical ("for me the greatest source of ideas and inspiration"), nostalgic ("hybrids...and the ones which most fascinate decorators") and prophetic ("rooms which will set the pattern for the future").

For Hicks, "The essentials of a really congenial bathroom are simplicity, style and utter cleanliness." He finds the small bathroom the most intriguing challenge to his design skill. And the most difficult in the world — bathrooms in New York apartment buildings because "They're invariably small and invariably have the same plan."

—JODY JACOBS

Women's Wear Daily.

By Royal Appointment

David Hicks, the smart decorator, has gone into publishing by forming Britwell Books Ltd., Britwell Salome (his own house), Oxon.

This will be a disappointment to his last publisher, Leslie Frewin, who published Hicks's previous books on decorating. Britwell Books Ltd's first publication is *David Hicks on Bathrooms* priced five guineas and distributed by Michael Joseph. This book has given him, presumably, less trouble than past books, since he has not restricted it to his own work or in fact to new work. He has even been able to publish, as it were, by default, an illustration of a bathroom on page 32 which I have reason to know one of his customers was too impoverished to re-do. David Hicks has apparently helped this particular customer to face this ignominy by putting himself forward as the John Betjeman of Odeon modern: Hicks says that he persuaded his customers to retain the features which were so evocative of the 1930s.

David Hicks, not unlike that other young courtier, Lord Snowdon, is, in spite of having reached middle age, a self-energising business swinger, as well as being married to a Mountbatten and cousin of the Queen. He has been able to outlive that warning which most of us would happily disregard: 'There is no foreign debt that brings more disaster to a man than to look for a wife who encumbers him with a great dowry if his own affairs are prosperous'.

Spectator

TAKING A LOOK AT BATHROOMS

INTERIOR decorator and designer David Hicks, who lives at Britwell Salome, Oxon, has published his third book on the subject—"David Hicks on Bathrooms" (Michael Joseph, £5 5s.).

Lavishly illustrated with 32 pages of colour, it takes an inquiring look into bathrooms of the 18th, 19th and 20th centuries aimed at highlighting details from the past which can be used now, or become the starting point for design inspiration of the future.

Mr. Hicks maintains that even the smallest bathroom can have atmosphere and luxury through an intelligent and creative approach.

This is an authoritative, original book, full of ideas and thoughts to stimulate the most unimaginative reader.

As the author comments: "In the past the taste of the masses was dictated for the fortunate few. The excitement of today is the freedom of the individual to make his own choice and the vast range of possibilities from which he may choose."—J.W.R.

Berkshire Mercury

In fact, in spite of initial homesickness, the Prince rather enjoyed Gordonstoun, did well and became head boy. As for all those cold showers, he insists he actually enjoyed them. Has had one voluntarily every morning ever since; shivering visitors to his Hicks-decorated Palace study maintain he still preserves a pretty Gordonstounian attitude to fresh air as well.

PUNCH, March 3 1971

the White House

The President

requests the pleasure of the company of

Mr. Hicks

at dinner

on Thursday evening, November 5, 1970

at eight o'clock

Black Tie

ONE OF A PAIR OF CAST-IRON DOGS OUTSIDE ST. GEORGE'S CHURCH, OFF HANOVER SQUARE

INCONSPICUOUS SENTINEL

SIR,—My photograph shows one of a lifelike pair of dogs, full-size and beautifully detailed in cast iron. As they stand in shadow in the porch of St. George's Church, off Hanover Square, London, many people must pass them by each day without a second glance.

Attributed to Landseer, they used to stand, I believe, outside a tailor's shop in Conduit Street, but when the building was destroyed during a second World War air raid the dogs were removed to their present position.—JOHN L. SPRINGETT, 25 *Boleyn Gardens, West Wickham, Kent.*

David Hicks Collection

Burrows Textiles

Calder Vale Mills
Ravensthorpe
Dewsbury
Yorkshire
England

Telephone Dewsbury 5715·6·7
Telegrams 'Arodes' Dewsbury

PHOTOS DAVID MASSEY

Sa manière douce : ce séjour noyé dans un camaïeu de brun, animé par le jeu des matières : liège mural, fourrure, cuir, Perspex, tissus ; cette géométrie confortable des sièges. Sa signature aussi, le graphisme décidé du rideau, et le choc d'un seul trait de bleu. Ci-contre, sa manière "forte" : enthousiasme dans le mélange des couleurs et des motifs. Six couleurs en tout, qui s'opposent mais surtout se répondent d'un imprimé à un uni, d'un motif à un siège. Cet essai brillant : son pied-à-terre new-yorkais, hymne à la couleur "plus importante, pour lui, que n'importe quel matériau au monde".

Les moquettes à dessins ? C'est lui. Ce vent de vigoureuse géométrie sur les tissus ? C'est lui. Cet art de faire vibrer les couleurs, de confronter les matières, de mélanger les imprimés ? C'est lui encore, l'initiateur. Et surtout cette inimitable façon d'avoir appris aux décors modernes à redire "Home, sweet home...", c'est vraiment lui, David Hicks, décorateur-designer londonien dont le tempérament britannique est sans doute à la base de ce sens inné du confort. Sa fantaisie, sa jeunesse - en réaction aussi contre une certaine Angleterre conformiste - sont venues en Europe réchauffer, adoucir, égayer le style contemporain et le retenir sur la pente de la rigueur esthétique et de la beauté froide.

A LONDRES UN CRÉATEUR DE RÉPUTATION INTERNATIONALE

DAVID HICKS
A la recherche du bonheur individuel

Maison et Jardin no. 169
Dec/Jan 70.

Daily Mail

April 13, 1971

Lucky America!

DAVID'S GOT DESIGNS ON YOU...

NEXT month David Hicks faces the biggest test of his skill as a commercial designer.

It will come in America during a three-week tour of 21 major cities to promote the launch of David's first massive collection of co-ordinating household linens.

The collection includes sheets, towels, fabrics, table linen and carpets which are being produced by several of the biggest American manufacturers.

Total

He will be accompanied by his wife Lady Pamela and business manager Leslie Button.

While they are there, American TV networks will be showing a glossy commercial featuring the whole Hicks family, with lovely shots of his three young children at home in England and France, and, of course, all the new designs.

In each city he visits at least one department store will show a Hicks-designed room set (like the dining room shown here) incorporating the 'Total environmental look' they aim to create.

DAVID HICKS in his own dining-room, newly decorated with 50 yards of his printed cotton fabric.

The designs are stunning. Neat, sophisticated patterns, their scale depends on the fabric on which they are printed. So you get large designs on objects like carpets, and sheets, tiny patterns on tablecloths and napkins.

All the favourite Hicks patterns are there, divided into what he describes as geometrics, geo-florals and geo-forms, disciplined and chic and they are in all the usual glorious Hicks colours, like palest apricot, blackberry, ginger, sharp greens and soft, warm browns.

So, for the first time, the American housewife redecorating her home for the spring will

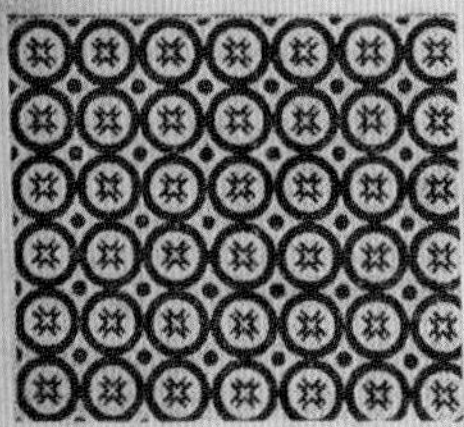

One of the striking new Hicks designs.

be able to furnish not only practically a whole room, but almost her entire home with these covetable, expensive-looking but moderately priced stylish designs—the first complete range to come from a designer in his own right.

In October the range will be extended to include even garden tools.

Soon, some of the designs, like the bed linen, and possibly some of the table linen, will go on sale here.

At least three important British furnishing manufacturers, recognising the tremendous Hicks flair, have turned to him for their newest designs.

by Angela Broadbridge

From Parker and Farr will shortly come the first Hicks-designed sofas and chairs.

Chlydema carpets, of Kidderminster, will market Hicks-designed rugs and carpets and Burrows Textiles of Dewsbury will shortly put on sale a wide range of Hicks-designed upholstery fabrics in plain colours and dazzling toning checks.

And in menswear you will soon be able to buy Hicks-designed neckwear—flamboyant patterns, brilliant stripes, even colourful geometrics making up one of the most dazzling collection of ties seen yet.

Behind David are two of the smartest organisation men in the business—Leslie Button and Billy Guinness.

Work on the Hicks projects takes place in a terraced Georgian house in Pimlico. Inside, the apple green walls and carpets make a calm background for the jumbled heaps of fabrics and rolls of carpeting and cuttings and the loaded tycoon-sized desks.

Daily Sketch

. . . hire an open Daimler and drive down The Mall flinging new pence to passers by . . .

. . . appear on a Vogue cover, snapped in red velvet hot pants between two Irish wolfhounds by David Bailey . . .

. . . ride in the Grand National and win. . . .

. . . buy a 20-bedroom house and call in David Hicks like he was the local decorator to do it all over . . .

So why not then? What's the difference between me and Mr. Webb. At a rough estimate about £72,314.

That's the Daimler at £14 an afternoon, Bailey at £200 a session, this year's National winner, £12,000 plus £100 entry fee, and David Hicks at £1,000 an hour.

HOUSE & GARDEN INCORPORATING LIVING FOR YOUNG HOMEMAKERS CREATE BEAUTY ALL AROUND YOU 02030 MAY, 1971

HOW YOU CAN CREATE BEAUTY ALL AROUND YOU

50 PAGES OF EXHILARATING IDEAS

NEW BEAUTY TREATMENTS FOR YOUR BEDROOM AND BATH

SHOULD A HUSBAND AND WIFE SHARE A BEDROOM AND BATH? What the experts say

EXCITING FACE-LIFTS FOR 3 HOUSES

HOW TO MAKE YOUR LAWN GROW GREEN

12 PARTY TABLES SET LIKE GARDENS

FRUIT COOK BOOK 55 QUICK DELIGHTS AND SURPRISING RECIPES

Main bedroom at Britwell.

WARREN
ne com-
design-
lents to
ns, not
rs have.
London
e for J.
ic., will
seventh
nt early
month.
for his
cs — he
think
started
of them
es—Mr.
number
pillow
sembles.
ly catch
at this
veryone
a floral
English

has done
at Wind-
Charles
is also
sheets,
els with

nens are
percale
and all
mark, as
ces for
for the
up to
towels
and all
h.

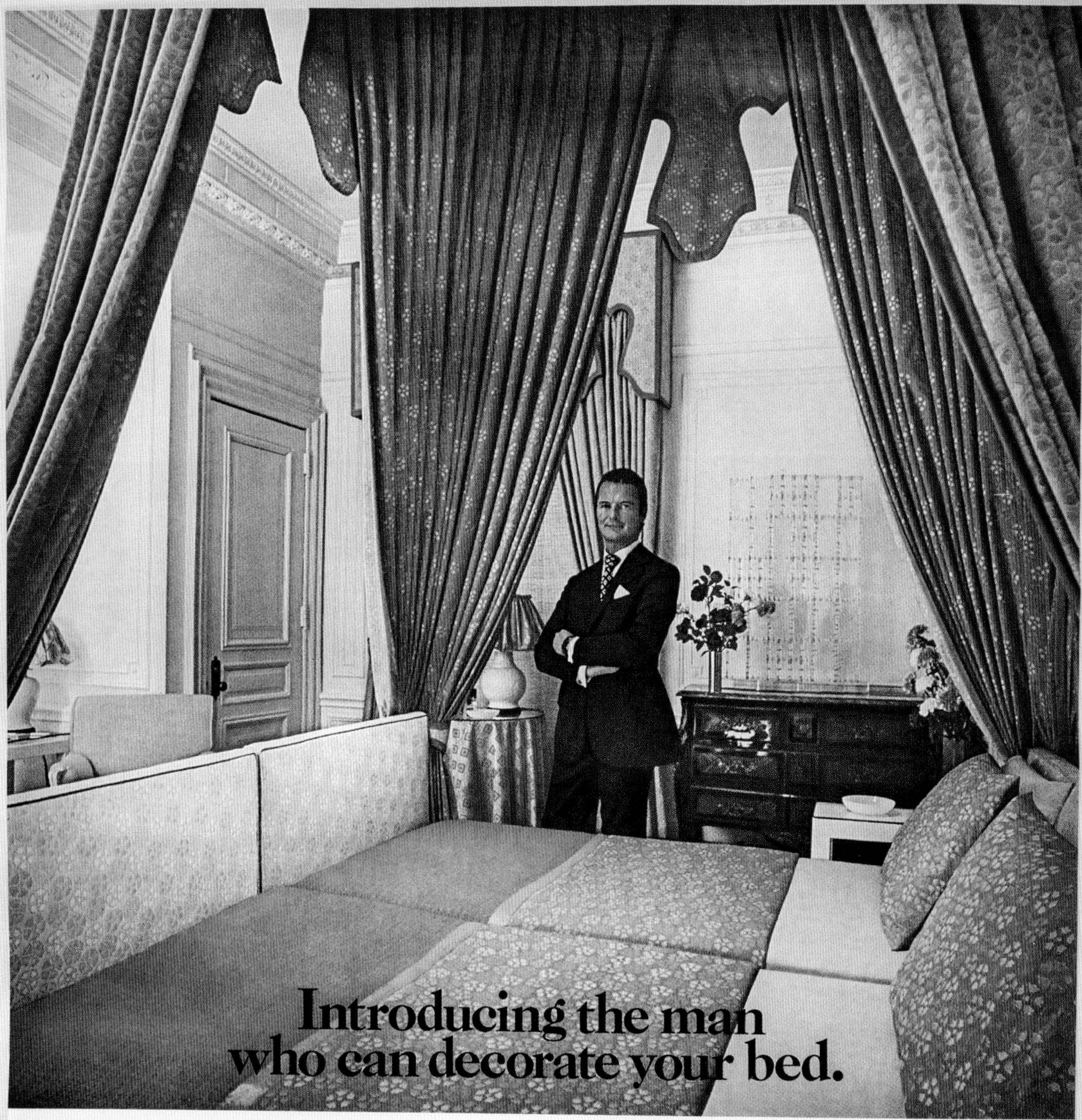
Introducing the man
who can decorate your bed.

The man is David Hicks.

He's the internationally famous interior designer responsible for the geometric explosion in home furnishings.

He's decorated homes all over the world and everything from ocean liners to castles.

This time, we asked him to decorate the interior of a bed.

The patterns you see here are just some of the designs he created for Stevens-Utica® No-Iron sheets (50% cotton/50% polyester).

You can use them alone, coordinate them with solid sheets or even mix them up and decorate a whole room.

If you want a famous interior designer to decorate your bed, see the entire collection of Stevens-Utica sheets by David Hicks. They don't just make beds. They make bedrooms.

Stevens-Utica No-Iron sheets and towels.
Designed and selected by David Hicks

J. P. Stevens & Co. Inc.

Use a pillowcase to trim towels for the luxurious look here. We've trimmed "Chelsea" with a contrasting pattern. All sheets are Designs and Selections by David Hicks for Stevens-Utica. Singer self-cover buttons. Talon piping cord.

Ideas that start with sheets

Cover a button form with a scrap of fabric to tuft a pillow. Use two contrasting patterns in the same pillow for an interesting look. The round pillow has a shirred side piece that gives it a real custom-made detail. "Chips" and "Zed" are the patterns used in these two pillows.

Glamour Magazine

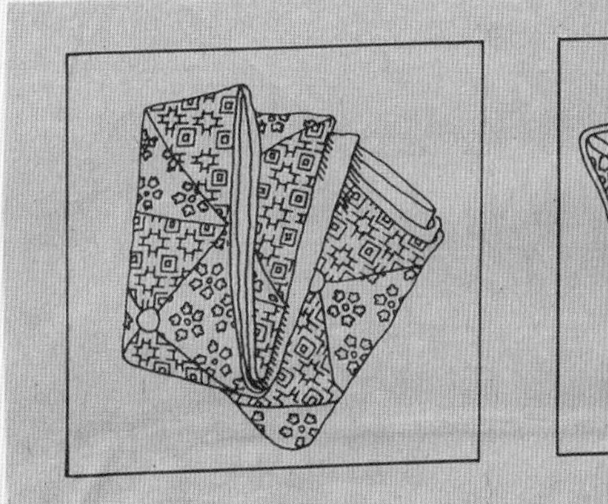

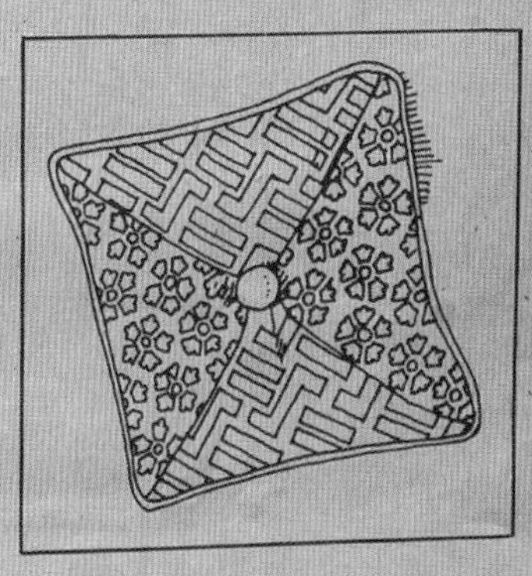

The British Consul General
and Mrs Franklin
request the pleasure of the company of

Mr. David and Lady Pamela Hicks

at a Cocktail Reception

on Monday, 3 May. 1971 at 6:30 o'clock.
- 8:00 p.m.

450 South June Street
Los Angeles 5

R.S.V.P.
383-7381 Ext. 20

Bed, Bath Fashions Will Be Introduced

David Hicks introduces geometrics for bed and bath and Joske's of Texas has the complete collection.

Hicks, the celebrated young English designer, who has created suites for members of the British Royal Family, for tycoons of industry and for the world's fashionables, has entered the U. S. market designing bed and bath fashions for J. P. Stevens & Co., Inc., the great textile name responsible for innovations in home fashions for generations.

David Hicks

Joske's will introduce Hicks' complete collection in the linen departments on the third floor in the downtown and North stores Monday.

In his Stevens-Utica designs, Hicks features geometrics, and also includes stylized and over-all florals and complementary, contrasting, or matching solid colors.

His designs and selections introduce a new approach to color—fresh, light clear pastels with strong but subtle contrasts inspired by the Riviera.

He, his wife, Lady Pamela, daughter of Lord Mountbatten and cousin to Elizabeth II, and their three children are frequent visitors on the Riviera where they maintain one of their four homes.

Geometrics are a new decorative idea for bedroom and bath. The designer recommends them alone or in combinations of different colors of the same pattern, different patterns in the same color, and in combination with florals, or combined with, or accented by, solid colors.

He sees far more uses for sheets than simply to cover a bed. He likes to use them to cover walls and ceilings, to cover mirror frames, for draperies at the windows, and for draperies to give a bed the effect of a four-poster.

Changing a standard bed into a four-poster can create an entirely new look for a bedroom—whether style is traditional, contemporary, "stark," "organized clutter" or "romantic."

Just as sheets can give a dull bedroom a look of magic, David Hicks points out, they can transform an old-fashioned bathroom into a decorative treasure, or turn an ordinary modern bathroom into high drama.

For bathrooms, the designer recommends sheets for wall and ceiling covering, shower curtains, lamp shades, a "skirt" on a washbowl, and to cover such often overlooked items as a waste paper or laundry basket.

H.M. YACHT BRITANNIA

Women's Wear Daily (Stella Fagan models.)

THE TUNIC AND HOTPANTS shape up in David Hicks' towels

Photo by Tom Colburn, Chronicle Staff

Designer David Hicks stands before a drape of his logo design, "Pimms." He also designed the tie, part of a future collection.

Promise Him Anything But Give Him His Own Sink

How to create a four-poster bed with sheets is the core of Hicks' tour presentation. This bed with canopy is in the Hicks home on the French Riviera. The pattern is melon "Zed," a mix of orange and pink, with the valances bound in red.

BY MADELEINE McDERMOTT
Home Furnishings Editor

Amid a growing trend of the bath-built-for-two, chic British designer David Hicks still believes in separate bathrooms.

"It's such a bore for a man to find himself surrounded by false eyelashes and makeup. Two baths are very practical for a couple and at the same time their No. 1 luxury," Hicks said.

"If a second bathroom is impossible, you should at least try to arrange for the man to have his own vanity alcove, a shower and maybe a second, separate basin. Personally, I don't like the twin basins," he said, mimicking bumping elbows in cramped space.

"The bath is the most neglected part of the home, especially in Europe. In the American home the bath is one of the worse features. The plumbing is good, but the space is usually cramped. No imagination is used.

"With imagination Mrs. America can give the bathroom atmosphere. Two impotrant steps are good lighting and good wallcoverings."

The subject of wallcoverings is Hicks' big involvement right now, as he races through 22 U.S. cities in 24 days to introduce the bed and bath fashions he designed for J. P. Stevens & Co., Inc. His Thursday whistle-stop was Joske's Houston. Today he's in Dallas, aimed at the West Coast.

Hicks' wife, Lady Pamela daughter of Lord Mountbatten and cousin of Elizabeth II, usually doesn't accompany him on his frequent, rushed business trips. She prefers to remain with their three children, ages 9, 7 and 3. But she is making this tour because, Hicks said, she has never seen America properly, nor Texas.

The project with Stevens began in May '70. Hicks did the initial sketches, then supervised the development of the designs in his studio. No work leaves Hicks' studio without his final approval.

The collection includes tailored geometrics — Hicks' favorites — and florals: "Pimms," a geometric created from the Hicks logo ("It's composed of Hs, for Hicks and Houston."), sheets and towels; "Zed," sheets only, geometric in three soft color combinations; "Chelsea," sheets and sheet spread floral; "Chips," a stylized floral.

Oh his passion for geometrics, Hicks elaborates: "When I first came to America some 18 years ago, I was overwhelmed by the high level of taste and the degree of sophistication in design and home furnishings. It was a challenge.

"What did I have to contribute? In geometrics, I found an answer. Geometrics brought a new strength and interest to designs for home furnishings. Geometrics can be strongly masculine, but, with the right accessories, the same patterns and colors can have a look that is soft and homey."

In the Stevens collection Hicks sought a "cool, crisp, clean, clear, pale look."

"I personally don't want to sleep on scarlet or black sheets. I think sheets should be cool and inviting. A classic look. These designs are classic, serious. Not amusing. I get sick of women asking for something amusing," the designer said.

Hicks' clientele has included members of the British Royal Family, industry tycoons and many famous Beautiful People. "I've probably done some of the most glamorous baths in the world — and some of the most inexpensive. At our home in South France (they have three others, one in New York City) I couldn't afford to redecorate so I painted it all white and used brilliant colored towels. The result is elegant but not cold because of the towels." A simple way to get a total new look.

In the suite Hicks remodeled at the St. Regis-Sheraton Hotel, New York City, the bathroom became Edwardian in feeling with clever addition of geometric fabric.

Houston Chronicle: Texas

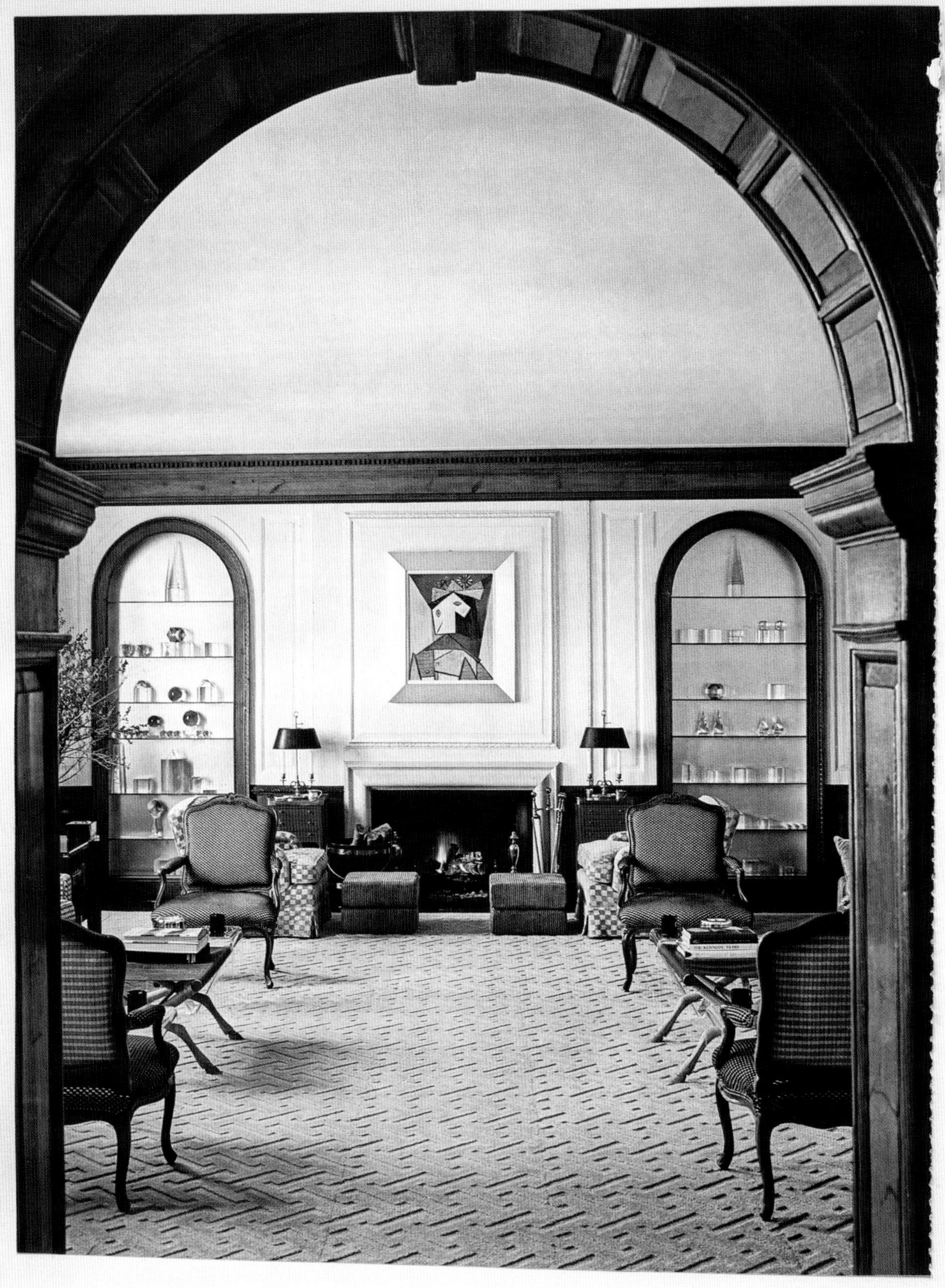

Connaisance des Arts
Fevrier 71.

Ten

1971
1972

Britwell Books Limited

In White House Alley

"TIME"

43 Conduit Street
London W1R 0NL
Telephone: 01 437 7722
Telex: 21820
Cables: Gubuhic London W1

Invoice

New York Times Sep 15 1971 DH wallpaper

United Press International

Mr. Nixon, unfazed by photographers and newsmen, then rolled a strike on second lane. He said his average was 152.

DH writing paper design

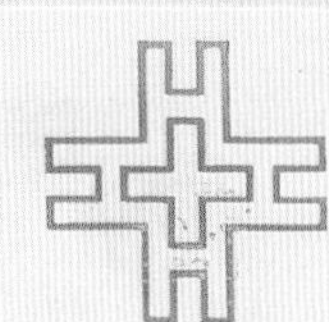

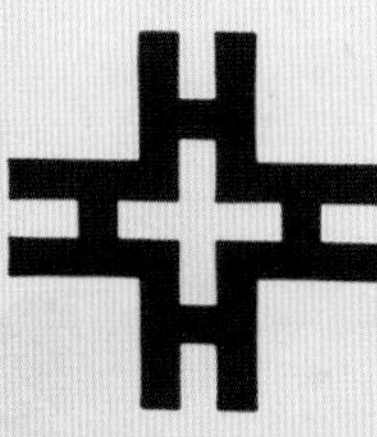

David Hicks Limited

vogue 71

David Hicks has put his patterns on American sheets and towels, *right*. His letter H on non-iron sheets, geometric cables on towels. Blues, suede browns, more colours, patterns, at Heal's; Tiarco, 47 Beauchamp Pl.

Some years ago in London I worked with Adelle Donen, who married the man who made the film Seven Brides For Seven Brothers, Charade and many other star-studded films. It was in Stanley Donen's flamboyant London apartment that I first met David Hicks who had done its interior design.

It has been a few years now, but our paths crossed again on Thursday night. He had just flown in from London to confer with the NSW Government, for which he is designing our new London offices under the aegis of Sir Jock Pagan. We met at Happy and Dolly Robertson Ward's super Christmas party. A tremendous assembly of well known faces were gathered to enjoy their marvellous hospitality.

Sydney paper

The David Hicks Suite / St Regis Hotel, New York City

From David Hicks

David Hicks Limited

23 St Leonards Terrace
London SW3
Telephone 01-730 4652
Telex: 21820
Cables: Gubuhic London W1

TELVA
Núm. 206 · 15 de abril de 1972 · 25 ptas.

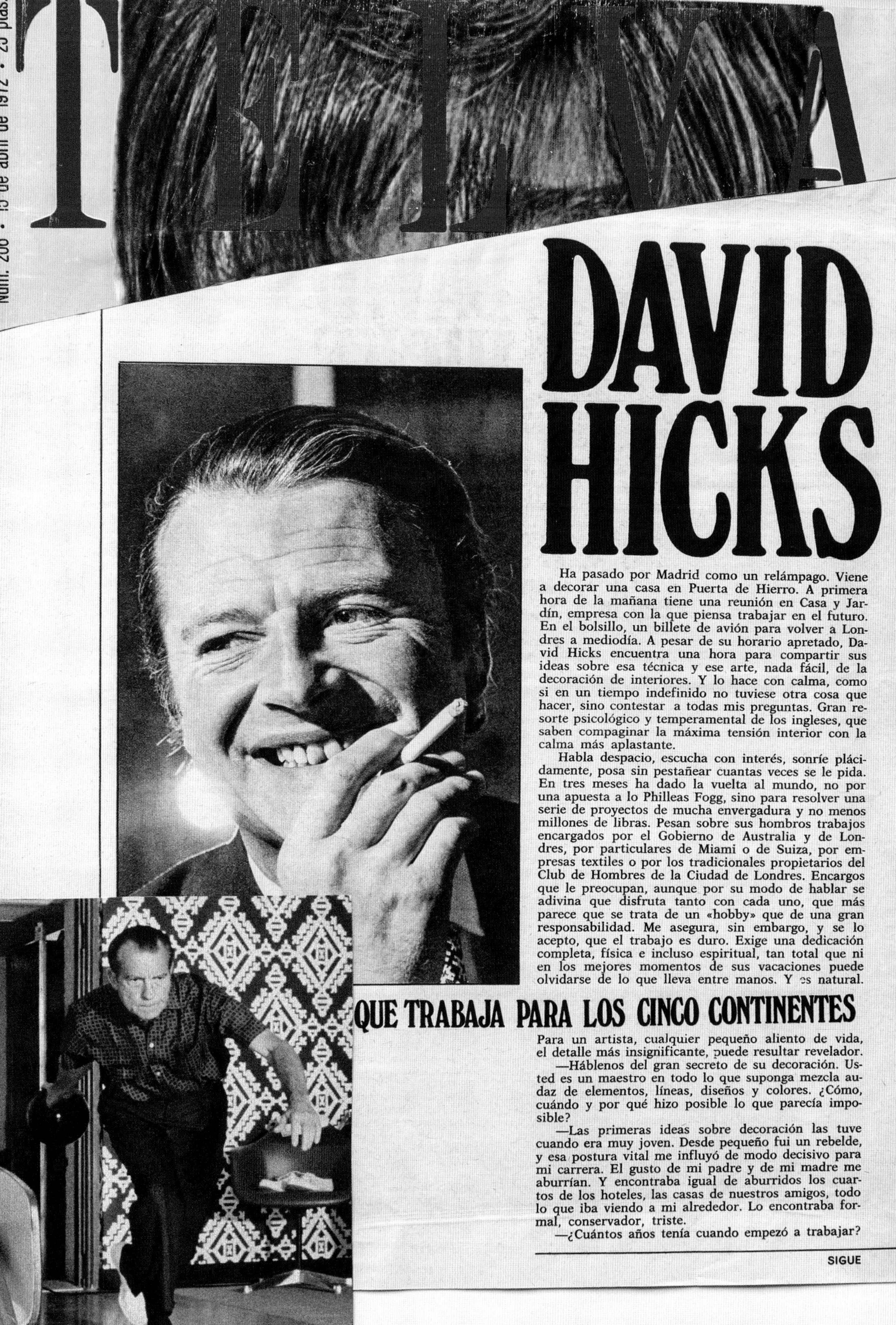

DAVID HICKS

Ha pasado por Madrid como un relámpago. Viene a decorar una casa en Puerta de Hierro. A primera hora de la mañana tiene una reunión en Casa y Jardín, empresa con la que piensa trabajar en el futuro. En el bolsillo, un billete de avión para volver a Londres a mediodía. A pesar de su horario apretado, David Hicks encuentra una hora para compartir sus ideas sobre esa técnica y ese arte, nada fácil, de la decoración de interiores. Y lo hace con calma, como si en un tiempo indefinido no tuviese otra cosa que hacer, sino contestar a todas mis preguntas. Gran resorte psicológico y temperamental de los ingleses, que saben compaginar la máxima tensión interior con la calma más aplastante.

Habla despacio, escucha con interés, sonríe plácidamente, posa sin pestañear cuantas veces se le pida. En tres meses ha dado la vuelta al mundo, no por una apuesta a lo Philleas Fogg, sino para resolver una serie de proyectos de mucha envergadura y no menos millones de libras. Pesan sobre sus hombros trabajos encargados por el Gobierno de Australia y de Londres, por particulares de Miami o de Suiza, por empresas textiles o por los tradicionales propietarios del Club de Hombres de la Ciudad de Londres. Encargos que le preocupan, aunque por su modo de hablar se adivina que disfruta tanto con cada uno, que más parece que se trata de un «hobby» que de una gran responsabilidad. Me asegura, sin embargo, y se lo acepto, que el trabajo es duro. Exige una dedicación completa, física e incluso espiritual, tan total que ni en los mejores momentos de sus vacaciones puede olvidarse de lo que lleva entre manos. Y es natural.

QUE TRABAJA PARA LOS CINCO CONTINENTES

Para un artista, cualquier pequeño aliento de vida, el detalle más insignificante, puede resultar revelador.

—Háblenos del gran secreto de su decoración. Usted es un maestro en todo lo que suponga mezcla audaz de elementos, líneas, diseños y colores. ¿Cómo, cuándo y por qué hizo posible lo que parecía imposible?

—Las primeras ideas sobre decoración las tuve cuando era muy joven. Desde pequeño fui un rebelde, y esa postura vital me influyó de modo decisivo para mi carrera. El gusto de mi padre y de mi madre me aburrían. Y encontraba igual de aburridos los cuartos de los hoteles, las casas de nuestros amigos, todo lo que iba viendo a mi alrededor. Lo encontraba formal, conservador, triste.

—¿Cuántos años tenía cuando empezó a trabajar?

SIGUE

J. P. Stevens & Co., Inc.

STEVENS TOWER, 1185 AVENUE OF THE AMERICAS, NEW YORK, N.Y. 10036

Thomas B. Price, President
Domestics and Allied Products Division

May 24, 1971

Mr. & Mrs. David Hicks
David Hicks Ltd.
23 St. Leonard's Terrace
London SW3, England

Dear David and Lady Pamela:

I would like to personally thank you for being such tremendous troupers. David, there is no doubt that in addition to being an excellent designer, you are a true salesman and showman. As we all know, it is a great combination.

Lady Pamela, it goes without saying, your gracious presence was realized and appreciated by all. I certainly hope that Tom Davis did not try to make you work too hard -- you have to be careful of him.

I really do not know how the two of you stood up under the grueling three and a half weeks. Again, my sincere thanks to both of you.

Sincerely,

Tom

EIIR

MENU

Crème Argenteuil

Suprême de Saumon à l'Anglaise

Poulet Poëlé Derby
Haricots Verts
Choufleur Glacé
Pommes Nouvelles
Salade

Bombe Glacé Royale
Friandises

WINES

Sherry Fino La Ina
Moselle Scharzhofberger 1967
Claret Château Pontet Canet 1961
Champagne Bollinger 1961
Port Dow 1955

le 10 Juin 1971 BUCKINGHAM PALACE

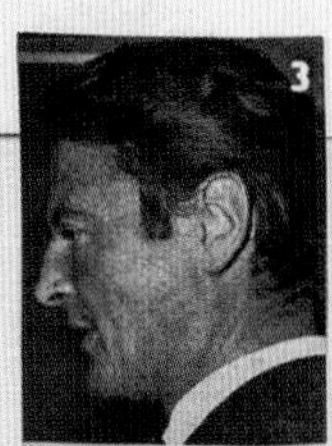

DH at Sainsbury opening: Vogue.

Dods & Pammy: Queen

Wall and chair fabric designed by David Hicks for Connaissance. Painting: Dorian Destenay. Dress by Ken Scott.

Good Housekeeping U.S.
Aug 71

7

8

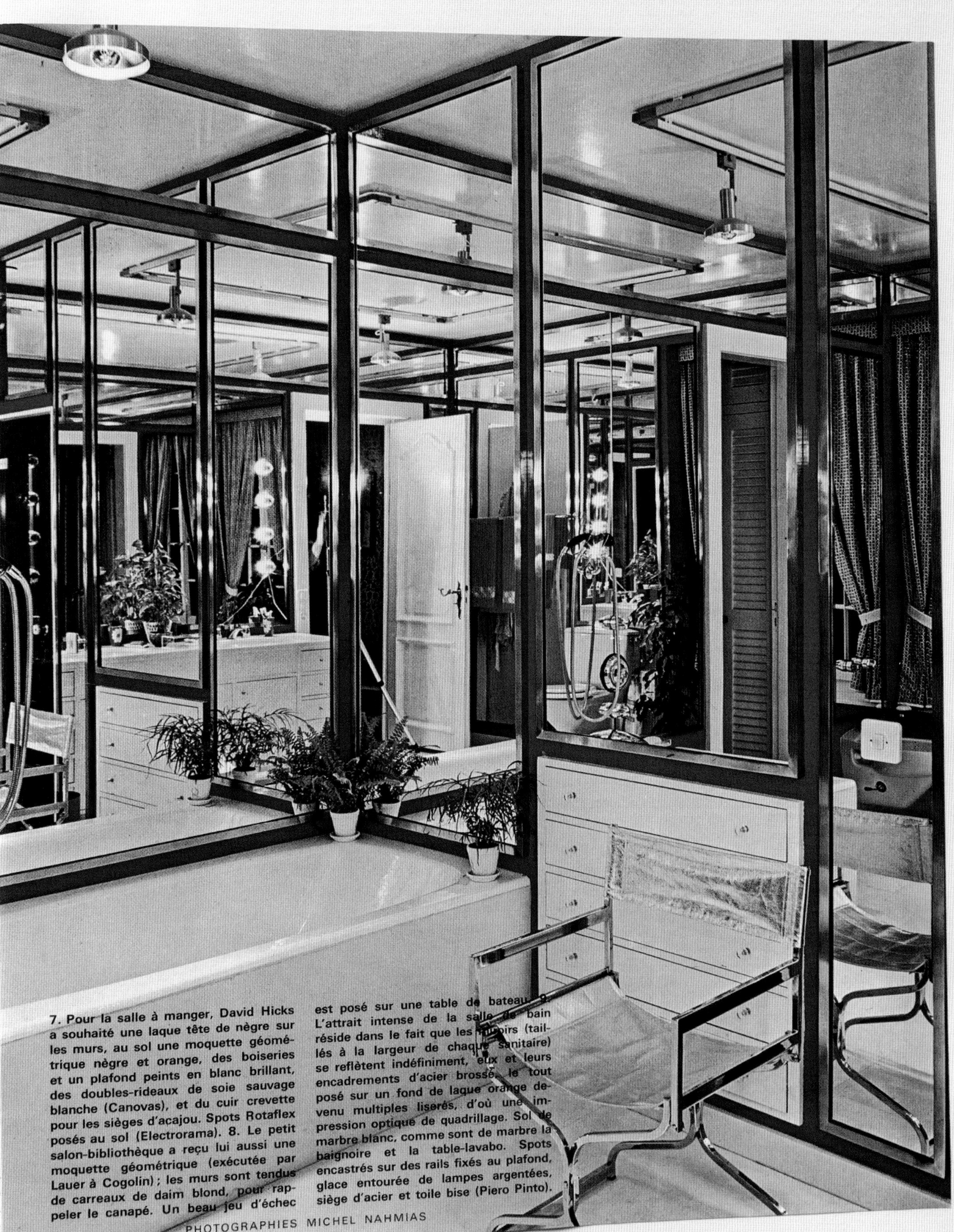

7. Pour la salle à manger, David Hicks a souhaité une laque tête de nègre sur les murs, au sol une moquette géométrique nègre et orange, des boiseries et un plafond peints en blanc brillant, des doubles-rideaux de soie sauvage blanche (Canovas), et du cuir crevette pour les sièges d'acajou. Spots Rotaflex posés au sol (Electrorama). 8. Le petit salon-bibliothèque a reçu lui aussi une moquette géométrique (exécutée par Lauer à Cogolin); les murs sont tendus de carreaux de daim blond, pour rappeler le canapé. Un beau jeu d'échec est posé sur une table de bateau. 9. L'attrait intense de la salle de bain réside dans le fait que les miroirs (taillés à la largeur de chaque sanitaire) se reflètent indéfiniment, eux et leurs encadrements d'acier brossé, le tout posé sur un fond de laque orange devenu multiples liserés, d'où une impression optique de quadrillage. Sol de marbre blanc, comme sont de marbre la baignoire et la table-lavabo. Spots encastrés sur des rails fixés au plafond, glace entourée de lampes argentées, siège d'acier et toile bise (Piero Pinto).

PHOTOGRAPHIES MICHEL NAHMIAS

Bolaffiarte october 1971

HICKS: LA SUA CASA A LONDRA

David Hicks è un famoso arredatore il cui nome è legato strettamente alla cronaca mondana internazionale per essere fra i più geniali ed i più richiesti creatori d'interni di questi anni dai personaggi del bel mondo. La sua multiforme attività è illustrata dalle riviste specializzate più qualificate e pubblicizzata da Hicks stesso nei 3 libri che ha finora dato alle stampe: *David Hicks: Decorazione*, del 1966; *David Hicks: Living con gusto*, del 1968 e il recentissimo *David Hicks: bagni*, prodotti dalla Britwell Books Limited, la sua compagnia editoriale. Ma già dal prossimo volume, *David Hicks: decorazione con tessili*, si propone per le edizioni una scadenza annuale: il 5 ottobre. La sua casa londinese di St. Leonard Terrace 23, distribuita tradizionalmente su quattro piani, si può a ragione considerare come la creazione più autonoma, libera ed aderente alle invenzioni dell'autore, committente di se stesso e quindi non condizionato che dalle proprie predilezioni espressive e dalle personali concezioni dell'abitare. Se è vero, come ha avuto più volte occasione di affermare Hicks stesso, che una dimora – o addirittura le singole parti di essa – devono rispondere e corrispondere al carattere di quali e di quanti ne saranno i fruitori, la sua casa di Londra dovrebbe risultare specchio non deformato che riflette il carattere e l'estro del proprietario-autore. In effetti gli ambienti che qualificano i diversi livelli dell'abitare secondo la consueta partizione verticale londinese, svelano a prima vista l'estrosità di un eclettismo insolito: gli echi di una suggestiva eco vittoriana sono avvertibili, appena abbozzati ma diffusi negli ambienti per il soggiorno e per il riposo. Dovunque hanno spazio tessuti disegnati da Hicks medesimo, insieme a mobili ed altri elementi di arredo di una "domesticità" invitante e quieta, nessuno di alta epoca, ma quasi tutti al più risalenti alla fine del XVIII secolo – o esemplati ad eleganti prototipi Luigi XVI e ottocenteschi – che si sposano a pezzi moderni.

Una concezione dell'abitare, per certi aspetti tradizionale, per taluni altri innovatrice: una cura speciale è stata infatti dedicata al colore di soffitti, pavimenti e pareti ed all'illuminazione indiretta, che orchestrano e costruiscono di per sé ogni ambiente – sia a puntualizzare gli elementi accessori dell'arredo, come nel soggiorno, sia a neutralizzarli quasi come nelle camere da letto – dimostrando l'attitudine più genuina di Hicks che è innanzitutto un *designer* di ambienti e sottomette alle proprie invenzioni spaziali (il gioco delle superfici murarie e il loro colore) l'arredo tradizionale (mobili e oggetti), strumento e quasi corollario compositivo.

Nell'apparente tradizionalismo, la sfarzosa intimità delle sale da bagno si potrebbe considerare come inconsueta e divertente estrosità se non la si riferisse alle concezioni che David Hicks ha dell'abitare, e di questo ambiente in particolare. Alle sale da bagno ha addirittura dedicato il suo ultimo libro perché esse sono « l'ambiente per iniziare e per terminare la giornata » ed il luogo « dove è piacevole avere un po' di distensione dopo una giornata di lavoro e sostare prima di rivestirsi per la sera ». Hicks sostiene ancora – e l'ha dimostrato nel proprio appartamento londinese – che, avendo a disposizione due locali, installerebbe il bagno nel più vasto e la propria camera da letto nell'altro. In realtà questo ambiente, quasi sempre negletto nella progettazione, è il più delle volte ridotto all'essenziale, inscatolato in un blocco asettico ed anonimo che risponde rigidamente ad una funzione mentre dovrebbe essere personalizzato e consentire *relax* e distensione, particolarmente terapeutici se agevolati da un consono arredo. All'ultimo piano della sua abitazione, sotto i tetti, morbidamente inguainata da un *tweed* color bronzo, accarezzata da una luce dolce e diffusa, la sala da bagno di David Hicks (chissà perché non compare nel suo volume?) è certo l'ambiente più "costruito" e più "di rappresentanza" dell'intero appartamento, quello che meglio può sintetizzare la ricerca di un nuovo modo di abitare di questo vate della decorazione contemporanea.

TESTI DI GIUSEPPE LUIGI MARINI
FOTOGRAFIE DI
FRANCA PARISI E ANNA PRESSI

Tre immagini a colori del salone: le pareti sono laccate di marrone; serramenti, finestre e soffitto bianchi. Il tappeto nero è un Cogolin. Il camino è copia ottocentesca di un modello Luigi XVI. Il grande quadro giallo e bianco è di Ellsworth Kelly. Il cassettone in stile Luigi XVI è stato costruito in Svezia ed acquistato da Pamela Mountbatten, moglie di David Hicks, in occasione di una visita a sua zia, la Regina di Svezia. Il divano è ricoperto da un tessuto creato da D. Hicks a disegno geometrico, *"Cross Purposes". Le sedie sono Luigi XVI. L'illuminazione è indiretta con faretti da terra e* spots *dal soffitto.*

Bryan Organ, "Ritratto di David Hicks".

Chi è David Hicks

È nato il 25 marzo 1929 a Coggeshall nell'Essex. Educato alla Charterhouse, ha completato la propria formazione alla London County Council Central School of Arts & Crafts. Ha sposato nel 1960 Lady Pamela Mountbatten ed ha tre bambini. Arredatore ed architetto d'interni di felice inventiva, pubblicista ed autore di scritti sulla própria fecondissima attività, ha operato soprattutto nel mondo anglosassone "inventando" le case e le dimore di molti illustri personaggi. Nel 1956 avvia la ditta di decorazione londinese "Hicks & Parr" in London Street, curando gl'interni delle abitazioni nella Londra *chic* (fra le altre quelle di Sir Rex e Lady Benson, dei Conti di Bessborough, dell'on. A. Berry, dei signori Middleton, del Conte Betty, di Sir H. Channon e di Lord Boyd), per Guido Venosta e il palazzo del presidente del Ghana Nkrumah. Nel 1960 apre la "David Hicks Limited and David Hicks Associates", la sua compagnia di prodotti di *design*. Cura a Londra nel 1961 l'arredamento dell'appartamento di Helena Rubinstein, quelli della casa della Marchesa di Londonerry e della Duchessa di Rutland. È in seguito impegnato dai dieci ristoranti di Peter Evan ed arreda il Carrosse and Garden e il Simpsons di Piccadilly. Dopo gli arredamenti nelle case Cook, Saunders, Creighton, realizza alcuni interni per il film "Petulia" di Richard Lester. Intensifica la sua attività con molti altri lavori e nel 1965 – mentre conduce a

DAVID HICKS LTD

23 St. Leonard's Terrace London SW3 4QG
Telephone 01·730 0608
Telex 21820 Cables Gubuhic

Business paper 72

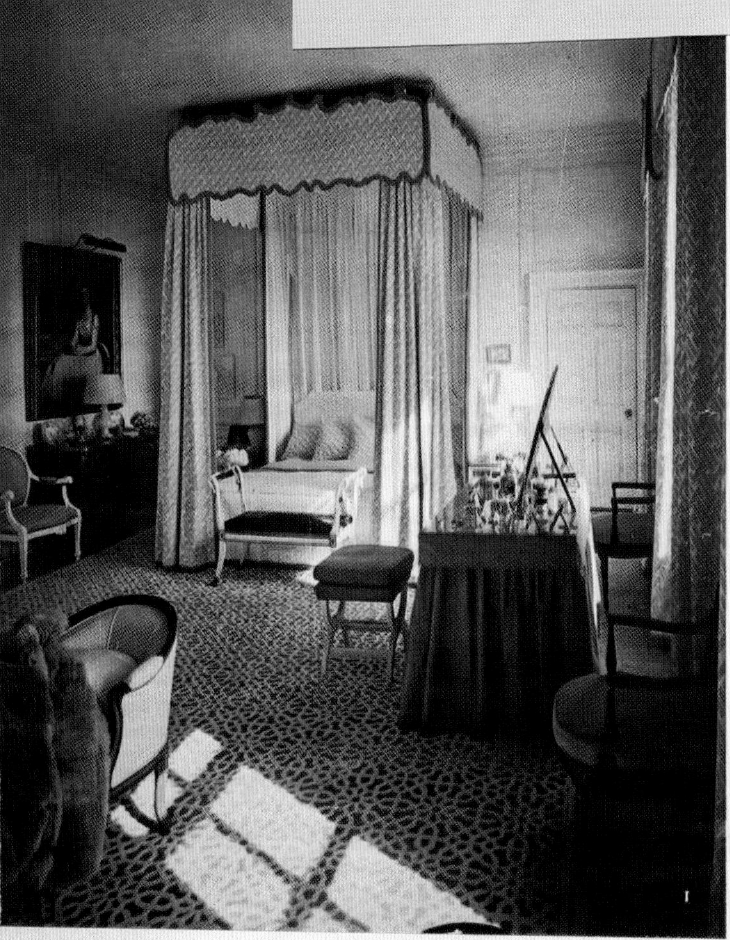

1

Total predominio del blanco y la constante del dosel.

2

1 Una cama con dosel, con un panel blanco del siglo XVIII, tiene una greca en dos tonos de verde y va ribeteado con un «tweed» brillante en tono verde esmeralda; la parte interior es de fibra vidriosa blanca. Las almohadas y las sábanas son del mismo material que llevan las cortinas de la cama y de las ventanas, son sábanas Stevens. La alfombra, tejida en Hong-Kong, es verde esmeralda y blanca; el tocador está cubierto con un azul turquesa brillante, y las sillas que van entre las ventanas tienen un «tweed» verde esmeralda.

2-3 Esta cama con dosel utiliza uno de los diseños geométricos de Hicks, hechos en blanco sobre blanco, con las líneas interiores trazadas en algodón. Las baldosas y todos los muebles son blancos.

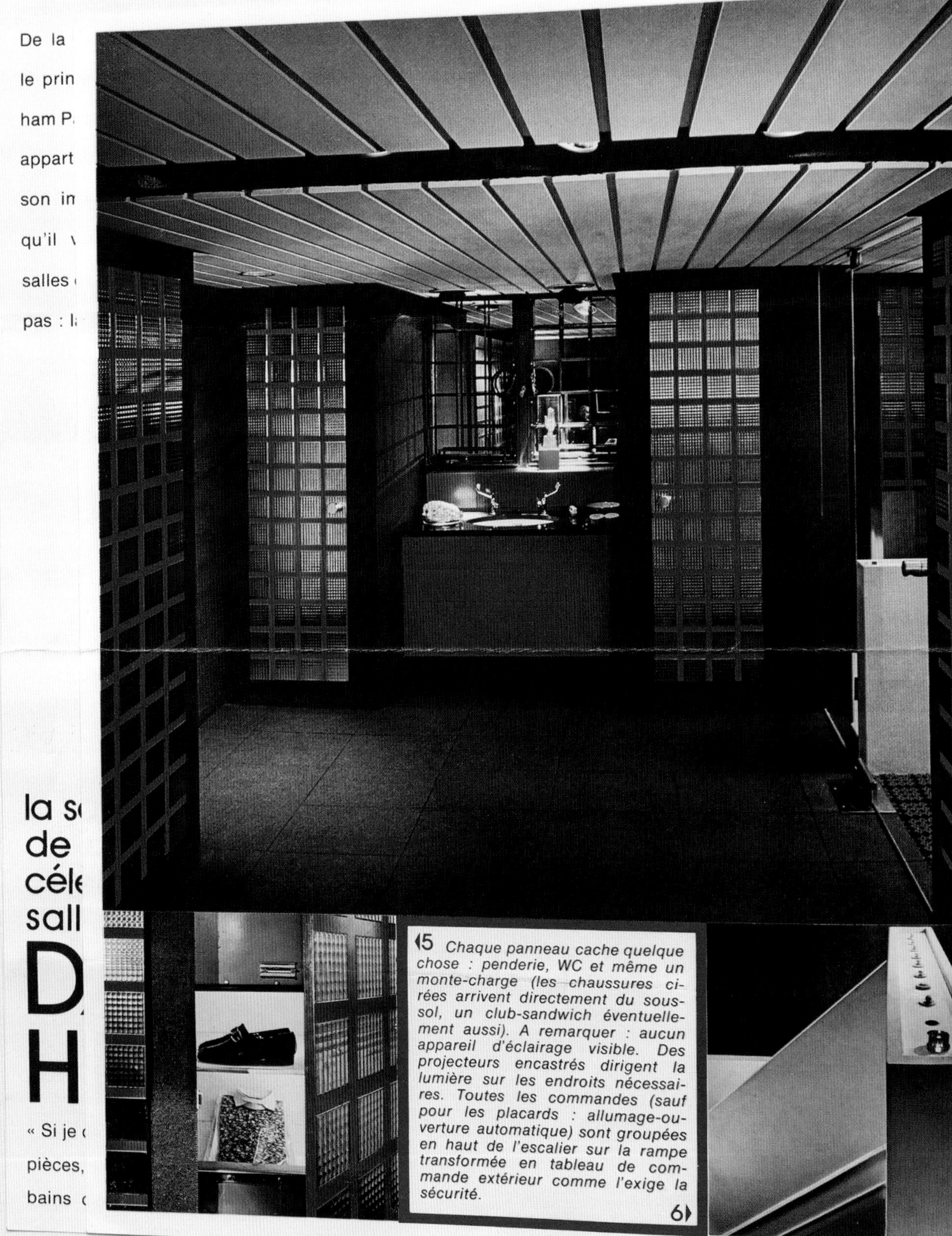

De la
le prin
ham P.
appart
son im
qu'il v
salles
pas : l

la s
de
céle
sall
D
H

« Si je
pièces,
bains

⟨5 *Chaque panneau cache quelque chose : penderie, WC et même un monte-charge (les chaussures cirées arrivent directement du sous-sol, un club-sandwich éventuellement aussi). A remarquer : aucun appareil d'éclairage visible. Des projecteurs encastrés dirigent la lumière sur les endroits nécessaires. Toutes les commandes (sauf pour les placards : allumage-ouverture automatique) sont groupées en haut de l'escalier sur la rampe transformée en tableau de commande extérieur comme l'exige la sécurité.* 6⟩

Connaissance des Arts

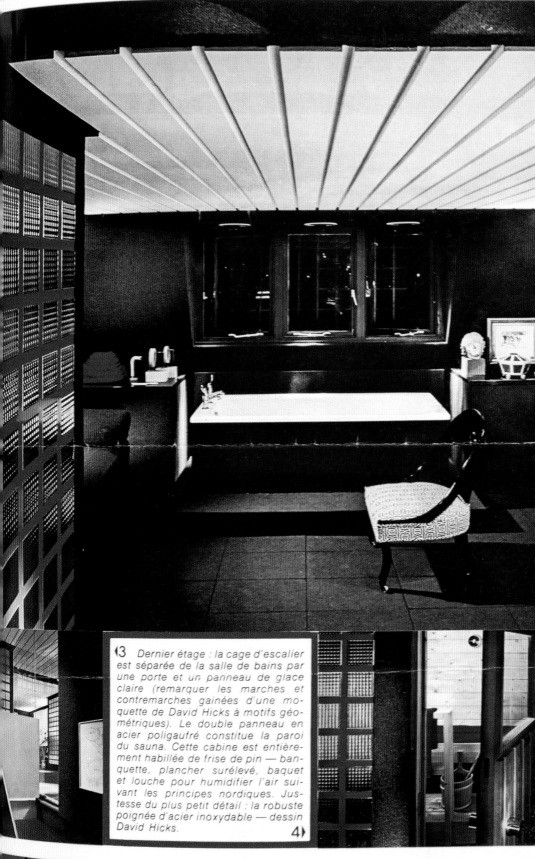

ma chambre
David Hicks,
ınglais bien
de bains est
trop souvent
énagée pour
d'un « rite »
ès peu modi-
si faite pour
it pouvoir s'y
Comme toute
a maison —
ıntage parce
— elle doit
aractère pro-
ceux à qui
La salle de
as un « bloc »
ie, mais un
et débordant
c'est pos-
préfère sé-
, comme au-
simples sont
ıs perdre de
l'ensemble :
matières de
ibuent à l'af-
urtout ouvrir
le de bains
Une salle de
s le bain où
aise où que
rd. »

-Jean Vinson

◂3 *Dernier étage : la cage d'escalier est séparée de la salle de bains par une porte et un panneau de glace claire (remarquer les marches et contremarches gainées d'une moquette de David Hicks à motifs géométriques). Le double panneau en acier poligaufré constitue la paroi du sauna. Cette cabine est entièrement habillée de frise de pin — banquette, plancher surélevé, baquet et louche pour humidifier l'air suivant les principes nordiques. Justesse du plus petit détail : la robuste poignée d'acier inoxydable — dessin David Hicks.* 4▸

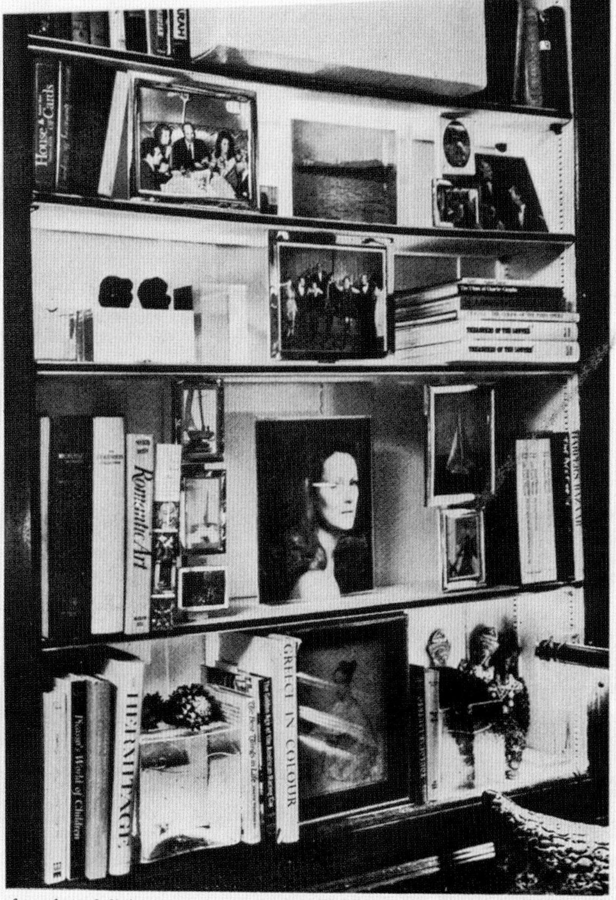

The two pictures above are taken from **David Hicks on Decoration 5** (*Britwell Books, £5·50) and show his interest in the arrangement of both larger and smaller objects. Left: One of his own octagon-design carpets used as a basis for a formal dining-room setting. Right: Photographs, books and personalia as a change from the more conventionally-filled bookshelves. The book is packed with sound guidance for decorators, lay and professional.*

Guide-lines about the house

Although the best way to learn more and more about design and decoration in the home is to do more, reading and studying books on the subject can prompt ideas for further practical experiment.

The *House & Garden* book of **Modern Furniture and Decoration** (published for Condé Nast by Collins at £6·00) is probably the most comprehensive book on the subject, beautifully printed and—most important thing of all in a book of this kind—every one of the three hundred illustrations is reproduced in colour.

The book deals with every room in the house and is thoroughly international in scope, with examples from the United States, France, Italy, Scandinavia and Japan. Without doubt, although it sounds like prejudice, the best book of its kind.

Quite a number of interior designers and decorators have written on the subject, of course, most notably David Hicks who is now on to his fifth volume. They are apt to deal with fairly grand projects, varying from his own country house in Oxfordshire to penthouses in New York,

UK "House & Garden"

Initialed David Hicks ties

—Staff photo by Roy Scully

IT IS POSSIBLE the name David Hicks is less well known, but Walter E. Schoenfeld is taking care of that — and Schoenfeld is the man who heads Seattle's Fashion Craft organization, which has expanded to a London factory.

Hicks is the great designer who, for one thing, has produced initial neckties in good time for the buyer looking for "something different" in Christmas giving ties.

Examples are illustrated here — the R. is in red-and-blue, and the H., more subdued in design, is in blue-and-silver.

These distinctive ties are found almost everywhere now, in plenty of time for you to tie one on to your early shopping list for the man in your life.

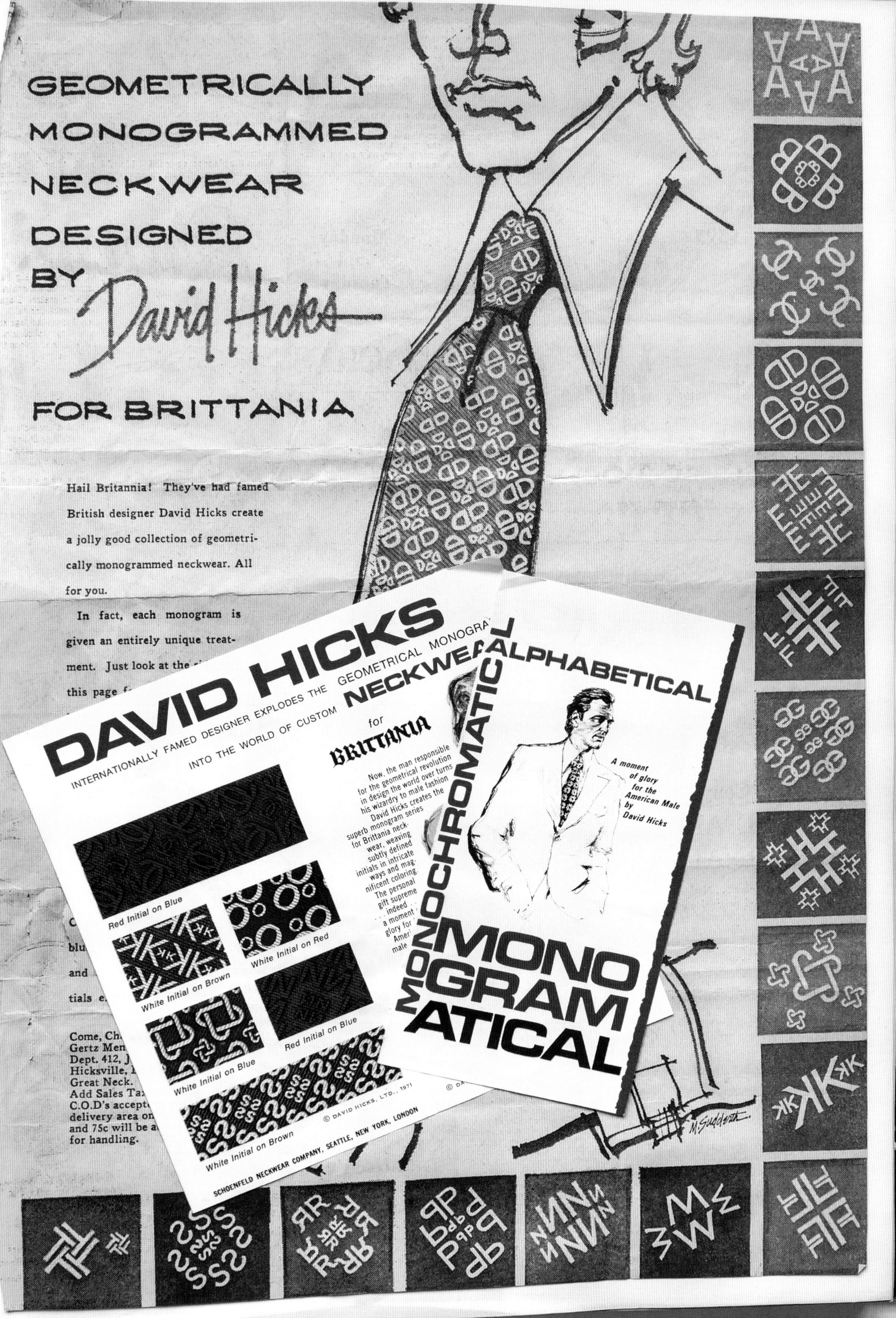
GEOMETRICALLY
MONOGRAMMED
NECKWEAR
DESIGNED
BY David Hicks
FOR BRITTANIA
Hail Britannia! They've had famed British designer David Hicks create a jolly good collection of geometrically monogrammed neckwear. All for you.
In fact, each monogram is given an entirely unique treatment. Just look at the
this page
Come,
Gertz
Dept. 412,
Hicksville,
Great Neck.
Add Sales Tax
C.O.D's
delivery area on
and 75c will be
for handling.
DAVID HICKS
INTERNATIONALLY FAMED DESIGNER EXPLODES THE GEOMETRICAL
INTO THE WORLD OF CUSTOM
NECKWE
for
BRITTANIA
Now, the man responsible for the geometrical revolution in design the world over turns his wizardry to male fashion
David Hicks creates the superb monogram series for Brittania neckwear, weaving subtly defined initials in intricate ways and magnificent coloring.
The personal gift supreme indeed . . . a moment
Red Initial on Blue
White Initial on Red
White Initial on Brown
White Initial on Blue
Red Initial on Blue
White Initial on Brown
© DAVID HICKS, LTD., 1971
SCHOENFELD NECKWEAR COMPANY, SEATTLE, NEW YORK, LONDON
ALPHABETICAL
MONOCHROMATICAL
MONOGRAMATICAL
A moment of glory for the American Male by David Hicks
M. Suddarth

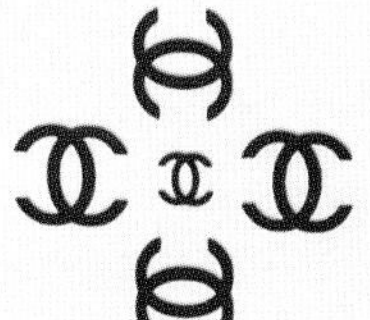
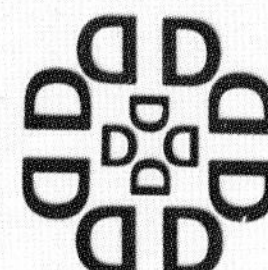
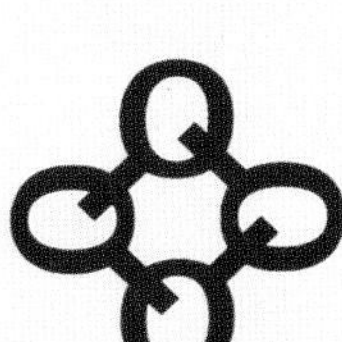

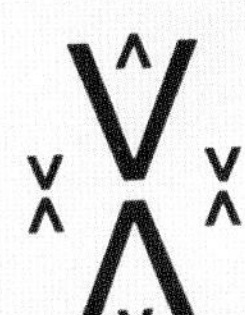

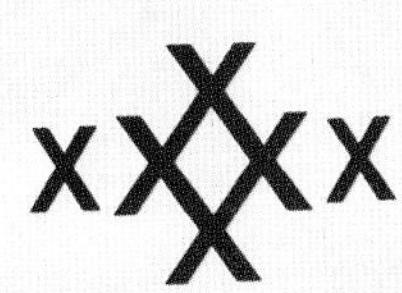
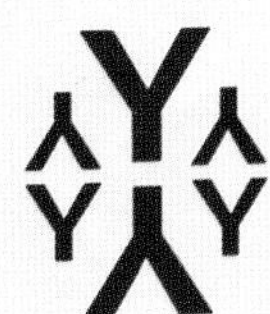

David Hicks Writing Paper

Tiles displayed in Miami Showroom

Birthdays today

Lord Hemingford, 68; Mr David Hicks, 43; Professor Sir Norman Jeffcoate, 65; Major-General S. W. Joslin, 73; Sir Geoffrey Keynes, 85; Mr David Lean, 64; Sir Bernard Miller, 68; Sir Kenneth Peppiatt, 79; Sir George Pope, 70;

The Times

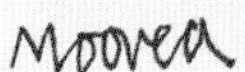

Moorea

Round the world with Pammy

Bali

Savanah on Eleuthera

1972 42

PASSERKORT
TILL
KUNGL. SLOTTET
DROTTNINGHOLM

S. B. Hegardt
Slottsfogde

RITE

ELA HICKS 23 STLEONARDSTERRACE
W3

To expedite y...
Denmark, Swed...
U.S.S.R. and Jap...
01 - 588 363...

D STOP SUGGEST YOU FOUR VISIT ME DROTTNINGHOLM
PRIL 14TH TO MONDAY APRIL 17TH

CLE GUSTAF

OTTNINGHOLM

Saturday, April 15, 1972

9.30 a.m.	Breakfast
10.00 (appr.)	Departure
	Vasa-Museum
	Northern Museum (Armoury, Folk Dresses)
1.00 p.m.	Lunch
2.15 (appr.)	Departure
	Cathedral (St. George and the Dragon)
	Treasury
	Apartments in the Royal Palace
5.00 (appr.)	Back in Drottningholm
7.00 p.m.	Dinner

uncle Gustaf's sittingrooms

with Ashley

NAVE

Entrance by South door

BLOCK A

SEAT 11

Front Row

ST. GEORGE'S CHAPEL, WINDSOR CASTLE

SERVICE OF

The Most Noble Order of the Garter

MONDAY, 19th JUNE 1972 at 3 p.m.

THIS TICK

Seats n

On the occasion of the Opening of
New South Wales House
by Her Majesty The Queen, accompanied by
His Royal Highness The Duke of Edinburgh
The Agent General and Lady Pagan
on behalf of Her Majesty's Government
of New South Wales
request the honour of the company of
Mr. David Hicks & the Lady Pamela Hicks
on Wednesday 24th May 1972

9 o'clock
Dinner Jacket

Please reply on the
enclosed card to the
Private Secretary
56 Strand, London WC2

Buckingham Palace Balcony after the Trooping of the Colour

"... and you designed the interior?"

THE RENTER

Mr. David Hicks

of the Salters Company

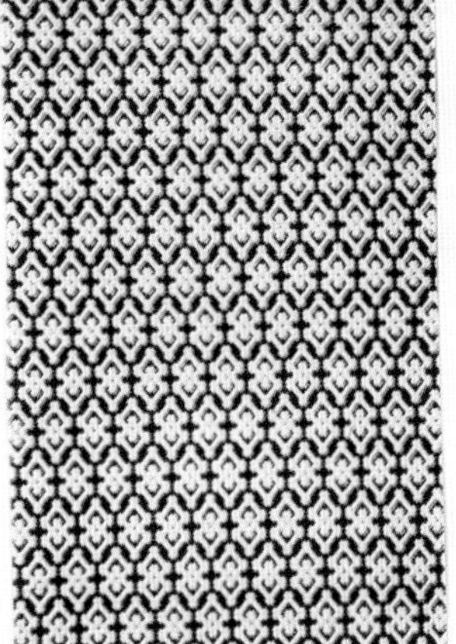

Burrows Textiles Three examples from the David Hicks Collection. Clinch, *top*, six colourways; Sergeant, *centre*, four colourways; Mint flower, *above*, three colourways. Range costs about £2 per yd

Bed and bath togetherness—matching sheets, towels and bathrobes by David Hicks in turquoise and brown on white. Sheets from £4.65, bath towels £3.10, man's robe £21 at Heals.

reportage Pascal Hinous

102

off to a ball !

Autre contraste, bien dans la manière de David Hicks. Entre une statue romaine antique et le matériau moderne qui lui sert d'écrin : des panneaux d'aluminium poli. Pour diminuer sa hauteur, le plafond a été retaillé en pyramide.

La salle de bains joue à fond, elle aussi, le jeu de la lumière et d'Athènes. Le miroir mural traditionnel est remplacé par une baie vitrée (on se contente fort bien d'un miroir sur pieds de côté). Le carrelage, par sa simplicité et sa fraîcheur, convient à un appartement méditerranéen.

Hicks: Designing man

David Hicks in his London home

David Hicks dresses impeccably, drives a Rolls Royce and is married to the daughter of an earl. More important, he designs everything from banks to yachts

DAVID HICKS and the Hicks' style have become synonymous with good taste and established chic. Mr Hicks labels himself as "a decorator, interior designer, produce-designer, and author". He is a jet-set designer who rules a steadily increasing clientele. Twelve associate designers from Athens to Australia carry out his dictates. What does Mr Hicks in all his power predict?

"A totally new design – all inflatable furniture or all environmental structures – is *not* for living except if you are very young. When I walk into a room I automatically see a sofa, a few chairs, and a couple of tables. More people are asking for the heavy, feather-cushion chairs and conventional comforts."

These traditional concepts however do not necessarily mean a total period room or house. Eclecticism in design is always interesting and Mr Hicks explains, "I like a balance within the room, soft elaborate drapery as well as modern metal-finishes on furniture." If the designer selects well, he intimates, a sense of refinement can be achieved with the most disparate elements.

The one thing Mr Hicks hates to talk about is fashion in connection with design. Whether pink butterfly chairs will or will not be the rage is of no importance to him. Yet he does acknowledge, although begrudgingly, that the general trend is toward 'elegance' (as all the Paris couturiers are telling us).

Gone are the days when 'decorating' meant a vase here, a screen there. "Today," he assures us, "it is a serious business with exacting professional standards. People want well-designed rooms – rooms built to last." He insists that fashion is merely whimsical and should be ignored.

Even so, some miscellaneous information did filter through. Colour he sees in paler, pastel shades. Light blues, greens, creams and roses are replacing primary colour schemes. All chalk white is becoming monotonous. Pattern intrigues him. The Islamic Near-East inspires much of his own controlled, geometric designs. And he has just created a new batch of formalised floral prints for wallpaper, tiles, carpets and fabrics.

Far from stopping, Mr Hicks' ambitions are ever-growing. He recently completed a line of bed and bath linen for the American company Stevens which is now available in London at Heals. Currently he has even stepped into the Fashion world designing alphabet ties for men (one naturally with the famous 'H') and slippers for all the family. Soon it is to be interiors and exteriors for cars and planes.

"Flair"

Part 5

1972–77

1972–77

David in his London store with monogrammed ties and porcelain balls; his daughters at Britwell; an apartment in New York. Luggage labels for all the family, colour coded for male and female; a flurry of excitement at the opening of his Paris boutique, pride of place given to Princess Grace of Monaco's letter saying she cannot attend. Dickie is there, and loves it, as he writes from Windsor Castle. Britwell is photographed outside in twilight, every window ablaze with light; David's new, modern living room is a riot of pinks and purple, while his butler shows off his own designs: sculptural table napkins.

Dickie on his fishing boat in Ireland; David's dried flowers in a galvanized bucket in New York; more geometric carpets. *Weekend* magazine covers a weekend at Britwell: David on the telephone, returning from a ride, giving a lunch party and smoking at his desk. With Dickie to the Isle of Wight in a royal helicopter; on another magazine cover as 'one of the ultimate arbiters of taste'; in the *Herald Tribune* bemoaning the globalisation of design. David's hexagon carpet design, 'borrowed' the next year by Stanley Kubrick for the Overlook Hotel corridors in 'The Shining'.

Dickie at a coronation in Nepal; the Prince of Wales in his sitting room, designed by David. His monogrammed notepads; opening stores in South Africa and Norway; licensing his name, face and designs to Japan; a new flat in London 'where his clever design gives the illusion of extended space'; recounting his day to *Vogue* (the editor says 'What a day!') Scarlet-heeled evening shoes and a suede-lined BMW. David against an H-logo made to his exact height in Johannesburg; David with Andy Warhol at Britwell; David looking Bond-like in his office for *Men in Vogue*.

David Hicks a rassemblé pour CA ses principales créations dans sa boutique située 39 Elystan Street SWA, Londres • 1. Des tissus : environ 3.10 £ le mètre/37,20 F • 2. Des papiers peints : le rouleau de 4,55 m, entre 12 et 21 £/145 et 240 F • 3. Des livres de décoration : le dernier paru a pour titre David Hicks on décoration-5 : 5.50 £/ 65 F • 4. Des carreaux de faïence : environ 8 £ le m²/95 F • 5. Des objets décoratifs : une paire d'obélisques en acier chromé, 20 £/ 240 F • 6. Des bouquets secs : entre 10 et 65 £, vase compris/120 et 780 F • 7. Des œufs en faïence aux couleurs gaies : 3.50 £/42 F • 8. Des cravates monogrammées (celle de David Hicks porte 4 H en croix, voir sigle en bas de page ; il existe une vingtaine d'initiales, 2,50 £ en fibre synthétique/30 F • 9. Des objets indécis : un éperon monté sur perspex rouge, 18 £/215 F • 10. Des objets utiles : un cendrier en faïence de couleurs vives, 3 £/36 F • 11. Des meubles : une table octogonale en bois recouverte d'un tapis (tissu au choix) et d'un plateau de verre, à partir de 40 £/480 F sur commande • 12. Des tapis : moquette à l'emblème de David Hicks, 6.70 £/80 F •

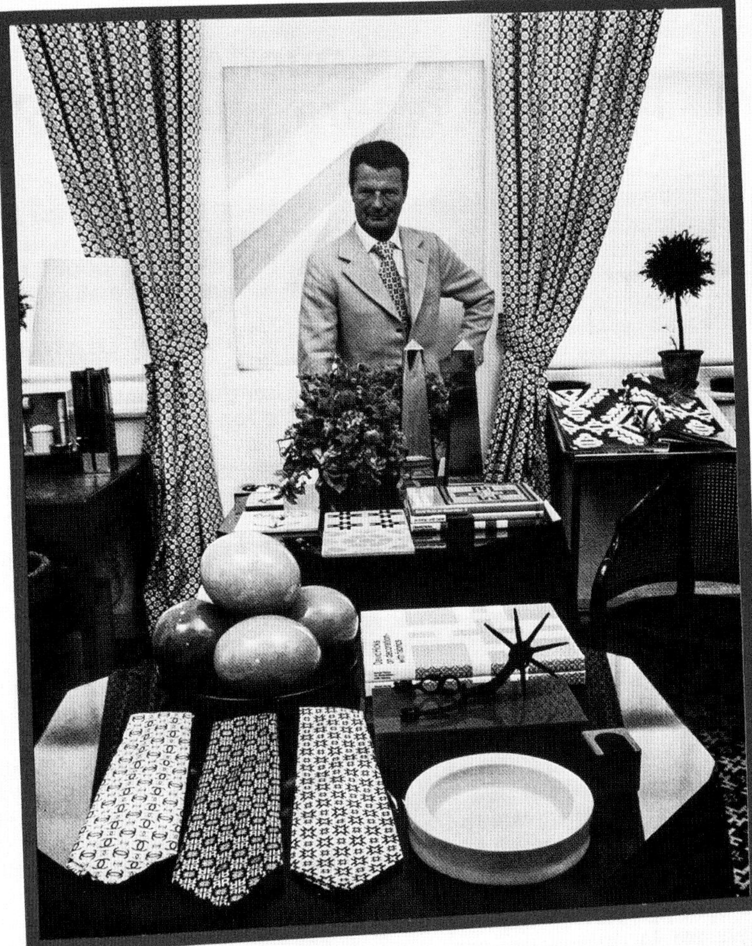

A LONDRES DAVID HICKS DIRIGE UNE GALERIE

 FIN

"DAVID HICKS ON HOME DECORATION" [World Publishing, $15] is the English author's fifth book, which is a handsomely printed volume with stunning pictures of elegant rooms. While the color illustrations are extravagantly beautiful, you soon realize that sometimes more than a dozen pictures are of the same room.

All of the captions for the photographs are brief; and tho Hicks usually says something cleverly different about the same home, he begins most of his paragraphs with "I." Quite a few of the photos used to fill out the book are closeups of the carpets Hicks has designed. If you like these kind of catalog shots, this book would be a beautiful purchase.

Chicago Tribune

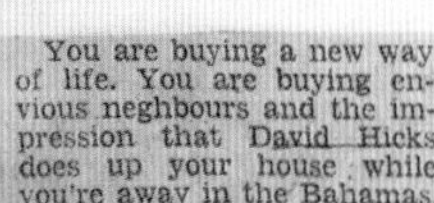

You are buying a new way of life. You are buying envious neghbours and the impression that David Hicks does up your house while you're away in the Bahamas.

SOULEIADO et les tissus d'ameublement

DAVID HICKS le fameux décorateur anglais de renommée mondiale est venu à TARASCON, au cours du mois de Décembre, et il a sélectionné une quinzaine de dessins qui sortiront au mois d'Avril 1973, sous l'appellation "Les anciens géométriques" de Charles DEMÉRY, sélectionnés par David HICKS". Ces dessins qui forment un ensemble compact et ont une ligne bien particulière, seront diffusés dans le monde entier soit par l'organisation de David HICKS, soit par le circuit commercial de Charles DEMÉRY.

Morning fellers....I have just been admiring the job.

ALAN:

What's he talking about? Do you know?

KEN:

David Hicks couldn't improve on it.

Feb 5th 1973

CORONATION STREET

Script

DH Fabric and Carpet

Left *Mahogany moulding in a bathroom and dressing-area designed by Victor Grandpierre for Yves Lanvin*

Above *Attic bedroom with* trompe-l'oeil *panelling painted by decorator Paolo D'Anna*

Below *Angular patterns in different shades of marble in another bathroom designed by Victor Grandpierre*

Right *Painted panels adding interest to a windowless entrance-hall in Paris, designed by David Hicks*

Right (below) *Another David Hicks design for an entrance-hall with painted borders, this time in New York*

[I]n England, David Hicks was [ma]inly responsible for this kind of [wa]ll treatment, using pastel Etrus[ca]n reds and browns to remarkable [eff]ect—rather as if he were framing [a] majuscule water-colour painting rather than the bare plane of a wall. Like all the best professionals, he practised his precepts in his own Chelsea home with highly decorative results. He has also shown that what might seem, when described, a somewhat austere decorative theme, can prove quite otherwise in practice. Applied to the walls of a hall or long corridor, this can enhance and dramatize an otherwise dull interior to a remarkable degree.

American and European decorators have also used these themes of emphatic angularity. Overleaf, American interior designer Mark Hampton shows how a huge

UK House & Garden

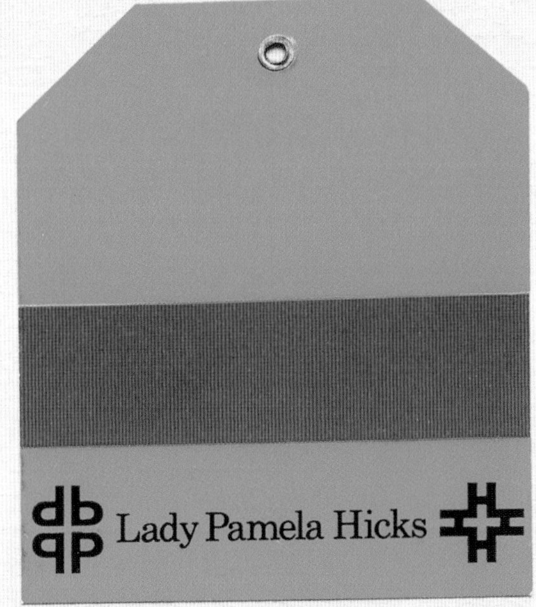

Luggage labels I designed for the family.

vol 11
1973-75

postcards

DAVID HICKS LIMITED

23 ST LEONARD'S TERRACE LONDON SW3 SLOANE 6288

American Embassy,
Grosvenor Square,

David Hicks France

May 24th 1973

DAVID HICK
Le C

David Hicks Fleur Vulliod

David Hicks Fleur Vulliod

30-5-73

On the occasion of the Inauguration of David Hicks France

Her Britannic Majesty's Ambassador and Lady Tomkins request the honour of the company of

Mr. David and Lady Pamela Hicks

at a *Buffet-Dinner*

on Thursday 14 June *at* 20.30 *o'clock.*

39 rue du Faubourg St. Honoré Paris
Black tie

Pour mémoire
~~*R.S.V.P.*~~
~~*Social Secretary*~~

PRIOR TO THE OPENING AT 11PM IN PARIS
OF DAVID HICKS FRANCE,
DAVID HICKS & MARY FOX LINTON
REQUEST THE PLEASURE OF THE COMPANY OF

AT THE OPENING OF THEIR SECOND SHOP
AT NUMBER ONE ELYSTAN STREET
ON 14TH JUNE AT 11AM.
CHAMPAGNE

RSVP 39 ELYSTAN STREET SW3

Dining-room

Table B

THE LADY PAMELA HICKS

Mr. David HICKS

DAVID HICKS LTD

Registered Office
43 Conduit Street
London W1R 0NL

Telephone 01·437 7722
Telex 21820 Cables Gubuhic
Registered Number 655568

Palais de Monaco,
May 11, 1973.

Dear David,

I am so sorry that Rainier and I will not be able to be in Paris on June 14th. So sad to miss you on this occasion.

All best wishes for your new venture in Paris.

Sincerely

Grace de Monaco

Mr. David Hicks

2 bis rue Emile Verhaeren
92-St Cloud

Mr & Mme DIDIER WIRTH

Diner le Vendredi 15 Juin

21h30

RSVP

225 0891.

DUC ET DUCHESSE DE LA ROCHEFOUCAULD

David Hicks, Christian Badin et Barbara Wirth
prient Mr. David and Lady Pamela Hicks
de leur faire l'honneur de venir inaugurer,
en privé, la nouvelle boutique
"David Hicks France" 12 rue de tournon paris 6e
le jeudi 14 juin à 23 heures

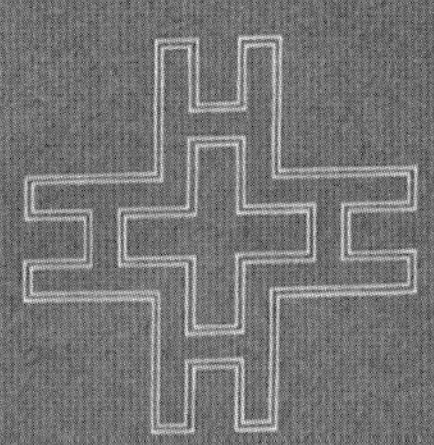

R. S. V. P.
12 rue de tournon 75006 paris

DAVID HICKS IN LONDON, *above, with: top row, from left, Mrs Jules Stein; Patricia, Countess Jellicoe and Doreen, Lady Brabourne; Mrs Robert Stokes. Second row: Mr John Stefanidis; Miss Julie Michel; the Hon. Mrs John Stuart; Mrs Paul Channon. Third row: the Knight of Glin; Mr Somerset de Clair and the Marchioness of Bristol; Lady Jane Wellesley. Fourth row: Miss Margaret Anne du Cane; Mrs Columbus O'Donnell; Mr Peter Coats.* **DAVID HICKS IN PARIS,** *below, with: first row: Lady Pamela Hicks; TRH Prince and Princess Paul of Yugoslavia and Mrs Pierre Schlumberger; Baronne de Courcel. Second row: HRH the Princess Michael of Greece, SAR Mme de Balkany; Margaret, Duchess of Argyll. Third row: The Duchesse de la Rochefoucauld; Mr Douglas Fairbanks, Lady Tomkins and Mme Jean Panchaud. Fourth row: HE the British Ambassador to France, Sir Edward Tomkins; the Duchesse d'Uzes; M Hubert de Givenchy*

THE WAY PEOPLE DO

DAVID HICKS

The way David Hicks does. Opening two shops in one day—first in London at 11 am with Mary Fox Linton (1 Elystan Street, S.W.3); on to Paris for "David Hicks France" 11 pm opening with associates Christian Badin and Barbara Wirth (12 rue de Tournon, Paris 6).

EnglishVogue

L'OEIL DE VOGUE

Les gardes républicains seront-ils un jour décorés, en voisins, par ***David Hicks,*** *le talentueux décorateur anglais qui vient d'ouvrir, (ci-dessus), sa première boutique parisienne en fête, rue de Tournon, à côté de leur caserne?...*

1

2

3

4

5

1. S.A.R. la princesse Marie Gabrielle de Savoie (Mme R. de Balkany) et David Hicks. 2. Lady Pamela Hicks. 3. La vtesse Paul de Rosière, Lord Mountbatten, Mrs Mary Fox Linton. 4. S.E. L'Ambassadeur de Grande-Bretagne Sir Edward Tomkins, Mrs Mark Littman et Lady Tomkins. 5. Barbara Wirth, M. Carl Flinker et M. Paul Louis Weiller.

Whoever owns Rolls convertible BLC 99H has had the bright idea of replacing the normal **dull car carpeting** with a patterned David Hicks design. (You'll need 6 yards 27-inch width for a Corniche, 3½ yards for a Mini. From Zarach.)

The way **David Hicks groups printed cottons into French rush baskets,** *top left.* French cottons, £4.95, English, £2.64 a yard. Baskets, from £3.25, depending on size. *Above left:* another way of showing still more eggs. Again, pine eggs plus ceramic eggs in off-white, £3.85, also available in strong and pale Easter egg colours. *Above centre:* who else would hang ties on a pine ladder? £3.52 each. *Above right:* top shelf, ivory and mahogany pieces mounted on Perspex; treen cups, from range. Andrew Yates picture; £63.80. Centre shelf, ceramic cigar boxes, £4.40. Square ashtrays, £2.42; circular ones, £3.85. Eggs, as *above.* Bottom shelf, ebony crabs, £46.50. Egg-shaped thimble holders, £4. Wooden boxes, from £6. All at David Hicks Mary Fox Linton, Elystan St. **How David Hicks designs for Paris,** *below.* Pine obelisks, about £18.70. Poplar bowls, about £68. Note: flowers are simply put in straw baskets, each variety clumped together as in a flower shop. The walls behind are rough natural poplar

WINDSOR CASTLE

16th June 1973

My dear David,

Often, when I have expected something to be good it has lived up to my expectations, sometimes it hasn't. But it is rare when it turns out so very much better than expected. In fact I cannot think of anything that has

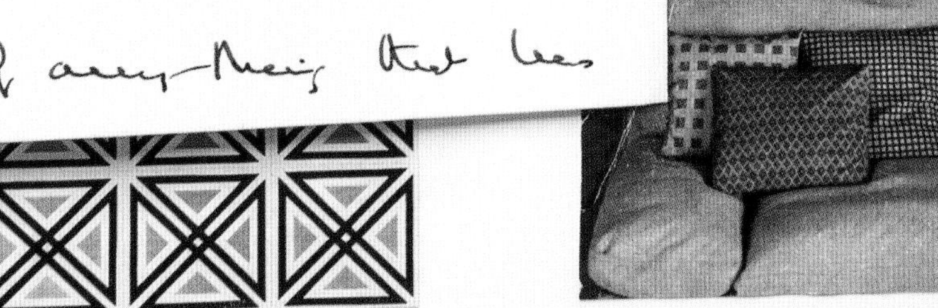

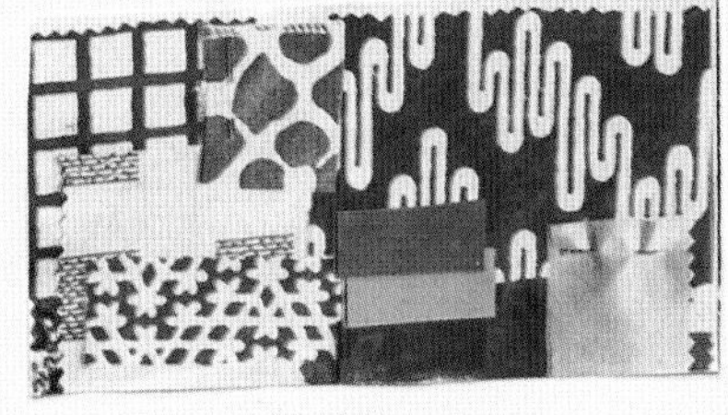

dans son château près d'Oxford

david hicks

le fameux décorateur londonien
aménage une aile : un corridor...

Rose acide, rouge feu, violet épiscopal : la stridence des coloris éclate comme un défi. Et le nouveau salon de David Hicks est bien un défi. Un défi à toutes les traditions de douceur et de sérénité des « country houses » anglaises, un défi à l'architecture du lieu (un manoir « early georgian », à quelques kilomètres d'Oxford), un défi à la paisible campagne environnante, tachetée de poneys et de moutons blancs. David Hicks s'explique. « Le corps de logis principal de Britwell Salomé remonte à 1728. Vers 1800, on y a ajouté deux dépendances symétriques à usage de communs, reliées à la construction centrale par deux corridors incurvés. Une de ces dépendances avait été donnée aux domestiques dès 1800. Je me suis attaqué à celle qui est à droite : une grande pièce fruste, sans corniche ni boiserie. Occasion inespérée de faire ce dont j'avais envie. Je me suis senti libre de créer du nouveau, un salon totalement différent de celui que j'avais installé dans la partie la plus ancienne de la maison et qui est, lui, parfaitement conforme à la tradition des demeures anglaises à la campagne. Dans celui-ci j'ai voulu faire oublier la campagne anglaise. J'ai voulu qu'on ne sache plus si l'on est aux champs ou à la ville. A Londres ou à New York. Ou n'importe où. » Par exemple en Inde, à Bali, ou aux îles Samoa. Cette pièce dépaysante, qui annonce si crûment ses couleurs — tous les mariages de tons aigus et chauds, du « rose triste » (dixit David Hicks) au « rose gai » et à l'aubergine, du capucine au pourpre en passant par tous les degrés de cuivre et de terre

C'est l'aile de droite — les deux ailes furent ajoutées vers 1800 au bâtiment principal — que David Hicks vient d'aménager : un vaste salon percé de cinq fenêtres et relié au corps central par un corridor en arc de cercle.
Le corridor incurvé de Britwell Salomé évoque le château de Groussay à Montfort-l'Amaury. « C'est mon hommage à Charles de Beistegui », dit David Hicks. Particulièrement « beisteguiens » : le mariage acajou-ébène aux socles des quatre continents; les brandebourgs noirs au tapis de la table centrale, les lampes à abat-jour verts éclairant les collections de boîtes. Sur les murs, tapissés de papier gris « royal navy », sont groupés des portraits de famille du 17e siècle, sans cadre.

reportage Roger Guillemot

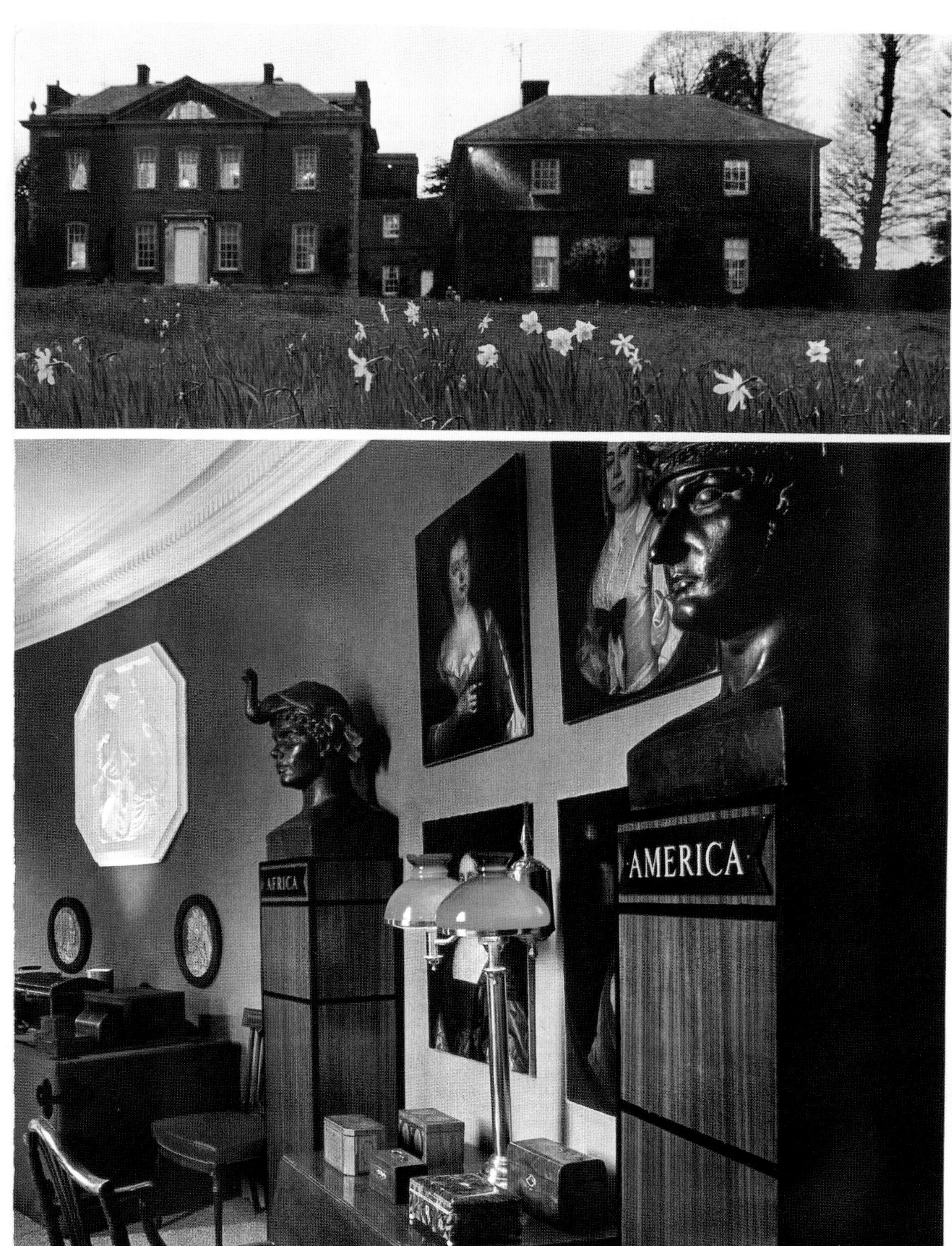

Connaisance des Arts

HICKS ON THE WING

Mr David Hicks, occupied as usual on the international front of interior design—in Miami, Madrid, New York, Geneva, Sydney and Tarrascon—has found a little time over to replan and redecorate three rooms in one wing of his beautiful 1728 country house, Britwell Salome. A series of farm buildings with no period detail, the wing was built and joined to the main block about 1790. He and his wife bought the place in 1960, decorated this bit, then closed it due to lack of servants. Now it's looking like this, very Hicks and very

nice too. The Garden Room, *above*, has stone floors and plaster painted on raw plaster walls, Scheemakers' bust of the first Earl Godolphin. At the chrome and white lacquer book table Mr Hicks inspects the *Grammar of Ornament* by mid-Victorian Owen Jones who compiled 10,000 designs—the source of Hicks' geometry. Now that others have found Mr Jones, he has moved to torn paper flower designs—big for the world, scaled down here not to frighten the English. The Long Room or Music Room, *right*, has Sony stereo, colours of off-pink, aubergine, flame red. Deep Royal Wilton carpet, a new Hicks' design. Louis XV fauteuils with puce tweed, a Hicks' Plain Colour. Chevroned curtains, a Hicks'

THE GARDEN ROOM, *ABOVE*. *RIGHT*, MR DAVID AND LADY PAMELA HICKS, INDIA, 5½, EDWINA, 11½, RETRIEVER BERTIE RETRIEVING

Printed Linen. Interested people find these at the new shop, David Hicks & Mary Fox Linton, 1 Elystan Street. The fireplace is by Lutyens, the red sandstone horse carved in Agra the other day, the Bruckner grand, lacquered black eggshell, had bulbous 1890 legs replaced by tapered ones. Details, *from top right*, include pot pourri in Navajo baskets, each with petals of a different rose. Gypsophila and papier mâché group from Goya's *Carlos IV and Family* by Equipo Cronica. Corn and baskets on Adinkra cloth given to Mr Hicks by President Nkrumah. In the main house breakfast room, *above*, the butler with his napkin masterpieces according to Bologna and Mrs Beeton—waterlily, clown's hat, vase, mitre, boat, Venetian boot.

MICHAEL BOYS

THE LONG ROOM, *ABOVE*. HICKSIANA DETAIL, VINCENTE CAMPAGNA WITH HIS AMAZING NAPKINS, *RIGHT*. HICKS ON THE SWING, *LEFT*.

English Vogue

23 ST LEONARD'S TERRACE LONDON SW3 01-730 4652

For the last two years my head office and studio have been at 43 Conduit Street, and my shop has been at 39 Elystan Street, while my private office has been at St. Leonard's Terrace.

In future, I will be based at Conduit Street, where my new secretary, Miss Anne Straughen, can make appointments to see me there for product design and contract work or at 39 Elystan Street for private work.

My new shop at 1 Elystan Street will open on 14th June, and, on the same day, our shop in Paris will open at 12 rue de Tournon.

From 1st May, my telephone number (at Conduit Street) will be: 01 437 7722.

David Hicks

DAVID HICKS

P.S. As you may or may not know, I have not been associated with Zarach, either in the Fulham Road, or in Sloane Street, for over three years, and this has caused some confusion. However, some of my carpets and my books are still available through them.

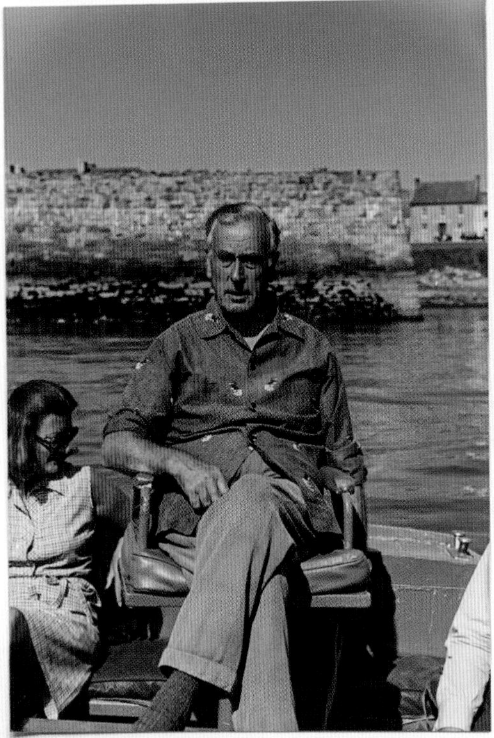

NEW SHOPS IN THE NEW YEAR

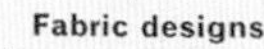

Fabric designs

Shown here is one of nine fabric designs in the David Hicks/Mary Fox-Linton range. Called 'Belgrave', it is in heavyweight cotton at £2·64 per yard. This is one of three collections of fabrics to be seen at David Hicks' shop at 1 Elyston Street, SW3. The others in the collection are 'Tarascon'—exclusive to, and styled by, David Hicks—with echoes of Provence; and the 'Armitage and Rhodes' collection consisting of geometric prints and wool weaves. The wool weaves are in three different weights and are available in 69 different colours devised by David Hicks. There are also some particularly unusual new designs in his range of Crossley Carpets, as well as some splendid wallpapers and vinyls. The shop has all kinds of home accessories to provide all the ingredients for successful decorating, and looks very smart indeed.

...mela Hicks I

wmp

Mrs Gilbert Miller

at Home

on Thursday, June 28th

at the Savoy Hotel.

(River Room)

R.S.V.P. to
40B Hill Street,
London, W1X 7FR.

Dancing 10.30 p.m.

Black Tie.

ARMITAGE and Rhodes who showed in the Design Council pavilion at Heimtex attracted great interest with their David Hicks collection of printed fabrics.

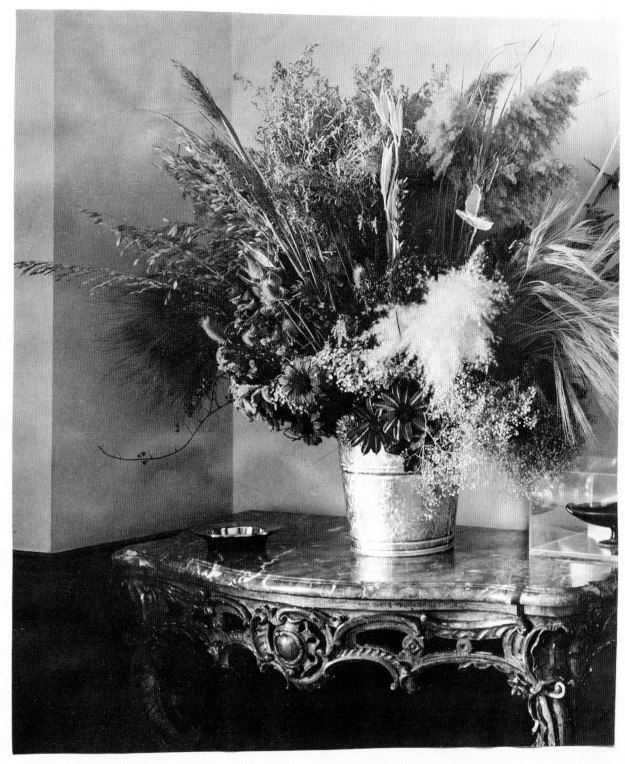

from 'Flowers and Plants in the House'

He showed her round the palace ('sub-Hicks, good Harrods, but if I'd had to do up an old monastery on a Lebanese hill top I couldn't have done it better myself.')

Shirley Conran : Observer

Among those displaying their talents were London's trend setter, David Hicks;

ref to S.F. show

LADY PAMELA MOUNTBATTEN was 18 when the Queen and Prince Philip married. She is Prince Philip's cousin and the younger daughter of the then Viscount and Viscountess Mountbatten. She was lady-in-waiting on the Queen's tour of Australia and New Zealand in 1953-54.

In 1960 Lady Pamela married interior designer David Hicks at Romsey Abbey in Hampshire, not far from the Mountbatten family home, Broadlands, where the Queen had spent part of her honeymoon.

Lady Pamela's mother died a few weeks after the wedding, leaving her two daughters a joint inheritance of something like $400,000 from a trust which had been set up for Countess Mountbatten by her grandfather, Edwardian financier Sir Ernest Cassel.

Lady Pamela and David Hicks have three children — Edwina, 12, Ashley, 10, and India, 6. They have three homes — one in Chelsea, one in Oxfordshire, and a villa in the south of France.

Lady Pamela, like most women close to the Royal family, is patron, president or chairman of a host of committees and organisations but says she is "quite content to stay in the country and read".

market

Hicks at Harmony

For Harmony Carpets, David Hicks has designed the first major collection since his geometric floor coverings started something of a trend following their debut at the 979 Third Avenue showroom in New York. ("That was eight years ago," says Hicks. "Six," says Harmony president Bernie Siegel. They settle on splitting the difference). Although occasional additions have supplemented the Hicks designs over the intervening years, the current collection is markedly different, relying on relief and texture variance rather than contrasting colors for visual impact. Said to employ a patented production technique, the all-wool floor coverings—available as carpets or rugs, with or without borders—consist of five designs, all with biblical names, and each in seven colorways or custom coloration. Several utilize only one color yet are precisely defined through high-low delineations, others combine vivid hues which still further heighten the three-dimensional quality. According to Hicks, the manufacturing process went through a two-year development stage, and makes possible considerable cost reduction. *circle 545*

Delilah from Harmony

Abraham from Harmony

BELOW RIGHT: *Mr. David and Lady Pamela Hicks at a preview of the exhibition of paintings and sculptures from the Spanish March Foundation Collection which was held at the Marlborough Galleries.*

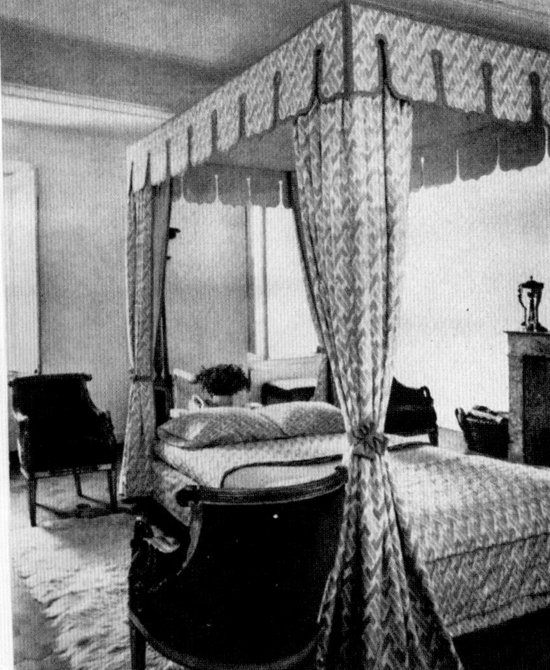

Geometric-patterned sheets, designed by David Hicks for Stevens-Utica, cover the freestanding four-poster in Hicks' French Riviera home, left. The sheets are used for quilted coverlet, pillowcases, and bed valance and draperies. Empire chairs surround French-style bed.

NORTH CHOIR — Mr. David Hicks — Q.55 FRONT ROW

WESTMINSTER ABBEY

MEMORIAL SERVICE

for

HIS MAJESTY THE KING OF SWEDEN

Friday, 5th October, 1973 at 12 noon

ENTRANCE
GREAT WEST DOOR

ERIC S. ABBOTT,
Dean.

Ticket Holders are requested to be seated by 11.45 a.m.

Lady Zia Wernher on Westminster A

me meet Mr. David Hicks, one of the world's most fascinating and most respected leaders in the art of interior design!

He'll be in our new Custom Carpeting Gallery Wednesday and Thursday, March 27th and March 28th, from noon through three...and he'll **autograph** any one (or all) of his beautiful books on decoration.

While he puts his "David Hicks" on his books, we'll show you his superb new collection of carpets. which, incidentally, you will be able to order for your home or office **"sans"** a decorator.

However, we all know that some people feel more secure (and well they should) in the hands of an experienced decorator. So if you feel just so, we'll **introduce** you to one of Altman's specialists in this field of design and décor. He'll be most happy to help you with colorings, patterns and particular projects.

Of course, if you are a **devotee** of the decorative world, you already know that Mr. Hicks made history with his ingenious **geometric** carpet patterns, and the stir it caused in the carpet world is a major design influence. In this new collection he gently moves away from the bolder geometrics to a more fluid design and a much softer palette.

David Hicks was really one of the very first to concentrate on mixing periods and mixing fabrics. He has such a **keen eye** and such sure and convincing judgment in décor that he has become the "decorator's decorator."

His decorating practice ranges from the United Nations Plaza to Johannesburg and from Cap D'Antibes to the China Museum at Windsor Castle. In fact, a very famous prince (now traveling about our country) has a beautiful new bedroom designed by Mr. Hicks.

a pagina precedente un'immagine nostro ospite ed una panoramica a settecentesca villa rittwell Salomè.

In questa pagina il maggiordomo italiano Vincenzo Campagna con i tovaglioli per la colazione (li sa comporre in ventidue modi diversi), la sala da pranzo e cinque immagini di David Hicks mentre controlla la disposizione dei posti a tavola, nel suo studio, durante la colazione con i suoi ospiti e nel soggiorno.

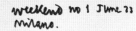

weekend no 1 June 73
Milano.

Security fit for a lord

The show goes on . . . Lord Mountbatten listening as his new role is announced yesterday

By Jack Hill

DETECTIVES searched 4,000 guests yesterday at a ceremony involving the Queen's uncle, Earl Mountbatten.

Police feared I.R.A. reprisals as he was installed as Lord Lieutenant of the Isle of Wight where martyred hunger striker Michael Gaughan died last week in Parkhurst Jail.

Handbags and pockets were checked as V.I.P. ticket-holders arrived for the colourful ceremony at ancient Carisbrooke Castle, two miles from the prison.

And plain-clothes men searched the rambling castle and its ground before Earl Mountbatten arrived to receive his letters patent.

Holidaymakers were banned from the castle during the ceremony.

No reasons were given for the intensive security screening, but an island official at the ceremony said: "It is an obvious sequel to the Parkhurst I.R.A. affair."

Lady Pamela Hicks, her husband David and son Ashley were there to see her father installed as the first Lord Lieutenant of the island which gained county status in April.

Strike

Meanwhile, in Parkhurst, former bus conductor Frank Stagg who joined Gaughan on his 67-day fast, continued to gain strength after ending his strike at the weekend.

● JAILED hunger strikers do not have public sympathy, according to a poll published today by the Opinion Research Centre.

It finds that seven out of 10 people say the Government should not act on demands by prisoners "deliberately endangering their lives."

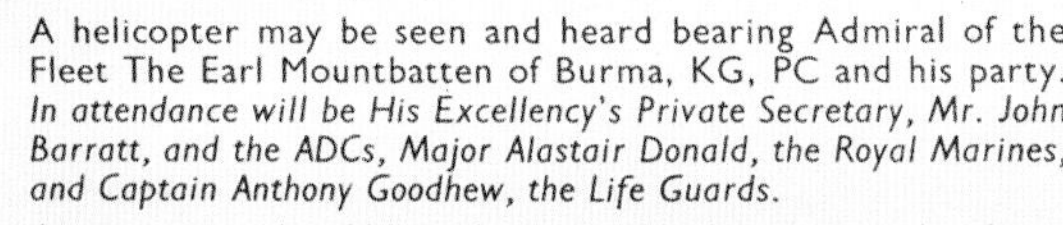

2.15 p.m. A helicopter may be seen and heard bearing Admiral of the Fleet The Earl Mountbatten of Burma, KG, PC and his party. *In attendance will be His Excellency's Private Secretary, Mr. John Barratt, and the ADCs, Major Alastair Donald, the Royal Marines, and Captain Anthony Goodhew, the Life Guards.*

Accompanying Lord Mountbatten will be his younger daughter, the Lady Pamela Hicks, her husband, Mr David Hicks, and their son, Ashley Hicks.

flying from Britwell

in a Queen's Flight helicopter

to Broadlands and then the Isle of Wight

Staying with the Buccleuchs

June

leaving Horseguards after the T

(H.M. Queen Elizabeth and the P

"Oxford" paper designed by David Hicks for Coloroll, £2·75 roll. Paint, Bronze Olive from Spectrum range by Sandersons

TARASCON
6 SYMONS STREET, LONDON SW3
(01 730 6571)

This is one of the prettiest restaurants to open recently. Decoration is by David Hicks and Mary Fox Linton—and there is no mistaking the designers' touch. The walls are covered with a decorative blue-and-white fabric and are hung with blue-and-white plates. The steel lamps on the tables are some of the most attractive designs I have seen, although I still think there is nothing to beat the flattering light of candles in tall glass holders.

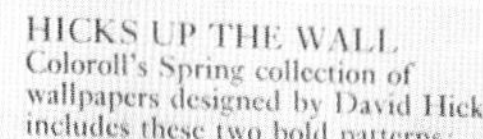

HICKS UP THE WALL

Coloroll's Spring collection of wallpapers designed by David Hicks includes these two bold patterns: Yorkshire and Northumberland. The collection features 16 designs and costs £2·50 a roll from Coloroll stockists throughout the country.

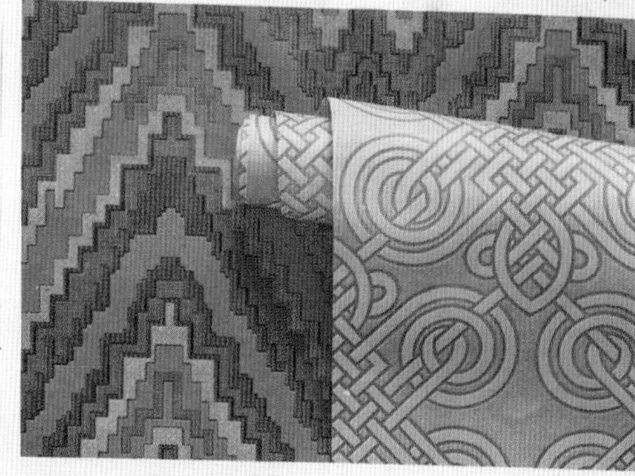

21st 22nd August

the Drawing room at Birr

THE DAILY
TELEGRAPH
MAGAZINE

INTERIOR DECORATION

David Hicks, one of the ultimate arbiters of taste, can ask £300 an hour for consultation. But what can an interior decorator do that you cannot?

Number 498 May 24 1974

Paper, Paint and Professionalism

Anybody can buy wallpaper, order curtains, find a painter in the telephone book. Why employ a stranger to plan and supervise the redecoration of your house or flat? What can an interior decorator do that you cannot? And surely he will charge a fortune? SELINA HASTINGS browses through a range of those who have made interior decoration their business – from international figures like David Hicks to the gifted amateur with confidence and flair. Photographs by GEG GERMANY

David Hicks, *arbiter elegantiae* of interior decorating, (above) discusses with a client final adjustments to his work. "I see myself as an interpreter of taste," he says, "although of course everything I do must be acceptable to me aesthetically."

ussé

If the first is the alternative preferred, then what you need is a great deal of money and a man like David Hicks, decorator and product designer.

HANDSOME and self-assured, David Hicks is the *arbiter elegentiae* of house decorating; but he is also, with his organisation, an interior designer of many restaurants, hotels and offices as well as a product designer. In this last role he has recently designed nine ranges of carpets and a collection of wallpapers. In the past he has designed men's ties, sheets, tiles and tablemats.

Much of his interior decorating is conducted by remote control, sometimes without even meeting the client or seeing the house – for he has associates for this private work in London, Paris, Geneva, Madrid, Sydney, Brussels and New York. This is not as impersonal as it sounds. Hicks always insists that the clients must already feel a sympathy for the Hicks look, otherwise they would not have asked for the associate's help. He also insists that a thorough brief be taken of the clients' existing possessions and of *their* likes and dislikes.

But, whenever possible, he likes to attend the initial meeting himself, either at Elystan Street in Chelsea, rue de Tournon in Paris or in the other cities where he is represented. The client gets a card showing all the colours to be used in adjacent rooms so that he has an overall picture before he commits himself. For larger projects his head office, at 43 Conduit Street in London, produces coloured perspective drawings; but there is a rejection fee if the scheme is not embarked upon for any reasons.

His newest venture is into architecture, designing medium-priced houses to counteract the bungaloid works which, he feels, disfigure the English landscape.

Except when given *carte blanche* in an hotel or restaurant, David Hicks is continually trying to fuse what his client wants with his own inspiration. "I see myself as an interpreter but everything I do must be acceptable to me aesthetically. If somebody said, 'I insist on using cut-glass vases with gladioli in them,' I would say, 'Well, *yes*, but we can't just take *ordinary* cut-glass vases, we must go to Steuben and have them made square with geometrical patterns on the side, and we'll take the gladioli and pick the flowers off and float them so they look like sweets in a box.' "

David Hicks levies a flat rate consultation fee of £300 an hour, whether or not his ideas are then carried out. But he is famous for being able to compose the scheme of an entire house within that time. If he is called abroad – to Switzerland for the day, for example – there is a minimum charge of £500 plus expenses. A room may come to £1,200, or more, according to the time spent upon it.

When you consult David Hicks you are buying the Hicks style, almost the Hicks way of life.

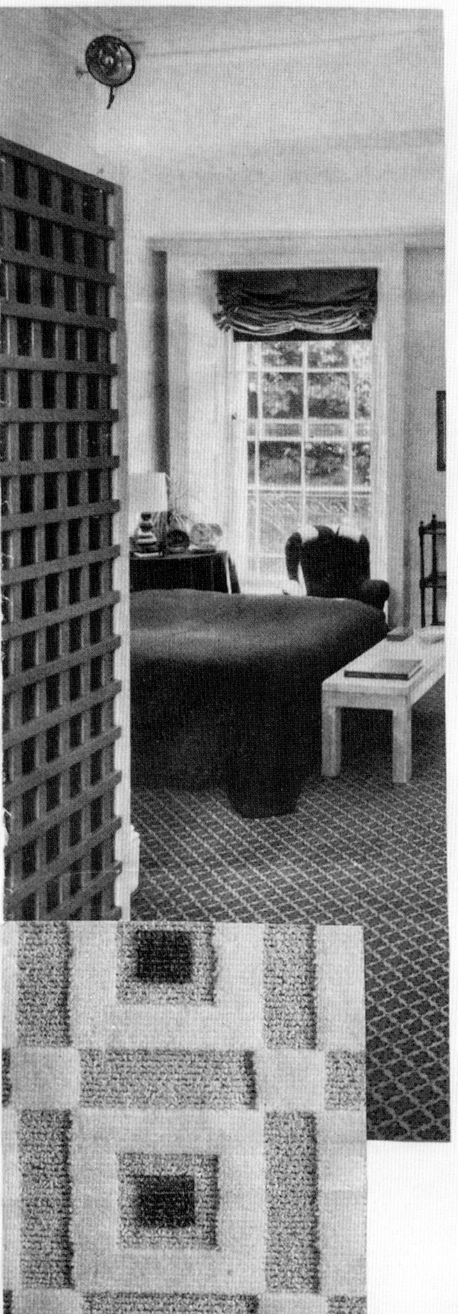

It is interesting to see what furnishings and decorations a well known restaurateur chooses, particularly when he has worked closely with David Hicks. Mr. Geoffrey Clarke, who owns The Grange restaurant, divides his time between a converted oasthouse in Kent and a Georgian house in a fashionable London square.

U IS FOR U AND NON-U, of which the latter is having zips not buttons on trousers, men wearing rings (except signet on left hand), catching non-specific uteritis, belonging to the Army and Navy (or even shopping there), David Hicks, feeling shame or guilt over anything, and mooring one's cabin cruiser at Kingston.

taste. .

David Hicks, interior designer, England: Taste means selection, decision, and sensitivity. Some of the best rooms I know are in such differing environments as 19th-century attics, stately homes, and 20th-century boxes—taste and selection make them great.

BED & BATH

Simple architectural look keynotes this bedroom, below, and adjoining bathroom, right, by Designers David Hicks and Robert Stokes. Colored with neutrals and pastels, the bedroom is serene, soothing, and simple—no lamps, no curtains, no frills. The sleek bathroom, too, has few accessories. A ceiling-high sliver of mirror is the focal point

PHOTOGRAPHS RIGHT AND BELOW BY HANS NAMUTH; OTHERS, GEORGE R. SZANIK

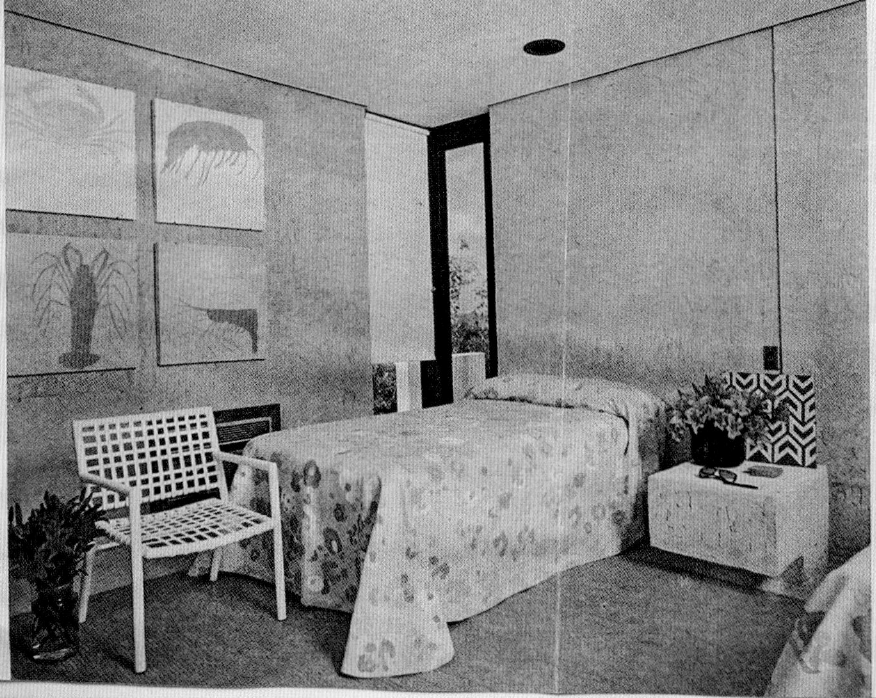

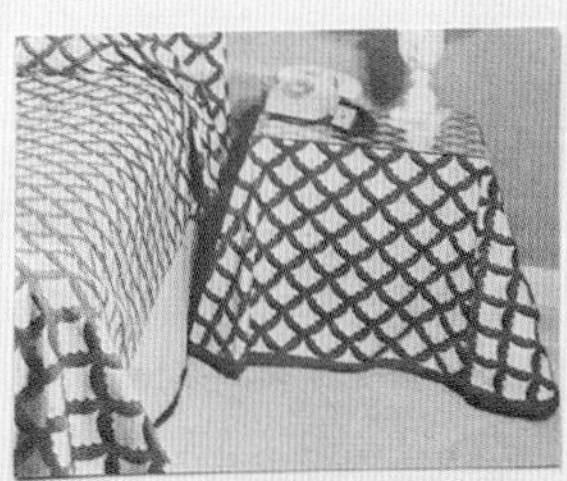

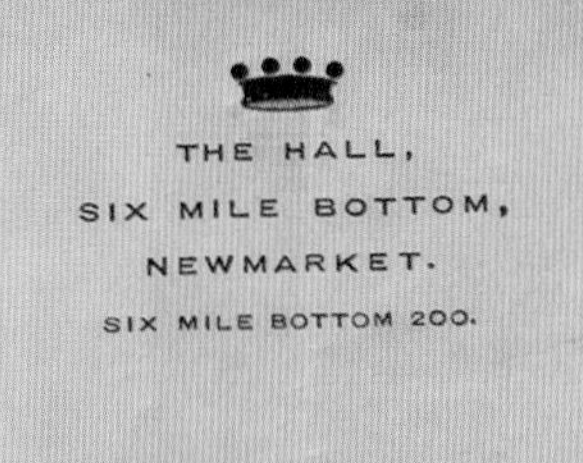

THE HALL,
SIX MILE BOTTOM,
NEWMARKET.
SIX MILE BOTTOM 200.

Shooting lunch with Aunt Mary

Prince of Wales's birthday photograph wearing DH tie.

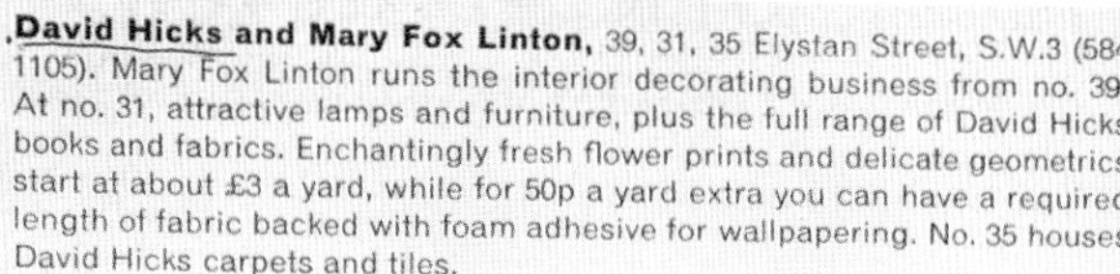

David Hicks and Mary Fox Linton, 39, 31, 35 Elystan Street, S.W.3 (584 1105). Mary Fox Linton runs the interior decorating business from no. 39. At no. 31, attractive lamps and furniture, plus the full range of David Hicks books and fabrics. Enchantingly fresh flower prints and delicate geometrics start at about £3 a yard, while for 50p a yard extra you can have a required length of fabric backed with foam adhesive for wallpapering. No. 35 houses David Hicks carpets and tiles.

As a result, he now lives austerely on Manhattan's East Side. The tiny, neat enclave ("It's scaled to my size—5′5″") is the epitome of his current philosophy, "Simplify, simplify, simplify!" The L-shaped room, painted a shiny brown that appears black at night, is sparsely furnished with two large sofas (one of which, tucked in an alcove, serves as a bed), several slipper chairs and a few choice antiques. All of the furniture is covered in plain white linen and cotton. It is, says a fellow decorator, England's David Hicks, "an homage to paranoid neatness—reflected in mirrors and seen three times over!"

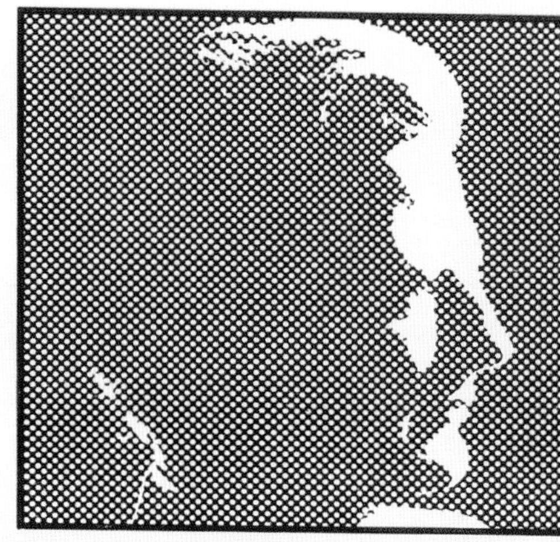

deux hommes

DAVID HICKS

ALPHONSE CATRY

une collection

En exclusivité pour la France, la Suisse et la Belgique, nous vous présenterons les moquettes à motifs créées par le grand Designer de renommée internationale :

DAVID HICKS

ARDI 17 DÉCEMBR
MERCREDI 18 DÉC

Un événeme
dans la décora

OLIVIER SEG

SCULPTEUR

DAVID HICKS

CRÉATEUR DESIGNER

allié leur art pour présenter
oquettes contemporaines éditées p

LPHONSE CATR

de 10 h. à 20 h. sans interruption

ALERIE ST-GERMAI

206, boulevard Saint-Germain, Paris

Réalisation : J.-P. TRACHIER - C. BABERT

24 PAULTONS HOUSE
PAULTONS SQUARE
LONDON SW3 5DU
01 351 0088

Alphonse CATRY a choisi le sculpteur Olivier SEGUIN . . .

pour présenter les nouvelles créations en moquettes de David HICKS, alliant la sculpture contemporaine au sol.

Il vous prie de lui faire l'honneur d'assister au vernissage de cette exposition franco-anglaise qui aura lieu le lundi 16 Décembre 1974 à 18h précises.

Galerie St Germain, 206 Boulevard St Germain, PARIS 6e.

En présence de David HICKS et sous la gracieuse présidence effective de

Lady PAMELA HICKS

Réalisation J.P TRACHIER . Caroline BABERT

Keeping Design Internationalism in Line

'It used to be, remember, that you could wake up in a hotel room, look at the walls, the ceiling and floor and know instantly that this is France, Germany, England.

By Jan Sjoby

BRUSSELS (IHT).—David Hicks, 45, British designer, admits that he is a man of contradiction: He laments the continuing process of internationalization in the applied arts, yet he jets around the world building an international network of internationally recognized interior designers.

"We can't beat the trend," he said, "we have to join. The mass media are bringing American culture to Europe, Indian culture to the States, Euro-American trends to the Far East. What we *can* do is to try to keep this new international culture developing in a graceful, tasteful manner."

Mr. Hicks, in Brussels for the opening of his Belgian branch in the Rue de la Concorde, designs for the high and the mighty. But, contradicting the record again, he maintains that he works primarily for the regular fellow, for John Doe and Monsieur Dubois.

"Look," said Nicole Cooremans, one of Mr. Hicks's Belgian associates, "we'll provide interior design for your Renaissance castle—if you have one—or we'll sell you a Christmas present for 300 Belgian francs and upward. The price of the product may differ but they have one thing in common: taste, by contemporary standards."

Stage Design

Mr. Hicks, a former student at the London Council School of Arts and Crafts, graduated in stage design.

"Interior design is the art of accomplishing a maximum with a minimum," he said.

"The important thing, as I see it, is to try to bring good taste to everyone, regardless of race, creed and income bracket." Mr. Hicks, at times, sounds like a sophisticated revival preacher.

"Regardez," said Mrs. Cooremans, holding a piece of wallpaper behind a sofa. "See how the design matches, how the colors harmonize."

"We consider color and texture most important," she continued. "Look at the carpeting, raise your eyes to the easy chair. The one goes with the other, *n'est-ce pas?"*

"In addition," said Mr. Hicks, "we try to mix psychology with interior design. We want to keep the setting in tune with the personality of the customer."

Contradiction again: Mr. Hicks appears to have a penchant for ultramodern geometric forms and square plastic tables. He talks about a "geometric revolution." But it seems that he almost always manages to include a piece or two from the past. An authentic Buddha may be next to a set of flowers, live or dried, and some geometric wooden sculptures in one of his "tablescapes."

Mr. Hicks has "overseas" (as the British call it) associates and offices/showrooms/shops in Madrid, Geneva and Paris. He plans to open in Amsterdam and Copenhagen and he is negotiating in New York and Tokyo.

National Trend

"All our showrooms are different in style, type and design," Mr. Hicks emphasized. "Our Paris showroom [in the Rue de Tournon, near the Luxembourg] is entirely different from our Madrid or Brussels locales. We try to keep a national trend in the international tide.

"We have been overrun, on a worldwide scale, with American influence," he said. "It used to be, remember, that you could wake up in a hotel room, look at the walls, the ceiling and the floor and know instantly that this is France, Germany, England . . . I and my associates would like to return progressively to that stage."

Alain V. d. Bussche

David Hicks with personalized tie.

Mr. Hicks is married to a former Lady Mountbatten.

"How can regular-weekly-paycheck people afford your services?" he was asked. "We try to make sure they can," Mr. Hicks said. "It is a question of diffusion. We aren't exclusively in the carriage trade."

Mr. Hicks pointed at his white-on-blue tie. "Look," he said, "at the geometric design. You can make out an 'H' for H in Hicks and an 'x' for 'icks'. We design ties for people with names ranging from A to Z."

"Do you plan to get into fashion design?" asked a reporter for a Brussels homes-and-gardens weekly. "Eventually," he said. "The Japanese want to dress like Europeans, but their legs are too short. The Europeans want kimonos, but their backs are too broad. I'd like to work that equation out."

Book on Bathrooms

Mr. Hicks is the author of five volumes on graceful living and interior design. One of the books is on bathrooms, a badly neglected sector, in his opinion.

A Hicks-designed bathroom is likely to have wall-to-wall carpeting, pictures on the walls, a television set and telephone. The tub, very likely, will be placed in the middle of the room, for easy access.

"You started out as a stage designer," he was asked. "Have you done any scenography?"

"No," said Mr. Hicks, "but I'd love to set the stage for a Wagner opera at the Metropolitan. I'm a Wagner fan and I'd do it more or less for kicks if they asked me."

"You spend a lot of time in the air," a journalist said. "How do you find time to work between London, New York, Tokyo and Brussels?"

"I spend two or three months each year relaxing in the south of France," he said. "Then I have my farm [1,600 acres of cattle and wheat land] near Oxford. There I manage to find time for thinking and doodling. I am basically a farmer at heart."

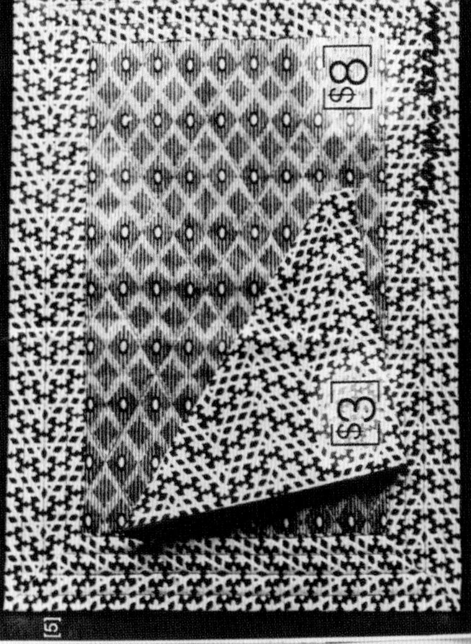

Call them team-ups, match-makers, near relations. In furnishing, no less than in fashion, one can mix and match with merchandise that has been designed specifically to co-ordinate. Thus we often see quite disparate manufacturers linking their separate skills to give us that coveted "total" look. On the one hand there is the grand design of carpet-teamed-wallpaper, teamed-fabric with parts of the same design repeated in different scale throughout (vide David Hicks)

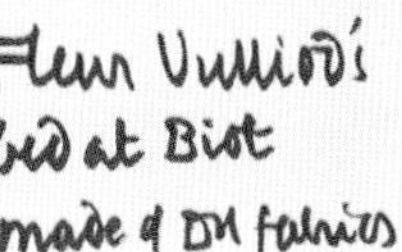

Fleur Vulliod's
bed at Biot
made of DH fabrics

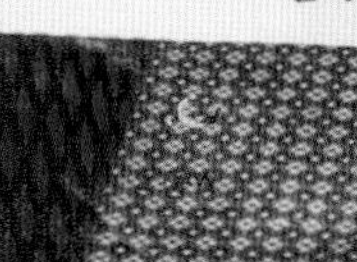

DH carpet

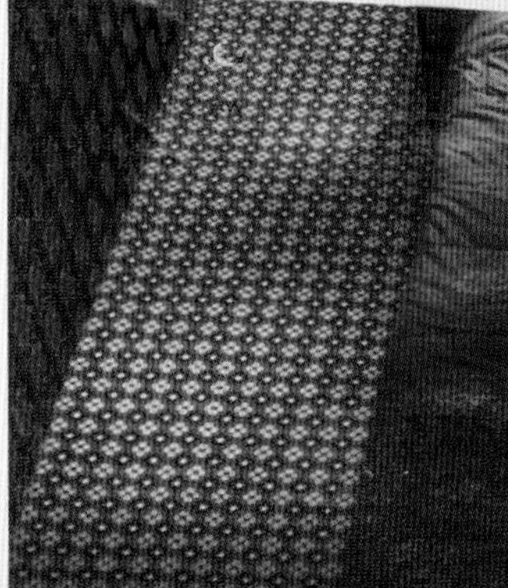

moquettes David Hicks
éditées par A. Catry

WHO WORE WHAT WHERE

Coronation in Kathmandu

Prince Charles and Admiral of the Fleet Earl Mountbatten of Burma

The King and Queen of Nepal and 4-year-old Crown Prince Dipendra. Nepalese girls, *below left*, welcoming Prince Charles with flowers; the Maharajah and Maharanee of Jaipur, *centre*, with the Maharajah and Maharanee of Jodhpur; and, *right*, the Crown Prince and Princess of Japan

David Hicks France - Bayonne
Christian Badin décorateur

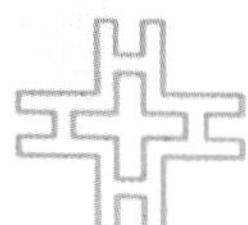

David Hicks France à Bayonne

David Hicks, Marion Hostein et Christian Badin
seraient heureux de vous recevoir
le Jeudi 18 Septembre 1975 à l'occasion
de l'ouverture de la Boutique David Hicks France
à Bayonne, chez Niéto.

RSVP
Niéto Place de Gaulle 64104 Bayonne

17 h à 20 h

Nieto Place de Gaulle 64104 Bayonne
Magasin (59) 25 02 28 Bureaux 63 01 45

David Hicks . . . "everybody should have beauty."

It's Mr Geometric

ARRIVAL—3 **Jane Fraser**

THE revolution is here — the geometric revolution in interior design and decor. And Mr Geometric himself, David Hicks, is in South Africa to see it launched.

Author, innovator in his field, debonair, erudite and impeccable to the tips of his manicured finger-nails, Mr Hicks arrived in Johannesburg yesterday, in time for the opening of David Hicks, South Africa — his newest shop, first in South Africa and seventh in the world.

David Hicks has become a by-word in the upper echelons of European society. He has designed rooms for Prince Charles and Princess Anne at Buckingham Palace, "done" the Marchioness of Londonderry's house, worked for the Soviet and Algerian governments by designing their airline offices in London, and, when he leaves here he's off to finish the Shah of Persia's palace on the Caspian Sea.

He also does designs for council houses.

But the message David Hicks brought here is that he is launching a whole new range of his products, including silk ties and scarves and an entirely new design in kitchen-ware.

He describes himself as an interior designer and interior decorator — yes, there is a difference. An interior decorator does private homes — with the odd palace or two thrown in — and an interior designer designs offices, hotels and government houses.

David Hicks is also a product designer, which is where the ties, scarves, kitchenware, sheets and shoes come in. One of his latest innovations has been in Japan where the men are now sporting black-and-white geometric umbrellas, and the women softer, more feminine ones with a flowing design.

This man who has so successfully captured the mood of the mid-seventies is also a family man. It is hardly surprising to know that David Hicks is on first-name terms with royalty.

His wife is the former Lady Pamela Mountbatten, daughter of Earl Mountbatten of Burma, Admiral of the Fleet, ex-Viceroy and first Governor-General of India. They have three children.

David Hicks is determined that his talents be channelled into the mass market.

"It's not fair," he said, "that only the wealthy should have beauty in their homes. Everybody should have it, and I'm going to do my best to see that they can get it."

1

2

The opening of David Hicks South Africa, in Rosebank, Johannesburg. 1 Mrs Carel Lion-Cachet, Mr David Hicks, Mrs Toinon Panchaud and Mr André Louw. 2 Mr Howard Cohen and Mr Len Miller.

I had three appointments in Johannesburg – to see David Hicks South Africa, to visit Mrs Doris Trace, and to meet Mrs Malcolm McLean. I was met at Jan Smuts Airport by Miss Rosemary Bennett, a charming young lady who had just started working at David Hicks South Africa; as I had labelled my luggage through to London from Cape Town, we were able to go off without delay. We drove straight to 173 Oxford Road, Rosebank, one of the chic shopping centres of Johannesburg, where the David Hicks South Africa double-fronted shop which opened recently while Mr David Hicks was present, stands out in its elegance. It is run jointly by Mrs Carel Lion-Cachet, who was there to greet me, and Mr André Louw, who worked with David Hicks in London for three years. I did not meet André Louw as he was away on a few days holiday. Monique Lion-Cachet, who is young and most attractive, took me round and I saw far too many pretty and useful things to mention them all. But I am sure many house-proud families living in and around this great city will be delighted to be able to have their houses really attractively decorated, and to buy at this shop so many lovely things from all over the world.

Among items that caught my eye were glasses from Biot, plates and dishes in Capis shell from the Philippines, a very practical perspex make-up-bath tray, which I was told one can buy in David Hicks shop in London; rather pricey exquisitely painted ostrich eggs, which make beautiful ornaments; most attractive fabric covered glass-top tables of all sizes; a variety of door handles, American card lampshades, a good selection of lovely lamps from England; chairs and sofas covered in French chintz; a large selection of patterns of David Hicks carpets that can be made locally to the correct measurements; a wide selection of really super furnishing fabrics, an enchanting four-poster bed, with green French cotton hangings lined with snow white glazed chintz, and a snow white quilted glazed chintz bed cover; and lastly I noticed some copies of David Hicks' very instructive book *David Hicks on Decoration-5*, published by Britwell Press. Monique Lion-Cachet, whose husband Carel has a financial interest in the shop, can for the present only work here part-time as they have two little daughters Jackie and Tracey who go to school in the mornings. But she has a very efficient staff at the shop whom I noticed looking after the many shoppers who came in while I was going round, and who, I noted, were buying and not just looking! It should be a great success.

From here Monique Lion-Cachet kindly ran me in her car to call on Mrs Doris Trace, a very old friend who lives quite near, in a new building of cleverly designed small modern apartments. I was able to spend nearly an hour catching up on all her news since I was last in Johannesburg in 1969.

MEN WHO ARRANGE FLOWERS

(Photo: Michael Boys)

David Hicks

I first met David Hicks in Australia. He was to give a talk on interior design in a Sydney store, but alas, the necessary settings had not arrived. Undaunted, he threw some soft carpets across a few tables with a panache that has now become expected of him, and in a few minutes the audience had become entranced with all he had to say.

Some years later I asked him to help me on a Forces Help Society Luncheon and, on the day, he hurriedly brought in a cylinder-shaped vase, and stuffed it full of what I think were mauve Alliums, or they could have been chives. It was certainly original, though not according to the one, two, three method. Soon he was off, for Mr Hicks is a very busy man.

Whenever he is at home and not on one of his international design travels, he arranges the flowers in his country house in Oxfordshire. He likes concentrating on one colour to achieve what he thinks is maximum effect. He prefers flowers tightly stuffed into simple containers, rather than large romantic arrangements.

He published a book *David Hicks on Bathrooms,* and likes his clients to have bathrooms large enough to have plants or flower arrangements in them. He says this gives life to an otherwise dull room. I agree with him, for although my bathroom isn't all that large I have shelves of plants separating the 'you know what' from the bath. His latest book is *David Hicks on Decoration – 5.*

He is just off to the USA with his wife, Lady Pamela, to introduce new designs for decoration, and I noticed in them most of the glorious colours he likes such as pale apricot, blackberry, ginger, sharp greens and warm browns.

When I asked him if there were any flowers he liked or disliked, he answered without hesitation that he doesn't like Gladioli, Bougainvillea and Polyantha roses.

A man of decision and action is David Hicks, you can tell it in his flower arrangements.

Julia Clements

Next issue: Cyril Fletcher

David Hicks Mary Fox Linton
1, 35 & 39 Elystan St, S.W.3; 581 2188. No 39 is where it all began and where David Hicks has his interior decorating offices. The carpet, tile and matting shop is at 35. At 1, the David Hicks fabrics and wallpapers, made-to-order blinds and lampshades, cushions, quilted table linen, presents, occasional pieces of furniture.

DAVID HICKS is one of the best-known interior decorators on the international scene today. Not only can his distinctive style be seen in houses, hotels, restaurants and offices from London to Tokyo, but his five books on decorating have brought him into the lives of everyone interested in interiors, whether amateur or professional

Mr Hicks was in South Africa last week to open the latest David Hicks shop, in Rosebank, Johannesburg — his fifth outside England.

His associates, from Paris, Brussels and Switzerland. had come with him to wish the new venture well, and all pronounced themselves delighted with the cool, airy shop in the newly-built mews.

David Hicks, South Africa, has been started by Monique Lion-Cachet and Andre Louw, who worked with David Hicks in London for four years.

Together, they're all rather like a family, deeply involved, with Andre and Monique, the welcome new additions.

"Each shop, though basically Hicks, has its own special identity," said David. "We all learn a lot from each other."

Meeting him, among a scurry of workers unpacking crates — wearing white gloves, no less, while they did so — it is easy to see what brought him right up top.

You are aware of total concentration, whether he is hanging a picture or positioning an ashtray.

Distinctively David Hicks . . . A simple double divan is transformed into a glamorous four-poster by hanging fabric from a tester, attached by chains to the ceiling.

S.A. Sunday Times Magazine.
November 30th 1975.

Kings College Hospital— Dining Room

Floor: This is close carpeted throughout with a Wilton grade, David Hicks geometric design, produced to the architects' specification of tan, brown and cream, by Crossley Carpets.

Paris

David Hicks en Rhodésie...

■ Après Rolle en Suisse, Londres, Madrid, Paris, Bruxelles, Amsterdam et Bayonne, le décorateur David Hicks ouvre sa 9e boutique à Johannesburg le 20 novembre. Elle sera dirigée par son ancien assistant à Londres, André De V. Louw et par Monique Lion-Cachet. A l'intérieur, tout le « style Hicks » *illustration : un salon très caractéristique, composé dans sa boutique parisienne l'an passé,* avec ses objets préférés, ceux qu'il sélectionne, ceux qu'il dessine (moquettes, cravates, etc.) et quelques nouveautés fabriquées sur place.

Pascal Hinous

David Hicks, 173 Oxford Rd., Rosebank, Jhb. Run under franchise of the London company: • Hicks' famous glazed chintzes (R13,50 a metre) and French cotton (R18,50). • Magnificent colour co-ordinating and quilting (headlines in London) done for you. • Green and white, quilted four poster with 70m of ebullient curtaining – R2 000. • Quilted 2-seater chintz couches, R645. • Vivid plastic envelopes, R9,50 – to fill with original and elegant Hicks stationery. • Asbestos circlets that fit on electric light bulbs – sprinkle them with a drop of Jasmin, Sandalwood or Hyacinth, and the heat gently vaporises the smell. The whole kit – R6. •

A KING AMONG INTERIOR DECORATORS

World-famous English interior decorator, David Hicks has recently opened a superb shop in Johannesburg's Rosebank — his first in South Africa. It's a cool haven from the hot, dusty heat of the city in summer. White ceramic tiles cover the floor and the furnishings are cool acid green and white, cream, pastels and ice-cream colours. Fabrics are mostly smooth glazed cottons — in fact everything gives a feeling of coolness.

As Mr Hicks put it: "The first and most important consideration when planning interior design is the climatic condition. Red velvet upholstery and deep pile carpets are ideal for a cosy atmosphere in northern Europe, but for a summer place in South Africa, they're totally unsuitable.

"I have been commissioned to design interiors all over the world and whether it's New York, Paris or Ankara, I always adapt my style to suit the climate."

What does he think of our local interior design?

"I love the Cape Dutch homes and I admire the work of Imré Loerinz as a classical decorator, although his style is completely different from mine."

Apart from his distinctive style of decorating interiors, David Hicks has designed a range of kitchenware which will shortly be available throughout the Republic. He has also designed men's ties which are obtainable from his Rosebank shop. And to bring a little Hicks atmosphere into your home, he has compiled and published four books: *David Hicks On . . . Decoration With Fabrics, Decoration; Bathrooms* and *David Hicks On Living With Taste,* price R13,80 each.

Sir James, Nicolea Lady Bottomley.

DH

Connaisance des Arts Jan 76

R.S.A. Jl.

R.S.A. journal.

South African 'Habitat'

DAVID HICKS IN PROFILE

at work at 9 Grosvenor Gardens SW1.

A self-confessed magnet — he attracts requests from all over the world, to open his shops. A perfectionist, he is totally dedicated to his work and is totally stimulating if exhausting to be with.

Spare body, definite features, greying hair brushed back and amused, calculating blue eyes all spell energy, perspicacity, authority. This is David Hicks a creative, clever man in full control of his situation and surroundings. He uses his ideas as a bulldozer uses its shovel yet nothing escapes his notice — 'write down everything or you'll forget it'.

Accompanying the charm is a distinct lack of humility — I overheard him relating how a certain English lady had offered to pay for the glory of lunching with him. Fame he obviously enjoys, as he does the company of people of high rank and standing (his anecdotes read like a juicy, social gossip column.) To celebrate the opening of his Paris shop, ninety two people (among whom, of course, were the best names in France) dined at the British Embassy and afterwards rode in a procession of Rolls Royces to the new shop on the left bank where they toasted the occasion with pink champagne.

The Johannesburg opening though perhaps not as sumptuous, was nonetheless an elegant affair worthy of it's predecessors. The fact that next day Hicks at lunch was able to recall, in interesting detail, a large majority of his guests, goes some way to explaining this man's success. During this lunch, where I was the only non-member of the "family" — "London," 'Brussels,' 'Paris,' and 'Geneva' having all gathered in Johannesburg to wish the new baby well — I asked Hicks whether the time and trouble he devoted to his promotions didn't interfere with and distract him from the actual business of designing. He was astounded, 'Of course not. Being present at an opening demands at the most two days flying time besides I adore travelling and learn something from every new place I see. I also have very efficient staff, not only in my shops but in my art department — there I instigate and originate ideas then leave it to my team of art students to do the dogsbody work, once the back of the scheme is broken I check, alter, change or give my stamp and seal of approval, without this nothing, anywhere, goes onto the production line. *No one* may interfere with my designs. The artists job is to interpret — if he thinks he has come up with a mind bender, then he is free to discuss it with me over a drink after working hours'.

His reply to the question of whether he is not diversifying his energies too much, was perhaps predictable, 'Not at all its marvellous to design bikinis for Japanese girls one day, carpets for a London bank another, then devote my attention to decorating a palace in the South of France and after that start thinking about my new range of kitchenware — this way any tendency to staleness is obviated, my mind is kept active and continually on the alert! He pointed to an arrangement of brilliant red and orange flowers blazing from a white table, 'That I did this morning — the colour combinations are splendid, I've noted them and will probably use them for a range of headscarves. Flowers and my children I think are among my favourite things, my next book is about flower arrangment.'

Although Hicks agreed that his work has a very definite stamp, there is a rigid spine that holds it together the result of his respect for discipline (a quality that few people and few places still possess, South Africa in his view counting among these) he would hate to become type-cast. The geometrics for which he became famous some fifteen years ago he still adores, but he is equally fond of florals, curls and arabesques. It was the Americans who first adopted his geometrics with such enthusiasm — everyone who was anyone had to be 'geometricked' by Hicks. Very gratifying, but he admits that the oft repeated request for having, 'My apartment done exactly like the one on page . . . of such and such a glossy' a trifle trying. 'Decorating is a very personal thing, when I do a job I take not only the client's personality and life-style into consideration but also the national and climatic influences. 'There is no way one can put Lady 'Highbottoms' drawing room into an American or South African context and expect it to work'. His other horror is of people who preserve, with reverence, every detail as he created it. He tells the story of an apartment to which he returned three months after completing the job. He found everything, down to the smallest ashtray as he had 'decreed' (discovering afterwards that the positions had been carefully marked with white paint). Even the pink carnations were still in evidence — despite the passing of the seasons.

That certain people have come to use his name purely for its snob value, a kind of social crutch for the clueless, Hicks concedes, and doesn't mind so much now that his work is encompassing a broader spectrum. 'What I used really to resent was picking up a journal boasting a Hicks interior to find that not only had I never seen it before but that at best it contained a carpet or table of mine'.

David Hicks to all accounts is not financially orientated, several advisors take care of that side of the business, what continued fame really means to him are more scrapbooks. These are his passion — he is on his fourteenth at the moment and says he will one day hand them down to his children.

The opening of David Hicks South Africa should add a new and welcome dimension to decorating in this country. We wish the venture every success and hope it will be worthy of yet another scrapbook. □

Coming from the country of the Queen Elizabeth.

When it comes to fashionable designs over the world, you may think of those of Paris, Rome, and New York quickly.
However, it is London's design that is most respected in the European fashionable design industry for its unique combination of the cherished tradition and the modernism.
In this London's design world, David Hicks is highly regarded as foremost among the prominent British designers.
He, cousin to Queen Elizabeth and designed private suites for the royal family, has started to introduce his sophisticated and fancy works in Japan's design market.

寝装品・インテリア商品のメーカー・問屋である松本繊商（本社・東京、松本栄造社長）は九日、英国王室デザイナーのデービット・ヒックスとライセンス契約を結び、デービット・ヒックスのデザインを取り入れたタオル、寝装品を六月ごろから売り出すことを明らかにした。
寝装品、インテリア業界では、すでにピエール・カルダン、イブ・サンローラン、エマニエル・ウンガロと提携、これらのデザイン商品を販売しているが、デビット・ヒックスは初めて。

デービット・ヒックス氏

同社では、これまで扱ってきたカルダン製品とともに高級寝具のリード役にしたい、としている。
カルダン、サンローラン、ウンガロといった従来のライセンス寝具は服装デ… とり入れた… うとカジュ… に対し、… は、紳士、…

日本的… ブル。…

Elegant Royal fashion for you!

British designer David Hicks has taken an important position in the fashion world of Great Britain. A cousin of Queen Elizabeth II, Hicks designs not only wearing apparel but is also an interior designer/decorator for members of Britain's Royal Family and high society world wide.

Described as his "elegant Royal fashion," Hicks' creations are a combination of his magnificent tastes and refined geometric patterns.

David Hicks

英国王室デザイナー

51年度デービッ

英国王室
陛下のい
がアルフ
模様をネ
につくり
シックな
51年春夏
ル、カー
秋冬にはドレスシャツ、スカーフ、婦人アパレル、寝装品、紳士ソックス、ナイトウェアなどの分野にも進出します。

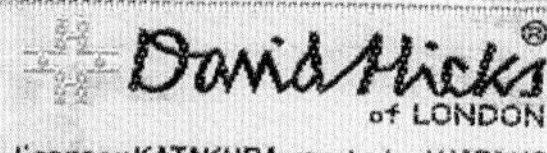

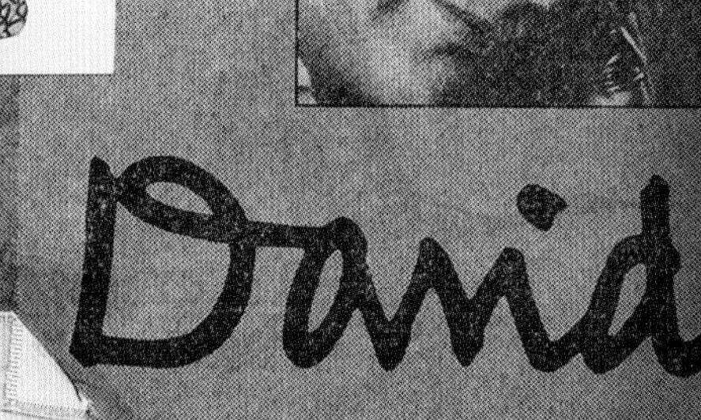

David

David Hicks, a versatile conductor of the beautiful, is now performing in more than 60 nations over the world.

He was born in 1929 in Essex in England and studied the design at London Central Arts and Creation School(literally translated from Japanese).
He established the David Hicks Organization in 1959, and has extended his business beyond his home country into more than 60 nations all over the world, including 15 boutiques in the U.S. and European countries.
His works are famous for his fine combination of cherished British traditional elegance and freely developed esthetic consciousness.
Among others, his unique geometric designs have been attracting lots of people by their flesh sensibility, classical elegance and quiet.
His brilliant reputation is established not only in the world of interior design but in other various fields.
His many-sided esthetic activities are ranging from the design of neck-ties to total interior decorations.
It may be some of reasons for his world-wide reputation as a versatile conductor of the beautiful that he is cousin to Queen Elizabeth and designed various decoration for royal family and homes of famous people in many countries.
From this time on, he will keep the mind of Japanese with his sophisticated fine works.

ファッションというとパリ、ロー

David Hicks

英国王室デザイナー　デービッド・ヒックス

カタクラ
片倉工業株式会社
東京都中央区京橋3-2〒104 TEL.03-281-3161

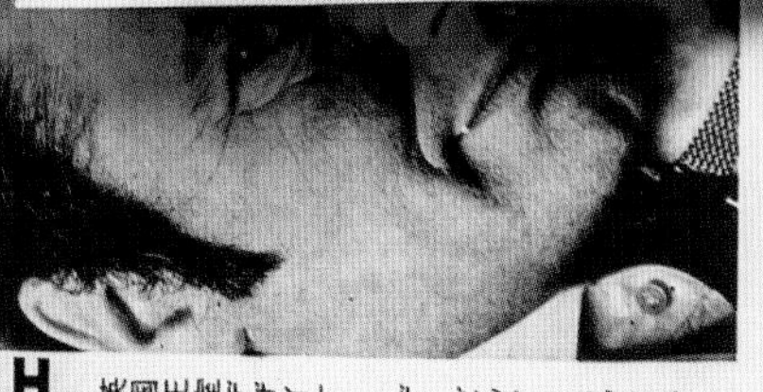

英国王室デザイナー・デービッド・ヒックス

英国王室デザイナー　デービッド・ヒックス

ファッションの世界に、いま華麗なる王室の感覚が。

女王陛下の国から、はじめて
日本にやってきた"デービッド・ヒックス"。
エリザベス女王の近親という名血。
エレガンスな美のコンダクターとして
世界60数ヵ国のステージで
活躍している実績。
その華麗なる美のコンダクターが
いま日本に、
"エレガント ロイヤル ファッション"の
真髄を披露します。

〈ネクタイ〉
渡公ネクタイ
ヤング・エース
〈婦人スカーフ〉〈紳士スカーフ〉
岡島
ムーン・バット
ヤング・エース
〈ハンカチ〉
岡島
シャトー平商
〈鞄・ハンドバック・小物〉
青木
〈傘〉
林道商店
〈タオル・寝装品〉
松本繊商
〈照明器具〉
山田照明
〈紳士セーター〉〈紳士・婦人ソックス〉
片倉工業

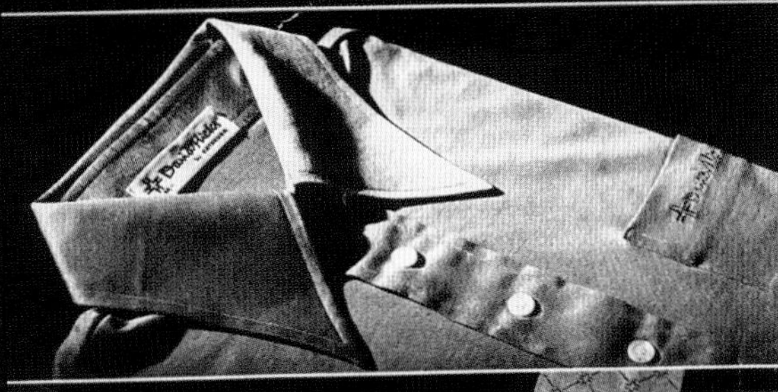

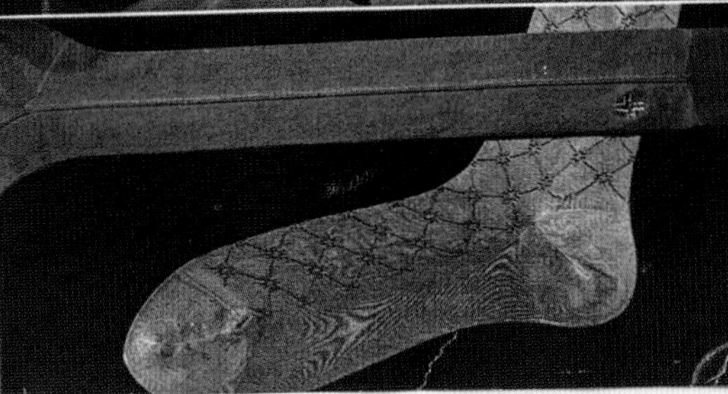

David Hicks
〈デービッドヒックス〉
OF LONDON

日本製
David Hicks
デービッド・ヒックス

David Hicks
デービッド・ヒックス
ENGLAND

DAVID HICKS' LONDON

where his clever design gives the illusion of expanded space

One illustrious interior designer interviews another:
John Siddeley visits David Hicks in his Chelsea flat

Two views of the living room. David Hicks specifically wanted to have only drawings on the walls; most of them are architectural.

PIED-À-TERRE

I have known David Hicks since he went into business with a colleague just around the corner from my own shop. His determination to succeed has been total. This in no way diminishes his talent—which is considerable—but does sometimes tend to alienate others from himself, which is a shame. Famous names roll off his tongue as though they had just left or were about to arrive. One is left breathless and after a while one begins to feel a definite 'jet-lag' and tries a change of conversation. He has charm that switches itself on—and off the moment one treads away from the path he has prepared. Several telephone calls interrupt the interview, which give me a chance to read back what I've written and think up more questions. At the end of the two hours I leave, being thanked and told it has been the funniest interview he has ever been through. I was trying to be serious so maybe some of his replies were quips and not for real. No matter, I enjoyed myself.

Continued overleaf

DAVID HICKS NORWAY A/S

MY DAY

...it stares at me from my black leather, gilt-cornered notepad...

David Hicks hour-by-hour design

My day is finalised by my office the day before and, as I shave at 8.15, it stares at me from my black leather, gilt-cornered notepad—given me by my first client many years ago. It is on a typed card and my next day is almost formulated on the reverse side. Photocopies of these are already with the redoubtable Peter Gutteridge and others. Peter, who has already cleaned the car, pressed my suit and is putting a 2½-minute egg to boil and squeezing a glass of one-third lemon and two-thirds grapefruit juice on the table, then allows me to drive the car—seat belt firmly fastened—to the office at 9.45.

Tea, and I look at the urgent European telexes and the letters to be read today. 10 am, the first appointment arrives. Miss Anthea Questionmark with her portfolio of fascinating but unusable designs—I try to be helpful but if only art schools would instil applicability into their students, though it is still worth seeing every young aspirant.

10.10, we call David Hicks France in Paris to see if the mosquito-man has finally fixed the netting at the Schlumberger house at St Jean Cap Ferrat—if he cannot by the day after tomorrow it is very dubious if we will get the second phase of the job. Detail is of paramount importance in my work, whether it is devising new interiors for motorcars or kitchenware for Metal Box—two important design commissions I am working on now. I am assured by our Alpes Maritimes architect Pierre Fevrier that all is well with the "moustiquiers".

10.12, I talk to Hugh Tunney, who has rented Classiebawn Castle, about the William Morris and Owen Jones wallpapers that I have proposed—both designers were friends of the Ashley Cowpers, so they are very suitable.

More tea at 10.15 and Psyche Pirie comes to see the running proofs of *The David Hicks Book of Flower Arranging* which she will herald, prior to publication, in her magazine.

10.30, a planning meeting with >6

A London drawing-room designed by David Hicks

MY DAY

Japanese telexes...Viennese plans... tomorrow's outline...

Sunflowers and marigolds: from "The David Hicks Book of Flower Arranging" (published September 2, by Marshall Cavendish, £2·95)

<4 my business manager, Leslie Button, financial director, Charles Warden, chief accountant, Peter Nixon, chief designers, Jane Wickens and Jean Pierre Geoffroy, head surveyor, Ron Gee, and quantity surveyor, Brian Street, to discuss the Saudi Arabian project—not large but something that *could* lead to great things. Questions, agreement but research needed. We'll meet again after my second briefing meeting the day after tomorrow. Then we discuss the Quatari Embassy in Paris which we recently completed.

All leave except Leslie who stays to discuss our future policy with Katakura who, he tells me, have now formed "the David Hicks Association of Japanese Manufacturers", fifteen separate and independent companies who want me to get into clothes designs besides luggage, sheets and towels, etc., etc. Very exciting, for ever since I left the Central School of Arts & Crafts I have wanted to be involved in fashion design—but how to get that and all the other products out of Japan and exported to Europe?

We have to break up as I have an 11.15 taping session with Madame Maingard of the University of Paris, with questions from fifteen students. I take them to see a David Hicks house of a Greek client in Chelsea which has still the finishing touches to be put to it.

At 12 I go to see pictures for a client at Christopher Gibbs' Gallery in Bond Street, and look in at the new Midas shoe shop which we are completing. I then see the Managing Director of Bally of Switzerland and see the prototypes of the line of men's evening shoes which they are making to my design. From there I go to 101 Jermyn Street where we shall move our headquarters, and where I shall open my big new shop in November.

I arrive at 79 Chester Square in time for one Bloody Mary before a delicious lunch at which I sit next to the wife of the chairman of the board of one of the biggest American chain stores. More interest again in my Japanese product design.

By 3 o'clock I am back in my refreshingly cool, air-conditioned office and I start to unravel Japanese telexes.

3.45, Tanya von Trauttmansdorff, who will open David Hicks Austria on October 21, blows in—I am always available—to tell me what merchandise she has ordered for the shop in Vienna. More tea.

I drive to London Wall to supervise the hanging of pictures at the Salter's Company of which I am now the Upper Warden. The Salter's Hall is perhaps the best of all Sir Basil Spence's buildings. I then go to see a flat in Eaton Place where the clients want to install air-conditioning and, now that their children are grown up, to re-allocate and redecorate a number of rooms. It is always interesting to go back to my original career although, of course, I can no longer handle the execution myself. It is for that reason that it is so useful having foreign franchise operations, each with their interior designers to carry out my proposals.

Back at the office for the last time I go over the day's work with my studio and vet the architect's drawings for the Caravelle Hotel in Athens. Then a cocktail party, not that I particularly enjoy them and never give them. I prefer to have a drink with two or three people and talk seriously. It is fun, though, to see old friends by chance and, as often happens, I meet people who want to talk to me, either because the husband wants his offices redesigned or the wife wants to know if I've designed any new fabrics.

Home to Paultons Square for a quick bath and to say hello to my daughter, Edwina, who is just home for holidays. Then out to dine with the Hamiltons, taking with me swatches of fabric and their carpet trial for discussions about the long gallery.

12.30. On getting home, Pammy and I discuss our different days over a whisky and soda and I translate the notes from my appointments card on to foolscap paper and jot down seeds of ideas for action and implementation by my office and my studio later today...

WHAT A DAY THANK YOU LOVE BEATRIX

editress of vogue

Brown and white printed cotton wall fabric is St. Pierre from the Tarascon range by Mary Fox-Linton & David Hicks in a room designed by them

The David Hicks decorating books have been out for some time, and the fact that they look as new as ever says a lot in their favour. **David Hicks on Decoration with Fabrics** and **David Hicks on Decoration – 5** (Britwell Books, £5.50 each, available from the David Hicks/Mary Fox-Linton shop, 39 Elystan St, London SW3) are probably the most useful. They're picture books (sumptuous photography, but more black and white than colour, which is occasionally frustrating) showing rooms and details of rooms, fabrics and carpets designed by the great man himself. Brief captions are sometimes helpful, sometimes not ("In a house in Eleuthera, I put two Bruce Tippets over two sofas"?). Some may be irritated by the name-dropping and by the "I, Hicks" slant, but you've got to give it to him – the man's got flair.

His books are particularly helpful for inspiration on using and mixing colour, patterns, textures. There's also the sheer *voyeur* pleasure of looking at the homes of the rich, the macabre fascination in wondering just how much some of the schemes *cost* – "I covered the walls in stitched panels of suède leather and had the geometric rug specially woven . . ." But there's plenty there for the Common Man.

I was very lucky, when I first began to consider the subject of wall treatments and fabrics, to have the chance to see **David Hicks**' country house, Britwell Salome, in Oxfordshire, because it is a catalogue of the things one can achieve, as well as proving the point that, properly handled, a number of treatments can be used successfully in one house. Mr Hicks has scarlet paper-backed felt in the main living-room, an off-white textured fabric in a smaller sitting-room (which has been up for ten years, by the way, and still looks crisp and new), hessian in the gallery, and black stippling done with a synthetic sponge by a local builder in his own bathroom. All this is used with both bold and small-scale wallpapers, plain paints, tiles, panelling, and most spectacular of all, magnificent murals in pale blue-greys by Rex Whistler in Lady Pamela Hicks' library, which she inherited from her mother Lady Mountbatten. Mr Hicks can do the same for you, or you can try your own hand by choosing from a carefully selected range of papers and fabrics, all reflecting his very special point of view, at his shop, **David Hicks & Mary Fox-Linton**, 1 and 35 Elystan Street, SW3 (589-4264 and 581-2188).

Having found so many ideas from one decorator, I tried another who works in quite a different, more traditional style:

. . . that interior design consultant David Hicks was allowed a free hand on the 3.3Li interior. It features uninspired suede facia covering, but very comfortable looking worsted seats. Cost? An extra £3,000 . . .

Geometrics here and everywhere are variations on themes that made their debut as David Hicks's decorating signature more than 10 years ago. It frequently takes that long, or longer, for ideas tested in high style decorating to spread to mass marketing carpeting selling at about $14 to $21 a square yard.

Pleasant David Hicks 'bro period' decor, swift, agile serv the **Grange, 39 King Street, W**

NOW PUT YOUR FOOT IN IT

The first of David Hicks' shoe designs for Bally of Switzerland: men's evening shoes in black—patent, kid, suede, velvet or grosgrain, all with dashing red patent heel with the Hicks' insignia in gold. Only at the Bally shoe shops in Savile Row, Bond St and Sloane St, £42·50

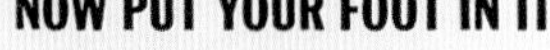

DICKIE AND A PRETTY GIRL

WHO IS the pretty girl that sometimes accompanies **Lord Mountbatten**, 76, on his many engagements?

She is tall, blonde and aristocratic. And she stands by his side, making arrangements and smoothly dealing with his affairs. Last week she accompanied him to Paris for a brief round of functions —and the Parisians were fascinated by her.

She is the **Marchioness of Hamilton**, 30, known as Sacha, the granddaughter of **Lady Zia Wernher** and the late Sir Harold Wernher. Born Alexandra Phillips, she married the **Marquis of Hamilton**, son and heir of the **Duke of Abercorn**, 10 years ago.

The marchioness, a charming and unaffected person, is a favourite god-daughter of Lord Mountbatten, whose wife died 16 years ago.

She lives with her husband, the former Ulster Unionist M.P. for Fermanagh and South Tyrone, and their two children, **Viscount Strabane**, seven, and **Lady Sophia Hamilton**, three, in London and at their stately home, Barons Court, in County Tyrone.

Says the marchioness: "Lord Mountbatten doesn't really need anyone to look after him, but he is great fun and I like being with him."

All the cars are in silver, except for the 320i which is in heliotrope with special trim designed by David Hicks, the famous interior designer.

They are downgraded if one's first reaction is John Fowler, David Hicks or David Mlinaric (all of whom have style in themselves).

Photo by Tim Jenkins

BALLY GOOD

LONDON — "I'm designing virtually everything that can be designed," David Hicks, the internationally known interior designer explained to FN when asked why he entered the world of shoes.

Actually, Hicks was approached by Peter Jellinek who heads the Bally London operation. Jellinek had read an article about Hicks' "ever widening" field of operations and arrangements for the first shoe designs was set.

While Hicks is best known for his interior designing, he also plays the name game in men's ties, umbrellas, lug-

See FASHION, Page 8

FASHION VIEWPOINTS

BY VIVIAN INFANTINO

Continued from Page 1

gage, women's silk scarfs, men's knitwear, socks, towels, tiles and carpeting.

"Bally got in touch with me and said they wanted Rolls Royce shoes by David Hicks," he said with a grin, "but not Rolls Royce prices (The shoes retail for about $75.).

"I was very excited about it. To have the English manufacturing side approach one—in these rather gloomy years for Great Britain—was a great challenge."

Hicks noted that he had very "definite feelings, "about what he wanted to do. "I wanted design, imagination, color, flair...something different, yet still disciplined." "This is just the beginning of a continuous relationship," he explained. "I'm also going to look into the realm of women's shoes, which will be totally complementary to women's clothes."

Discussing his design for Bally he said he thought of doing evening shoes first. The inspiration for them came out of an old experience, he said, explaining a little of how a designer works. "You must use your eyes continuously. Certain things you see over a period of years get left like discarded eggs in a bird's nest. But sooner or later you remember. At Versailles 25 years ago, I saw red heels on a painting of Louis XIV and I thought, 'How marvelous to have shoes like that."

That experience is what provided the basis for the red-heeled evening shoes just launched. He sees them worn with "black tie or its equivalent—a velvet coat." "Plain black trousers with an evening stripe would be good with the grosgrain shoes, " he pointed out.

"I selected the materials," he emphasized, which include black patent, kid suede, velvet and grosgrain all set on a red patent covered heel with his "H" signature.

The concept behind doing just one shoe many ways is to offer customers selectivity instead of a whole range. The Hicks evening shoe is the beginning, and next it might be the Hicks casual, then the Hicks boots and perhaps accessories. The idea is THE SHOE, not a range.

Because Hicks' interest covers such a wide area and since so much of his day is spent working on colors he said he dresses in a "boring, conservative way" (He wore a gray suit, his own blue/white signature tie, black patent Bally mocs.) and described where he lives as a "beige area. I want something totally plain after working with color all day."

All of his designs can interrelate and help each other, he said. "For example, the shoe idea of scarlet and black suede or patent could work for a man's library with patent walls and red suede sofa."

A complete cosmopolitan, he admitted, "I'm nervous before a presentation." But he was very pleased by the reception his shoes received at an introductory party by Bally.

"I detest enormously thick soles...they're appallingly bad for the feet."

He said the evening shoes could be a "marvelous Christmas present for a wife who can't think what to give her husband."

While Hicks won't project the specifics of his next shoe effort, he does indicate what it won't be. "I detest enormously thick soles," he said with the expression of someone who has just had an unexpected bitter taste in his mouth. "They're appallingly bad for the feet."

Talking about customers he said he feels, "The young and middle aged long for something to get away from drabness. I'm not talking about the long hairs (most give that up at 27 or 28). These shoes give them an opportunity for just that slight breakthrough into color, into stylish controlled fashion. Actually, it's just the beginning of what I plan, the tip of the iceberg."

As an experiment, Hicks wore a pair of the evening shoes with his dinner clothes at Broadlands, where his 75-year-old father-in-law (Lord Mountbatten) thought them very dashing. "My brother-in-law (50) thought them unsalable and my nephew (28) cannot wait to buy a pair...the first market research results," Hicks concluded.

De Wet House Cape Town

Appartement londonien.

– Je les désapprouve totalement. Je n'ai pas encore vu le Musée Pompidou mais je suis déjà outré! Je sais que le président Pompidou a créé des appartements soi disants modernes à l'Elysée qui sont de la plus grande vulgarité et qui resteront le « Kitch » de la décade passée. J'applaudis à la régénération du Marais. Paris a été préservé et reste la grande ville que l'on connait, celle d'Haussmann et de Louis XIV; c'est une ville merveilleuse comparée à Londres qui a été chambardée par les promoteurs et qui a été littéralement violée sans aucune intervention du gouvernement.

– *Quelle est la règle d'or de la décoration?*

– Avoir l'esprit de décision. Aujourd'hui, il y a tant de marchandises! Le choix est écrasant. C'est dans ce domaine que des professionnels peuvent aider le public à créer quelque chose de personnel, de varié, de calme, d'apaisant, d'agréable à l'œil, pas trop riche, pas compliqué. La grande faute de l'amateur-qui-pense-avoir-du-goût est d'utiliser toutes les idées à la fois et à l'avenant.

Le goût, c'est la décision et le choix entre un objet et un autre; c'est un entraînement de l'œil. Depuis l'enfance, j'ai étudié la peinture avec de très bons professeurs comme William Roberts, ou Keith Vaughn, (de bons peintres anglais inconnus en France mais qui resteront). Ils m'ont appris à chercher certaines qualités, certaines compositions, certains concours, certaines techniques que j'applique à tout ce que je vois.

Il faut que les jeunes et vieux aillent dans les musées, dans les églises, dans les expositions, qu'ils se promènent à la campagne et comparent sans cesse : Aiment-ils les bouleaux ou les châtainiers? moi, j'aime le chêne, l'orme, mais pas les arbres à bois tendres, excepté le sapin. Je n'aime pas

DM Marguerite Littman Paul Hull Andy Warhol

Designer is 'editor of taste'

26 AUG 1977

He deserted cornflakes for royalty

By SUSAN HELLER ANDERSON

LONDON — David Hicks once drew cornflake boxes for the J. Walter Thompson advertising agency. He now designs residences for royalty like Princess Anne and Prince Charles and untitled nobility like Jacqueline Onassis and Mrs. Paul Mellon.

He made this graceful transition in 23 years, thanks to his marriage to the queen's first cousin, Lady Pamela Mountbatten, and a sophisticated decorating style of stripped-down refinement and bold use of color that is at once contemporary and timeless, and his smooth charm and good looks, which have improved with the crinkles of age.

Hicks, 48, describes himself as an editor of taste rather than a decorator. "I'm only an interpreter," he said. "After all, it's Princess Anne, Mrs. Onassis, the Duchess of Argyll who have to live in their houses, not me."

Now he is "editing" and showing his new range of furniture, fabrics, carpets and accessories in airy new quarters that opened last month.

Through the story-high windows, passersby can get a good look at the Hicks look. In the right window, a four-poster bed extravagantly canopied in a Hicks red cotton fabric, set off by Aubergine tweed walls and a sugar-pink quilted chaise longue. In the left window is a living room, one of seven room settings in the shop, with a sofa and two chairs squaring off opposite a wall hung with a Charles II gilt boiserie mirror.

Both window displays are done in a calculated melange of red, orange and pink and all shades in between — delicate salmon, deep coral and vibrant tangerine. The living room carpet is a typical Hicks geometric pattern in mulberry, bordeaux and white.

The shop's furniture was designed by Hicks; the more elaborate wood pieces are signed. Chairs and sofas are mostly straight-sided and cleancut. There are a few traditional armchairs, some upholstered in Ultrasuede, with bleached wood frames.

Furniture is new for Hicks, already a one-man design industry, with fabrics (32 new patterns at about $6 to $13 a meter), carpets (19 new designs, $30 to $34 a meter), wallpaper, notepads, vases, ashtrays and ties with the wearer's initials woven into the fabric.

Hicks sports a red-and-blue one with H's and is conservatively elegant in white shirt and gray worsted shirt with cuff buttons that unbutton. "I wear the same thing every day," he said.

Downstairs (the store has two floors), an austere setting in black, white and gray flannel is softened by a warm Chinese yellow ceramic lamp. Hicks is proud of the lamps, made by a retired colonel and his family. Glazed spheres, by the same people, come in golf ball to bowling ball sizes and are piled in shallow banana-leaf baskets.

There are brass-bound tables in scagliola — chips of marble with dye and powder reconstituted to resemble semiprecious stone. The artisanal accessories artfully placed about are a far cry from the chatchkas of our grandmothers — fragile porcelain pots in delicate colors, horn beakers from shot glass to tumbler size, and hand-carved wood boxes. The quality of workmanship is exceptional.

Hicks put the bathroom on the map by treating it like any other room, and there is a good example in the shop. The free-standing tub is encased in blond oak, and an upholstered chair for the back washer sits alongside.

"I'm a great advocate of putting bathtubs in the middle of the room," he said. "It's easier to clean, and you can furnish around it." The tub has old-fashioned brass faucets with white "hot" and "cold" porcelain disks lettered in black. Details count, and Hicks has given considerable thought to them. A galvanized wash bucket holds massed spruce branches.

"I love using very simple things as long as they have good manners," Hicks said.

There is a pair of retour d'Egypte bookshelves in mahogany inlaid with ebony. "We've had too much metal. I'm into lacquer and beautiful quality wood." He caressed the silken leg of a sycamore table.

The grim economic situation here has affected the Hicks business somewhat less than he expected. He has about six large private residences in progress, plus the jobs in his other shops in Johannesburg, Oslo, Geneva, Brussels and Paris, for which he often acts as consultant. He also designs for the Japanese market. "It's no more expensive to have me than any other designer," he said.

He described "the Hicks look" as "elegant, simple, direct, honest. A relish of pattern, texture, shiny and matte with nubbly tweed and geometric carpet. Muted lighting. And I'm always intensely practical."

But he is not contemptuous of antiques. "I'm an inveterate collector," Hicks admitted.

THE DAVID HICKS BOOK OF FLOWER ARRANGING, as told to Maureen Gregson, 88 pages, indexed by plants, illustrated (color), Van Nostrand Reinhold Co., New York, $9.95.

David Hicks, a British designer of international renown, has here applied himself to designing with flowers. The results are stimulating. Many of his pictured arrangements are mere parts of total settings, but his eclecticism is eye-opening. In the text he goes into surprising detail to explain his attitudes in such areas as cutting and care of flowers for arranging, using vases and containers, and suiting the flowers to the occasion. It is a fresh and inspiring view of a familiar subject.

Staying in Oslo with Cousin Olav

nursery which is being designed by decorator David Hicks, a Royal relative by marriage. He is the husband of Lord Mountbatten's daughter, Pamela.

"not tone!"

DAVID HICKS, INTERIOR DECORATOR.
Tailor: Mr Hammick at Huntsman;
shirts: Hawes & Curtis;
tie: own design; shoes: Bally;
barber: Nicholas of Sloane St

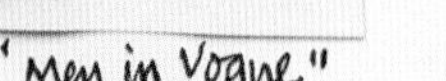

Hang fire

THAT dapper house decorator **David Hicks, 48,** is about to become a resident of that exclusive Regency enclave Albany in Piccadilly.

But everything must hang fire until he can provide the right references and prove himself acceptable to that honourable body, the trustees.

Now David (middle-name Nightingale) made a good marriage to **Lord Mountbatten's** daughter **Lady Pamela Hicks** and is always anxious to improve himself.

The chambers which David has cast his eye on are currently occupied by shy millionaire **Stanley Vaughan** and his Colombian heiress wife **Gloria.** It's really quite modest—"only three rooms, a pied-a-terre," explains the secretary of Albany, **Colonel Gilbert Chetwynd Talbot.**

Quite a comedown from the Hicks's current 10-bedroomed pad Britwell House in Oxfordshire.

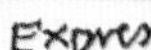

Part 6

1977–98

1977–98

'Interpreter of Taste' David opens a new store on London's Jermyn Street; he denies that Princess Anne's house, which he is decorating, will look like his own; he writes to his book designer Nick Jenkins. Sunday in the country, bluebells in the wood and a marmalade label by his son. David is Master of the Worshipful Company of Salters and rides in a carriage in a fur-trimmed scarlet robe, a brief moment of perfection before everything goes wrong. David has to sell Britwell and his collection but creates a beautiful still-life for the catalogue cover. His prized Horace Walpole Strawberry Hill chair goes to the V&A. He decides the best place for a Rolex is on his wrist. He devises a beautiful minimal desk in Formica for his new office.

David moves his London home from Chelsea to a set of chambers in Albany and is photographed 'breakfasting' on a cigarette. He moves out of Britwell to The Grove and is photographed in his unfinished library. Slim Aarons takes his picture in the Bahamas, and Derry Moore in London, again smoking at the breakfast table. He decorates the British Ambassador's library in Washington DC. His new drawing room in the country has walls of pink cotton; the dining room has Edwina Mountbatten's Rex Whistler panels. 'Mr Hicks picks classics': David designs womenswear and a garden at the Chelsea Flower Show.

Here are David's own pictures of his Hanae Mori house in Tokyo and a story titled 'Building on the Hicks image', where he later deletes his business manager's face and every mention of the disgraced man's name. The great projects of his last years are Vila Verde, his spectacular Palladian essay for Nahid Ghani in Portugal, and his own garden in Oxfordshire. His old friend Tony Snowdon photographs David and Pammy by the bed in Albany. 'All about me: the making of a man of taste', a hilarious record of his monologue to a would-be biographer, makes him cry with laughter. He squeezes into the royal family's balcony group in 1995, and redecorates Albany in all-male Vandyke brown.

He dies in 1998, but is frustratingly unable to stick the extensive press coverage into his scrapbook.

An Interpreter Of Taste

By SUSAN HELLER ANDERSON

LONDON

DAVID HICKS once drew cornflake boxes for the J. Walter Thompson advertising agency. He currently designs residences for royalty like Princess Anne and Prince Charles and untitled nobility like Jacqueline Onassis and Mrs. Paul Mellon.

He made this graceful transition in 23 years, thanks to his marriage to the Queen's first cousin, Lady Pamela Mountbatten; a sophisticated decorating style of stripped-down refinement and bold use of color that is at once contemporary and timeless; and his smooth charm and good looks that have improved with the crinkles of age.

Mr. Hicks, 48, describes himself as an editor of taste rather than a decorator. "I'm only an interpreter," he said. "After all, it's Princess Anne, Mrs. Onassis, the Duchess of Argyl who have to live in their houses, not me."

Now he is "editing" and showing his new range of furniture, fabrics, carpets and accessories in airy new quarters that opened last month at 101 Jermyn Street.

Through the story-high windows, passersby can get a good look at the Hicks look. In the right window, a four-poster bed extravagantly canopied in a Hicks red cotton fabric; set off by aubergine tweed walls and a sugar-pink quilted chaise longue in the left window is a living room, one of seven room settings in the shop, with a sofa and two chairs squaring off opposite a wall hung with a Charles II gilt boiserie mirror. "Always a very intense sense of the placing of objects and furniture," Mr. Hicks said of his arranging.

Both window displays are done in a calculated mélange of red, orange and pink and all shades in between—delicate salmon, deep coral and vibrant tangerine. The living room carpet is a typical Hicks geometric pattern in mulberry, bordeaux and white.

The shop's furniture was designed by Mr. Hicks; the more elaborate wood pieces are signed. Chairs and sofas are mostly straight-sided and clean-cut. There are a few traditional armchairs, some upholstered in Ultrasuède, with bleached wood frames. "I'd never put an antique finish on an 18th-century copy," Mr. Hicks said distastefully. "But stripped—unpretentious."

Furniture is new for David Hicks, already a one-man design industry, with fabrics (32 new patterns at about $6 to $13 a meter), carpets (19 new designs, $30 to $34 a meter), wallpaper, notepads, vases, ashtrays and ties with the wearer's initials woven into the fabric. "To keep people from wearing YSL," he explained.

Mr. Hicks himself sports a red-and-blue one with H's and is conservatively elegant in white shirt and gray worsted suit with cuff buttons that unbutton. "I wear the same thing every day," he said.

Downstairs (the store has two floors), an austere setting in black, white and gray flannel is softened by a warm Chinese yellow ceramic lamp. Mr. Hicks is proud of the lamps, made by a retired colonel and his family. Glazed spheres, by the same people, come in golf-ball to bowling-ball sizes and are piled in shallow banana-leaf baskets.

There are brass-bound tables in scagliola—chips of marble with dye and powder reconstituted to resemble semiprecious stone. The artisanal accessories artfully placed about are a far cry from the chatchkas of our grandmothers—fragile porcelain pots in delicate colors, horn beakers from shot-glass to tumbler size, and hand-carved wood boxes. The quality of workmanship is exceptional.

Mr. Hicks put the bathroom on the map by treating it like any other room, and there is a good example in the shop. The freestanding tub is encased in blond oak, and an upholstered chair for the back washer sits alongside.

"I'm a great advocate of putting bathtubs in the middle of the room," he said. "It's easier to clean, and you can furnish around it." The tub has old-fashioned brass faucets with white "hot" and "cold" porcelain disks lettered in black. Details count, and Mr. Hicks has given considerable thought to them. A galvanized wash bucket holds massed spruce branches.

"I love using very simple things as long as they have good manners," Mr. Hicks said.

There is a pair of retour d'Egypte bookshelves in mahogany inlaid with ebony. "We've had too much metal. I'm into lacquer and beautiful quality wood." He caressed the silken leg of a sycamore table.

The grim economic situation here has affected the Hicks business somewhat less than he expected. He has about six large private residences in progress, plus the jobs in his other shops in Johannesburg, Oslo, Geneva, Brussels and Paris, for which he often acts as consultant. He also designs for the Japanese market. "It's no more expensive to have me than any other designer," he said.

•

The shops, franchises over which Hicks keeps strict control, diffuse the Hicks look throughout the world. "My look?" he pondered. "It's elegant, simple, direct, honest. A relish of pattern, texture, shiny and matte with nubbly tweed and geometric carpet. Muted lighting. And I'm always intensely practical." He has combined coco-mat floor covering with 18th-century furniture in the living room of the Marchioness of Hamilton's Irish castle, Baron's Court.

But he is not contemptuous of antiques. "I'm an inveterate collector," Mr. Hicks admitted. He is assembling a collection of white vellum-bound books for their bindings rather than their contents. He wears Victorian gold cuff links, but has concocted modern settings for some of his wife's jewelry. "I'd adore to design jewelry," he said wistfully.

It is one of the few things he has not tackled. Initialed notepads designed by him, at $1.40 each, are his shop's least expensive item. Most expensive is an inlaid wood backgammon table at $1,700, with a reversible top that flips over to become a beige suede card table. Slim sliding coasters pull out to hold glasses; while Mr. Hicks pushes cold salmon around his plate during lunch, he shows a certain appreciation for the liquid parts of the meal.

"I never eat except in France," he said.

Mr. Hicks has a small house in St. Jean Cap Ferrat, one in Eleuthera in the Bahamas, an 1870's castle in Ireland that he says is hideous and is redoing "in the spirit of the period, which is hard because I don't admire it," and an 18th-century residence set in a 58-acre park in Oxfordshire. He is gleeful today because he has just wangled a set of rooms in Albany, the post-Victorian pile off Piccadilly where bachelors live in butlered solitude overlooking the Burlington Arcade. Lady Hicks stays in the country with their three children, ages 9 to 16. Mr. Hicks visits his far-flung homes once a year.

He is in a jet once a week on business and, to recharge, he travels some more. "I go to Venice to look at the floor in St. Marks. India is full of ideas—the smells and the color. Every variation of pink and purple. And the variety of whites." His youngest daughter is named India, and Mr. Hicks's father-in-law was the last viceroy of India.

Derry Moore

London's David Hicks

"I find New York very electric and exciting. There are more people with good taste than anywhere else," he said. "I've learned a very great deal about design from people like Philip Johnson. He has a sense of immaculacy. Is that a word?"

Mr. Hicks has invented another word—"tablescape." "They're objects on stands connected in some way by texture, color or interest." Tablescapes are not haphazard. "It is the discipline of selection. Taste is simply the choice between alternatives. You need spectacles to edit."

There are some "editing" jobs he will not discuss. "I did Anne's flat in Windsor Castle but we don't talk about it." He's now doing Gatcombe Park, the house in Gloustershire given the Princess by Queen Elizabeth.

Princess Anne was a bridal attendant at Mr. Hicks's wedding 17 years ago, as were Princess Clarissa of Hesse and Princess Frederica of Hanover. The entire Royal Family came, the Queen excepted, and Prince Philip is godfather to one of the Hicks children. Lady Hicks's family is related to most of Europe's royalty.

"When you marry someone with such a background you relax totally. I loathe pretentious people and I'm totally unimpressed. Owning a Rolls is a disadvantage in my eyes."

New York Times.

Staying with Derek Hill in Co Donegal.

Bedroom

Dining Room

Drawing Room

Bathroom

Harry Creighton's house, "Drovers" by DH.

View of St Jean Cap Ferrat harbour

A WAY WITH COLOUR
David Hicks' New Shop in Jermyn Street

by Corinna Wildman, photographs by John Miller

Below: the winter drawing room. Opulent red tones create an inviting surround to an antique mantelpiece and large decorative mirror. Opposite right and below right: applied chevron pattern is used only in the carpet of the other main room, the bedroom. The cleverly balanced combination of vivid shades, not the easiest of colour schemes, adds all that is necessary for a sparklingly interesting room. Opposite below left: a small print is used in profusion in the dining area. Tablecloth, chair and bench seat covers are in a neat geometric pattern (almost a David Hicks trademark) that features the red, which is a recurring theme, throughout the showroom's ground floor.

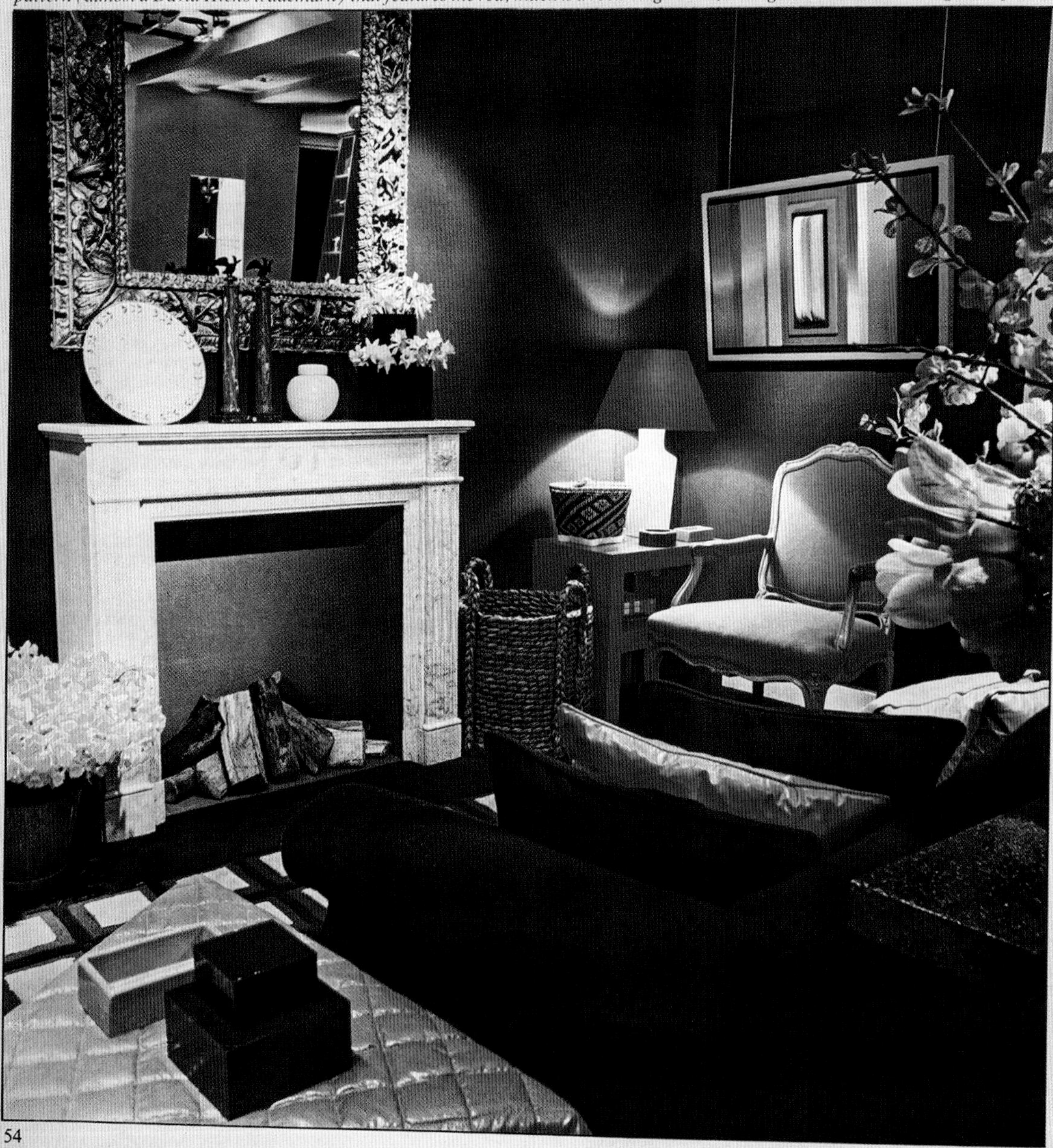

Stepping into 101 Jermyn Street, London, it is clear that David Hicks is blessed with an eye for colour far superior to most people's. The first impression is of intense light and colour while closer scrutiny reveals a masterly blending of subtle shades.

The two main rooms are in shades of red. David Hicks describes the colour of the tweed on the bedroom walls as oxblood. This he has mixed with a shocking pink quilted chintz *chaise longue* while the four-poster bed is covered in a soft corally pink tweed with matching hangings edged with bright orange chintz. The carpet picks up all these colours and cushions and tables are in pillar box red with a couple of bright mauve chintz cushions thrown in.

The living room is also in reds but aubergine and orange have been used in larger quantities with the same oxblood tweed on the walls.

The dining area has blood red walls with the furniture covered in scarlet, brown, beige and white printed cotton. Also on the ground floor, a small study area has red in the print of the two chairs and in the patterned carpet.

Downstairs are more rooms and corners, but here the colours are cooler and/or softer. A small seating area has a sofa covered in bright turquoise on a grey and black carpet. Vivid apple green, peacock and navy blue chintz covered cushions make as lively a combination as the reds upstairs.

Down yet another floor is a summer drawing room. The carpet is in blocks of colour like Neapolitan ice-cream. The sofa is a soft off-white against plain white walls with a large modern

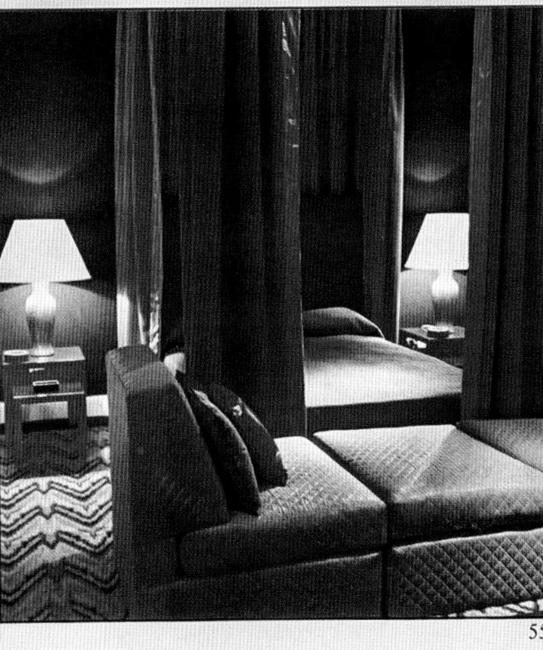

Homes and Gardens.

IS THIS WHAT PRINCESS ANNE'S HOUSE WILL LOOK LIKE? NO!

DH.

"A girl of the Seventies"—that's how top designer David Hicks describes Princess Anne, and for him the Seventies is "a time of mixing and matching old and new—beautifully". This is the look he has captured in his own elegant home, Britwell Manor . . . and this is the design talent that will bring Gatcombe Park, Anne's new house, back to life again. Here, he talks to Woman's Own about his ideas

STORY: GILL PREECE

PICTURES: LORD LICHFIELD

"When they write my obituary," says David Hicks, "I hope they will credit me with the revival of geometrics and the use of colours." The study, where he is pictured at his desk (above) and guest bedroom (right) show what he means. The study, with its antiques and books, is a period classic, except for his own 20th-century geometric carpet. For this bedroom (they all have four-posters) he chose palest blue and white and did it thoroughly; everything in the room—walls, drapes, curtains, carpet—fits the theme

Eye-catcher in the drawing room is David Hicks' latest idea, a "blue table" (far left). Best gift for him right now is something blue, anything from a lump of quartz to a butterfly wing, to add to the group. Even a hallway (below) is unmistakably Hicks, with his own geometric wallpaper, and yet more objects in a cabinet

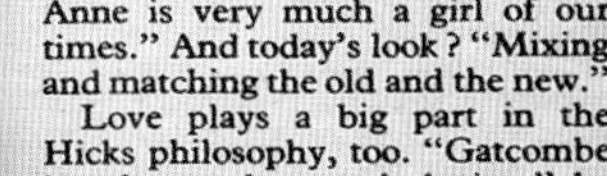

Anne is very much a girl of our times." And today's look? "Mixing and matching the old and the new."

Love plays a big part in the Hicks philosophy, too. "Gatcombe is a house that needs loving," he said. "It hasn't had any love for a hundred years. It was in such a sad state of repair when I first saw it and yet it is fundamentally a beautiful house. It just craves for care and thought. But these are ideal conditions for me to work in."

He loves decorating period houses most of all, so naturally Gatcombe—pure 18th century—is a gift of a job. The rambling homestead was originally owned by a strange family of Italian bankers who (*Please turn to next page*)

woman's own.

24 PAULTONS HOUSE
PAULTONS SQUARE
LONDON SW3 5DU

01 351 0088

26th January 78

Dear Nick,

I enclose a c.c. of a letter to Leslie for your information. Forgive me for quoting you so liberally and don't think that I am too critical – I just don't want either of us to burn our fingers.

To help you budget I have jobs in Switzerland (4 unphotographed) in Geneva and Lucerne, in Brussels and Antwerp (2 unphotographed) in Paris (2 unphotographed) South of France, one in Australia, 2 in Ireland (1 unphotographed) and several in London and the country.

We have almost nothing, Singapore airlines lost 60 original transparencies in September

At chapel a resounding and emotional *Jerusalem*, visiting the new house, a glorious ride, making notes for the next books

My Sunday David Hicks

My Sunday varies. Travelling a good deal, it can be spent in Tokyo, Australia, on Eleuthera or at St Jean Cap Ferrat, but my favourite Sundays are those in Oxfordshire. But even there they can vary considerably, because I use Sunday partly as a day of preparation for the coming week and for entertaining people to do with my own work and, of course, friends. However, fortunately, the children are nearly always involved which gives an animation and warmth to the day of so-called rest, which I never spend in London.

When I was a child, before I went away to preparatory school, Sundays were spent at Little Coggeshall, the mornings in my "house in the tree". Lunch was always late because of "Pops" Turner, who called in for sherry and would never go, which annoyed my punctilious Victorian father. Yet, for as long as I could remember, this benevolent country doctor had dropped in for sherry before lunch on Sunday. Sunday as a teenager was porridge and cream with moist brown sugar, and church in the evening in the minute, candlelit Pattiswick church. Sunday at Charterhouse was Evensong in the Gilbert-Scott Chapel – dramatic war-time lighting, and fantastic acoustics.

Now, at Britwell Salome, our ten-year-old daughter, India, wakes us up by jumping on our bed early. I doze on until my wife Pamela's breakfast tray arrives with Pat Millett – as it has done for 16 years on Sundays – at nine o'clock. I cross the gallery to my dressing room and start the process of waking myself up. I gargle, I shave at the basin in the window recess, gaze down on the canal where Julie, the groom, is feeding the ducks, peafowl, pigeons and peacocks, and then I get into the bath. It is in the middle of the room, and across the bath I have a reading rack; I browse through *The Illustrated London News* for the year 1891. I put on my favoured Sunday clothes – tweed coat and grey flannel trousers, and one of my geometric alphabet ties.

I then saunter down to the breakfast room, where my eldest daughter, Edwina, joins me for kippers at about 9.45. India has long since disappeared for the first of several rides on Badger. Fleur Vulliod telephones me from Switzerland in a great state of agitation because of the airport strike at Heathrow. She is afraid that we may lose two of our Swiss clients – who were to come to London – because of it. I call my shop in Jermyn Street which is open because they are arranging a special window display, and dictate a Telex for Tokyo. "Oh, and could someone make reservations at Rowleys, and could you get six rolls of wallpaper to Eaton Square so that they can be brought down by someone coming to lunch?" I had forgotten to put them into the car on Friday night and I need them for my Dublin flight tomorrow.

The 18 members of The David Hicks Association of Japanese Manufacturers are flying with us to see my work at Classiebawn Castle and at Barons Court. The Association, which I believe is unique, was formed three years ago, by manufacturers in Japan, who make umbrellas, costume jewellery, shirts, bedroom slippers etc., under licence to my designs. At 10 o'clock I meet Steve Madgen in the courtyard and discuss the new avenue of trees we are planting, then we drive over to the Grove, the dower house we are moving to, to see the vista he created on Thursday by making a wide gap in the garden wall.

Next I drive as fast as safety permits through the staggeringly beautiful countryside to Stowe. How incredibly lucky we are not to live in polluted, industrialised, desecrated northern Europe. My son Ashley is waiting on the steps of the chapel and we sit together for the remembrance service. We sing *Jerusalem* and, as usual, tears come to the eyes – my brother lies buried below Assisi. I suppose I should feel embarrassed in front of all those flaxen-haired stoics. The *boutonnières* in their lapels remind me of Sir Peter Vanneck in his crimson robes, carrying a posy of scarlet Flanders poppies when I saw him sworn in at the Law Courts the

Judith Aronson

David Hicks and daughter Edwina (top) off for a ride, while David's wife Pamela watches them from the doorway of their Oxfordshire home. David (above), Edwina and her brother Ashley settle down in the drawing room with their scrapbooks

The working man in a blue denim bathroom

❛ If the newspapers know you have designed Princess Anne's new home, they publish only that side of you. But there is another side ❜

Interview by JANICE MORLEY

THE NOBILITY are not renowned for their business sense. In fact it is often a surprise to discover them working.

Two concepts that David Hicks, interior decorator and designer, knocks on the head right away.

As pleasant as it is to be Earl Mountbatten's son-in-law and Lady Pamela's husband, it tends to tempt diary writers to bracket David Hicks with those who rise late, linger over lunch and strike out at six for pre-supper champagne.

When we met in the office behind his new shop in London's chic Jermyn Street, he had been up long before me, had two appointments and was fitting in our talk before lunch.

Mr Hicks had just closed a file on office premises he has designed for a firm in Paddington and placed it in concealed compartments of a large white, square desk, in a small room of plain red, white, grey and black. The same colours were in the tie he had designed and wore with a grey suit.

Pocket

David Hicks, a tall, slim 48, took the first of many cigarettes from a case in his inside pocket, put it in a holder and lit it.

"If the newspapers know you have designed Princess Anne's new home they tend to publish that and all the other rich and wealthy people I design for . . . but there is another side."

He made the comment casually. He doesn't mind the publicity, but the rather reserved manner he maintains to describe those projects breaks down when it comes to the far reaching commercial side of his company.

With a certain pride, he took me round his lovely shop full of furniture, prints and all manner of modern design; colourful creations in wood, plastic, glass—the majority Hicks'-designed.

"I hate people to think only the rich can afford these things. There are things in this shop from 60p upwards," he said. The man who once designed a council house at Tyneside to prove that good design is open to all said: "I think my greatest ambition now is to start a school to educate people on how to think about design."

He says frankly but without criticism: "My mother, an actress, was artistic but she did not have taste. I don't think you're born with it."

David Hicks was artistic too, and built on it. "At my public school, Charterhouse, I did not even get the school certificate, but I liked art."

And when he left he capitalised on his instinct.

His father, a stockbroker, died when Hicks was 11 and he lived in a London flat with his mother. His first attempt at interior design was decorating their home. Meanwhile he studied and graduated from art college.

Eighteen years ago, when he married Lady Pamela, he was established in his professions. "I made the decision not to live off a wealthy wife," he said, "I am basically a worker, and I think if you are, you are."

Clock

If you substitute "energy" for "work" you have David Hicks summed-up. His mind, like an electric clock, almost visibly turns over.

He was far too polite to give me anything but his full attention, yet you suspect he is mentally ahead of us—wondering what damage the storm has done to the roof of the magnificent Georgian mansion at Britwell Salome, Oxfordshire, where he lives with his wife and three children.

A house up for sale at £1m. "It is simply a question of economics, the running costs are too high," he said. "But we won't be short of space. We are moving to a six-bedroom eighteenth-century house on our estate with 1,300 acres of ground."

Hicks does the decor of all their homes—in France, the Bahamas and London—and the problems of their new period house are not new to him, at Gatcombe Park, the home he finished for Princess Anne two weeks before her baby was born, is all eighteenth century.

He deftly side-steps discussing what's in the home, but admits it's nice to do the house of someone whose personality you know — she was one of the bridesmaids at his wedding.

David Hicks is no stranger to royal designing — he also did Prince Charles's flat at Buckingham Palace.

Be it an office block or a mansion, Hicks is always positive in his ideas: "I have no doubts about what I want to do," he said, "I avoid gimmicks and the outrageous and cannot be dishonest.

"If I cannot design a room round someone's certain favourite carpet I say so . . . either it goes or I go.

And these days, with a design team working flat out in the office above to carry out his designs, and shops all over the world, Hicks cannot afford the time to linger or supervise each job personally. Instead he delegates.

"There is so much I want to do. I never stop making notes. If we're at the cinema and I see a design on a dress, I note it down and remember the colours visually."

"There is nothing I don't want to design," he said. "I'd like to do something for hearses and coffins—they're so ugly."

He loves to combine the old with the new. In his magnificent mansion he is covering the walls of his bathroom in blue denim. "My wife is driven mad by people asking her if she lets me decorate our own home," he said. "Like everything else, we work it out together."

Stylish

Their children, Edwina, 16, Ashley, 14, and India, 10 have their own bedrooms, and they have just formed a committee to decide how to design the sitting room their parents have given them.

But David Hicks could not resist adding: "I think I might give them some guidance on it."

During the week, Hicks has an apartment at the stylish Albany, conveniently near his shop, and his latest commission. He is just completing a men's and a women's shop for Simpsons of Piccadilly—just opposite his own shop.

If he is not in London he is abroad. At the moment, finalising plans for shops in Australia and Pakistan.

Nobility is giving commerce a great deal of style.

Daily Express
Centre pages

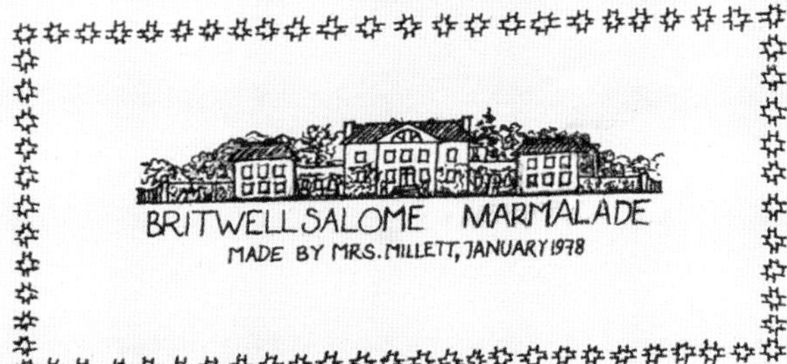

BRITWELL SALOME MARMALADE
MADE BY MRS. MILLETT, JANUARY 1978

Inexpensive gifts

Two useful and attractive gift ideas from *David Hicks* furniture and accessories, 101 Jermyn Street, SW1: the David Hicks book of Flower Arranging, gorgeously illustrated with blooms for all seasons; and a desk set, diary and memo pad trimmed in one of the delicate Hicks house fabrics. Each of these items is priced under £5.

Arlene Gould

HICKS TO REVAMP SIMPSON'S

HAVING finished revamping the interior of Gatcombe Park for his cousin Princess Anne, David Hicks, the top society designer, has now started an even more lucrative commission.

He is revamping the whole of Simpson's, the traditional Piccadilly men's stores. His brief is to make one of London's most traditional stores the most up to date emporium of 1978.

Hicks, 48, married to Earl Mountbatten's daughter Pamela, is living right on top of the job. He has taken a spacious apartment in the Albany, across the road.

He is still looking for someone with £1 million to buy his country mansion Britwell Salome, in Oxfordshire.

Dinners

Lady Mayoress

The Lord Mayor and the Lady Mayoress, entertained the following guests at dinner at the Mansion House yesterday:

Marshal of the RAF Lord and Lady Elworthy, Lady Mary Strachey, the Archdeacon of London and Mrs Woodhouse, the Admiral President Royal Naval College and Mrs Weston, the Master of the Salters' Company and Lady Pamela Hicks, Mr and Mrs Humphrey Brooke and Mr Lanning Roper.

□ IF David Hicks, THE interior decorator, who did Princess Anne's new home, does "do something about coffins, because they're so ugly," I suppose the best people would't be seen dead in anything else. What you might call going down with the Joneses. If anyone paid to have me panelled and upholstered in a Hicks I couldn't show off to my friends, I'd come back and haunt them.

Lord Mayor: Sir Peter Vanne

at Guildhall

in the "Britska" with Lord Aldenham →

in the Court Room

in the entrance hall

in the hall

DAVID HICKS

AVENA CARPETS
pour
DAVID HICKS

La première moquette à motif géométrique tissée ainsi a été le célèbre "Hexagon" de David Hicks. Depuis, David Hicks a dessiné plus de soixante dessins exclusifs tissés en "Brussels" par Avena Carpets.

By Bevis Hillier

DAVID HICKS SAYS GOODBYE TO HIS DREAM HOUSE

From March 20 to 22 Sotheby's is selling the collection of England's most famous interior decorator. Photographs by Shaun Skelly

David Hicks at Britwell Salome House. Among the objects he is selling are (below left) a copy of a horse's head made in India and (below right) a bust of Oliver Cromwell

SOTHEBY'S
Britwell House
Sold by direction of Mr David and the Lady Pamela Hicks

Catalogue cover by DH.

Half million pound house

Designer David Hicks' Oxfordshire home has been sold to a Swiss company for a sum believed to have been about £500,000.

David and Lady Pamela Hicks lived at Britwell House, a beautiful Georgian mansion, but last year said the upkeep was costing too much.

The contents of the house will be up for auction at a three-day house sale in March.

continued from previous page

PICTURES:
DENIS JONES

hall, the first carpet you see is in camel-coloured jute.

"On a very grand staircase it's wonderfully understated," says Mr. Hicks.

One of the more classic Hicks tricks may be missing in this lovely but now-stripped house — the cylindrical vases filled with one tightly-packed species such as marguerites or carnations — but there are still a few of the famous "tablescapes" left.

For, if Mr. Hicks could be said to have one, special, gift, it is for "arranging things."

Indeed, there are said to be clients who have even pencil-marked the position of ornaments put down by Mr. Hicks, so that they could be exactly replaced after dusting.

As it is, one of the tablescapes — a collection of objects whose link is that all are made of lapis lazuli — will be sold with a cardboard cut-out indicating their precise positions.

Of furniture Mr. Hicks remarks simply: "I think there is really an inevitable plan for furniture — you move it round till you find it.

"People should spend more time rearranging their furniture, trying unexpected combinations, until they find that solution. Obviously, with my experience, I find it very quickly."

Influences

Mr. Hicks' seventh book, Living Design, due out in September, will detail much of that experience.

"It's really how I went about becoming what I am—it's slightly autobiographical. I've quoted the influences that guided me on my journey.

"From when I was about 11, I suppose, I was conscious that there were people with a way of looking at things other than that of my parents, who had very boring taste, though they did buy objects and pictures.

"For instance, every Saturday morning when Mum was at home, one would go round the local antique shops.

"It was then that I bought my first antique, a Regency black and gold chair for a pound. I still have it."

Today, Mr. Hicks is under contract to 24 different Japanese designers, and has a "you name it, he's done it" list of private and commercial commissions to his credit. April sees the opening of the latest of his shops —in Munich—and another is planned later this year for Sydney.

But 30 years or so ago, he was no academic high-flyer. "I never even took School Certificate. I went to art school instead."

Some of his drawings and paintings figure in next week's sale, including an impressive "graphic" portrait of Cecil Beaton on orange perspex.

One item, however, definitely won't be going under the auctioneer's hammer. And that's the Regency chair that, for just £1, set David Hicks on the road to startling success . . .

V&A from our sale

STRAWBERRY HILL
a turning point in the Gothic Revival of the 18th century. The back is based on Gothic window tracery, and was designed by Walpole for his house at Strawberry Hill, Twickenham, which he transformed into a Gothic fantasy. Dated 1755, it is one of the rare documented pieces made by the great Georgian cabinet-maker, Hallett

Sunday Times.

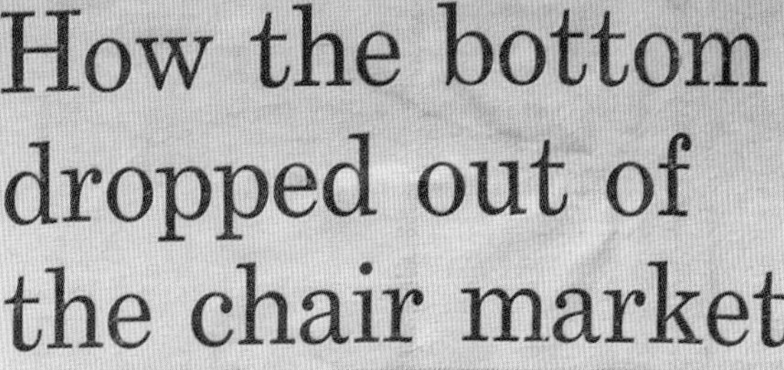

How the bottom dropped out of the chair market

By JANE GASKELL

ANYONE living in a large house these days 'has a hell of a struggle,' said Princess Anne's interior decorator, David Hicks.

He has given up the struggle with rising costs and inflation. The Georgian mansion where he has lived since marrying Earl Mountbatten's daughter, Lady Pamela, 19 years ago has been sold, and next week the contents are going the same sad way.

Sotheby's reckon the furnishings will bring in £250,000. Mr Hicks hopes for rather more—around £450,000.

Stars of the show are 20 George II scarlet and gilt dining room chairs, expected to fetch more than £1,000 each.

David Hicks and one of the £1,000 chairs.

Marble

At a preview yesterday, a woman journalist sat thankfully in one and went straight through the cane seat.

Fifty-year-old Mr Hicks took it extremely well. 'How sad,' he said. 'It shouldn't affect the value, though. The chairs were a mixture of old and new caning anyway.'

Five minutes later, however, there were white ribbons across all the chairs as though they were driving away from a wedding.

They'd been a wedding present from his father-in-law, said Mr Hicks. Yes, he was sorry to part with them. 'But how often does one have a dinner party nowadays for 20?'

Furniture, pictures, curtains and carpets designed by Mr Hicks are among the lots to be sold by Sotheby's in a marquee in the grounds of the mansion, Britwell House, near Watlington, Oxfordshire.

Ribbons

Mr Hicks said members of the public could pick up a bargain, a set of six sherry glasses for £20-£40, or a comfortable armchair for £150-£200.

Other presents to be sold include a red marble mortar given by Queen Helen of Rumania, a pair of white, Swedish, 18th-century chairs from Queen Louise of Sweden, and a gold embroidered, green silk robe from the late King Saud of Saudi Arabia.

Queen Helen's mortar is expected to make between £400-£800 and the two chairs £300-£500.

The house itself, built in 1728, was sold for half a million pounds to a Swiss corporation, who remain anonymous.

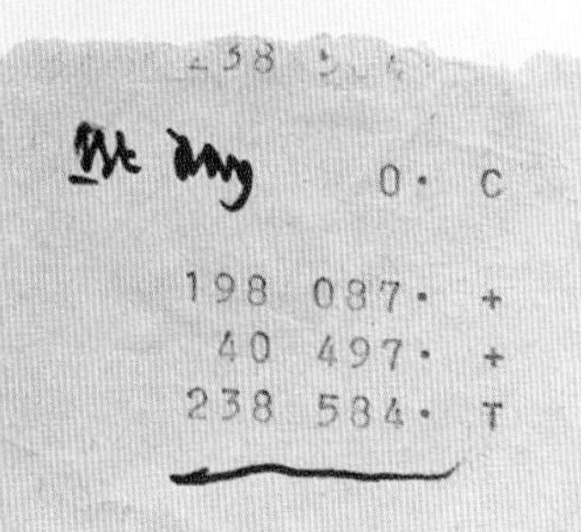

238 5..

Bt day 0· C

198 087· +
40 497· +
238 584· T

David Hicks has decided that the perfect place for a Rolex is on his wrist.

David Hicks is undoubtedly the most famous interior designer that Britain has ever produced.

The quality and invention of his designs for, and books on, carpets, fabrics, clothes and wallpapers have placed him at the absolute peak of his profession. Equally outstanding have been his interiors for the residences of some of the wealthiest and most influential people in the world.

"I realised I didn't have sufficient talent to be a painter," says Hicks "so I turned to interior design because it encompassed all my interests – architecture, houses, writing, furniture, colour. It seems to have gone quite well so far."

Hicks considers the minutest details in his design recommendations, even down to the positioning of the objects in the room. Indeed, some of his clients value his opinions so highly, that they mark those positions in pencil, so that the candlestick or clock in question can be precisely replaced after dusting.

Rolex are delighted with David Hicks' positioning of their watch.

"I wouldn't be without it," he says.

"When I first see a room, I make up my mind very quickly and it was the same with my watch. This Rolex Oyster Day-Date looks exactly as I think a watch should look, which is traditional, yet it is modern, accurate and reliable in the way that it functions. That's completely in accord with my own design philosophy."

After receiving David Hicks' recommendations, Rolex wouldn't dream of changing a thing.

ROLEX
of Geneva

Pictured: The Rolex Day-Date Chronometer. Available in 18ct. gold with matching bracelet.

Above: Lady Mountbatten's London sitting room in 1938. Regency antiques are effective against Whistler's murals.

By Ke[n]

DO W
AN OFFICE

Millions of offices look the same – a few chair[s]
necessary? Or does it impede efficiency?

David Hicks in the office he created to provide a neutral background for his work. Its most prominent feature is the desk, made to his own design, which has l

David Hicks, noted as a designer, makes a point of deliberate simplicity in his white-walled office. Part of his new shop and design premises in Jermyn Street, London, it is strictly a background.

"Basically, there is nothing to look at in this room, so that the eye can be clear," he says. "I want a neutral background like this, against which to create colour schemes."

A white desk of his own design, Formica-topped and eight feet square, fills half the room. "It's a version of a partner's desk", he explains. "A quadruple partner's desk, perfect for a conference of four people." It hides incoming and outgoing papers under lift-up panels, leaving a vast clear top on which to spread plans and samples.

The only colour in his white work place comes from a tomato red black-edged carpet set on a dark stained wood floor, four French chairs covered in scarlet wool, and a red telephone. A wooden screen across the window filters the daylight.

It is an office which insulates Mr Hicks. "I dislike open-plan working," he says. "But a sense of contact with the rest of the office is important, so the double doors facing me are usually left open."

Mr Hicks chose the neutrality of white as his own aid to good concentration, but adds "An office can be any colour that creates a good working mood for you."

h Carlson

NEED
EVOLUTION?

lesk, a filing cabinet. But is such uniformity really
ook at unusual answers to the problem

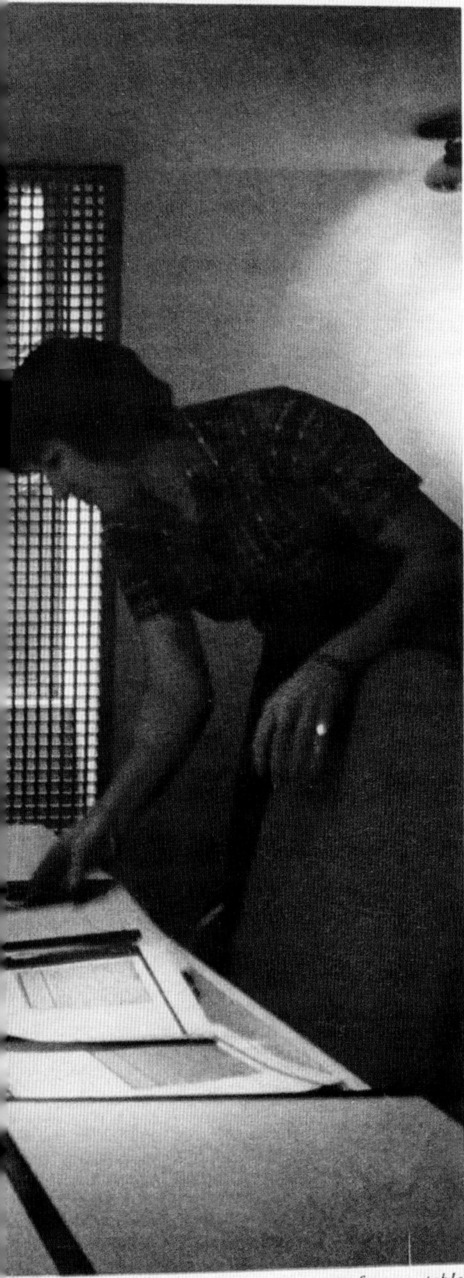

panels for papers and doubles as a conference table

Sometimes, you wonder if it's worth the effort.
One little slip and your room looks like badly-tuned colour TV.

Short of calling in David Hicks, what's the answer?

Well, our latest pattern book has one or two suggestions up its sleeve.

David Hicks' Piccadilly pied-à-terre

A JEWEL IN THE ALBANY

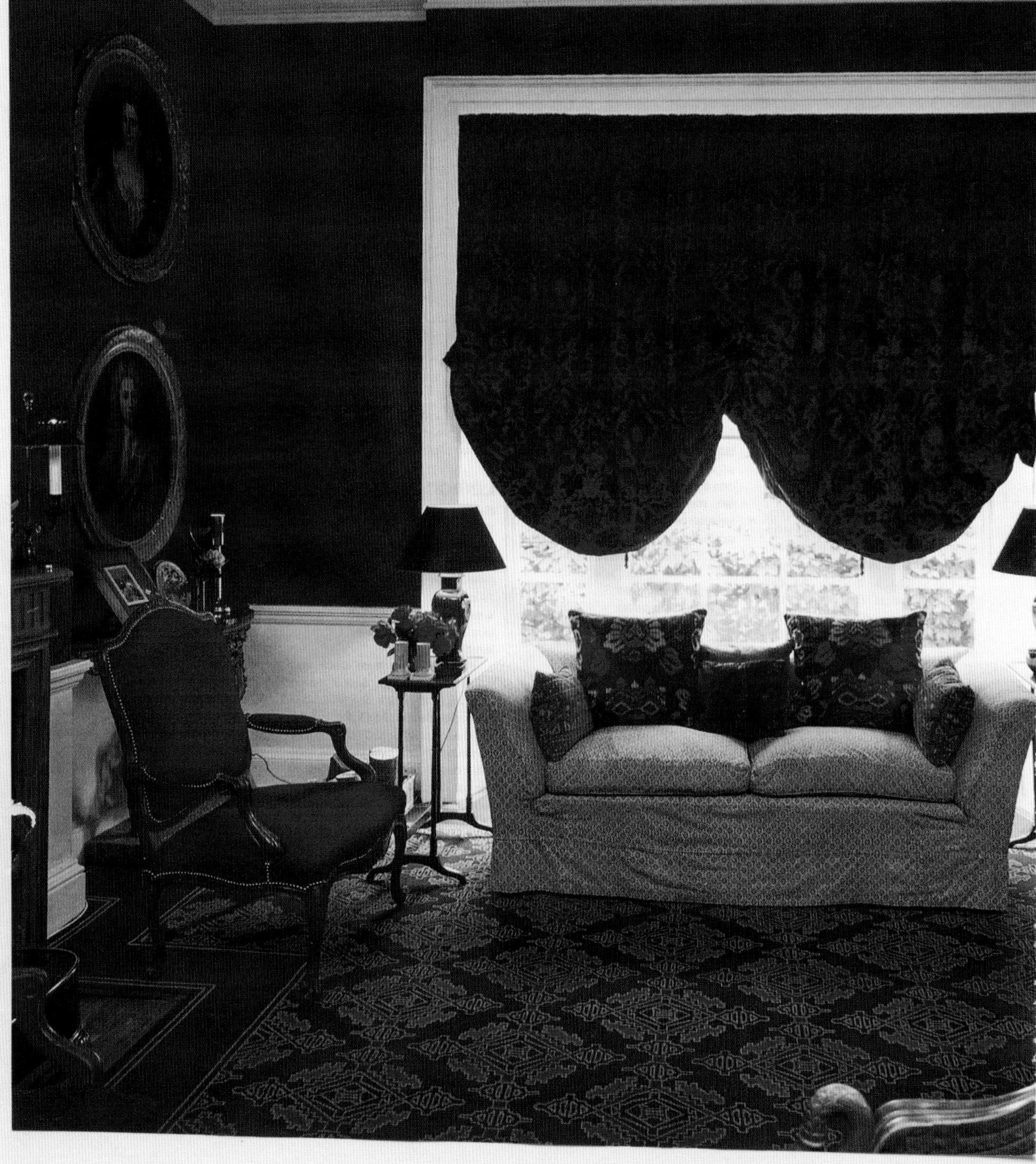

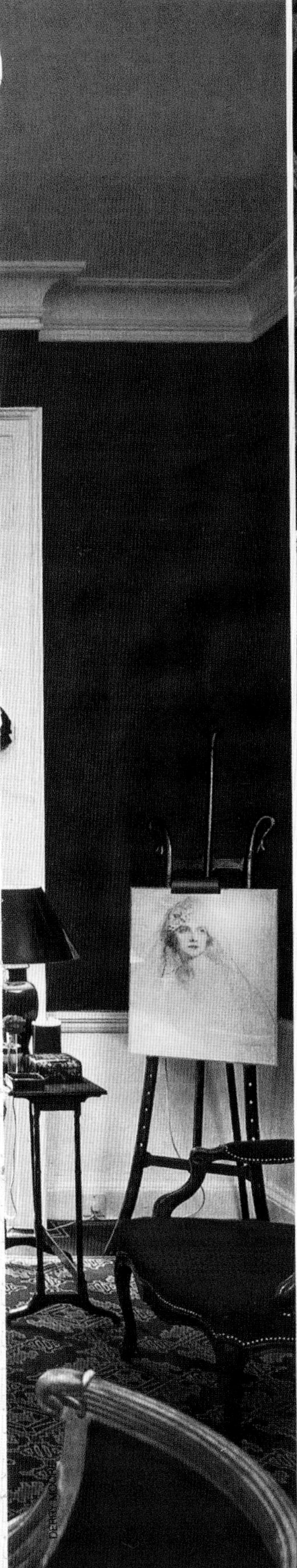

Steeped in history

"When I come home in the evening, I like to relax in this lush, early-nineteenth century atmosphere," says David Hicks, interior decorator extraordinaire and son-in-law of the late Earl Mountbatten of Burma, talking to Michael Love in his exotic chambers, Albany, London. "These two terraces were built in 1804, when the developer turned what had been Melbourne House into Albany House, making them, in fact, the first flats (as we now call them) in the world. When I opened the shop in Jermyn Street, it seemed absolutely essential that I should move from Chelsea and live in this part of the world." ▷

Left, the sitting room where the carpet (based on an early Turkish design), offsets the glowing etruscan red walls and the Louis XV and Directoire 'swan' chairs. Above, Coalport plates hang above a doorway flanked by a pair of Queen Anne mirrors and 'eagle' tables by William Kent. Right, in the bedroom, the silk damask-festooned tester bed.

Australian Vogue

Madeleine Masson visits David Hicks at his London home and reveal

BREAKFAST WI

ALBANY, in Piccadilly, London. It is one of the most exclusive blocks of flats in Europe. It is among the oldest, pre-dated only by that ravishing building which forms part of the Palais Royale in Paris, in which Colette and Jean Cocteau lived.

The original building was erected on the site of Sunderland House. Known as Piccadilly House until 1770, it was then sold to Viscount Melbourne, who, in his turn, exchanged it for a mansion in Whitehall with the Duke of York and Albany. In 1803, the Duke, mortgaged to the hilt, sold the property to a developer who commissioned Henry Holland, the architect, to design two terraces in Lord Melbourne's old garden. Holland, influenced by Eastern design, also built the famous *Rope Walk*.

The rooms were originally let out as bachelors' chambers, and were inhabited always by men of talent, and sometimes, as in the case of Lord Byron, of genius; and, since the beginning, having chambers in Albany has been the ambition of many a rising politician, publisher and man of letters.

David Hicks has all the qualifications of the ideal tenant. He is brilliantly successful in his work — considered to be one of the world's top interior designers and he is well connected. The husband of the Lady Pamela, daughter of the late Lord and Lady Mountbatten, he is quiet and considerate of his neighbours (rowdies are given short shrift in these time-hallowed premises).

David Hicks, who says that living at Albany is like living in an Oxford College, is able to enjoy the best of all worlds. Part of his week is spent in London and the rest of the time — when he is not travelling — takes him to his country estate in Oxfordshire and to the delights of domesticity, gardening and farming — he farms 1,300 acres — while get-away-from-it-all family holidays are spent in their house on the island of Eleuthera, in the Bahamas.

David Hicks makes no secret of the fact that he much prefers the country to cities; and he also makes it plain that an ornamental, but solid wall, divides his

Right: One of David Hicks' most famous themes is that of the tester bed. He has studied the subject thoroughly from early medieval manuscripts to old paintings. He has devised a simple and inexpensive way of making tester and canopy beds. He makes most of his tester beds on frames which are fixed directly to the ceiling. This treatment is very effective, and can be allied to all manner of pelmets, curtains, and bed coverings.

the personal taste of one of the world's most influential interior designers.

TH DAVID HICKS

KEITH McMILLAN

Above: Lord Byron would certainly have applauded David Hicks' taste which he would have recognised as being of his time. The drawing room in his chambers in Albany has panache and great dramatic quality, decorated, as it is, in various shades of red, which enhance the quality of the fine French furniture and bibelots in the room.

Left: This room-setting, carried out in shades of pink, from pink fondant to Persian rose, looks deceptively young and simple. It is, in fact, a background of great sophistication and elegance.

family life from his career.

While it is evident from the many photographs displayed in his chambers that he is immensely proud of his wife and three attractive children, he prefers to keep his family separate from his professional life. He is, in fact, a real professional and a perfectionist, being as interested and passionate about detail as the overall picture. He is also patient and hardworking and has a unique track record of achievements in his field.

His practice ranges from Australia to Japan, to Europe and the United States. It includes interiors for private homes, offices, hotels, shops and restaurants. In addition to designing the accessories traditionally associated with interior decorating — fabrics, carpets, furniture and wallpaper, his work includes a plethora of other products such as tiles, china, handbags, lights and logos, of which his own, a very chic 'H', appears in fabrics, wrapping paper and carrier bags. He has designed picture galleries, cinemas, luggage, pubs, scarves, shades, sheets, suits, sun glasses, ties, writing paper and yachts.

In the 25 years of his working life he has been responsible for the decoration of 28 restaurants, the most recent of which was on the sixtieth floor of a tower block in Tokyo.

I recently joined David Hicks for breakfast at Albany. He always starts the day with the same menu; cornflakes, fruit juice, grapefruit, boiled egg, toast and home-made marmalade, all served at a round table before the fire. The table is, of course, spread with a cloth made from his own fabrics.

I thought, as I drank my excellent coffee, that Lord Byron, had he walked through the door, would have been perfectly at home here, in the rather grand, classical decor of his time.

The walls of the drawing room are painted a matt Venetian red and are hung with eight oval portraits, each with its own picture light. The Directoire style swan chairs are covered in scarlet tweed, while the Louis XV chairs are upholstered in puce tweed.

A Louis XVI *Bonheur du*

David Hicks

Interviewed by Angela Levin
Photographed by Dmitri Kasterine

Interior designer David Hicks's favourite room provides 'the perfect antidote' to his London life, which is 'hectic and sophisticated'. 'Everything in my London apartment, my office, my shop and my showroom has to look right,' he explains. 'Whereas this room is totally relaxing and therapeutic and contains nothing I have to make a decision about.' It is a small square study on the ground floor of his detached house in 1,400 acres of land in Oxfordshire, and contrasts sharply with the rest of the house, which he has designed in his inimitable style.

The thought of returning to his room from his pressured life in London is so pleasing that 'on the motorway I feel a whole skin peeling off me'.

The room is lined with books and filled with memorabilia 'which aren't here because they are decorative, beautiful or valuable, but because I always seem to have had them'. It is near the front door and was chosen because he felt it was 'a good room to use at night to think and work in. People know that if the door is shut it means don't enter.'

David Hicks, a cigarette in a long black holder never far from his lips, gives detailed descriptions of the exact style, design and period of all his possessions as he talks about the room.

He explains that as he has been in the house for only a little over a year, the decorations are not yet finished. The place being a showpiece of his talents, so to speak, it was naturally difficult to know what to choose. 'I am normally very decisive,' he says, 'which is the whole art of being a design adviser. But one is supersensitive when choosing for oneself because one knows all the alternatives.' But once he has chosen a colour scheme he doesn't change it. 'Decoration is something very serious, not like clothes. Once I have the right solution to a room I try to prevent it being altered.'

His collection of books from floor to ceiling on three sides of the room is always growing. 'If one is a book person one never stops. I particularly like biographies and art books.' They are kept in specially designed shelves 'based on architectural ideas of about 1820' – which is also the date of the main part of the house. The shelves will eventually be painted 'dark bronze brown and varnished very, very bright', the missing shelf replaced and the books arranged in order of height.

Among his collection are 19 scrapbooks all expensively bound in black and red leather. David Hicks sticks 'everything from tickets to museums and art galleries to Press cuttings' into them.

An antique rug covers most of the floor. It was made 'about 1850' and bought by his maternal grandfather. 'I used to hate the colours,' he says, 'but now I like them. It has become a thing of enormous nostalgia for me by reminding me of my early childhood. The rest of the carpets in the house are my own designs, so it is restful for me to live with a traditional rug.'

The bordering floorboards are painted mid-brown, as David Hicks dislikes polished wood. 'Floorboards should either be carpeted or painted,' he declares, 'as they were until about 1860.'

There is a large white marble fireplace with a white interior, which was freshly touched up for the photograph. 'I always paint the interior of country fireplaces white because I like the pattern the black smoke makes on it at the back,' he explains. There is no fender. 'It stops you getting near the fireplace. If you leave the ash all winter it creates a good heat.'

The red velvet on the wall in the recess above the fireplace is part of what was once his grandmother's evening dress. 'It had been in the dressing-up trunk, but there comes a time when you can no longer keep things there. I decided to isolate it in time and stretched it on to the walls. Silk velvet doesn't get moths, so it should last about 100 years.'

He works at a desk 'with an incredible clutter', made for his wife's great-grandfather. (He is married to Lord Mountbatten's daughter.) When he wants to relax he sits in one of the winged chairs by the fireplace. 'I grew up with them and they are like old friends.' There are numerous sculpted heads around the room, both of his famous in-laws and unknown people. On the mantelpiece are Prince Albert, his wife's great-great-great-grandfather and Princess Alice, her great-great-grandmother.

'It's typical of this room and my attitude to it that one bust is bronze and the other white,' says David Hicks. 'A traditionalist would say I should have both in one or the other.'

Other favourite possessions about which he is 'romantic but not sentimental' include a pair of glazed pottery ashtrays made by his son when he was 12. 'The colour scheme is grey and black, which I think is very sophisticated for a 12-year-old, don't you?' There is also one of the first antiques he acquired, a small octagonal table of 1740, bought for £2 in 1948.

The only recognisable David Hicks designs are two table lamps. 'They are based on the classical column,' he says, 'and only the colouring is different. I will unite them soon by painting them the same colour. I designed them in 1954. I didn't want anything new in this room. Just treasured old friends.' ■

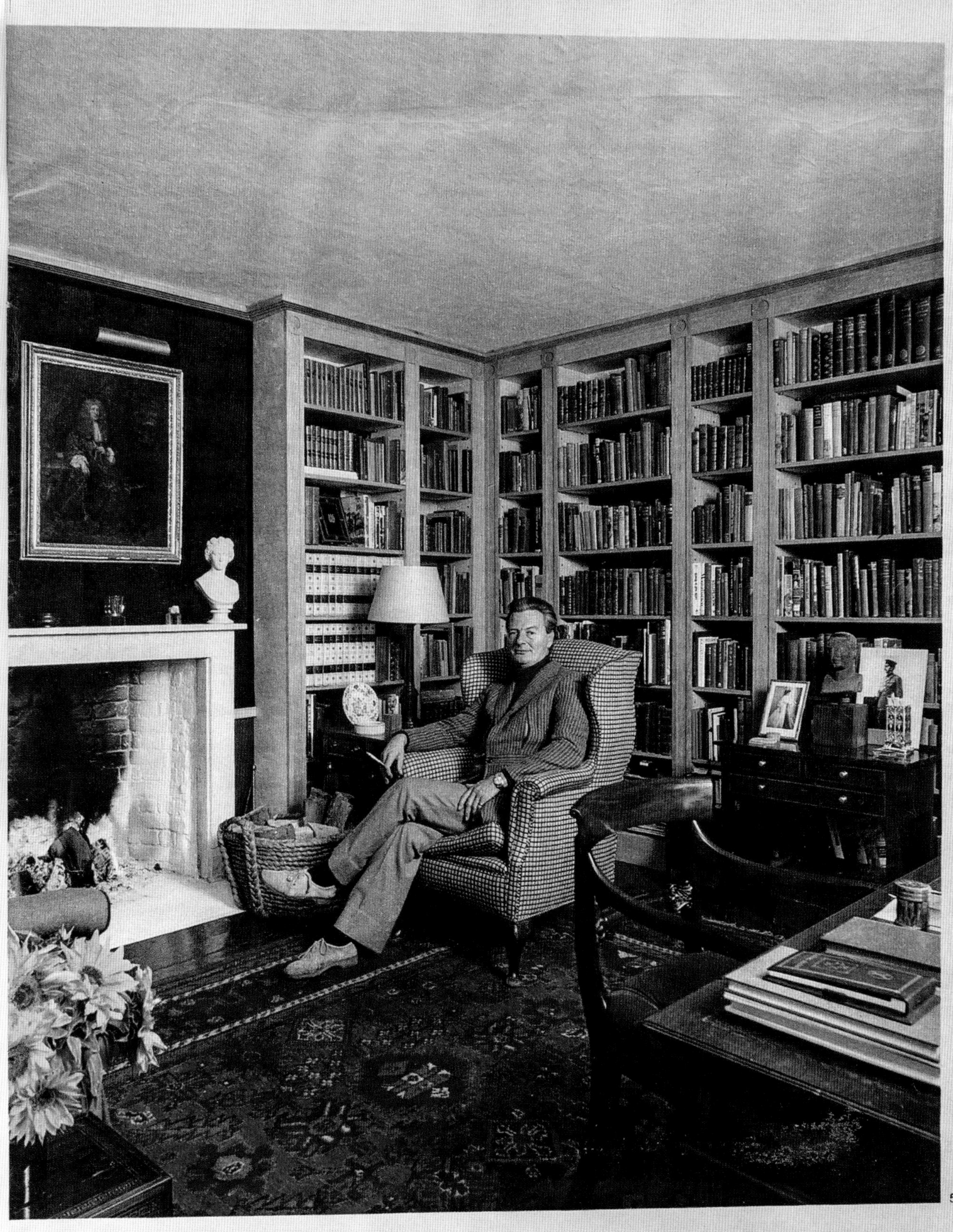

Observer 22.2.81

Singing with Colour

The problem was a small impersonal shell in Mayfair—the answer was to call in David Hicks. Christine Coleman went to see the result

Mr and Mrs Ghani, whose main house is in Portugal, spend several months of the year in London where they have a small flat a stone's throw from one of London's parks. Primarily, they chose the flat

Facing page: French antique furniture and a few modern pieces mingle in the beige drawing room whose colour scheme is accented with sugared almond pastels. Silk covers the walls and seating and is used for curtains, but the effect is pleasantly subdued. The carpet has a textured design.
Right: cinnamon felt walls soften the look of the hallway and set off the large flower prints which are lit by ceiling spotlights. At the far end hang framed collections of Roman intaglio seals. David Hicks designed the geometric-patterned brown and beige carpet to complete the scheme.
Below: the simplicity of the entrance hall heightens the impact of the ornate Empire console of silvered wood with a lapis lazuli top. Tall, slender lamps light a display of silver objects reflected in the mirror behind. French antique chairs add interest.

JOHN MILLER

PHOTO: SLIM AARONS

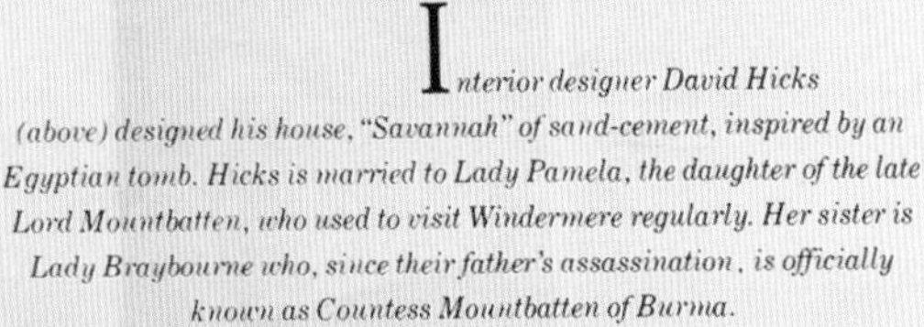

Interior designer David Hicks (above) designed his house, "Savannah" of sand-cement, inspired by an Egyptian tomb. Hicks is married to Lady Pamela, the daughter of the late Lord Mountbatten, who used to visit Windermere regularly. Her sister is Lady Braybourne who, since their father's assassination, is officially known as Countess Mountbatten of Burma.

The geometric pattern above is actually a modern one, designed by David Hicks and executed in sunny French colors.

1. Interior designer David Hicks (foreground), with wife Lady Pamela and daughter Edwina. In the background, daughter India and son Ashley with the reclining Marquis of Milford Haven, head of the Mountbatten family and cousin to Lady Pamela.

"I have never seen or tasted such an extraordinary meal," David Hicks exclaims during dinner, his blue eyes blazing with pleasure. "But tell me," he says, turning to Marie, as cream-filled petits fours are passed on a silver tray, "Are the Bernini columns real?" He is, of course, referring to what are Marie's pride and joy—wooden columns supposedly carved by the sculptor Gian Lorenzo Bernini for the Basilica in Rome.

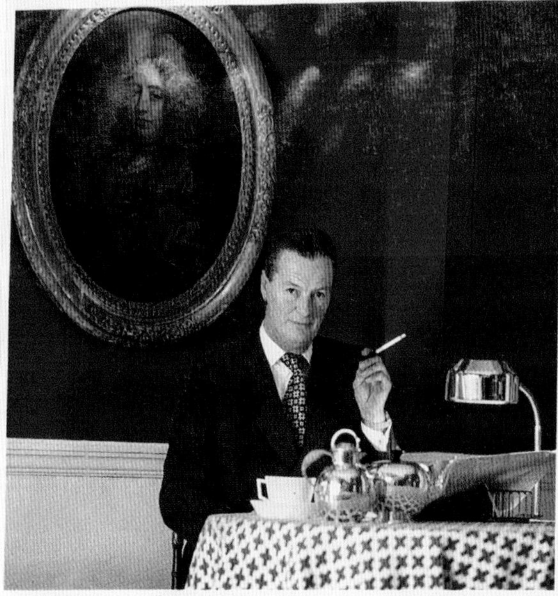

David Hicks, left, stationed at the breakfast table in London, wears a tie made of interlocking "H"s. The clerk's desk, right, is a small biography in its choice of books, from "Mountbatten" (a biography of his father-in-law) to books on Egypt and the eighteenth century. Somehow they manage to be the books he needs and still have predominantly red covers

LIVING

INSIDE OUT

A new chapter for David Hicks

David Hicks has written a book about designing gardens. It is not about how to grow things, it is about where to grow them and what shape they should be when they are grown. He has taken his taste for geometry outside into the open, applying his sense of order, balance and proportion to the unruliness of nature. However, the result is not municipal and insensitive to the spirit of plants; he has developed a theory that order and clarity of shape can evoke order in the lives of the people who walk in such a garden. It is a bold thought; for years he has made use of it indoors, and, surprisingly, the more one looks at his work the more it seems an obvious move to tackle what lies beyond the windows. For one thing, his sense of colour, which has often seemed to rely for its effects >

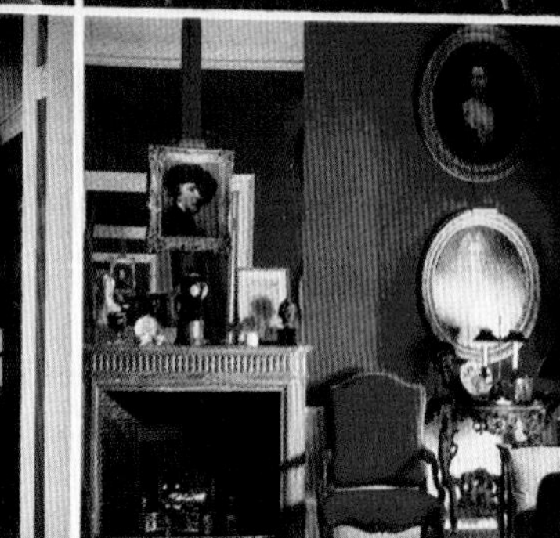

Four views of the London apartments. A secret door, far left, complete with moving cabinet, painting and flowers; the drawing-room, left, with pattern of plates over double doors, very grand eagle consoles and Empire swan armchairs; canopied bed, below far left, with mirrored chimney-breast behind, reflecting endlessly with its counterpart in the drawing-room, below left. Just visible in both bottom pictures, a splendid Reynolds

DERRY MOORE

Vogue: April 1982

The Argentine/British crisis has hit Embassy Row again.

Last week, the Embassy of Argentina pulled out of the Goodwill house tour. This week, the British decided to have a supper instead of the gala dinner they had planned for tomorrow to show off the house, redecorated by British designers using donated British products.

But yesterday, guests were called and a spokesman read a statement saying: "The Falklands' crisis makes it inappropriate to be planning the gala dinner at the British Embassy May 6. Nevertheless the purpose of the evening is a display of British design and products. We will therefore be having a presentation with supper at 7:30 p.m. that evening instead of the dinner and look forward to your attendance. Her Royal Highness Princess **Alexandra** will be honoring us with her appearance."

And what's the difference between a gala dinner and a supper? The menu is the same, and it will still be served in a tent in the garden, said the embassy. It's still black tie. Ah yes, but no television cameras or still photographers. "And it isn't a gala."

—Michael Goldfarb

'Before this time the colours mainly used were pale grey, pale green and ivory. David Hicks had first broken this up, and with John Fowler dominated the whole of English decoration. Most interior design was influenced either by one or the other and those with eyes to see and the sense to edit could learn from both. This was pre-motorways, pre-package tours, people were longing to break from austerity.'

↑ Photographed by Nico Henderson

New features at Broadlands

CHANGES and additions have been made at Broadlands, the former home of Earl Mountbatten at Romsey, which has reopened to the public.

During the winter restoration, repair and redecoration have taken place in the house, Lady Romsey inviting David Hicks, the interior designer, to advise her on the redecoration of the dinning room and drawing room.

The Mountbatten Exhibition features a new showcase display of a bridesmaid's dress and pageboy uniform from the wedding of the Prince and Princess of Wales. The costumes are those of Miss India Hicks, Lord Romsey's cousin, and Lord Nicholas Windsor, son of the Duke and Duchess of Kent.

Both of these young people performed similar roles at Lord and Lady Romsey's wedding.

And appropriately, in Maritime England year, new nautical exhibits are featured in the Mountbatten exhibition and the house.

The downstairs library was designed by David Hicks, possibly the British designer best known in the United States. The colors are sort of Pompeii red with blue. The roman shades on the arched windows are in Hicks' parrot fabric. The color sets off the room's elaborate wood caving in the Grinling Gibbons manner. The carpet has a small geometric, also designed by Hicks.

Fortunately, the ambassador's downstairs library, decorated by David Hicks in Pompeii red and blue, and off limits to Sir Nicholas since January, had been completed just in time for after-dinner discussions on the Falklands.

David Hicks' downstairs library

DAVID HICKS
FASHION FAIR
デービッド・ヒックスファッションフェア

主催：デービッド・ヒックス会
片倉工業㈱商事部 〒104 東京都中央区京橋3-1-2

DAVID HICKS FASHION SHOW

デービッド・ヒックスファッションショー

ご案内 ●日時

●会場

●構成

ホテル センチュリー HYATT

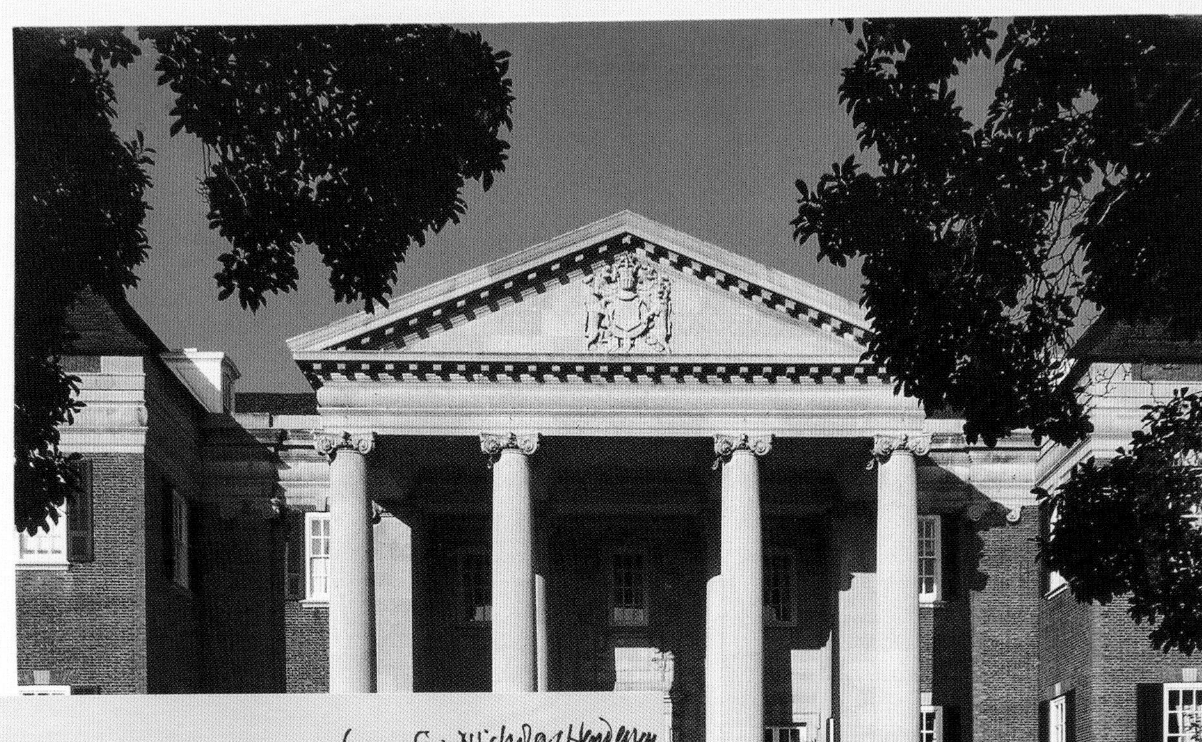

from Sir Nicholas Henderson

26 APR 1982

BRITISH EMBASSY,
WASHINGTON, D.C.
TEL: (202) 462-1340

FROM THE AMBASSADOR

14.4.82

Dear David,

Your library is better than Melk, Chatsworth or La Bibliothèque Nationale. I mean it. Deliciously soothing to the eye – and feet, because the carpet is the greatest attraction of all. Kidding that you

---

...rincess Alexandra
...tton. Angus Ogilvy

...David Bruce

...leasure of the company of

...id Hicks

...ner

... May 5th at 7:45

1405 Thirty Fourth Street N.W.

...ks

at a Gala dinner
on Thurs. 6 May at 7.30 o'clock.

please respond

British Embassy
3100 Massachusetts Avenue N.W.
Washington D.C.

BLACKTIE

R.S.V.P.
(202)462-1340

by 20 April

IN KEEPING with the sombre mood of the times, the British Embassy in Washington has downgraded tonight's longplanned 'gala dinner' to a 'supper'. Although the embassy now prefers to call it 'snacks', the menu, in fact, stays the same.

HICKS COUNTRY

In the drawing room, left, what makes a Hicks-designed room so charming and special: soft warm colors, a cloud of dried baby's breath (a favorite) on the Louis Seize commode, a great English painting, plaster bust of John, the first Duke of Marlborough, stripped back to the original 1720s paintwork, English medallion chair (1770) that Hicks freshened with white paint and yellow silk, the Hicks-designed rug in a Brussels weave custom-made in England. Above right: David Hicks in the library; bust of "Queen Victoria (Ena) of Spain's brother" is by Edward Onslow Ford, [illegible]

◆

With his unique sense of style, romance, comfort, reigning British designer (houses, gardens) David Hicks turned an eighteenth-century English farmhouse "of great simplicity" into a ravishing twentieth-century retreat

◆

David Hicks has assembled some of the most beautiful interiors in the world; but a house's surroundings are equally important to him—the trees, the gardens, the pool that one sees from indoors and enjoys outdoors—and so he also designs complete landscapes. (His latest book, *David Hicks Garden Design*, Routledge & Kegan Paul, became available in this country in September.)

And, while not trained as an architect, Hicks welcomes the opportunity to make the kinds of architectural changes and additions that give a house more style.

"I've always been passionate about architecture," he says, "and I love, whenever I can, getting the *bones* of a building right—working with cornices, redoing windows, making those changes that last. Decorating, on its own, lacks that kind of permanence."

All of his many talents came into play when Hicks took on the task of revisualizing and revital- *(Continued)*

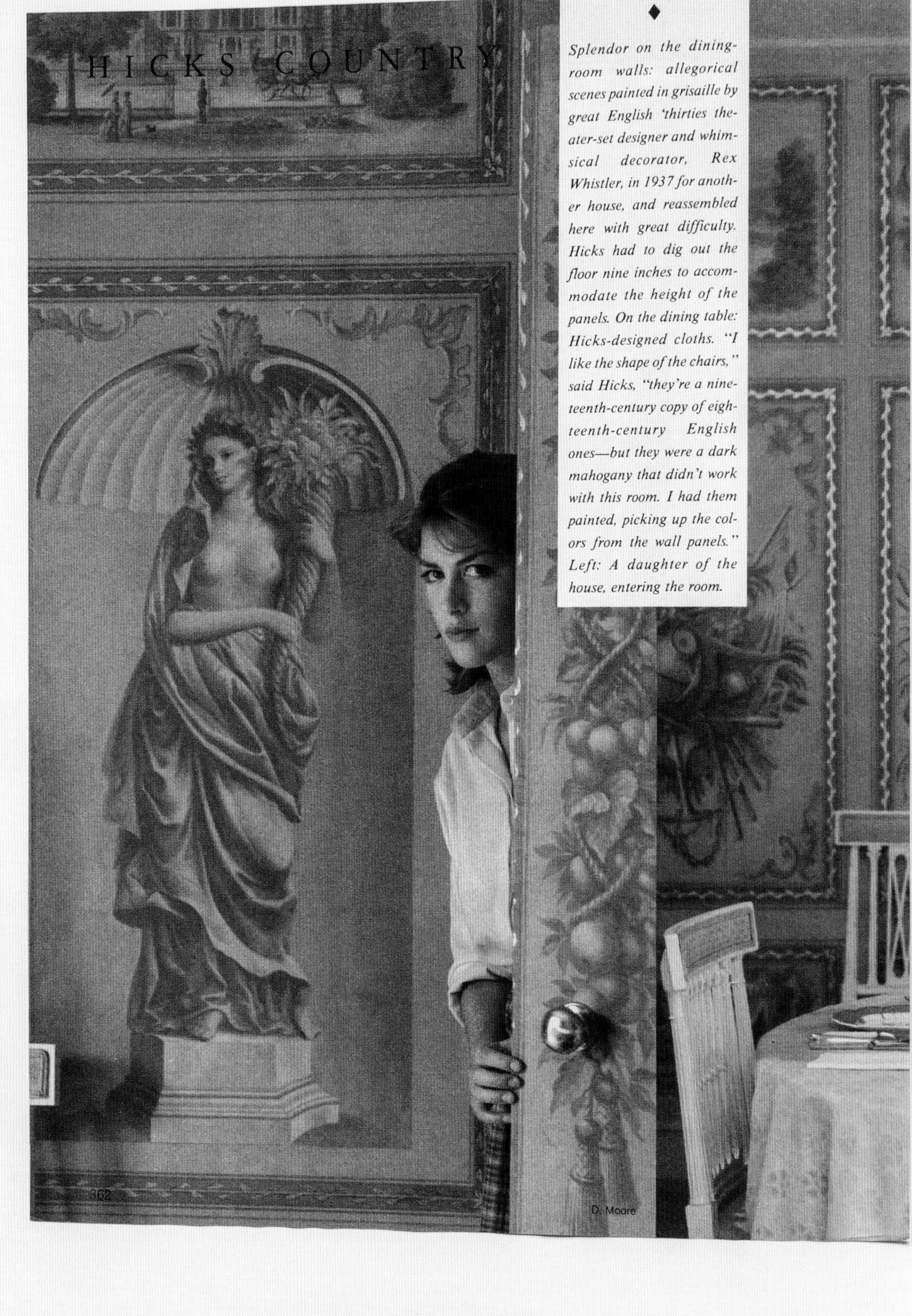

Splendor on the dining-room walls: allegorical scenes painted in grisaille by great English 'thirties theater-set designer and whimsical decorator, Rex Whistler, in 1937 for another house, and reassembled here with great difficulty. Hicks had to dig out the floor nine inches to accommodate the height of the panels. On the dining table: Hicks-designed cloths. "I like the shape of the chairs," said Hicks, "they're a nineteenth-century copy of eighteenth-century English ones—but they were a dark mahogany that didn't work with this room. I had them painted, picking up the colors from the wall panels." Left: A daughter of the house, entering the room.

D. Moore

Fashion

MR HICKS PICKS CLASSICS

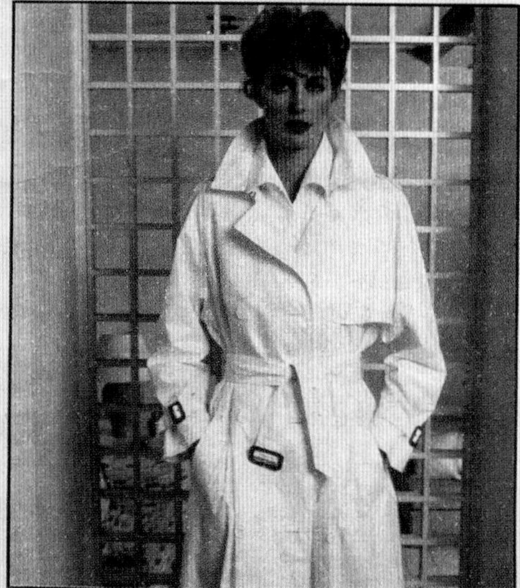

Famous interior designer David Hicks has turned his talent to fashion and designed a collection which is cool, elegant and very English

Marguerite Littman & Baba Metcalfe

David Hicks, whose work as an interior designer includes suites of rooms at Windsor Castle, Buckingham Palace, an African palace and the original bar on the *QE2*, feels that his move into the fashion world is a natural progression. He studied costume design at the Central School of Arts and Crafts before deciding on a career in interior design. For the last ten years he has designed fashion accessories for the Japanese market. His collection for spring consists of "very English, elegant, classical clothes" in pale colours and muted plaids. "I am very conservative", says Hicks. He feels that the "Englishness is precisely what people want". **Town and country** (left): David Hicks in his Jermyn Street, London, showroom approves two of his versatile styles. The cream linen pleated skirt, £90, is worn with a long-sleeved linen shirt, £73·50, and a double-breasted wool jacket, £190. The shoes, £59·99, are by Russell and Bromley. Equally at home for casual or more formal occasions, the beautifully-cut "cricket" trousers, £67, are teamed with a short-sleeved linen blouse, £71·50, and long-line, flannel blazer, £195·50. Russell and Bromley shoes, £69·99. **Country classics** (top, far left): white cotton blouse, £48·50, worn with straight, pure wool trousers, £83, and cotton "cricket" sweater, £80·50. **Go to town** (bottom, far left) in a white, cotton chintz trench coat, £212, over cotton blouse, £37, and culottes (not shown), £92. The clothes, all by David Hicks, are available from Fortnum and Mason, Piccadilly, London W1, and J. Carter Furs, Sauchiehall Street, Glasgow. Tartan jacket, double-collared linen blouse, pink jacket and trench coat also from Liberty, Regent St, London, W1 Fashion Editor, RUTH LYNAM. Photographs by DMITRI KASTERINE. Make-up by Terese Fairminer, using the new Etienne Aigner Decorative Cosmetics range. Hair by Hetta Keller at Ellis-Helen. Ⓣ

DAVID HICKS

DHIM AUSTRALIA PTY. LIMITED
70 BARCOM AVENUE, RUSHCUTTERS BAY 2011
PHONE: 331 2281 TELEX: AA71892 DHIMA

NICHOLA PAGAN

COMMERCIAL AND RESIDENTIAL INTERIOR DESIGN

The Joyes house at Palm Beach N.S.W.

ANGELA LEVIN

AT HOME WITH

David Hicks

The man who describes himself as 'undoubtedly the best-known interior designer in the world' gives a guided tour of the interior designs of his own home

David Hicks with his wife, Lady Pamela, in the drawing-room of their 'very small house'

'I hope it doesn't sound too egotistical,' says David Hicks, 'but I am undoubtedly the best-known interior designer in the world.' As well as Mayfair, he has offices in France, Belgium, Germany, Switzerland, Australia and Pakistan, and works under contract for many designers in Japan.

With a wealth of experience of designing other people's houses, it was going to be a fascinating experience to see how he furnished his own home. I might even pick up a few tips.

I wasn't disappointed. Mr Hicks has such ingrained ideas on every aspect of house and garden and is so generous with his advice, that at times I felt like a student taking an A-level in Setting Up Home. I came away with at least 101 Ways to Improve One's Domestic Environment.

Enviably, he knows exactly how a stamp-size sample of paint and a magazine-size piece of material is going to look spread over four walls and across two windows, though, unlike most of us, he needs to look at neither to make decorative decisions. Instead, he has the problem of knowing too much and explained how it was much more difficult designing for himself than other people.

'One knows so well the different effects that certain decisions will have on a room and the possibilities of colour, fabric and lighting are absolutely limitless. Budget becomes the main consideration and one cannot, of course, change all one's furniture whenever one moves. The other main consideration is that one doesn't want to live in a showroom. One wants to feel relaxed.'

We were talking at Mr Hicks's home in the country where he feels most at peace. He moved into the detached house about three years ago with his wife, Lady Pamela (daughter of the late Lord Mountbatten), and his three children – Edwina, 21, Ashley, 19 and India, 15. He also has a flat in London and another house on one of the outer islands in the Bahamas.

'This is a very small house,' he says. 'Although there are seven bedrooms and five bathrooms, most of them are quite small.' Downstairs there is a drawing-room, study/library, dining-room and television room. The house is surrounded by his 450-acre farm and the overall impression is the clever use of space.

No corner however small is wasted, but the

David Hicks's inner sanctum, a combination of bedroom, dressing-room, bathroom and small library. 'In the autumn of one's life I like a single bed'

BRIAN MOODY

Economy of space: under the stairs, a drinks table and a pile of logs; over the lavatory, a tie-rail

Everything in the garden's lovely . . . including its owner in Hicks-designed tartan

general effect is never cluttered. One example of maximising space is underneath the stairs where a marble cocktail table and a pile of logs stand side by side. Another is the conversion of part of a cloakroom into a flower-arranging area complete with small sink and shelves for his vast collection of vases.

The decor reflects his love of the geometric, from carpets (many of which have been specially woven) to upholstery. Even the ornaments fall into line. He loves symmetry and the house is like an inanimate Noah's Ark. There is never one salt cellar, side-lamp, ashtray, tin of tomato juice without its partner, both usually positioned equidistant from a central object.

As in his designs, so in his conversation. He speaks clearly and logically and when it comes to matters of style, there seems nothing he hasn't thought through and come to a positive decision about. 'I have,' he says, 'very definite views on what I do like and what I don't like.' In no particular order, he 'loathes', 'abhors', or 'finds an abomination' the following: toilet paper (Kleenex is used instead), cut-glass flower vases, drink mats, photographs on pianos, chiming front-door bells, standard lamps, hearth rugs, Persian carpets on plain Wilton carpeting, indeed any Persian carpet woven after 1600.

For a man of such fixed opinions, is it not difficult for him, I wondered, to go to other people's homes where things might not be quite as he would like them. 'Indeed,' he agreed. 'If things are not done the way I like, I would rather not be there. When I go into a room of a good friend of mine, I will often say "Do you mind if I move this?" Of course, there are occasions when one can't. Then I grin and bear it and never go again.

'In the 1950s I went to lots of cocktail parties because they were important for business. I loathed them because you cannot hear what people are saying and the drinks are never what you want. I don't go any more because I am in the fortunate position that business mostly comes to me. I have become somewhat reclusive.'

Does he know what sort of person he likes in the same way he knows how a room should look? 'Indeed. Certain people irritate me intensely. I am a snob you see. At least it is called being a snob, but I think it is actually being selective. I don't care a damn whether someone has a title if they have the right attitude to life, a *joie de vivre* and know how to be a good host or hostess.'

How does his reclusive nature affect his wife? 'She is less social than I am, so the more I stay at home, the more she is pleased. Our life revolves round my career, our children and, for her, horses and walking.'

When he can, Mr Hicks spends nearly half his week in the country. 'I have such different feelings here from the ones I get in the dreadful city.' His days also run on carefully regulated lines. He is not an early riser, has breakfast about nine and then goes into the garden, rides or shoots. If the children are at home he may play tennis. He enjoys a big, cooked breakfast. 'I will have one wherever I am in the world – Saudi Arabia, America, Sydney or London. I have a mixture of grapefruit juice and lemon juice ▷

Rather scotch than rocks

Picture: RICHARD YOUNG

No thanks, Albano . . . Margaret is unimpressed

★ AN eager PRINCESS MARGARET arrived on the dot of opening time when millions of pounds worth of jewellery went on display at London's Dorchester Hotel. Yet alas, she appeared unimpressed as ALBANO BAUCHATORY, European manager of New York jewellers Harry Winston, tried to tempt her with trinket after trinket. She bought nothing. And was certainly given no free samples.

Eventually the Princess retired to a corner, sipped scotch, puffed on her cigarette holder and chatted with dainty designer DAVID HICKS. Imagine her surprise when veteran socialite MARGARET DUCHESS OF ARGYLL hove alongside, eager to say hullo. The Princess slowly inclined her head away from this intrusion and the poor old duchess was left socially stranded, having to execute a kind of foxtrot out of royal range.

Who else was there? Well, TED HEATH turned up. Somebody calling herself COUNTESS DOMINIQUE DE BORCHGRAVE, who organised the event, explained: "Monsieur 'Eat . . .'e turn up every year, but 'e nevair buy anysing." He'd look good in a coronet, too.

Boat comes in for Hicks with an £11m haul

INTERIOR designer **David Hicks** has won a contract worth £11 million—just to decorate a boat.

Hicks, 54-year-old son-in-law of the late Earl Mountbatten, has snapped up the contract in immense secrecy to fit out **King Fahd of Saudi Arabia's** yacht.

The Abdul Aziz, hidden from prying eyes, is down at Southampton at Vospers Yard being turned into the world's most luxurious floating palace.

One of the King's men tells me: "David Hicks has won the contract, but at the request of the King everybody involved has been forced to take an oath of secrecy."

Hardly surprising, since Fahd is not exactly known for his modest ways. Earlier this year he bought the world's largest plane, a glorified Boeing 747 for £70 million. He is even now in the middle of doing a few

King orders top secrecy over new toy

alterations on his house in Kensington . . . £24 million worth.

Aboard the Abdul Aziz Hicks will deck out the King's bathroom in the blue gemstone lapus lazuli. Other bits and bobs include a helicopter pad, swimming pool, fully-equipped hospital and bullet-proof windows.

Voyage

Hicks was up against fierce European competition to clinch the deal, but work is well under way and the gleaming white, two-funnel Abdul Aziz will make her (or should it be his?) maiden voyage to Jeddah next May.

An admiring Hicks cohort sighs: "It will be the most spectacular yacht ever."

And why not. Dainty David knows his stuff. He did up **Prince Charles's** former Buckingham Palace suite, **Princess Anne's** Gatcombe Park, and even the London offices of Aeroflot. What's a boat after that?

DAVID HICKS

"There's a very interesting parallel between women's fashion and interior design. Design colour follows, almost inevitably, 18 months after what has been happening in fashion.

"Now a new element has crept in. The modern architecture that we've all been so excited about for the last quarter of a century is being knocked sideways and there's a tremendous revival in neo-classicism. More and more we are going back to classical styles and traditional furniture.

"We fully recognise that even a prince cannot afford to buy 40 Louis XV or Chippendale dining chairs, so we're finding craftsmen to build traditional sofas, chairs and bookcases to our design. It's a complete reaction to the ultra-modern, brutalist view of architecture — and indeed of interiors.

"Gathered curtains? No, they're not popular with me. Curtains have to be very bland, very straightforward and very down-to-earth — touching the floor, but not lying on it. I think that's a theatrical affectation.

"To me, lighting is one of the most important elements of an interior. You must have a lot of switches and you have to be able to raise or lower the amount of light emitted. Lighting can transform a dreary bedsitter, just as a simple tablecloth of felt draped over a perfectly ordinary table can give a feeling of glamour and style.

"As regards colour, I've got my own preferences, but I never impose them on my clients. I'm always tremendously against journalists asking me what the latest trends in interior design are. I think it's slightly immoral. People might actually listen to you, and redesign their homes in a colour that would be out of fashion three years later . . ."

Stein's designs

Cyril Stein, Chairman and Chief Executive of Ladbroke, the betting-to-property development group, has a legendary head for figures. But it is said to be second only to his eye for detail —particularly when properties built by his company are being fitted out and furnished. He insits upon good design and impeccable finishes.

All of which may explain why Ladbroke has just bought a 20 per cent stake in David Hicks International, the design group started 27 years ago by Lord Mountbatten's son-in-law, and still well known for its aristocratic clients and connections. Hicks remains a sizeable shareholder.

Nowadays the company has contracts as far afield as Australia and Pakistan. Stein — who is joining the board — is seen as an important recruit to an organisation which may well seek a public flotation within the next couple of years.

Leslie Button, chief executive of Hicks for the past 15 years, has been striving to change the company's image recently. He explains: "We are not just decorators for blue-haired ladies or designers of royal yachts for Saudi Arabians. We design biscuit tins for Metal Box and, in Japan, we design everyting from ladies' knickers to spectacles."

Button is behind the company's more aggressive new approach to life. He inspired a rethink after a public company made an offer for Hicks last year. "We had to decide if we were to continue as a family affair, or if we were to grow into something much bigger and capitalise on all our hard work. We chose growth."

Button, himself a large shareholder, is delighted that Stein has come on board. He says: "We are already doing considerable business with Ladbroke and we both saw tremendous value in some form of tie-up. We fixed it over breakfast in 20 minutes."

The latest result of the combined efforts will be unveiled today. The once-stately town house, 100 Piccadilly (it later became the Public Schools Club), has been turned into nearly 50,000 square feet of top-quality West End office space. It is expected to command the highest rents in that well-heeled corner of London.

David Hicks, designer: "Since my daughter India stole my Panama I've worn this terrible old cap"

. . . David Hicks used to wear his father's old Panama "although the mower had gone over it at least twice", until his daughter India took a fancy to it and carried it off to London. The *Sunday Times* gardening correspondent, Graham Rose, pinched his Westminster boating cap from his daughter, who liberated it from a boyfriend.

Sunday Express magazine 12 May 1985

THE MOST BEAUTIFUL

Domestic Interior

Chosen by
DAVID HICKS

Interior designer, who has designed for the Queen, the Prince of Wales, the British Embassy in Washington, and Aeroflot

From the first time I saw it in 1946, the **breakfast parlour in the Sir John Soane Museum** in Lincoln's Inn Fields, London, has been, for me, one of the most beautiful rooms in the world. I find that it has atmosphere, style, character, intimacy and warmth as well as a particular fascination that no other room has.

Soane was an incredible innovative character who gave not only to his exteriors but to the interiors of all his work a classic simplicity with a hint of grandeur, a whimsical inventiveness and an amazing sense of room. Here this is achieved in a relatively small space by curiously contrived domes, throwing daylight and vistas from room to room.

This room contains over 60 pieces of mirror, including 32 convex circular ones ranging in diameter from two inches to two feet. The shallow domed ceiling with its delicate incised plasterwork details, the Vuillamy clock with its elaborate and evocative chimes, combine with the relief plaques behind amber glass. The black and white marble fireplace and the view through to the antique sculpture collection, including my favourite Piranesi vases, also evoke an atmosphere more scholarly, caressing and stimulating than any room I know.

Soane's work has been the starting point of many of my own ideas in interior architecture. This incredibly rare combination of qualities inspires me every time I revisit the room.

The Queen has asked me to let you know that when she goes to Chelsea on 21st May she would like her attention directed to the Homes and Gardens Magazine garden, which I understand has been designed this year by David Hicks. I expect this will be on your itinerary anyway, but I thought I would let you know Her Majesty's wishes well in advance.

OUR CHELSEA

THE GARDEN

Our garden, which won the Royal Horticultural Society's Silver Gilt Medal at the 1984 Chelsea Flower Show, was designed by David Hicks to be a small (33 x 38 ft) and relaxing urban retreat. In association with Spear and Jackson, we asked the world-famous designer to create the sort of garden where one might invite friends to drinks or an informal supper.

The stunning result: cobble-edged grass leads the eye from a central cascading fountain down to a paved seating area centring on a carpet of ground-hugging plants. The beds are planted with a blending of shrubs. In front, a low box hedge outlines small fruit trees underplanted with salad crops.

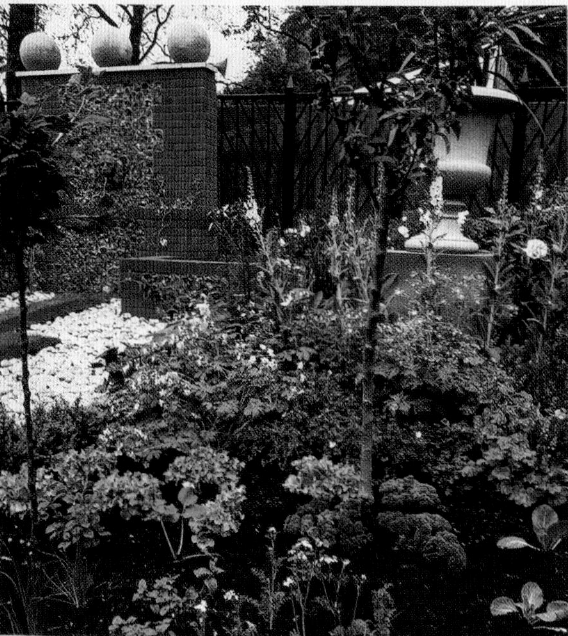

Top: *elegant garden seats and tables were specially designed by David Hicks.*
Above: *strong lines flow from the fountain to a parterre of green saxifrage, cream helxine and grey* Raoulia australis.
Right: *apple trees bearing three varieties, Victoria plums and standard gooseberry bushes underplanted with lettuces. Construction, Dilan Site Developments, Aldenham, Watford. Shrubs, Hillier Nurseries (Winchester). Herbaceous plants, Blooms Nurseries, Bressingham, Diss. Fruit trees, Deacons Nurseries, Godshill, Isle of Wight. Aquatic plants and pool equipment, Lotus Water Garden Products, Chesham. Paving, ARC Conbloc, Chipping Camden.*

GARDEN PARTY

THE PARTY

The weather was bitter but the rain held off and the party that launched our elegant town garden was a delicious success. The "green" lunch – that went with the Vinho Verde and with the very smart hunter-green chairs and tables – was every bit as chic to look at as it was delicious to eat. The lovely English Garden restaurant in Chelsea provided what must have been quite the finest fare being nibbled that day.

It was a thoroughly international event, and guests from far-flung parts were received by our editor, Jenny Greene, and David Hicks himself with his wife, Lady Pamela. They included Mrs Charles Price, wife of the United States' Ambassador; ex-King Simeon of the Bulgarians and Queen Marguerita; HH Rajmata of Jaipur whose book, *A Princess Remembers*, had just been published; the Marchioness of Salisbury, a very keen gardener; the former Prime Minister of Australia, Malcolm Fraser, and his wife. Lady Romsey, a niece of the Hicks', also dropped in.

A constant source of fascination and discussion was the oblong "carpet" of tiny green and cream and grey ground-hugging plants, boxed in geometric wooden shapes and set in carefully levelled gravel to give a striking oriental effect. So, too, were the dwarf fruit-tree canopies over neat rows of lettuces – an unexpected sight in an herbaceous border.

Above: *Later HM the Queen honoured us with a visit. She is seen here with Jenny Greene, the editor, Mr Robin Herbert, President of The Royal Horticultural Society, and Mr David Hicks (right).*
Left: *among the many royal visitors, who included TRH The Prince and Princess of Wales, Princess Alice Duchess of Gloucester and Princess Alexandra, was Princess Michael of Kent, seen here chatting to Mr Hicks.*
Far left: *David Hicks arranges a geranium display.* ▷**103**

Hanae Mori contd.

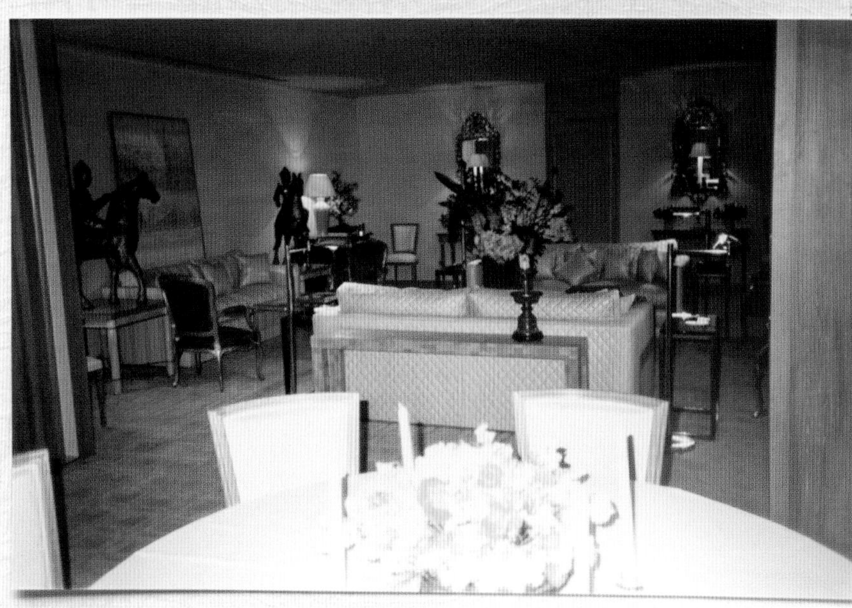

some trade secrets

"It's what David Hicks doesn't do that he does best. I don't add fidgety things to clutter up a room, or bounce in too many colours."
DAVID HICKS

This show flat designed by David Hicks, in a block of 15 residential units managed by Ladbroke Properties, was sold immediately it opened.

"We are always given the worst flat to decorate, the one the estate agents can't easily sell. The first had its arched windows quite ruined by a partition wall between the drawing room and the study and we had to camouflage it with blinds and a screen.

"But you see, I am 58 and have been decorating houses since I was 23, so I do consider myself an expert. Where in these rooms, tell me, is the vulgarity of so many

of the modern-day scheme
Good taste carries a price
the three-bedroomed flat in sca
and brown sold for £695,000 w
a studio is priced at £155,000.
That certain look Hicks bri
to any project is faithfully follo
by his design team, headed
Stephen Ryan: furniture grou
with perfect symmetry to "tal
each other"; an alteration of
level interest with furniture f
the tall limed oak corner cupbo
to the low Perspex tables; mir
that bounce back light into
room and double up the images
that element of surprise.
There are other "Hicksi
touches like the use of the m
patterned Brussels weave carp
designed by David Hicks, the
urious yet practically finished
holstery, even the flowers. D
Hicks always uses flowers in
schemes: he loathes wired arra
ments, and certain flowers
chrysanthemums and gladioli
never given house room.
"It's what David Hicks doe
do that he does best," he s
enigmatically. "I don't add fid
things to clutter up a room,
bounce in too many colours. A
never agree with such flashy i
as which colours are fashiona
Who am I to tell people to h
black felt all over their dining r
walls? It depends on where
live, the light, their belongi
and preferences."
David Hicks felt it would
difficult to walk into a dark fla
he intentionally kept the co
scheme light and attractive. He
an instinctive response to co
combinations, reacting like lit
paper to a scheme. Even wor
quickly, he can see when a r
needs toning up or down.
colour combinations can be bri
ened or dampened with a few s
changes, from scatter cushion
loose covers on the sofa, a favo
decorating device he uses—"
Slipper always made mine t
like a glove".
Rooms are lit carefully,
downlighters for background
mination, and lamps to cast p
of light to read or work by. And
designs are always attractive, "n
those ghastly ecclesiastical can
sticks with ruched shades".

David Hicks, 101 Jermyn Street, London W1.

Japanese wrapping paper

David Hicks

Building on the Hicks image

William Dawkins on the management of a style

David Hicks (left) [illegible] in the reception of Citibank in London's Strand, designed by David Hicks International

BEING the eminence grise of British interior design is one thing, but making a profitable business out of it demands quite different skills.

That realisation drove David Hicks to team up 17 years ago with [illegible], a former production salesman for a maker of printed circuit boards, who since then has provided the commercial brainpower behind what is now a household name for style among the rich and aristocratic.

Like a miniature version of Laura Ashley—which it will be following on to the full stock market next year—David Hicks International depends heavily on one person's personality, yet also like the fashion group, it has devoted much effort to evolving a business and design style that could run almost independently of its founding name.

For Hicks, now 57, and the group's elegant showrooms in London's Jermyn Street are only the most visible parts of the company. The real power behind the throne is the 43-year-old [illegible], whose 49 per cent equity stake makes him by far the most influential shareholder.

It was at the down-to-earth [illegible] insistence three years ago that most of the group's staff—including himself—moved out of Jermyn Street into a faceless high tech box in Nine Elms, south London. The new office fits the Hicks image about as well as a filing cabinet matches a Chippendale table, but, says [illegible], it is cheap and efficient.

It is also one of the most important elements in [illegible]'s crusade to change David Hicks from a comfortable family occupation into a fast growing little business fit for public ownership. The process has seen a doubling in staff numbers to 62 over the past three years, while turnover has risen over the same period from £1.7m to £9.6m for the 12 months ending in December, when the group made a £750,000 pre-tax profit.

However, achieving that change of gear has not been easy for a company which since its formation had idled along with annual sales of between £1m and £1.5m. Personalities have been bruised: 11 staff left last year because, according to Button, "they felt they could not keep up." Meanwhile, Button has had to strike a delicate balance between expansion and not jeopardising the exclusive image which has permitted the business to survive.

The way in which David Hicks reached for growth could be instructive to the many small businesses which find it hard to get off an earnings plateau. For one thing, the management might never have withstood the strain of expansion if the two partners had not ensured that their responsibilities could not clash. "David doesn't know what a pound coin looks like and I keep out of design," says [illegible], nonchalantly leaning back in one of the Hicks reject chairs with which he furnishes his office.

Ironically it was the enormous success of the Jermyn Street showroom after its opening in 1977 (by [illegible]'s wife) that made [illegible] realise that the group could not be run as a family business for ever. "Within months, £4m to £5m of business came off the street from passers-by. We spent so much time executing the work that we pushed the source of interest (the shop) aside. We were too busy to think about the future, so the shop became stale. As a result, the outside perception of us was that of a blue-haired ladies' decorator," says [illegible].

His solution was to hire a commercial manager and open a new business department, so that sales and operations were kept separate from design, allowing the creative team to get on with what they knew best.

The new commerical manager, Clifford Standen, had a hotel and catering background—appropriate in view of [illegible]'s feelings that the group needed to reduce its dependence on a fickle private market in favour of interior design for commercial property owners. Indeed, this was why David Hicks later sold 20 per cent of its shares for £600,000 to Ladbroke, the betting to property development group.

Ladbroke has not done badly out of its investment, which is valued at £1.2m in a private placing being arranged by stockbrokers Capel-Cure Myers. However, [illegible] admits that the group has not picked up as much Ladbroke business as it hoped.

Until last March [illegible] was in practice managing the non-design side of David Hicks alone. Fourteen managers reported to him and there was very little delegation. "That situation just couldn't go on if we were to grow," he recalls.

Accordingly, [illegible] made all the managers personally responsible for the contracts in their care and added a carrot in the form of profit bonuses for all staff and an increase in salaries to above market average for the first time in the company's history. Delegation was made easier by the completion in early 1984 of a computerised accounting system, which allowed the group to estimate costs and profit margins on individual contracts in advance, thereby providing managers with easily recognisable targets.

"Under the old system, we didn't know what our profits were until the project was over. There was a tendency on our part to over-run on costs, which meant that we started off with large margins that gradually got whittled away," says [illegible]. David Hicks depends on a small number of large contracts—only 12 last year—which take up to nine months to complete and arrive at erratic intervals. That means that cost estimating mistakes can have especially uncomfortable results, a risk which makes delegation doubly difficult.

[illegible] cannot disclose how much individual clients spend, though by way of illustration a recent David Hicks refit for the Saudi Arabian royal yacht cost $1m in design fees alone.

Financing the costly materials for which Hicks is famous, long payment times for overseas projects (more than 80 per cent of last year's turnover), and the group's increasing exposure to institutional clients who do not put up large initial deposits so easily as private customers, have all put a growing strain on working capital requirements. Last year's borrowings peaked as a result to £1.3m, just over the group's £1.2m equity base. It is to eliminate that strain that the company is about to raise £1.5m in new money from the City in a private placing underwritten by Capel-Cure Myers.

A smaller but important part of [illegible] campaign to put David Hicks onto a more stable footing was his introduction a year ago of daily written contract reports. While small businesses are believed by many to thrive on a lack of bureaucracy, [illegible] points out: "When the company gets to about 60 people, you cannot know what is going on in every area at all times. So if you can't do everything, you can at least read everything."

The Hicks redesign is not quite complete. [illegible] would like to stand still further back from routine administration so that he can concentrate on strategic matters like the flotation and the acquisitions which he feels will be essential if David Hicks is to go on growing in its small and fragmented industry. Even so, he claims, "we now have a system where we can grow to £18m or £19m turnover without changing very much."

Top designer eyes hotels

On April 1st, superstar English interior designer David Hicks will join forces with Australia's architectural firm **Peddle Thorp & Walker.** The new company, to be a division of Peddle Thorp, will be called **David Hicks Peddle Thorp.**

UK designer David Hicks
After local hotel market.

Hicks, who handles gilt-edged projects like the $44 million fit-out of the King of Saudi Arabia's yacht and the home of Japanese designer Hanae Mori, is also well known for commercial work, including the **International Wool Secretariat** in London.

While the Hicks PT group will handle everything from factories to the occasional private luxury project, it is believed that both Hicks and Peddle Thorp will be aggressively pursuing the booming hotel market.

Elizabeth Farm
70 Alice Street Granville, Sydney, Australia.

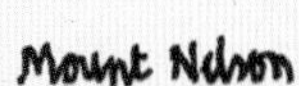

Three Designs On Space

How do design experts transform unpromising rooms into something that makes visitors gasp? Here are some demonstrations by Britons David Hicks, Pierre Botshil and Mary Fox Linton.

When David Hicks says there should be a chandelier, he means the biggest the ceiling will take. He covered the bathroom (above right) with mirror. It's a lot of cleaning," he says, "it must look immaculate."

DAVID HICKS, never known for his modesty, says quite simply that he is the best decorator in the world.

A "wealthy foreign family" asked him to convert this flat overlooking Hyde Park in London and, to his delight, they gave him free rein. "The flat had three completely separate living-rooms. I felt we should open it up and make these into one area. It really works, giving a much greater feeling of space. Standing at one end you have a long vista for such a small apartment, increased by mirroring the end wall in the study. You go from blonde light, pale and summery, through the red dining area, the colour of sun awnings in Venice, into the dark of the study."

Tulips at Albany from the Grove.

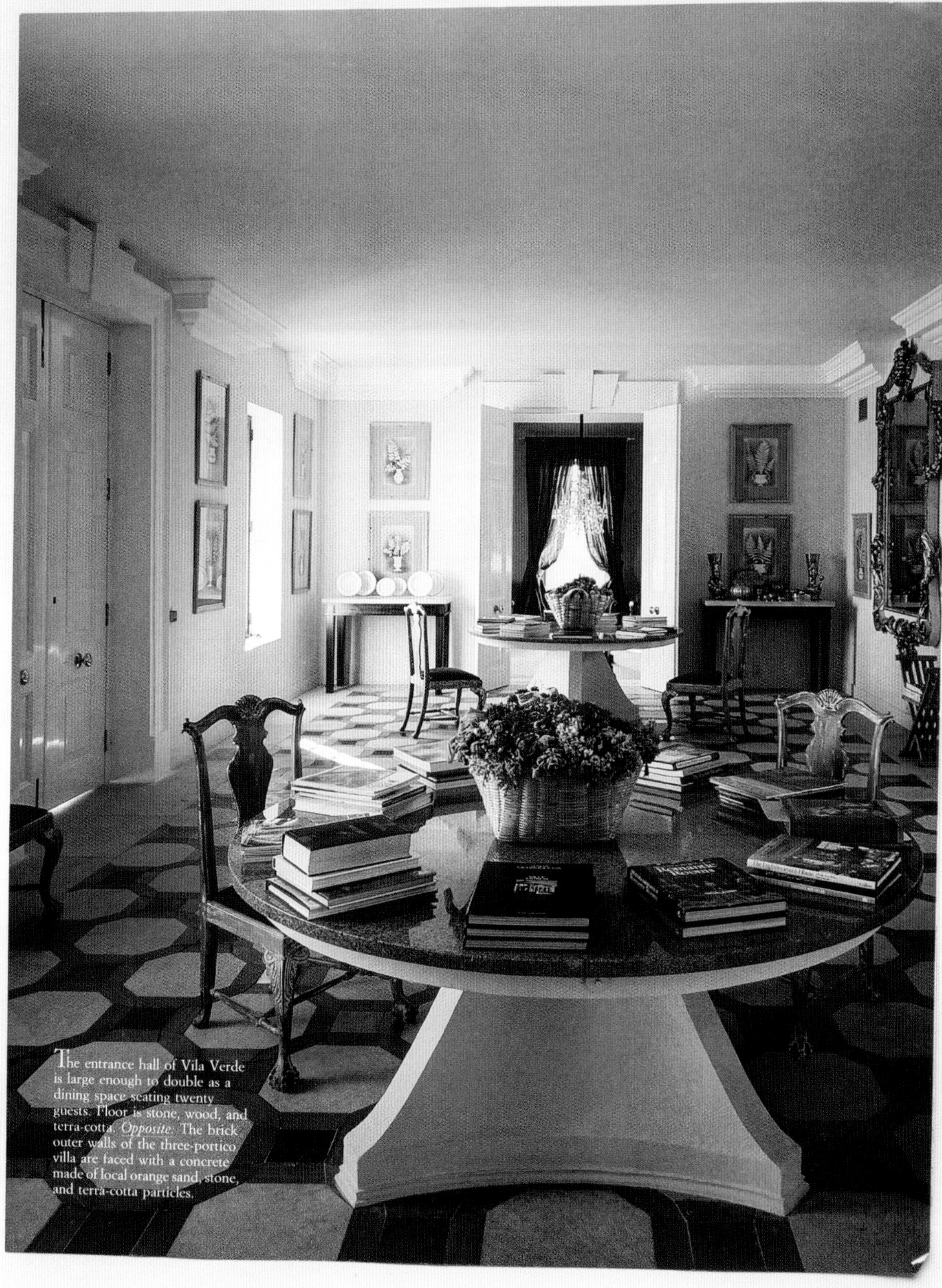

The entrance hall of Vila Verde is large enough to double as a dining space seating twenty guests. Floor is stone, wood, and terra-cotta. *Opposite:* The brick outer walls of the three-portico villa are faced with a concrete made of local orange sand, stone, and terra-cotta particles.

VILA VERDE
LAMEIRO
ALGARVE

October 19

Dear David,

What a great surprise & what a marvellous design. A great addition for the North lawn. I like it. Can hardly wait to see it done. Most probably will be in process while you're here. Will be fun.

I especially admire your contribution to V.V. in giving me

THE CLASSICAL VILLA RESTATED

David Hicks's total design for a magical new estate in Portugal

BY MARK HAMPTON

PHOTOGRAPHS BY FRITZ VON DER SCHULENBURG

At the beginning of the sixties, a decade before the term Post-modernism was coined, David Hicks was combining strong architectural elements of the seventeenth and eighteenth centuries with contemporary and antique furniture in a way that was prophetic. From the start the Hicks style was bold and solid-looking. Geometry prevailed over everything. The arrangement of furniture, the placement of objects (often the objects themselves), the designs of the carpets, and the patterns of the materials—all these elements shared a strict geometrical quality. The backgrounds against which they were placed were sturdily architectural. Clean moldings were set off by plain expanses of flat color or highly polished lacquer, the latter achieved by coat after coat of carriage varnish. Where no architectural details existed, new ones were created in an idiom that combined the sleekness of the twentieth century with a keen interest in the architecture and decoration of the past, and by the past I

American "House & Gardens"

born, Palladio had barely finished the Villa Rotunda, the inspiration for this house. (It is interesting to think that English Palladianism started so close to the time of Palladio himself). Vila Verde is proof of the current vitality of that venerable movement.

The interior continues the evocative mood of the exterior. The stair hall reminds one of the seventeenth century and the great divided staircases that were the logical development of Elizabethan stairs. The *sala*, or 'big room', as David Hicks and his clients call it, has a spare, monumental quality that is both imposing and quiet. The five round openings and the gigantic cornice immediately draw the eye upward. Then you look around, and you see a room of great comfort with the more usual accumulation of furniture from the owner's previous houses, the most recent of which was an apartment in London, the result of

1 *and* **2** *The flat wood balusters of the divided staircase stand out against the charcoal grey stippled wallpaper. Against the walls hang panels of architectural fragments.* **3-5** *In one of the guest rooms, a granite-encased bath sits at the foot of the four-poster bed draped in cotton printed to one of David Hicks' designs. The hand-made terazzo floor contains terracotta, stone and sea shells, and the Louis XVI chimneypiece (4) is of marbled pottery from Apt. The windows are shaded by dark-brown-stained wooden Venetian blinds.*

another collaboration with David Hicks. For years, his clients have travelled around the world collecting the furniture and objects that have finally come to rest on this hilltop in Portugal. The Vila Verde is the first complete house and garden that David Hicks has architected and decorated from start to

3

4

5

Caroline in the Lib

Interior designer David Hicks and his wife, Lady Pamela, a Mountbatten, find their Albany chambers a "haven from the horrible world outside."

little garden out back. To the people lucky enough to own or rent one of the seventy apartments there, Albany is not so much a London address as a way of life—albeit a somewhat eccentric and reclusive one. For instance, you cannot live there if you are under thirteen, so families are not exactly encouraged. You cannot keep pets, alter any of the interior architecture, whistle, or run down its corridors. Nor can you take photographs without very special permission, which can sometimes take months to acquire. Nor can you ever sell your apartment, assuming you somehow managed to buy one in the first place, without first making sure that your prospective buyer is acceptable to the other residents. Albany is, in short, that most English of institutions, a block of mansion apartments so exclusive and impenetrable that most of those who live there will, if possible, deny that they do so for the sake of their own privacy. It is much like having a small flat somewhere in the Vatican, only without the religion; the ceilings are not a lot less impressive.

To find out how Albany got to be Albany, it's best to start at the beginning, with the help of the current secretary to the trustees, Peter Davison. In 1770–71, Lord Melbourne had a house built on the north side of Piccadilly going up toward the circus, diagonally opposite both Fortnum & Mason and Hatchards bookshop, and approached through a small courtyard that can accommodate roughly one car for every ten residents. The Melbourne mansion cost all of £30,000 to build, an astonishing sum for the late eighteenth century, and it now houses thirteen of the Albany apartments,

Decor by David Hicks, designer for the British Royal Family.

Completing the tasteful decor of each guest room is a view of Kobe Port's glittering harbor lights. Designed by the celebrated British interior designer, David Hicks, all furnishings have been coordinated in a simple design that emphasizes their beauty and creates a sense of composure and relaxation.

oKura, Kobe.

ツインルーム

プレジデンシャルスイート

スイート

Gandee AT LARGE

"I think I have been rather boring," said David Hicks at the end of lunch. But it wasn't true

When the waitress tried to escape from our table with a bowl of mayonnaise, David Hicks stopped her. "The war is over, my dear," said the famous British decorator in a voice reminiscent of Winston Churchill's. "We're not rationing anymore." The poor woman placed two additional dollops next to my luncheon companion's dismembered lobster, which satisfied him—and freed her.

Hicks and I had adjourned to Bentley's restaurant on Swallow Street after meeting for an aperitif in his rooms at Albany in Piccadilly where, I was told, "Lord Byron once lived" and where the interview had gotten off to a somewhat dangerous start with my host's announcement that America had become bored with him. "In the early sixties," recalled Hicks, picking up where he had left off twenty minutes before, "I introduced geometric carpets and fabrics to the United States. And I did it with great panache, and I was very much sought after. But you know Americans do tire of a look—you people are very fashion-conscious. So in 1972 I looked to Japan as a marvelous market waiting to be exploited." And exploit it Hicks did, designing "every kind of thing for sale in department stores"—including, but not limited to, panty hose, costume jewelry, luggage, womenswear, menswear, and sheets. "I am a very well known designer in Japan," he boasted—then, apparently to prove the point, proudly added that his current commissions include a 900-room hotel in Tokyo and a 600-room hotel in Kobe.

Since Hicks has enjoyed such a long and distinguished career, I asked him what he thought about the current state of decorating, in general. Which proved to be a mistake: "I am really just bored with the interior design scene. I think it has become an uninteresting subject because everything has been said, everything has become sort of tired and finished." Thinking that a more specific tack might be advised, I solicited Hicks's opinion on a diverse group of his high-profile friends and colleagues. But that, too, made for less than happy conversation. Referring to some of the best decorators in Paris, London, and New York, he said: "Ugh. Dreadful work. Not a shread of taste. A complete poseur." "He's terribly nice, but there's no guts to his work." "I have known him a long time. It won't last very long." "He's hopeless, but he's sweet and nice and funny and knowledgeable and charming and fun." "It's dreary, it's tired, it's finished, it's worn out." "She's a nice girl, hardworking; there's nothing interesting about her at all."

Hicks was even less reserved on the subject of architects. "All my interior designing career I've been fighting and grating against these idiot architects. I mean, most of them have never seen a drawing room—they just don't know how ladies and gentlemen live." Of London's two premier practitioners of high tech, Hicks said of the one, "I don't like anything he's ever done in his entire life," and of the other, "He's an absolute lunatic."

In search of safer ground I asked if Hicks thought the Prince of Wales was on the right track with his highly publicized war against Modernism. "I won't speak about him because I'm related to him—he's my wife's first cousin once removed. I think it's very good indeed that someone in such an influential position has made a strong statement about architecture. I think it's marvelous." Also marvelous, according to Hicks, is the Classical architecture of Prince Charles's favorite, Quinlan Terry: "I'm a great admirer." When prodded, however, it seems that "Quinlan is too Italianate."

So what succeeds in snaring David Hicks's attention and talent these days? "I am very very interested in garden design because when I plant an avenue of trees, when I plant a formal rose garden, those things will remain for fifty or one hundred years. And then I am also building, I am actually being an architect." Specifically, Hicks reported that he was working on a "very compact and very Classical" house for a businessman in Miami. "You wait and see what I do in Miami," he said. "That will be very fresh, very different, very strong, very original."

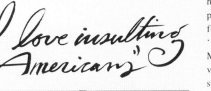

"I love insulting Americans"

CHRIS GARNHAM

As we left the restaurant, I asked Hicks what his day-to-day life was like. He reported that on this particular Wednesday morning he had been to Savile Row to his tailor, Huntsman—"He's the best, really"—and that he planned to drop by the office sometime later in the afternoon. "Sounds as if you don't spend much time there," I said. "Familiarity breeds contempt," explained David Hicks.

Charles Gandee

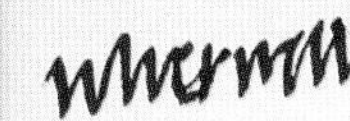

THE GRASS IS GREENER

Flowers make way for foliage. PENELOPE HOBHOUSE explores two luxuriant gardens where green takes centre stage

The textured greens of leaves form the background frame to almost every garden scene. Green, in a multiplicity of shades and tones, provides a quiet and cool contrast to all the more vivid flower colours which are a garden's decoration. Floral colour is fleeting and ephemeral; the more solid and lasting greens of foliage shape the garden landscape through all the seasons.

The "greens" in a garden composition, whether used formally or informally, are the province of the garden planner. By using architectural rules of symmetry, balance and perspective a logical design rhythm is created. Tree canopies composed of different weights and densities of foliage frame the sky; at lower levels the shapes of trees and shrubs define vistas to focal points or to distant countryside. In the foreground, sweeping lawns, edged with low-growing foliage plants, make pools of light; contrasting areas of mown and longer grass give further texture and colour >

***Top** and **right**, The Grove, designed by David Hicks. **Above**, 19th-century Brockenhurst*

1. Deux portes d'inspiration gothique dessinées en 1979 ouvrent sur le jardin.
2. Des fenêtres en avancée, d'autres de style gothique, d'élégantes colonnes, un porche en treillis blanc dessinés par David Hicks.

EN ANGLETERRE

DAVID HICKS AT HOME

DAVID HICKS NOUS OUVRE LES PORTES DE SA MAISON ET DE SON JARDIN PRÈS DE LONDRES. UNE INTERPRÉTATION PLUS PERSONNELLE- ET PEUT-ÊTRE UN PEU INATTENDUE DE SON PROPRE STYLE.
PHOTOS MARIANNE HAAS

A.A. Est-ce que la décoration et l'architecture d'intérieur ont été pour vous une vocation précoce ?

D.H. Je crois avoir vécu avec une sensibilité d'artiste, très intéressé surtout par la façon dont vivent les gens. C'est une activité où l'on cherche à changer l'optique des gens sur la façon dont ils utilisent et vivent les choses. Nous cherchons à les influencer afin qu'ils en tirent le maximum. Ce qui m'a rendu inventif, c'est d'avoir été élevé dans la période austère de la guerre et de l'après-guerre. Ce qui m'a contraint à toujours utiliser au mieux ce qui se présentait. De là ce goût que j'ai pour les choses simples et naturelles, et souvent les objets les plus simples sont ceux qui donnent le plus de bonheur.

A.A. Cette époque vous a donc beaucoup marqué.

D.H. Elle nous a tous marqués, et elle m'a donné conscience d'être Anglais. Et c'est peut-être ce que les gens recherchent en faisant appel à moi. Mon style et mon talent sont Anglais.

A.A. Qu'entendez-vous par là ?

D.H. Je ne sais pas. C'est à vous d'en décider. En revanche, je sais ce que j'apprécie chez les Français : leur précision intellectuelle, leur culte pour la nourriture et le vin. Leur grande connaissance de l'architecture et de la littérature. Et puis les femmes françaises ont du chic.

A.A. Vous reconnaissez-vous des influences ?

D.H. Bien évidemment, et elles sont nombreuses. D'abord les livres où j'ai découvert des photos, des dessins qui m'ont intrigué. Il y a eu une expérience, entre autres, qui m'a profondément marqué. Lorsque j'étais enfant, mes parents m'amenèrent chez des amis. Lui était le rédacteur en chef du magazine « Studio ». Il avait un sens artistique exceptionnel. Je me souviens que dans son immense bibliothèque, il y avait, au milieu de la pièce, l'énorme maquette d'une cathédrale qu'il avait dessinée et construite. J'étais complément subjugué par ce morceau d'architecture. Il y avait aussi un jardin merveilleux, tout à fait magique. Quand je lui fis une visite beaucoup plus tard, il avait inventé une extraordinaire décoration dans la maison d'une amie. C'était au début de la guerre, lorsqu'on ne pouvait rien trouver. Ils avaient fait ça pour s'amuser. Ils avaient ac-

NOON

pool pavilion

Tennis pavilion

Tennis Court

electricgates

For Rose garden

Doors.

1. Move urns by house
2. " urn, near garage, to Rose Gdn

The Carlton
Main Street/Mainstraat
P O Box/Posbus 7709
Johannesburg, 2000
South Africa/Suid-Afrika
Telephone/Telefoon:
(011) 331-8911
Telegrams/Telegramme:
Carltonotel

Pergola for Wisteria

Shed

POOL

Rose gdn

40 trees

16 M

seats for E front.

Plaster seat for ex. vista?

a slope

Entrance archway

4 M

1 M

2 M

DH.

garage

THE CARLTON

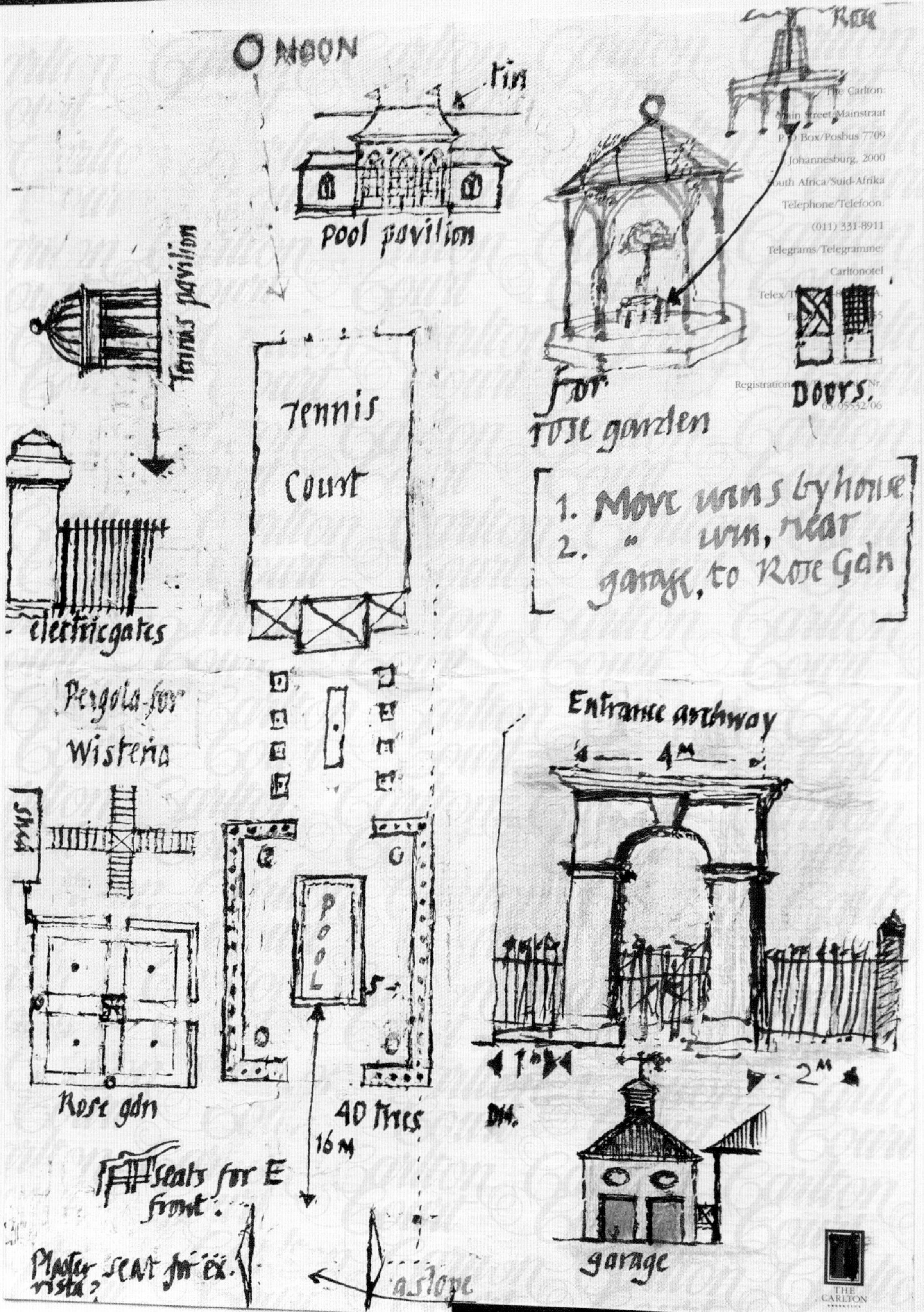

" David Hicks proposes a "Fountain of Freedom . . . 12 metres tall with water falling, from 32 places, representing releasing the masses from oppression".

Exterior design: David Hicks among his roses and foxgloves with, left, the display of bronze silhouette, coral and seashells commemorating Lady Mountbatten and, right, three roses that put the finishing touches to a statue

seed bought at Woolworth's, and scarlet geraniums which he now regards as hideous.

As a boy, he lived in Coggleshall, Essex. His father, who was born in 1863, died when Hicks was 11, and his elder brother was killed in the first world war, so he was brought up almost as an only child. Consequently, he says, his naturally indulgent mother spoilt him.

Not in the least bit academic ("I write, but don't read"), he never took his School Certificate, went straight into the army at 17 and on to the Central School of Arts and Crafts in Holborn, London.

His mother then encouraged him to take a year off in his twenties and travel through Europe. There he developed a love of classical architecture and a feeling for history. Now he has visited nearly every big house in England, going up drives and knocking on doors, if necessary. From his mother he also inherited a great sense of theatre.

She had studied acting, although her husband – who claimed that all actresses were tarts – allowed her to perform only in amateur productions. But she revelled in dressing up as Queen Elizabeth I and, together with Hicks (aged seven) attired as Essex, they would go around in a pony cart to raise money for charity. "We had a sort of tumbril and, with the gardener on foot, leading the pony, we progressed from village to village," he says.

He remembers trawling the local antique shops every Saturday with his mother. He bought a regency chair, which he still proudly owns, for £1. From that piece of furniture, he says, his love of classicism stems. It was also partly a reaction against his mother's taste. They lived in an Elizabethan cottage crammed with clutter.

So when he started interior decorating, aged 24, his imprimatur was always purist and distinctive. Ever since, he has stamped his mark on all manner of objects: trays, umbrellas, tights, sunglasses, bedroom slippers, even a circular gravestone. He has also written numerous books on style and one on gardens.

Now, he devotes his time mainly to gardens, and is immersed in writing and organising the photography for his

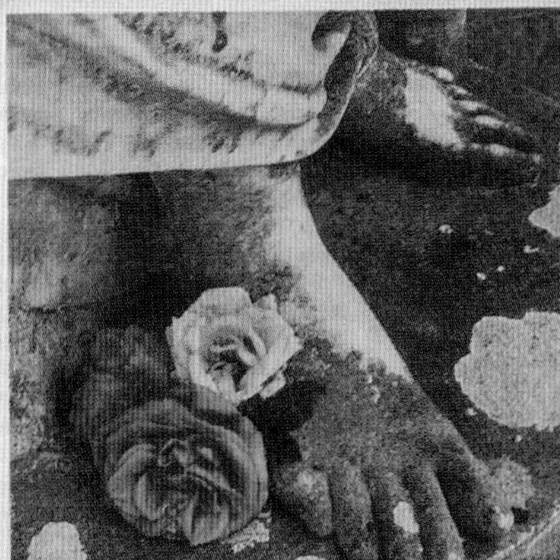

new book, to be called *My Kind of Garden*. To be published next year, it is a collection of his favourite gardens all over the world. The Prince of Wales has allowed him to photograph the entire garden at Highgrove, and the Queen her herbaceous borders at Buckingham Palace. Hicks's own garden will also feature. Essentially a picture book, it will also contain drawings, plans and hints from Hicks.

He is inclined to feign insouciance about horticultural and botanical details. But, of course, he need not. It is obvious – since he can reel off names of plants and flowers as a sort of litany – and spends most of his day pruning, planting and tending his ground, that he knows his stuff.

When he is not personally "torturing and twisting" his trees into shape, he is planning fresh schemes or supervising his two willing, enthusiastic but untrained gardeners, as they work.

"Gardening is just common sense," he says. "But I am told that I am a better gardener than a designer. That amuses me a lot." ●

5

6

7

DAVID HICKS ESQ
& Pammie
to Compiègne
St Denis &
Ecouen.
LONDON/PARIS
AF809 CLUB CLASS
809
ATHROW TERMINAL 2
0845hrs

sessions accumulate?

Most people have a fair idea of their own likes and dislikes as regards colour. If my clients say they do not, I simply draw their attention to the colours in their clothing and take it from there.

It's always a good idea to select colour schemes, fabrics, carpets and lighting that will make the most of the internal architecture or furniture you have. The overall scheme should flatter the owners. When I was confronted with a series of small living rooms in the London apartment of Helena Rubinstein, I knocked them all into one long reception room. Then I covered the walls in a brilliant purple tweed which flattered the exotic but diminutive owner and was an exciting background for her collection of Nigerian sculpture and nineteenth-century North American Belter furniture.

If you are starting from scratch, it is probably best to begin with the carpet. This is, after all, probably the most expensive and long-lasting item in the living room apart from antique furniture and a really good sofa. However the sofa can always be recovered as your ideas develop and change. It is sensible to choose a neutral colour for the carpet – I often recommend grey.

When choosing fabrics, I enjoy mix and matching strong coloured plains with small geometric prints and perhaps a damask.

I also enjoy the contrast in texture – take for example a polished wooden-framed chair covered in a matt tweed fabric. And I am not shy about using strong and sometimes dark colours on walls and enjoy the effect of dark lacquered walls with matt white paint on the woodwork such as doors, windows, dado and skirting. But there has been a trend in recent years towards too much overdecoration with pattern on pattern and flowers on flowers, frills and fringing everywhere.

Some people are fortunate enough to possess or be able to collect entirely antique furniture. But this is not always possible and in any case, there is today a great choice of competitively priced and newly made traditional pieces which, if well upholstered, can be equally stylish. I have always liked the mix of antique with modern, for example, a fine antique dining table with six simple but elegant contemporary chairs.

The positioning of furniture is of the utmost importance – I place furniture at right angles. Pieces of furniture, like people, should 'talk' to one another. And always try to find an unusual arrangement. For instance, if you have a roughly square living room with a fireplace, position on the left of the fireplace two elbow chairs at right angles to each other and on the right of the fireplace, place another pair of elbow chairs facing each other and flanking a sofa. This will allow two people to have an intimate conversation whilst a group of four can have a more general conversation.

When lighting a room, it is essential to be practical and yet subtle and to avoid visible light bulbs. I even like to shade real candles. To avoid shadows in the ceiling, put copper discs on the shade carriers of table lamps.

Pictures work best if they are grouped together. If you have only four fairly small pictures, I try grouping all four together on one wall rather than one on each wall.

When you have made the big decisions you can enjoy putting together the final touches – the pla-

Lydiard Tregoze

Venice

All about me: the making of a man of taste

The news that David Hicks, the interior designer, has finally chosen his biographer is a sad day for fiction, says Byron Rogers

A FEW years ago David Hicks approached me with a view to seeing if I would make a suitable biographer. We met and I found him fascinating, having previously encountered such an ego only in fiction, so that when I came to write a specimen chapter I made it a dramatic monologue, for the man never stopped talking about himself. It was prefaced with two quotations, one from Hicks ("I enjoy being me"), the other from Earl Mountbatten's diary for September 13, 1959 ("walked with Pammy barefoot on the lawn for one hour hearing about David Hicks. As a result had blood blisters on both feet. Very painful.")

Here is the chapter. The scene is Mr Hicks's apartment in Albany, Piccadilly.

Exterior: David Hicks

'I'm so glad you could come. It is nice here, don't you agree? You come into this building, you have this impression of great dignity, then you come up here and it's the perfect antidote to today. I'm excited by tomorrow and I did love yesterday, but today's different. You have to work at today.

"Of course people in my profession would recognise this room as being *me*. They'd see the geometric patterns, the festooned curtains. But do you know why these are festooned? It's because the people opposite haven't replaced their windows properly; I've had to cut out the view. I'm an extraordinary mixture of — well, perhaps not genius — but quick thinking and practicality. When I'm in a tight corner aesthetically I'm at my best, I have to fight to get out. Would you like to see their windows? No, I couldn't do that to anybody. They're such dreadful suburban things.

But what's really *me* are the colours, the *vibrating* colours. Before I came along people said that colours clashed. "The carpet's magenta, the chairs scarlet. Is my wife going to like that?" Your wife, I tell them, will find it *exciting*.

Some colours I don't like to see together, like peacock blue and orange, but even then it depends on how they're used. There are so few definites in life and so many "I should prefer not" situations. Don't you agree? I knew you would. I hate everything which matches up, it's so suburban. Is there anything worse than suburban? Not in this world.

A company in Yorkshire once asked me to select and name 39 colours for a new range of fabrics. I did so and I told Mountbatten this. He said, "I simply don't understand. Are you trying to tell me that hard-headed Yorkshire businessmen are paying you to name colours?" Yes, I said. "But there are only so many colours." I said no, there were millions. Of course, he had no taste, Germans never do. The only thing that ever interested him about my family was that my grandfather had been born in the reign of George III.

It's very new, my profession. It only became a profession after the Second World War, and I'm the one who did it. Before this century, apart from William Morris and the Adam brothers, it just used to be an architect who also did a bit of interior design. Then in the 1930s it was people like Syrie Maugham, Somerset Maugham's wife, after a chat over tea — "you have such a pretty house. *Do* help me with mine."

People have to be told, "pencils massed in a container both look decorative and are useful. *But they must all be the same colour and be sharpened.*" I put pencilled marks on mantelpieces where the objects must go. After the dusting they must be put back.

I've lived here since 1977. I was at a party and someone said, "Now you've got a shop in Jermyn Street you could come and live here." So I asked the chap who arranged such things if he couldn't *squeeze* me in. He was very apologetic, said there was a waiting list of 25 years, so I went back to the office but then the phone rang. "You

Heirlooms do so help a room

ALBANY AT LARGE by Kenneth Rose

Silver lining

LUNCHING with the Court of the Salters' Company last week, I was shown an unusual feature of a City livery: a promising garden newly laid out to mark its sexcentenary. It stretches between Salters' Hall in Fore Street — built by Sir Basil Spence to replace the 18th-century hall in St Swithin's Lane, destroyed in the Blitz of 1941 — and part of the original Roman wall of the City. The cost has been shared by the Salters and the Corporation of London. Members of the public are invited to share this tranquil retreat.

It has been designed by David Hicks with the same attention to detail as he brings to interior decoration. There are hornbeams clipped into green walled arbours containing benches, a tunnel of honeysuckle as in a medieval monastery, lavender and lilies and English roses.

Hicks, Master of the Salters in 1977, also designed the interior of the hall with lots of cheerful reds. He is the 23rd member of his family to become a Salter and the 19th to be Master.

The company is also indebted to his wife Pamela, the younger daughter of Lord Mountbatten, for the loan of a magnificent collection of silver. Acquired by the financier Sir Ernest Cassel, it descended to his granddaughter Edwina Mountbatten and so to Lady Pamela.

I was diverted from my crab mousse on a bed of asparagus with Pouligny Montrachet 1989 by the rarest of all pieces. In front of me stood a gilded silver beaker of 1496, with vertical ridges for a firm grip — known as horsenail decoration.

THE SUNDAY TELEGRAPH MARCH 19, 1995

PHOTOGRAPHS BY FRITZ VON DER SCHULENBURG/INTERIOR WORLD

icksville: the battle of *eau de nil* won, Earl Mountbatten's son-in-law fearlessly took on boring plain carpets

't believe how lucky you young man. I've just n some people who are ving out and they asked, I know anyone nice?" He suggested Lord Snow- and David Hicks but they thought Lord Snowdon sounded a bit *complicated*. So here I am.

I've written nine books, you know. I may only have been responsible for very few words in them but, my God, those words were carefully chosen. The whole place was painted pale green when I came. *Awful*. All my life I have fought that colour.

In the Army it was a sort of creamy green, all my barrack rooms were like that. And when I started to work on grand people's houses it was *eau de nil*. All right once in a while, but people did whole houses out in it. Broadlands was like that when I married. I remonstrated, but in a very tactful way. "Tell me, what do you have in *mind*? Are you keeping this furniture and those curtains?" Very slowly I would *destroy* the whole room.

This is basically two interconnecting rooms, a living room and a bedroom. I keep the door open between them so the carpet had to go through. A patterned carpet.

I do hope you realise I am solely responsible for the revival of patterned carpets in England. There wouldn't be any if it weren't for me. Twenty-seven years ago I found a company that would do carpets to *my* design. Now half the carpets sold are patterned. I designed this one. Gives the room a cosiness, a pattern. You agree, of course.

The only things I liked here were the Louis XVI marble fireplaces, well, not quite, just late 19th century copies. I loved the depth of the shelf, you can set out so many things on them. Vases, Etruscan red and black. Mercury, head of, 17th century. Pewter plates, 17th century, a pair. Some Lowestoft china. A Christmas card from the governor of the Himalayas, another from an interior decorating lady with a dog on the front. There you have the range of the Hicks's acquaintance.

My life after 30 years is completely entwined with that of the Mountbattens. You may not like my in-laws but you must admit they were fascinating.

You will notice the matching mirrors in this room and the bedroom. That gives an illusion of space. But note that the mirror here is the width of the entire chimney breast, not just of the mantelpiece. To have it the width of the mantelpiece would make it look *squalid*.

The portraits? Oh, family portraits, eight oval 17th-century pictures. I've hung them against this rich red background, you have to have a *serious* background for pictures like these. Notice how they hang on silk damask ribbons. But see, the ribbons hide the wiring.

There are 28 sources of light in this room, and you can't see a single bulb. I have this rule: *I never want to see the bulb*. There are picture lights and lights in bookcases. There are two in the bed, for who knows when I might want to sleep at the other end? No centre lights. Yes, you are learning, that would be *suburban*. I lived in rooms with central lights when I was small, but when my mother and I moved to a timbered cottage in 1945 I decided then that it was an end to them. It is such a gradual evolution, the making of a man of taste.

And no television, I hope you noticed that. It is hidden away under the table. I can't *bear* them to be up anywhere in a room. I hate those legs, they're so wobbly, and people will put the *Radio Times* on the thing. Even when it's on I like it to be on the floor. That way it's like being in the dress circle.

I love my bedroom. What, you've never seen a bed in the centre of a room? Have you never been to Malmaison? Dear me. I just love canopy beds, they give one a feeling of luxury and protection. It's a wonderful bed, an important bed, it's a bed to die in and to receive one's doctors. It has to be in the centre of the room.

I suppose you think my ego is terrific. Some people do, you know. I have to be careful: I am very famous and clever, and I am also married to a very rich lady. So I mustn't brag. Mind you, I've known some bad times. School was bad, and the Army. Being marched through Bury St Edmunds with a lot of smelly young men my own age was the lowest point of my life. Then there was the time I first met the Queen and after dinner went into their little cinema. I was sitting next to the Queen as the film started and I fell fast asleep.

Sometimes I sit here and I remember the good moments. When I was 16 I took the train south from Paris to Avignon, and in the morning I found myself looking out at this Van Gogh world, the corn and the blue, blue sky. Not that long ago I went that way again, in a very expensive car with white leather seats, but it didn't work; I'd had too much to drink.

Things are so neat here, don't you think? I spend a lot of time here on my own. I shall keep things like this.

And that was the end of the book.

COTSWOLD GARDENS

by David Hicks (Weidenfeld & Nicolson, £25)

A temperate climate and a history of prosperous patrons have endowed the Cotswolds with an amazing number of fine gardens which, together with the natural landscape, make them one of the most beautiful and best loved areas of England. David Hicks begins the book with a tour around his garden, which epitomizes his distinctive approach to garden design – preferring neat, clean lines and angles to the gentle chaos of many traditional gardens. Andrew Lawson's magnificent photographs convey the richness of horticultural styles, from charming cottage gardens to historic designs by 'Capability' Brown and William Kent. The gardens of Blenheim, Buscot, Hidcote, Sudeley and Broughton (featured in *House & Garden*, July 1995) are included, and the author's notes provide a good preparation for visitors. For those who admire the Cotswolds, beautiful gardens and the style of David Hicks, this book is a sound purchase.

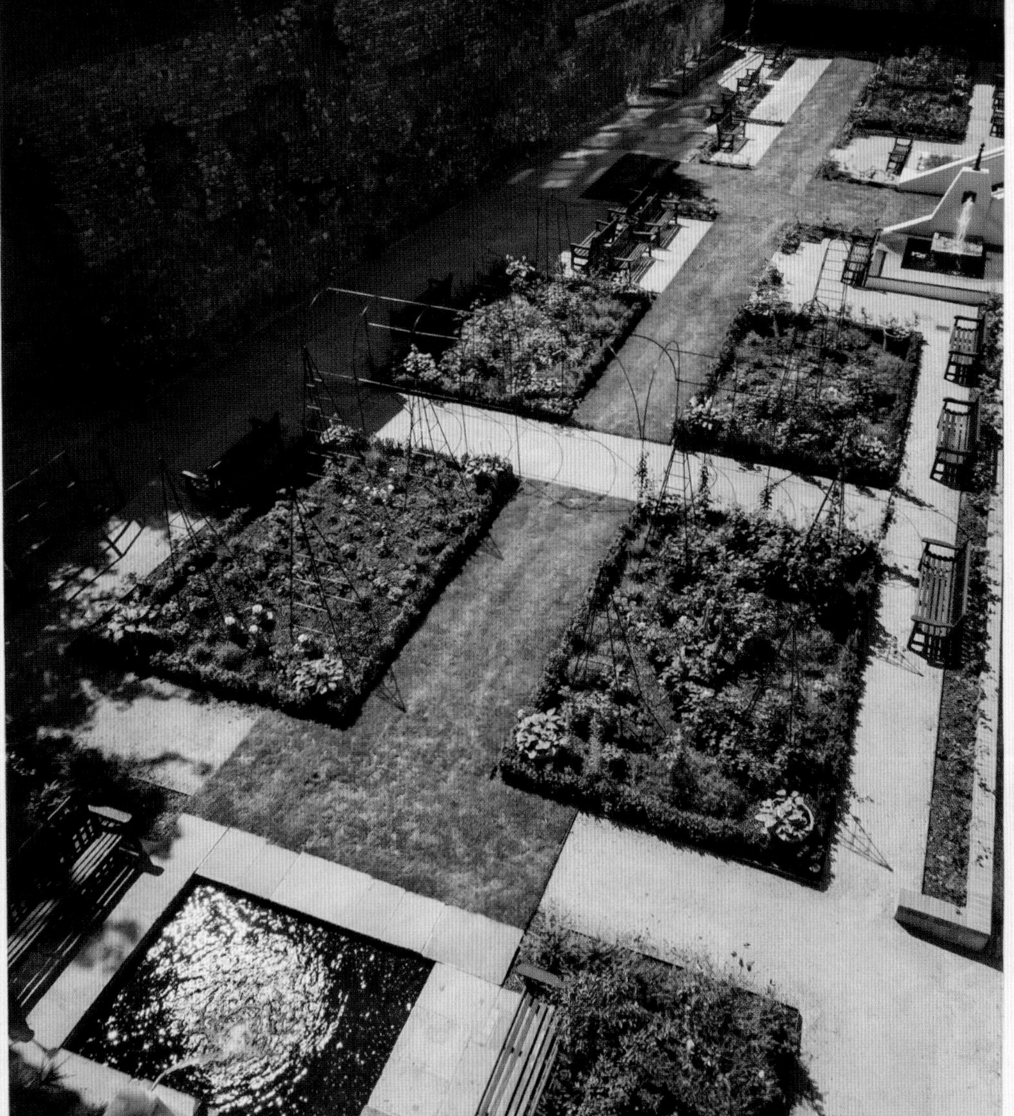

Salters' Hall
garden by DH

The Queen's Birthday Parade 1995.

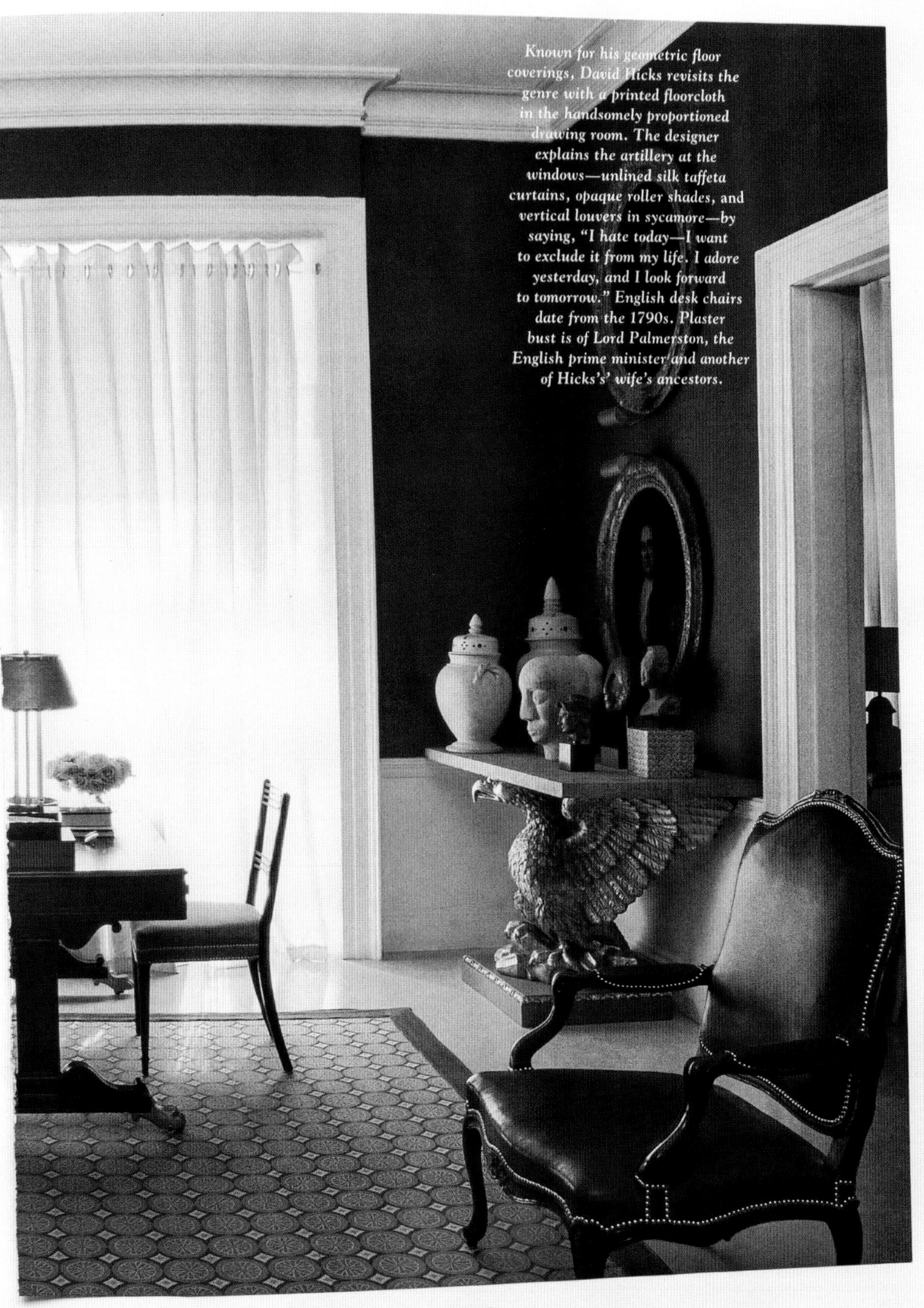

Known for his geometric floor coverings, David Hicks revisits the genre with a printed floorcloth in the handsomely proportioned drawing room. The designer explains the artillery at the windows—unlined silk taffeta curtains, opaque roller shades, and vertical louvers in sycamore—by saying, "I hate today—I want to exclude it from my life. I adore yesterday, and I look forward to tomorrow." English desk chairs date from the 1790s. Plaster bust is of Lord Palmerston, the English prime minister and another of Hicks's' wife's ancestors.

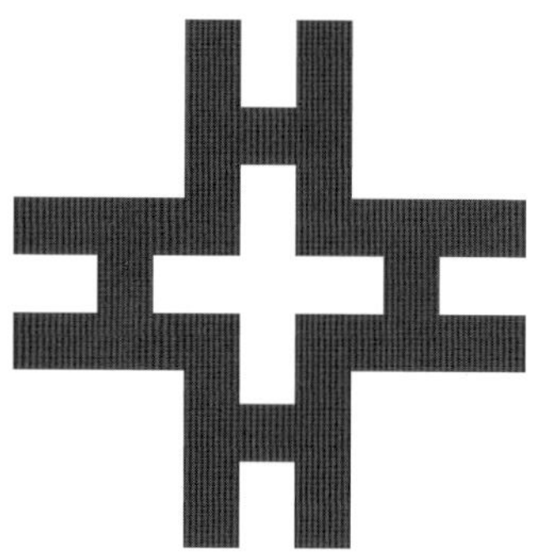

ACKNOWLEDGEMENTS

This edition presents the late David Hicks' scrapbooks as he left them, his original works that include excerpts from the many magazines and newspapers with which he collaborated over the years, and the work of the many talented photographers, illustrators and writers that appear in them. The publishers and editor would like to express their gratitude and appreciation to the publications and contributors who are too many to list here, but are acknowledged throughout in the excerpts and in David Hicks' own captions.

First published in 2017 by **The Vendome Press.**

Vendome is a registered trademark of The Vendome Press, LLC.

NEW YORK
Suite 2043
244 Fifth Avenue
New York, NY 10011
www.vendomepress.com

LONDON
63 Edith Grove
London,
UK, SW10 0LB
www.vendomepress.co.uk

Publishers: Beatrice Vincenzini, Mark Magowan & Francesco Venturi

Distributed in North America by Abrams Books
Distributed in the UK, and the rest of world, by Thames & Hudson

ISBN: 978-0-86565-345-0

First Edition
1 3 5 7 9 10 8 6 4 2

Library of Congress Cataloging-in-Publication Data is available upon request.

Printed and Bound in China by 1010 Printing International Ltd.